Photography

Photography

Phil Davis
University of Michigan

Second Edition

Wm. C. Brown Company Publishers
Dubuque, Iowa

Consulting Editor

Willard F. Wankelman
Bowling Green State University

Copyright © 1972, 1975 by Wm. C. Brown Company Publishers

Library of Congress Catalog Card Number: 74–14216

ISBN 0–697–03215–9

Third Printing, 1976

Printed in the United States of America

Contents

Preface

When this book was first published in 1972, formal instruction in photography in high schools and colleges was on the upswing, and students were turning to photographic expression with great enthusiasm. There was also growing interest—apparently worldwide—in photographic exhibitions and collecting and the increasing acceptance of photography as a legitimate art form. Now, some three years later, I am pleased to say that these trends, although somewhat tempered, seem to be continuing. In spite of diminishing enrollments, increasing costs, and shrinking revenues, more schools than ever have found places for photography in their programs, and courses continue to be oversubscribed by eager students. New collections of photographs are appearing in museums, universities, and banks, and private collectors are no longer rare. Photography seems, more certainly than ever, to be the art of the people—more widely accepted, appreciated, and practiced than any other art form in history.

Photography is a technological art, too. Materials and processes change; equipment evolution and improvement is rapid. It is no wonder that beginners find their first experiences with the medium bewildering and frustrating. But there is an order in this chaos. If taken step-by-step and if the experiences follow each other in a logical sequence, the processes are comprehensible and the fundamental skills can be learned quickly. The purpose of this book is to try to provide the essential bits of information clearly and in a format which will aid learning. I have tried to make the text informative and interesting to read. I believe it is also accurate. I hope you will find it valuable in advancing your knowledge and appreciation of photography.

Although this second edition is changed considerably from the first, the modifications are generally evolutionary. There are a great many detail alterations intended to clarify, simplify, and correct the meaning of phrases and sentences, but the essential character of the text is retained. The history summary has been expanded; several chapters have undergone extensive reconstruction; two new chapters, dealing respectively with the use of hand-held cameras and the Zone System, have been added; the bibliography has grown in size and variety; and the index is now more completely cross-referenced. Most significantly, a great many new photographs have been included throughout the text, with particular emphasis on the history and the portfolio sections.

I would like to express my appreciation again to those photographers who allowed me to include their work in the portfolio section of the first edition. Theirs was an act of pure faith. I am particularly grateful to Jerry Uelsmann for his interest and patience in repeatedly offering prints. George Tice, Todd Walker, Clyde Dilley, Anne Noggle, Bill Garnett, and Betty Hahn also continue to be represented in this new portfolio. I thank them all. While I am grateful to each of the new photographers whose work appears in this edition, I'd like to thank Yousuf Karsh, especially, for his cooperation. I must also acknowledge with real appreciation the help and cooperation of Ms. Christine Hawrylak of the International Museum of Photography at George Eastman House. Her cheerful patience made my dealings with Eastman House a pleasure.

All of the photographs in this book, which are not specifically credited to some other photographer, are my own. I would like to acknowledge gratefully the cooperation of Ms. Martha Kinney, Editor, of the University of Michigan Press, for permitting me to reproduce photographs which I did for their publication, *The University*, in 1967, and express similar thanks to Mr. Lee Buzan, Head of the Technical Information Department of the General Motors Research Laboratories, for allowing me to use two ad illustrations from a series completed for them a few years ago. I must also acknowledge the help I've received from the reviewers whose comments and criticisms of the original edition, and of the manuscript of this one, pointed out a number of weaknesses and offered many constructive suggestions for the improvement of the text. My particular thanks go to Walt Craig of Ohio State University, whose reviews were extraordinarily thorough and helpful.

Finally, I have been extremely gratified by the favorable response to the first edition. I hope sincerely that this revised text will be even more useful and effective and that through its use, students at all levels will find the agonies of photography minimized and its ecstacies enhanced.

PHIL DAVIS

A Survey of the History of Photography

1

It is almost impossible to imagine what the world would be like if photographs and photographic processes were suddenly taken from us. We take television for granted, and accept motion pictures, photographic magazines, and newspaper illustrations as a matter of course, but these are only the more obvious signs of the influence of photography on our lives. It is involved, directly or indirectly, in almost everything we experience.

Photography is involved in almost everything we experience

It wasn't always like this. There are people alive today who can remember the first Kodak camera. Newspaper and magazine reproduction of photographs was still something of a novelty at the beginning of this century. Color photography was in its infancy in 1910. Sound-on-film recording was introduced in the motion picture industry in the 1920s. And television, which seems to have made the whole world picture-conscious, was still new to most people in 1950.

Photography is a medium completely familiar to today's youth, and they have accepted it as their own. Everyone seems to be interested in photographic images—stills or movies, in black-and-white or in color, straight or contrived, fantastic or documentary, beautiful or brutal—and everyone seems to have at least one camera. Photography is the language of today. It is the "now" medium.

It is the language of today

Considering the fascination that photography has always held for people, it sometimes seems surprising that it took so long to be invented. In fact it wasn't just invented, it evolved. That evolution was a long and often frustrating process for those patient, thoughtful men who, one by one, generation after generation, gradually and painfully put the bits together.

Photography wasn't invented; it evolved

The camera came into being long before there was any real use for it. It was probably inspired by the observation of some naturally formed pinhole image. Aristotle mentioned the images of a solar eclipse formed on the ground by sunlight passing through little gaps in tree foliage, and his comments indicate that he had some grasp of the principles involved.

Aristotle observed pinhole images

The *pinhole* image, or the formation of an image by a simple aperture, is not too difficult to understand. Every visible object radiates light, or reflects it, in all directions, and the individual rays travel in straight lines. If a box with one tiny hole in it is pointed at some illuminated subject,

1

some light rays from every portion of the subject will be reflected directly toward the hole and will pass straight through to the opposite side. Each ray, as it strikes the inside surface, forms a tiny spot of light at a point which corresponds exactly to the subject point it came from in both position and brightness. The blending of these points of light produces the image.

The pinhole image can never be quite sharp since it is not a focused image. Each light spot which comprises it is actually the image of the pinhole itself, and it can never be smaller in diameter than the pinhole. In fact the image spots get larger as they travel toward the screen, so that the larger the image gets the more diffused it will appear. Obviously, enlarging the pinhole will also degrade image sharpness. Aristotle was aware of this fact.

No one knows when the first camera was constructed

No one knows when the first "camera" was constructed, but in view of Aristotle's obvious recognition of the principles, it could have been done by some unknown Greek. It's more likely, though, that it came more than a thousand years later. Roger Bacon discussed the *camera obscura* knowledgeably about 1267 and is presumed to have learned about it from the writings of tenth-century Arab scholars.

Leonardo da Vinci described the camera obscura in some detail

In its earliest form, the camera obscura was what the name implies, a dark chamber or room. Leonardo da Vinci described one in some detail in about 1490, pointing out that the image was viewed through the back of a screen of paper which "must be very thin." He also specified that the hole "should be made in a piece of very thin sheet iron."

della Porta refined the camera obscura

In 1558 the camera obscura was described fully by Giovanni Battista della Porta who, in the first edition of his remarkable *Magiae Naturalis*, specified that a conical hole be installed in the shutter of a darkened room and that the image be shown on a white screen. He mentioned the fact that the image will appear upside down and reversed from left to right, and that the image size is proportional to the distance from the hole to the viewing screen—all of which are equally valid observations for the cameras we use today.

He was accused of sorcery

Porta recommended that the camera obscura image be used as a guide for drawing and then went on to invent a method for producing an erect image using lenses and curved mirrors. With this apparatus, he astounded viewers with the images of elaborate theatrical productions staged outside and is even supposed to have been accused of sorcery for his trouble.

Lenses appeared about 1550

The application of lenses to the camera obscura after 1550 was a significant step. The image could then be made both sharper and more brilliant because a lens can admit much more light than a simple hole and also focus the light rays to finer points. Cameras began to be refined in design and construction as more and more people became interested in them, and by about 1575 the first movable cameras appeared. They were, at first, wooden huts or tents, still completely enclosing the viewer and viewing screen. Later more elaborate models, such as sedan chairs, were constructed.

Movable camera obscuras were built by about 1575

From that point on, the evolution was rapid. Smaller models were designed which permitted the operator to view or trace the image from outside the main enclosure, and finally completely portable cameras appeared. A *reflex* camera, that is one in which the image is reflected up onto a top-mounted viewing screen by an inclined mirror behind the lens, was built in 1676; a *ball-and-socket mount* (like some modern *tripod heads*) appeared in 1680; and a *telephoto lens* was installed in a camera obscura in 1685. The camera was ready, but for what?

By 1680 the camera was ready, but for what?

Photographic chemistry started late and proceeded slowly. Angelo Sala mentioned in 1614 his observation that silver nitrate, exposed to the sun, turned black, but apparently saw nothing of significance in the change and did not ascribe it to the action of light.

In 1614 Angelo Sala observed the blackening of silver nitrate

The first discovery of importance was made by Johann Heinrich Schulze, a professor of anatomy at the University of Altdorf, in 1725. He had mixed powdered chalk into a solution of nitric acid in an attempt to make a phosphorescent material (the "luminous stone" of the alchemist, Balduin) and was amazed to discover that the mixture turned dark violet in sunlight. He traced the discoloration to a contaminant in the acid—silver—and eventually proved that silver nitrate and silver carbonate were visibly changed by the action of light, rather than heat or exposure to air as had been previously suggested. Schulze made numerous stencil prints on the sensitive contents of his bottles but apparently never applied the solutions to paper or made any attempt to record natural images.

Schulze made stencil prints in 1725

A few investigations of interest, but no great significance, occurred in the next few years. Then, in 1777, the year after the thirteen American colonies had declared their independence from Britain, the Swedish chemist, Carl Wilhelm Scheele, investigated the properties of silver chloride and made some interesting discoveries. Like Schulze, he established that the blackening effect of his silver salt was due to light, not heat. He also proved that the black material was metallic silver and noted that ammonia, which was known to dissolve silver chloride, did not affect the blackened silver.

Scheele overlooked the significance of his discoveries

If Scheele had realized the importance of this last discovery, he could very well have become the inventor of photography, for now the essential processes were known. Silver chloride could be reduced to black metallic silver by exposure to light; ammonia could serve to preserve the image by dissolving the silver chloride without harming the image tones; and, of course, the camera was still waiting in the wings. But Scheele's investigations were only noted in passing. The world was not yet ready for photography. The fantastic possibility of producing images by the action of light had simply not occurred to anyone as a serious thought.

This essential idea finally came to Thomas Wedgwood, the youngest son of the famous potter, Josiah, who, in addition to being an outstanding craftsman and artist, was a brilliant and respected member of the English scientific community. Thomas was familiar with the camera obscura because his father had used it as an aid in drawing scenes for use on his pottery. The family also owned the notebooks of William Lewis, who, in 1763, had described Schulze's and his own experiments with the silver compounds. These circumstances, and his own natural curiosity, prompted young Thomas to begin experiments of his own, probably about 1795.

Thomas Wedgwood tried to invent photography, but failed

**Wedgwood and Davy
could not fix the image**

Thomas Wedgwood narrowly missed becoming the inventor of photography for two reasons. He gave up, as hopeless, attempts to make pictures with the camera obscura (his exposures were not sufficient), and he was not able to fix the silver images he did produce by direct printing.

It's strange that he failed to take note of Scheele's experiments with ammonia and silver chloride, particularly in light of his father's familiarity with things scientific and his own close friendship and part-time collaboration with Sir Humphry Davy, a famous young English chemist. Wedgwood's experiments with prints on paper and leather were published in 1802 with Davy's wistful summary, "Nothing but a method of preventing the unshaded parts of the delineation from being coloured by exposure to the day is wanting, to render the process as useful as it is elegant." This same problem continued to frustrate experimenters for the next thirty years; it was as if Scheele's work had never been done at all.

**Meanwhile, back at
the Nièpce family estate . . .**

In France, meanwhile Joseph Nicéphore Nièpce and his son Isidore were busy experimenting with lithography at the family estate near Chalon. Then Isidore, who had been copying drawings onto the stones for his father, joined the army; and Nicéphore began to explore light-sensitive varnishes, hoping to find a coating for the stones which would record the drawings by exposure to light. He must have had at least some success because in 1816 he set out to take pictures from nature using a camera and paper sensitized with silver chloride.

**Joseph Nicéphore Nièpce
experimented with silver chloride**

He had limited success almost immediately, but he was not pleased by the fact that the image tones were reversed from nature (they were *negative*), nor could he make the image permanent. He realized that the tonal reversal was an inherent part of the silver process and tried to produce a *positive* print by reprinting one of his negatives but was unsuccessful. He also found that nitric acid helped to preserve the image for a while, but it only postponed disaster and could not prevent it. He began to experiment with other materials.

**But he had more success
with asphalt coatings**

Finally, in 1822, he produced a copy of an engraving by exposing through the original onto a glass plate coated with Bitumen of Judea, a kind of asphalt. Light hardens this material, and when Nièpce washed his exposed plate with normal solvents, the unexposed portions were floated away, leaving the image in permanent lines. He called his process *heliography* (sun-writing). He made a number of similar heliographs in the next few years and continued his efforts to record a camera image. At last, in 1826, he succeeded.

**In 1826 Niepce made the world's
first camera image**

The world's first permanent camera image shows the view from Nièpce's second-floor window and is little more than an impression. It is a bitumen image on pewter, showing only masses of light (the bleached and hardened asphalt) and dark (the bare pewter) tones. The exposure is supposed to have taken about eight hours!

Daguerre wrote to Nièpce in 1826

In January 1826, Nièpce received a letter from a Parisian painter named Louis Jacques Mandé Daguerre who mentioned that he, too, was working with light images and inquired about Nièpce's progress. Nièpce was initially cautious, but after visiting Daguerre on a trip through Paris, his suspicions were somewhat allayed; and after occasional correspondence, he finally suggested to Daguerre in 1829 that they form a partnership to do "mutual work in the improvement of my heliographic process." Daguerre accepted and visited Nièpce to work out the details. They became friends and corresponded frequently, but they never met again.

They formed a partnership

Until the time of their partnership, Daguerre had not produced a useful light image, although he had implied that his work was rather well advanced. The agreement with Nièpce seemed to spur him on. He became a tireless experimenter, and mentioned in a letter of May 21, 1831, his growing interest in silver iodide. "I think after many new tests that we ought to concentrate our researches on 20," he wrote, "this substance is highly light-sensitive when it is in contact with 18." They were writing in code; "20" meant iodine, "18" meant silver plate.

They corresponded in code

Nièpce could not contribute much in this direction. His early experiments with silver compounds had left him prejudiced against them. Finally, impoverished and discouraged, he died. Daguerre was heartbroken but resumed his work with Isidore Nièpce as partner. He was now completely committed to working with the silver compounds.

**Nièpce died.
Daguerre and
Isidore Nièpce continued**

In 1835 Daguerre discovered (quite by accident if the story is true) that treatment with mercury vapor would produce a visible image on an iodized silver plate which had been only briefly, relatively, exposed to light. He also managed to stabilize the image with a strong solution of salt. In spite of the fact that Isidore had contributed nothing to the discovery, Daguerre included him in a new contract and set about trying to find a market for his process. He did not have much luck.

Finally, late in 1838, he contacted a group of leading French scientists, among them François Arago, and solicited their help. Arago was immediately impressed with the invention and made a brief announcement of it at the Academie des Sciences in January 1839.

**Daguerre made his discovery
and approached Arago**

Daguerre had supported himself quite handsomely during most of the period of his researches with the proceeds from his "Diorama," a kind of light show which employed enormous paintings on translucent screens combined with some real objects, controlled light effects, and music, to create illusions of famous scenes or ceremonies. It was a disaster for him, then, when the Paris Diorama was totally destroyed by fire in March.

Arago immediately sprang to his aid and succeeded in convincing the government that French national honor was at stake. A bill was passed granting life pensions to Daguerre and Nièpce, and the details of the process were announced to a frenzied public in August 1839. Although the French government had announced that the process was now public property, this was not entirely true. Daguerre had secretly patented it in England just a few days before the formal French announcement.

**The daguerroetype was given
to the world—except England**

News of the daguerreotype process spread like wildfire. Enthusiastic experimenters, French and foreign, were soon happily engrossed in the new technique. But there was dismay in England. A respected member of the Royal Society of London, named William Henry Fox Talbot, saw the new process as a threat to his own investigations, and, in an attempt to establish priority, had written Arago on January 29, 1839, to claim that

**William Henry Fox Talbot
was dismayed**

he had been the first to find a method for taking pictures with the camera obscura, and for fixing them. He overstated his case. He had not accomplished much more than had Nièpce in his experiments with silver chloride, and his method of fixation was far from satisfactory.

Talbot was not an artist, but he was a brilliant, well-educated man. He apparently conceived the notion of capturing the camera obscura images while trying to draw some landscapes in Italy and later wrote in his famous picture book, *The Pencil of Nature,*

> And this led me to reflect on the inimitable beauty of the pictures of nature's painting which the glass lens of the camera throws upon the paper in its focus—fairy pictures, creations of a moment, and destined as rapidly to fade away. It was during these thoughts that the idea occurred to me—how charming it would be if it were possible to cause these natural images to imprint themselves durably, and remain fixed upon the paper!

Talbot's experimentations began in 1834

On returning to England in 1834, Talbot began experimentation. Having heard that silver nitrate was light-sensitive, he made his first attempts with silver nitrate-coated paper. He quickly found it unsatisfactory and turned to silver chloride, at first coating paper with the prepared salt, then producing it in the paper by successive washes of sodium chloride (common salt) and silver nitrate. He soon found that too much salt reduced the sensitivity of the paper and turned, as Daguerre had done, to the use of a strong salt solution for fixing the image.

Talbot experimented with paper images

Before long, Talbot ran across the accounts of the experiments of Wedgwood and Davy and investigated them fairly thoroughly, apparently without discovering much of real value. He had not yet heard of the work of either Nièpce or Daguerre.

He took pictures with "mouse traps"

Although his early experiments were confined to making prints of objects laid directly on the paper surface, Talbot had succeeded by the summer of 1835 in taking pictures with a tiny camera obscura fitted with a microscope lens (his wife called his little cameras "mouse-traps"). The pictures were only about an inch square, but he had found larger ones impossible to make due to the length of the exposure required.

Talbot made little progress in the next three years, and his attention was diverted to other things. His interest and concern were apparent, however, when he received word of Arago's announcement of Daguerre's fantastic discovery.

The news which stunned Talbot also greatly intrigued Sir John Frederick William Herschel, son of the famous German-born English astronomer, and a prominent mathematician, astronomer, and chemist in his own right. Within a week, Herschel was at work in his laboratory near London, investigating the various known processes and keeping careful notes of his procedures.

Herschel made the process practical— in two weeks

It is an indication of Herschel's intelligence and acuity as an investigator that in less than two weeks he succeeded in testing several silver salts for sensitivity (he preferred the nitrate and carbonate), taking several successful pictures, printing a negative to make a positive paper image, and fixing the images with a chemical he had described twenty years before that he called hyposulphite of soda.

At the height of this investigation—less than two weeks after hearing of Arago's momentous announcement—Talbot visited Herschel at his laboratory, bringing with him samples of his work. Talbot begins to appear, at this moment in history, as a somewhat unlovely character. His treatment of the frank and generous Herschel was rather shabby. Herschel showed Talbot his results and described them in full detail, including his use of *hypo* for fixing. Talbot, on the other hand, revealed nothing. He referred airily to his own method of fixing the image without explaining how it was done and convinced Herschel that he should not mention the use of hypo until Talbot had announced his process. Herschel agreed, later writing admiringly that Talbot's method of fixing "must be a very chemical jewel," and gave Talbot permission to announce the use of hypo with his own process.

Talbot learned of hypo from Herschel

In fairness to Talbot, it must be acknowledged that he credited Herschel with the application of hyposulphite of soda. In his letter of disclosure to a member of the French Academy, he outlined his own methods of fixing, then described Herschel's hypo as being "worth all the others combined." Daguerre immediately applied it to his own process.

Niépce, Daguerre, and Talbot can each be called the "inventor of photography" with certain justification, but so can a fourth man who is less well known, Hippolyte Bayard. Bayard lived in Paris and was a minor employee of the Ministry of Finance. His experiments with light-sensitive materials probably began about 1837 and, initially, seem to have paralleled Talbot's. His first images were negatives on silver chloride-treated paper. On learning of Daguerre's discovery, he set out to produce direct positive images. Within a few months, he succeeded with a process that involved blackening a conventional silver chloride paper in light, then coating it with a solution of potassium iodide, and exposing it in the camera. The exposing light bleached this paper, producing a direct positive image, which was then fixed in hypo (Fig. 1.1).

Bayard also invented photography

Figure 1.1   Hippolyte Bayard (1801–1887), *Windmills at Montmartre* (IMP GEH)

Figure 1.2 William Henry Fox Talbot (1800–1877), *The Cloisters of Lacock Abbey*, ca. 1844 (IMP GEH)

His attempts to gain recognition were not very successful

Bayard was apparently a very quiet and retiring man of modest means. Many of his pictures are still-life arrangements or details of his house and garden. In some of these views he himself appears seated in a doorway or in his garden, surrounded by flowerpots and garden tools. Although he did make a few tentative attempts to gain recognition and support, they were not very successful. Perhaps, too, he was unlucky in his choice of consultants. He showed some prints to Arago in May 1839, and asked his help. Arago, who was very much interested in Daguerre's career at that point, arranged for a token grant of 600 francs to help Bayard finance his experiments and counselled him to remain quietly in the background until Daguerre's process had been publicly revealed. After that revelation, of course, Bayard's work seemed anticlimactic and insignificant, and he was virtually ignored by the public and the government alike.

Bayard photographed himself as a corpse

Understandably bitter at this callous treatment Bayard expressed his hurt by photographing himself as a half-naked corpse and explained in a long, piteous caption that this was the dead body of the unhappy Bayard who, unrecognized and unrewarded, had thrown himself into the water and drowned.

Although in his lifetime he was never given the credit he deserved, he did eventually receive a little prize of 3,000 francs. Now he is remembered as a significant figure, a victim of circumstances who might have been as well known as Daguerre if things had worked in his favor.

Talbot patented his processes

Photography (a name which is generally credited to Herschel) languished in England. The daguerreotype process was patented, and Talbot began immediately to secure his own processes by patents so restrictive that even amateur experiments were inhibited. Talbot improved his original paper negative process by subjecting the exposed paper to development in gallic acid and silver nitrate solution, thus shortening the neces-

Figure 1.3 David Octavius Hill (1802–1870) and Robert Adamson (1821–1848), *St. Andrews. Baiting Lines, Fishergate* (IMP GEH)

sary exposure time considerably. He called the new process *calotype* (it was later referred to also as *talbotype*) and included in its patent the use of hypo for fixing—blatantly appropriating Herschel's discovery (Fig. 1.2).

His calotype patent included Herschel's hypo

The calotype process could not compete with the daguerreotype in fineness of detail and delicacy of tonal scale, but it did permit the making of any number of identical copies. If it had been free for public use, it might have flourished. Probably the most significant work in calotype was done in Scotland where it was not patented, by Robert Adamson and David Octavius Hill who, working together, produced portraits which still rank with the very best (Fig. 1.3).

Talbot must receive credit for inventing the photographic process as we now know it, but he also must be remembered as a stumblingblock in its evolution. As new procedures were announced, Talbot promptly filed claims to them on the grounds that they were only modifications of the basic principles of his patented processes. Although these tactics created a great deal of antagonism and various suits were threatened, Talbot was generally successful in controlling photography in England until 1855.

Two significant processes were announced during this period. In France, Abel Nièpce de Saint-Victor, a cousin of Nicéphore's, invented in 1847 a process for sensitizing a glass plate with an emulsion of silver iodide and fresh, whipped egg white (albumen). The process, although slow, was capable of rendering fine detail and good gradation and produced prints free from the annoying paper texture which was a common objection to the calotype. Talbot patented a modification of the albumen process in 1849.

Nièpce's cousin invented the albumen process

The other invention, and one which was a real milestone in photography, was given freely to the public by a gentle and unassuming English

Frederick Scott Archer introduced the wet-plate process in 1851

sculptor named Frederick Scott Archer. He had learned the calotype process in 1847 and had set out to improve on it by exploring various paper pulp materials and surface coatings. He finally hit upon the idea of using a film of iodized collodion on glass and introduced the process to the public in March 1851.

Figure 1.4 Brady Gallery, *Gen. Jefferson Davis* (Library of Congress)

The collodion process was a demanding one. A glass plate had to be cleaned, then flooded with iodized collodion to form a uniform and blemish-free coating. It then had to be immersed in a bath of silver nitrate and rushed into the camera for exposure while still wet. Development in pyrogallic acid or a solution of ferrous sulfate had to follow immediately before the plate dried. For obvious reasons, it came to be known as the *wet-plate* process.

The process was not free for long. Talbot, with typical lack of scruple, claimed that it was covered by his patents and announced that he would prosecute anyone who used it without license. A number of challenges were made to this outrageous claim, but it was not until December 1854 that the courts finally found Talbot's claim illegal. His tyranny had ended.

Frederick Scott Archer died in 1857, exhausted and penniless. He had received no money from his invention and very little fame. His importance in the history of photography is recognized now, however. The wet-plate process was used almost to the exclusion of all others for thirty years.

Samuel F. B. Morse is well remembered as the inventor of the telegraph. He is less well known as a portrait painter and photographer. Morse had experimented with silver nitrate paper before 1839 but had given it up when he discovered that the images were always negatives. He visited Daguerre in Paris (he was demonstrating his telegraph to Daguerre in the hour the Diorama burned) and was enchanted by the images that Daguerre showed him.

Samuel Morse visited Daguerre

After his return to America, and after news of the daguerreotype process had been released, Morse was one of the first to try it. He had a camera built in September and soon applied himself to portraiture. He had only fair success because of the long exposure time required, ten to twenty minutes in full sunlight, and soon joined with John W. Draper in experiments in speeding up the process.

American daguerreotypists made rapid strides

Improvements came rapidly as other experimenters also applied themselves; and by 1840 the required exposure time had been reduced to a matter of seconds, both as a result of chemical improvements and the introduction by Alexander S. Wolcott of a concave mirror to replace the lens of the camera. Portrait studios sprang up at a rapid rate as the American pioneers, Morse, Draper, Wolcott, and the rest, instructed others in the art and techniques of this fascinating new medium.

One of Morse's students was a young portrait painter named Mathew Brady who very soon became one of the country's most renowned daguerreotypists. He specialized in portraits of famous persons and was also considered an expert in children's portraiture (Fig. 1.4).

The ambrotype

Although the popularity of the daguerreotype (Fig. 1.5) continued to increase for a time after 1850, the introduction of the collodion process

Figure 1.5 Daguerrotype of an unknown gentleman. The highly reflective surface of the daguerreotype is demonstrated in these two views; the image is obscured by reflection of the white table surface, but shows clearly when the daguerreotype is placed on a black surface. This unusually fine example is elegantly mounted in a tooled leather case. (Collection of the author)

made it obsolete. Before long daguerreotypists were experimenting with collodion, and they soon found in the *ambrotype* process a cheap and acceptable substitute for the more delicate, and more difficult, daguerreotype. Ambrotypes, which were used mainly for portraiture, made use of the fact that a very lightly exposed and developed collodion negative will appear to be a positive image if it is suitably bleached and mounted on a black background (Fig. 1.6). Because of the speed and economy of the process and the durability of the finished images, ambrotypes became very popular. They could not match the range and beauty of the daguerreotype's silvery tones, and, like the daguerreotype, only one image existed for each camera exposure, but they were cheap and convenient.

A variant of the same process, originally called *ferrotype* or *melainotype* (Fig. 1.7), produced a positive image on a thin sheet of varnished iron. These images were inferior to a true ambrotype, which was on a

Figure 1.6 Ambrotype of an unknown gentleman. Although generally superior to tintypes, ambrotypes are no match for the earlier daguerreotypes in brilliance and delicacy. (Collection of the author)

Figure 1.7 Tintype of seated lady. This portrait has been rather inexpertly tinted. The lady's cheeks are rouged and her necklace and bracelet are gilded. The case is moulded plastic. (Collection of the author)

Figure 1.8 A typical tintype. Outdoor views of this kind are common. Notice the reversed lettering in the signs. (Collection of the author)

The ferrotype, melainotype, or tintype

glass plate, but they were even cheaper, easier, and faster to produce, and they were unbreakable. They were produced in great quantities by itinerant photographers and bargain portraitists and soon became familiarly as *tintypes* (Fig. 1.8). By 1860 the daguerreotype was virtually extinct.

Cartes-de-visite became popular

In the mid-1850s there was a great public demand for the *cartes-de-visite*, or photographic visiting cards. Cartes-de-visite were small photographs, about 2½″ × 4″, often full-length portraits, and generally bearing the name and address of the pictured person or the name of the photographer who made them, or both (Fig. 1.9). They were made, usually eight-to-a-plate, on collodion negatives, then printed and cut into individual pictures. They were novel and cheap, and their popularity was enormous. They were collected and exchanged like baseball trading cards, and cartes-de-visite of famous persons were sold by the thousands (Fig. 1.10).

With the advent of the Civil War, there came a greatly increased demand for cartes-de-visite and tintypes as the recruits and their families exchanged their likenesses as keepsakes. Mathew Brady, and all the other photographers, did a brisk business as the war threatened. To Brady, now internationally famous as "Brady of Broadway," the impending conflict

Figure 1.9 Mathew Brady (1823-1896), *Portrait of Lincoln.* Carte-de-visite, obverse and reverse. (Courtesy of William A. Lewis)

Figure 1.10 The album shown open, and a detail of one of the pages. This small tintype has been placed in a carte-de-visite-sized, heavily embossed mount so that it will fit the album's oval mat opening.

was a momentous historical event. Brady's sense of history was already well known. For years he had made it a practice to photograph famous people and had published *The Gallery of Illustrious Americans* in 1850. Now he felt impelled to document the war.

President Lincoln gave Brady his consent, but no financial backing. This was enough; Brady was a moderately wealthy man, and he had no reservations about spending his own money for such a significant purpose. He assembled a staff of several men, outfitted them with the materials and equipment needed to make wet-plate photographs, and went to war. The photographs these men made are well known (Fig. 1.11). Taken and processed under the most awkward and dangerous conditions imaginable, they form a remarkable pictorial history of that desperate struggle (Fig. 1.12).

Brady emerged from the enterprise practically destitute. There was little market for his war pictures, the war was too recent and too horrible, and no one wanted to be reminded of it. His plates were stored in warehouses and eventually auctioned off. Ironically one lot of them was bought by the government for storage charges. Except for a belated government grant of $25,000, Brady went unrewarded for his labors. He died, penniless, in 1896.

Mathew Brady and his staff documented the Civil War

Figure 1.11   Alexander Gardner (1821-1882), *Ruins of the Gallego Flour Mill, Richmond, Va.,* ca. 1865 (Library of Congress)

Figure 1.12   Timothy O'Sullivan (1840-1882), *A. R. Waud Sketching Battlefield, Gettysburg, Pa., July 1863* (Library of Congress)

**Timothy O'Sullivan and
William H. Jackson
did Western Survey work**

The world has been pretty well documented in photographs since the 1850s. Photographers have been present wherever there was action of any sort, and many of them were attracted westward by the rumors of wealth and promise of adventure. Typical of these explorer-photographers were Timothy O'Sullivan and William H. Jackson.

A one-time Brady assistant who accompanied a U.S. Geological Expedition along the 40th parallel in 1867, O'Sullivan photographed the Isthmus of Panama in 1870, then returned to Western survey work in 1873 (Figs. 1.13 and 1.14). His pictures show the contrast between the ugliness of the mining boomtowns and the beauty of the yet-unspoiled wilderness areas —a clear warning of what was to happen to the West before many more years of senseless exploitation.

Jackson served in the Civil War

The career of William H. Jackson is, perhaps, even more significant since, among other things, his photographs of the fantastic hot springs and geysers of Yellowstone were instrumental in persuading the Congress to establish that region as the first of the National Parks. Jackson was born in Keeseville, New York, in 1843. His mother encouraged him to draw and paint. His father, an amateur daguerreotypist, introduced him to photography by allowing him to play with discarded camera equipment. His first job, "improving" the prints of a Vermont photographer, was interrupted by the Civil War, and William and his brother, Edward, joined the 12th Vermont Infantry in 1862. He returned to Vermont after the war, intending to settle down, but in 1866, two months before he was to have been married, his engagement was broken. In a sudden desire to "get away," he caught the first train to New York City. There he happened to meet an ex-army buddy and, together, they joined a covered wagon train headed for Montana.

After the War, he headed West

Jackson left the wagon train in Wyoming and struck out on his own. For two years he wandered from job to job, covering most of the mountain states, finally arriving in Omaha where he was hired by one of the local photographers. Soon he owned his own studio, but his wanderlust was

**He opened
a photographic studio in Omaha**

Figure 1.13   Timothy O'Sullivan (1840-1882), *Cañon of the Colorado River near the Mouth of the San Juan River, Arizona,* 1873 Wheeler Expedition (Courtesy of William A. Lewis)

still strong. Outfitting a horse-drawn wagon as a portable darkroom, he began to range the country north and west of Omaha, photographing the prairies and the Indians who inhabited them. Before long he was attracted by the dramatic expansion of the railroads and, redesigning his equipment to fit on packmules, he began to travel in earnest. In 1869, he met Dr. F. V. Hayden who was conducting a U.S. Geological Survey of the Territories, and was persuaded to join him. During the nine years that he worked on the Survey, Jackson produced thousands of magnificent negatives of both scientific and scenic value. An extract from his diary gives us some inkling of the difficulties of working in the mountains with the wet-plate process.

He joined the Hayden Survey in 1869

Aug. 2, (1878) Upper Wind River Lake. Returned to upper lake. Wilson, Eccles, his man Payot and Richardson going with me. Fine morning and got good 11 by 14 exposure first trial. There were two or three small defects but impossible to take it over and get as good a lighting. Time 9 m. with Portable Symmetrical, single lens, at F.32. Made 5 by 8 of same subject. Came up too thin, but intensifying made it as much too dense. Took camera up high for a general view. Exposed 2 m., F.16, Portable Symmetrical, with some over-exposure. In packing up to return, I forgot to remove the two 11 by 14 plates that I had put in the bath holder to bring the solution up to its proper depth. Hoggie, the pack mule carrying the outfit, traveled so roughly that when I opened up the bath holder later I found the plates smashed to pieces and one side of the bath holder punched full of holes. It is going to bother me now to replace it. Was two or three hours making general repairs. I don't think I ever had so inconvenient an outfit.

In 1879 Jackson moved to Denver, set up a studio, and returned to his earlier interest, photographing the railroads. For twenty years he traveled through every state in the Union and from Montreal to Mexico City, often in "Jackson Special" cars supplied by the railroads, making photographs of all sizes from 20″ × 24″ to the popular stereo views (Fig. 1.15).

In 1879 he returned to photographing the railroads

In 1898 he moved to Detroit and set up the Detroit Publishing Company, specializing in views and postcards printed in color, derived from his vast store of negatives. When he "retired" in 1924, Jackson took up

The Detroit Publishing Company

Figure 1.14 Timothy O'Sullivan (1840-1882), Stereo view, 1871 Wheeler Expedition (Courtesy of William A. Lewis)

Figure 1.15   William H. Jackson (1843-1942), *The Rocky Mountains, Scenes along the line of the Denver and Rio Grande Railway* (Courtesy of William A. Lewis)

painting again and was commissioned by the National Park Service in 1935 to do a series of pictures for various national park museums. Still vigorous in his nineties, Jackson continued to tour and paint and photograph the West each summer until his death in 1942.

Some nonsilver photographic processes

While most of the prints made for commercial purposes after about 1850 were done on albumenized paper, it was not entirely satisfactory. The color was not altogether pleasing, and, like the other silver papers, the image was likely to fade or discolor, especially if the photographer was less than meticulous in his processing. For these, and other reasons, considerable attention was devoted to the perfection of nonsilver photographic materials.

Ponton, Becquerel, and Poitevin

This was not a new thought. In 1839 Mungo Ponton had discovered that a solution of potassium dichromate (he called it bichromate of potassa) spread on paper would be insolubly stained by exposure to light and had used this principle to produce simple images. Edmond Becquerel pointed out, shortly thereafter, that the reaction was largely due to the effect of the dichromate on the starch size in the paper. This soon attracted the attention of the ubiquitous Talbot, who, in 1852, patented *photoglyptic drawing* based on the tanning effect of dichromates on a number of organic colloids, including glue, gelatin, starch, and various gums.

The honor of applying this technique to the production of photographic prints belongs to Alphonse Louis Poitevin, a French chemist and engineer.

His researches led to the eventual discovery of several methods of printing, including the *carbon* processes and the *collotype*. In the carbon process, a layer of gelatin containing powdered carbon and dichromate was spread on paper, dried, and exposed under a negative. The image, composed of hardened gelatin and carbon, remained on the paper after the unexposed—so still soluble—portions of the gelatin area had been washed away in hot water. This first form of the technique produced an image of black and white without gradation, but later modifications resulted in a complete range of tones, making it one of the best of the nonsilver processes.

The collotype process also used a dichromated gelatin layer, often on glass, but without the carbon pigment. Exposure tanned the gelatin making it less absorptive to water, and therefore capable of holding a coating of greasy ink. When properly dampened and inked, the collotype plate could be used for printing like a lithograph stone. The exposed portions, holding ink, printed dark, while the unexposed portions, holding water and repelling the ink, printed light in tone. When competently done, the process was capable of a complete range of tones, and is, in fact, still considered to be one of the finest methods of printing known.

Another interesting and ingenious process, which was used for production runs of a few thousand printed impressions, was the *woodburytype* (Fig. 1.16). Making use of the fact that the image on an exposed dichromated gelatin film is in low relief, the woodburytype process involved pressing the relief image into a lead plate to form an intaglio image. The depressions thus formed were filled with liquid pigmented gelatin which was then impressed on paper. The image was formed by the varying thicknesses of the pigment.

In addition to these well-known and eminently practical processes, there were at least dozens, if not hundreds of others, for which great claims were made on announcement but which almost immediately disappeared. Many of the experimenters were possessed of more enthusiasm than scientific objectivity, and they concocted some real witches' brews. No doubt some of them suffered as a result, for the chemicals they dealt with in some of those processes were lethal. One example is potassium cyanide, which was widely used in fixing baths, particularly in the ambrotype process, and there were many others. The collodion itself was made by dissolving a form of guncotton in ether and alcohol, and the daguerreotype process employed iodine and bromine vapors as well as the potentially deadly fumes of hot mercury.

While the chemical and physical aspects of photography were being zealously investigated, there was, almost from the outset, a group of photographers who were offended by the emphasis on mere technique. One of the first and best-known was Oscar G. Rejlander, a Swedish-born London portrait painter. He became interested in photography, as did many other painters, as an aid in painting but very soon became interested in the medium for its own sake. His fame results largely from an allegorical composition he completed in 1857, called *Two Ways of Life* (Fig. 1.17). Done in the best traditions of the fleshpot painters, it depicts two young men being introduced to life as exemplified by groups of figures in various attitudes and occupations. One youth is attracted toward a languid group-

The collotype is still one of the finest printing processes known

The woodburytype used an intaglio plate

Figure 1.16 Étienne Carjat (1828-1906), *Charles Baudelaire* (IMP GEH)

Oscar G. Rejlander and the "Two Ways of Life"

Figure 1.17   Oscar G. Rejlander (1813-1875), *Two Ways of Life* (IMP GEH)

ing of scantily clothed ladies, representing Dissipation. The other is gazing earnestly toward a more discreetly clothed and posed group, symbolizing Industry.

As corny and sentimental as this picture seems now, it was an enormous success, and Rejlander had to make several prints of it. This was no easy task, because the picture had been taken in more than thirty separate pieces which he cunningly joined together by multiple printing techniques. The finished image was 16″ × 31″ in size and had to be done on two sheets of paper joined together, since no single sheet could be found which was large enough to hold it.

Henry Peach Robinson

Another Englishman, Henry Peach Robinson, also a painter of some skill, was influenced by Rejlander. He felt that photography was capable of more than the simple recording of things and set out to produce pictures with real emotional appeal. Starting with a beautifully arranged composite image called *Fading Away*, which shows a lovely girl presumably dying while two women and a man mourn, he went on to even more sentimental themes and more elaborately faked compositions (Fig. 1.18).

Julia Margaret Cameron used a long lens

Julia Margaret Cameron must be remembered as one of the greatest portrait photographers of all time. She was a forty-eight-year-old mother of six when she began photographing in 1863, and within a year she had taught herself the rudiments of the craft. She was obviously familiar with traditions in art and certainly must have been influenced by the work of Rejlander, but her pictures are less slick than his and much more "photographic" in character. She was a ruthless person to sit for, sometimes subjecting her subjects to extraordinarily long exposure times (in dim light) if she felt the visual effect was pleasing. She worked with a very long-focus lens to make close-up portraits of outstanding expressiveness (Fig. 1.19). She was not entirely untouched by the romantic sweetness of the era. Most of the illustrations she did for Tennyson's *The Idylls of the King* were simply silly; but on the whole she brought a new directness to photographic portraiture which is still impressive.

For almost thirty years after its introduction by Archer, the collodion process reigned supreme in spite of its obvious shortcomings. It was not sensitive enough, it had to be used wet, and the large glass plates were fragile and bulky to handle. In the mid-1870s gelatin began to be used, first as a coating for printing papers and then for camera materials.

Gelatin emulsions began to appear in the 1870s

The first of these required elaborate handling. The emulsion was coated on a paper base for exposure in the camera, then developed and stripped off the paper to another support material, such as glass, for printing. Glass plates were also coated directly for camera use, but the growing public desire for smaller and lighter cameras spurred on experimenters in their search for glass substitutes.

Gelatin is an unusually compatible material for use with silver halide emulsions. It not only holds the halide crystals in suspension but enhances their sensitivity and tends to prevent reduction of the unexposed crystals during development. It also adheres well to many materials, can be either softened or set by temperature changes, and allows rapid penetration of processing solutions without dissolving. But most importantly for photographers in the 1880s, it produced emulsions which could be used dry and stored for extended periods, both before and after exposure. Although albumen paper continued to be used until about 1900, the collodion wet plate was obsolete for general photography by 1880.

Gelatin is a remarkable material

By 1890 *roll film*, consisting of a spooled strip of celluloid coated with a gelatin emulsion and protected by opaque paper wrapping, had arrived. Companies were formed, cameras and materials were put into production, and the era of photography-for-everyone was at hand.

George Eastman, founder of the Eastman Kodak Co., was at the forefront of this industrial surge, and he was quick to take advantage of the opportunities. Eastman was not an educated man, but he was shrewd and intelligent. He foresaw the potential in the amateur market and set

George Eastman and the Kodak

Figure 1.18   Henry Peach Robinson (1830-1901), *Fading Away,* 1858 (IMP GEH)

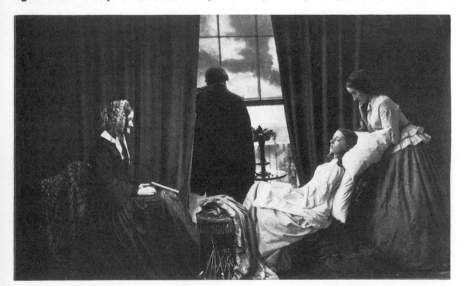

Figure 1.19   Julia Margaret Cameron (1815-1879), *Mary-Mother* (IMP GEH)

out to exploit it with a portable, simply operated camera which could be bought, loaded with 100 exposures of roll film, for about $25. He selected the name *Kodak* for it quite arbitrarily. He wanted a name that was easy to remember, and one which was not liable to be mispronounced in any language; also, one which could be registered in the patent office without confusion. Additionally, he is supposed to have admired the firmness of the letter *K*.

"You press the button; we do the rest"

In practically no time, the name Kodak and the slogan which accompanied it, "You press the button; we do the rest," were household words. The slogan was no idle boast. When the 100 pictures were taken, the owner simply mailed the entire camera back to the company; where, for $10 the film was removed and processed, prints made, the camera reloaded, and returned with the finished pictures, ready for the next 100 shots.

Hurter and Driffield pioneered in sensitometry

With the formation of large manufacturing corporations like the Eastman Kodak Co., technical research in photography spurted ahead. The heyday of the amateur kitchen-chemist was definitely over. A significant step in this direction was the publication in 1890 of a paper by Dr. Ferdinand Hurter and Vero C. Driffield, entitled "Photochemical Investigations and a New Method of Determination of the Sensitiveness of Photographic Plates." This was the first serious attempt to analyze the effects of exposure and development and to organize the findings into useful form. This effort was not lost on Henry P. Robinson, who, in a magazine article in 1892 said:

> Two very clever scientists, whom I much respect, Dr. Hurter and Mr. Driffield, have proved to everybody's unsatisfaction that photographers have no control over the gradations; but this does not alter the fact that—to put the simplest case—he (*sic*) knows when a negative is over- or underexposed or developed too dense or too thin to properly represent his idea of nature. . . .

Eadweard Muybridge was commissioned to photograph a running horse

Almost from the beginning photographers were intrigued by the possibility of taking "instantaneous" photographs. In 1851 Talbot used an electric spark to record the image of a page from the *Times* which he had fastened to a rapidly revolving wheel, and by 1860 several other photographers had managed to take outdoor views which showed walking figures caught in midstride. The first really serious attack on the problems of arresting motion, however, is attributed to Eadweard Muybridge who, previous to 1870, was a professional specializing in landscape and industrial photography. In 1872 Muybridge was commissioned by Leland Stanford, one-time governor of California, to photograph a running horse. Stanford financed this experiment, so the story goes, to settle a bet which he had made with a friend, Stanford claiming that all four of a trotter's feet leave the ground at some point in his stride, his friend insisting that at least one foot was always on the ground. Although his first attempts were failures, Muybridge finally managed to prove that Stanford was right.

He continued his motion studies at the University of Pennsylvania

In 1874 Muybridge was tried and acquitted for murdering his wife's lover. He left the country for a time, returning to resume his work in motion with Stanford in 1877. By 1880 he had refined his procedures considerably and was able to project a crude motion picture sequence on a screen with a device he called the *zoopraxiscope*. In 1883 he was invited to continue his experiments at the University of Pennsylvania, an invitation that Thomas Eakins, the American painter, may have influenced.

Figure 1.20   Eadweard Muybridge (1830-1904), Plate 156 from *The Human Figure in Motion* (IMP GEH)

In 1887 a set of his motion sequence photographs analyzing both animal and human activities was published under the title *Animal Locomotion* (Fig. 1.20).

Although his work was denounced by a number of influential painters and photographers as "inartistic" and "untrue," Muybridge was clearly an influence on men like Etienne Jules Marey and Thomas Eakins, both of whom devised cameras for making multiple exposures of moving figures. Their work, in turn, quite clearly foreshadows the Futurist painters, Duchamps, Balla, and others.

One of Muybridge's critics was Peter Henry Emerson, a physician, an amateur art historian, an avowed opponent of H. P. Robinson, a photographer of considerable skill, and a highly opinionated critic-at-large. Emerson's work is certainly impressive. Done in platinotype or photogravure, his prints have a delicate softness of outline and exploit the subtle midtone grays with genuine sensitivity (Fig. 1.21). They are in obvious contrast to Robinson's sentimental composites, and Robinson was sharply critical of them. Emerson retorted that nothing that Robinson had ever done or said had affected him in the least "except as a warning of what not to do" and continued to write and lecture energetically in support of his views.

Peter Henry Emerson: physician, art historian, photographer

In 1889 Emerson published a rambling philosophical and instructional book called *Naturalistic Photography* in which he defined photography as a pictorial art and emphasized that a photograph should be (1) true in natural sentiment; (2) true in appearance to the point of illusion; and (3) decorative. Then, incredibly, he published in 1891 a pamphlet renouncing his previous teachings, declaring that photography could never be an art and apologizing for having led astray so many followers. Called *The Death of Naturalistic Photography*, the little pamphlet

He published
Naturalistic Photography

**And *The Death
of Naturalistic Photography***

Figure 1.21   P. H. Emerson (1856-1936), *A Stiff Pull* (IMP GEH)

labels photography as "the hand-maiden of art and science" and Emerson closed it by saying that when his thoughts were in order he would write another book but, he said, "In the meantime, let students avoid all spurious imitations."

Emerson's influence was considerable

Emerson's influence on photography was considerable. In 1887, while judging a photography contest, he awarded Alfred Stieglitz the first prize for a picture called *A Good Joke* and told Stieglitz in a letter that it was the only truly spontaneous picture he had seen in the show. In 1903, acting as a judge of an exhibition sponsored by the Royal Photographic Society, he awarded the first prize to Frank Fraprie, a young American college student who later became a driving force in the pictorialist movement and editor of several photographic publications including *The American Annual of Photography*. Although Fraprie and Stieglitz were poles apart (Fraprie referred disparagingly to "Stieglitz and his crew of Photo-Secessionists" and the "Photo-Secession clique" in one of his articles) both remembered Emerson's appreciation of their work with satisfaction. Fraprie's account of the 1903 judgment is descriptive of Emerson's manner:

Frank Fraprie's account of Emerson's manner

The judge . . . was P. H. Emerson, the author of the celebrated book *Naturalistic Photography* which inaugurated a pictorial revolution in our art, and the most esteemed photographic critic of his time. Emerson, who was a man of decided opinions and choleric manners, walked into the room, cast his gaze around the wilderness of great frames, landed upon a minute white speck, which had been stuck in a convenient cranny by a door, walked up to it and said: "Gentlemen, you may do what you like with the rest of this show—this picture gets the pictorial medal."

It's interesting to note that Stieglitz carried on Emerson's philosophy of naturalism into "straight" photography and championed it as an art form in its own right. Fraprie, on the other hand, fixed superficially on

Emerson's "naturalistic focus" and "truth in sentiment" recommendations and, with the other pictorialists of the '20s, '30s, and '40s, let those noble aims degenerate into out-of-focus images and contrived situation photographs of the most cloying sentimentality.

The decade before the turn of the century brought a change in the way photography was used. It was no longer simply a scientific curiosity, and the camera image was becoming familiar to almost everyone. It was no longer a difficult or prohibitively expensive process either—George Eastman and the other entrepreneurs had seen to that. The snapshot era had arrived. Films were sensitive enough to record images in a small fraction of a second, and lenses had been vastly improved with the introduction in 1886, by the Schott glassworks in Germany, of new types of glass which permitted far better correction of the lens aberrations than had been previously possible.

One of the results of these improvements was the popularity of *detective* cameras. These took many forms, some of them ridiculous, but their common characteristics were small size and ease of operation. Cameras appeared disguised as waistcoat buttons, hats, books, cane handles, and almost anything else imaginable. Most of them were simply novelties, but some were workable enough to produce candid photographs in previously impossible situations. They brought informality to photography and led to the eventual appearance of the 35-mm *miniature* camera.

The snapshot and the detective cameras

The techniques of photography by 1910 were very much the same as those in use today. Cameras of all shapes and sizes were available; films were sensitive enough to make action pictures possible; lenses of large relative aperture and good correction existed. Stereoscopic pictures had been popular since about 1855 (Fig. 1.22) and color photographs, long a theoretical possibility, became a practical reality with the commercial production of *Autochrome* film by the Lumiere brothers in 1906. Photography had been used in the sciences and the arts; for business and pleasure; on the ground, in the air, and underwater; for good and for evil (photographic counterfeiting of dollar bills was noted in 1841).

1910 techniques were much the same as those we use today

Is photography an art or a science?

Figure 1.22   Francis Frith (1822-1899), Stereo transparency on glass (Courtesy William A. Lewis)

While the industry forged ahead purposefully, there was considerable dissension in the ranks of the photographers themselves. The question "Is photography an 'art' or a 'science'?" was, and still is, vigorously debated by opposing groups. An outstanding figure in this controversy was Alfred Stieglitz.

Alfred Stieglitz was introduced to photography in 1883

Stieglitz was born in Hoboken, New Jersey, on January 1, 1864. He spent his student years in Europe and was introduced to photography in 1883 during his first year as an engineering student at the Berlin Polytechnic. He became obsessed with photography almost at once and experimented constantly while studying photochemistry at the University. He was a nonconformist from the very beginning. He was also intelligent, artistic, and perceptive. He spent nine years in Europe, during which he studied and travelled on a modest income from his family, apparently leading a life which any young man would envy, and taking pictures. By 1890 he was internationally famous as an exhibitor of photographs.

By 1890 he was famous

He returned to New York in 1890 and was fascinated by the city (Fig. 1.23). An abortive attempt at business occupied him briefly, but he was soon out of it and devoted himself to photographing (Fig. 1.24) and promoting interest in photography by publishing *Camera Notes*, a quarterly, for the Camera Club of New York. The little group of sympathizers which soon surrounded him could have been called the "who's who" of American photography: Clarence White, Gertrude Käsebier (Fig. 1.25), Alvin Langdon Coburn (Fig. 1.26), Edward Steichen (see portfolio section, p. 284), Frank Eugene, Joseph Keiley, and others. In 1902 they formed their own informal group which Stieglitz, on impulse, named the "Photo-Secession."

Figure 1.23   Alfred Stieglitz (1864-1946), *The Terminal* (Courtesy of the Art Institute of Chicago)

Figure 1.24 Alfred Stieglitz (1864-1946), *The Steerage* (Courtesy of the Art Institute of Chicago)

In 1903 Stieglitz published the first quarterly issue of *Camera Work*, a lavishly printed magazine devoted to the promotion of photography as a form of art. The magazine and the Photo-Secessionists flourished for a while, and their gallery—three rooms at 291 Fifth Avenue, next to Steichen's room—became a crossroads and meeting place for artists as well as photographers (Fig. 1.25). It was an exciting time. The "ashcan" painters had stunned New Yorkers and the world with their notorious Armory Show of 1913, and the art scene was in ferment (Fig. 1.26).

Frederick Henry Evans was one of the several photographers whose work was publicized by Stieglitz. A London bookseller-turned photographer in 1898, Evans specialized in architectural photography, concentrating on the great cathedrals. His prints, on paper sensitized with iron and platinum salts, had a brillance and luminosity which few modern materials can approach. Evans must be considered one of the real masters of the photographic medium; his photographs are outstanding for their great tonal range and their delicate gradation (Fig. 1.27). He gave up

**The Photo-Secession,
"Camera Work," and 291**

**Frederick Henry Evans
made magnificent platinum prints**

Figure 1.25   Gertrude Käsebier (1852-1934), *Turner Family, Woburn, Mass.* (IMP GEH)

photography when the increasing cost and rarity of platinum made the commercially prepared paper unavailable during World War I. His prints are now collectors' items and command very high prices.

Stieglitz encouraged Paul Strand

Among the many photographers who frequented 291 was a young man named Paul Strand. For several years he observed the exhibitions and talked to Stieglitz, eventually becoming almost a protégé. With this kind of encouragement and an innate creative talent. Strand soon began making photographs of impressive strength (Fig. 1.28). Stieglitz gave him his first one-man show in 1916 and published six of his photographs in *Camera Work*. In further tribute, Stieglitz devoted the final issue of the magazine, June 1917, to Strand's work and praised his photographs as being "brutally direct . . . devoid of trickery . . . devoid of any attempt to mystify. . . . These photographs are the direct expression of today. . . ." Paul Strand's contribution to photography has since been outstanding. He is well known as a cinematographer and as the illustrator of numerous books and continues to be highly respected as an image-maker of exceptional vision and superlative skill.

Figure 1.26   Alvin Langdon Coburn (1882-1966), *St. Paul's,* gravure (Courtesy of the University of Michigan Museum of Art)

By 1914 Stieglitz was becoming disenchanted with the Secessionists and began to show the work of painters in 291 and *Camera Work*. It lost him the support of photographers, and in 1917, with the final Strand double issue of the magazine, he gave up the struggle. It had been a magnificent effort. Stieglitz's influence on modern art, and especially photography, had been immense. Never, before or since, has more missionary fervor been devoted to the advancement of photography as an independent art form.

It should not belittle Stieglitz to point out that he was outspoken, opinionated, and a bit arrogant; since without these tendencies, he would never have been successful in exerting the influence he did upon the art world. He was a highly visible and controversial figure, and his very presence tended to obscure the work of other less aggressive but quite significant photographers both here and abroad.

Eugene Atget was born in Libourne, France, in 1856. He was raised by an uncle and went to sea as a cabin boy in his youth. Later he became an actor and toured the country playing minor roles until he was about forty-

Figure 1.27 Frederick H. Evans (1853-1943), *Kelmscott Manor: Attics, 1896* (IMP GEH)

Figure 1.28 Paul Strand (1890-   ), *The White Fence* ("The White Fence," copyright © 1971, Paul Strand)

two. His entry into photography dates from about 1898. He was self-taught, largely ignorant of the technicalities of the medium, and not much concerned with other than the necessary materials and procedures; but he was a man possessed with the idea of documenting Paris. His love of the city and its inhabitants is evident in the direct, simple photographic records he produced. Working with an enormous old view camera with a simple set of lenses, and recording his images on glass plates, he prowled the streets of Paris from dawn 'til dusk, planting his tripod wherever a picture possibility appeared to him (Fig. 1.29). His views of boulevards

Eugene Atget documented Paris

Figure 1.29 Eugene Atget (1856-1927), *Un Coin de la Rue Reynie* (Courtesy of the University of Michigan Museum of Art)

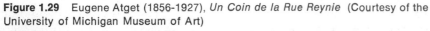

and shops, storekeepers and prostitutes, and all the rest of Paris, are only now being generally recognized as significant. Atget died in 1927, impoverished, alone, and almost totally unrecognized. What we know about him is due almost entirely to the efforts of Berenice Abbott, herself a fine photographer, who obtained many of his plates and has published many of his images.

Lewis Hine was a sociologist

Lewis Wickes Hine was a sociologist. His interest in photography appears to have started out of necessity in 1905—he wanted illustrations for his writings. He is best remembered for his documentation of the plight of immigrants and the Pittsburgh iron-workers (Fig. 1.30). Hine was not the first to document the ills of society—John Thomson had produced a magnificent series of pictures of London slums in the 1870s (Fig. 1.31), and Jacob Riis had exposed the conditions in the New York "sweatshops" in 1888—but he was a noteworthy social influence. His work points clearly to the magnificent documentation of the American depression years, accomplished by the FSA photographers some twenty-five years later.

Amateur photography was in a decadent state

If the photographic journals of the times are any indication, photography was in a kind of lull in the 1920s. Technical advances had certainly been made, but they were largely evolutionary (a notable exception was the introduction in 1924 of the *Leica*, not the first, but certainly the most successful of the pioneer 35-mm cameras). Photography, as practiced by the amateurs and the hobbyists, was in a decadent state. This was the age of the photographic pictorialist, and photo-clubs were flourishing. There was great interest in the nonsilver processes, especially those like gum and bromoil, which permitted great liberties to be taken with the image. Soft-focus images were the rule, and artificial textures which simulated paint or etching surfaces were much admired.

But new areas were being explored

Fortunately, there were some photographers who were not caught up in this superficial imitation of the established art forms. At least three sig-

Figure 1.30   Lewis Wickes Hine (1874-1940), *Forging the White-Hot Steel* (IMP GEH)

nificant new areas were being explored. The "super-realism" of the photographic image entranced Edward Weston; the jarring surrealism of the manipulated photographic image was exploited by Man Ray and Moholy-Nagy, and others; and the unique power of the photograph to communicate ideas was very shortly to be demonstrated by Salomon and Eisenstadt, and others in anticipation of what is now known as *photojournalism*.

Weston worked with the super-real image

Born in 1886 in Highland Park, Illinois, Edward Weston moved to California in 1906 and opened a portrait studio. He married and had four sons, but the marriage was not a happy one, and in 1922 he travelled to New York where he met Stieglitz. His daybook account of the two-hour meeting says it "focussed" him, and anxious to concentrate on a personal expression in photography, he travelled to Mexico City with Tina Modotti, an artists' model. There he worked for about two years producing portraits, nudes and cloud studies, and working in quite close contact with Mexico's leading artists.

Figure 1.31 John Thomson (1837-1921), *The Independent Shoe-Black* from *Street Life in London,* 1877 (IMP GEH)

He returned to California for good in 1926 and in 1929 settled in Carmel where he spent most of the rest of his life. Most of his work there was done with simple equipment; a rickety 8″ × 10″ view camera and the most rudimentary darkroom facilities, but there is no indication of this in his photographs. They are still exceptional for their glorification of natural forms in light, their sharpness of detail, and delicacy of texture. (Refer to portfolio section, p. 289.) Weston was a master of light, shade, form, and surface, who had strong convictions about photography and pursued them without fanfare.

His work introduced a major new direction in photographic imagery and philosophy, both of which have had profound effects on a generation of photographers. Fortunately for us, he kept a diary during most of his productive life and it has been published, in edited version, as *The Daybooks of Edward Weston*. It is a revealing and inspiring record of the life and creative struggles of one of the major artists of this century. He was the first photographer to receive a Guggenheim Foundation fellowship and was given a major retrospective exhibition in the Museum of Modern Art in New York in 1946. He died in Carmel in 1958.

Although photography had been used almost from its infancy for documentation and social commentary by various workers, it was not until the 1920s that its potential for reportage of current events began to be exploited extensively. A number of factors probably influenced this new development: the increasing public awareness of world and national happenings; the refinement of rapid printing and engraving processes; and, probably most important of all, the new cameras and improved lenses which were constantly increasing the capabilities of the photographic medium itself.

Salomon— father of modern photojournalism

Dr. Erich Salomon—often called "the father of modern photojournalism"—was one of the first to concentrate in this area. Like many of the earlier workers, he began taking pictures rather late in life (at the age of about forty-two), and almost out of necessity rather than real interest. Employed by a German publishing house, he found that working with hired photographers was a time-consuming and expensive business, so he bought a camera and set out to learn to use it.

The camera which made him famous was the Zeiss Ikon (Dresden) *Ermanox* which was introduced in 1927. It took $4\frac{1}{2}$ cm $\times$ 6 cm glass plates in individual holders and featured an amazingly fast f/1.8, *Ernostar* lens of 85 mm focal length. (Salomon's own camera was equipped with an f/2.0 lens, according to his son.)

Salomon experimented briefly with artificial lighting, but soon gave it up in favor of the more natural and pleasing effect of *available light*. Using the little Ermanox on a tripod because of the long exposures required (usually from about $\frac{1}{5}$ second to one full second), he specialized in photographing political notables, usually unposed, in their meetings and conferences. His ability to work quietly and surreptitiously produced some remarkable spontaneous portraits as well as a great many valuable documentary photographs of famous statesmen at work. He had an uncanny knack for catching his subjects unawares in the midst of some characteristic or expressive gesture, somehow managing—in spite of the relatively long exposure times required—to avoid excessive blurring of the image (Fig. 1.32).

He was a master of persuasion and subterfuge when it was required to get the picture, often concealing his camera in a flower vase, a brief case, a stack of books, or in his own clothing. He once smuggled a camera into the U.S. Supreme Court, where pictures were strictly forbidden, by putting his arm in an enormous sling and concealing the camera in the wrappings on the "cast." He was so successful in these efforts that he eventually became quite accepted in international political circles; so much so that a famous diplomat was once heard to remark, "Where is Salomon? If we begin without him people will think this conference is not important!"

Like Brady, he had a sense of history

Like Mathew Brady, Salomon had a great sense of the historical significance of his work. Much of it was done without thought of personal gain, simply to document the events that he knew were shaping history. It is ironic that he died in a German prison camp; a victim of a political

Figure 1.32 Erich Salomon (1886-1944), *Supreme Court, Chief Justice Hughes presiding,* 1932 (IMP GEH)

system that he had watched and documented and opposed. Characteristically, he managed to conceal his precious negatives from his captors. Just before he was arrested, he arranged for some of them to be left with the librarian of the Dutch parliament and was able to bury the rest, safely wrapped and sealed, in a friend's garden.

Salomon's "candid cameras" (the term was originally applied to Salomon's work by an editor of the *London Graphic*) caught the fancy of amateur photographers as well as other professionals, and 35-mm cameras began to become popular. With the introduction of the Zeiss *Contax* in 1932, the Leica had its first real rival, and the era of the precision *minicam* (as it was later sometimes called) had arrived. It was many years before the 35-mm camera dominated the amateur market, but the trend was clearly indicated. The introduction of the *Exacta* (it is now spelled Exa*k*ta) in 1937 gave photographers their first single-lens reflex 35-mm precision camera and forecast the development of the presently popular *prism-reflexes*. The Exacta was extremely successful. It was manufactured without any major changes in design for more than thirty years and has only recently been withdrawn from the market.

The 35-mm camera began to become popular

In 1932 Weston and a little group of serious young photographers had banded loosely together in an organization they referred to as "Group f/64." The name referred to one of the smallest apertures normally found on view camera lenses and implied the group's interest in sharp focus and precise detail rendering as opposed to the popular soft-focus images of the camera club pictorialists. The work of one of the original members, Ansel Adams, was, and continues to be, outstanding.

Group f/64

Originally trained as a musician, Adams was interested in photography only as an avocation until he encountered the work of Paul Strand in 1930. The experience changed his life and he was soon redirected to a career in photography. Within a very few years he had so thoroughly mastered the skills and vision of straight photography that he had produced a beautifully printed textbook, *Making a Photograph*, and had shown his work in Stieglitz's New York gallery, "An American Place." Since that auspicious beginning Ansel Adams has become perhaps the best-known photographer in America. He is a master craftsman, a prolific producer of images, a perceptive critic, author of numerous books, and the acknowledged master of the still-vital school of "West Coast" straight photography. (See Adams' photograph in the portfolio section, *Frozen Lake and Cliffs*, p.300.) Adams' influence on photography has been profound and he has had, and still has, an army of enthusiastic followers. He has taught photography and conducted workshops for many years and his *Zone System* of image tone control through previsualization and control of exposure and development has become a standard feature of most American college courses in still photography.

Ansel Adams was trained as a musician

The 1930s were significant years in the history of photography. *Fortune* magazine was launched in late 1929 and did well in spite of the great stock market crash of 1929 and the subsequent depression. *Life* magazine began in 1936, starting a whole new trend in journalism based on the concept of the picture story. *Life's* Alfred Eisenstadt (who had worked beside Salomon in covering the Geneva League of Nations conferences) and Margaret Bourke-White were original staff photographers whose names soon be-

The picture magazines arrive

came household words. It was not long before other publishers got on the bandwagon. *Look* appeared in 1937, followed closely by a number of others such as *Pic* and *Click*. Pictorial supplements were added to Sunday newspapers, too, and suddenly the nation was picture-conscious.

The Farm Security Administration Photographic Unit

No summary of photography in America would be complete without mention of the documentary work done by the Farm Security Administration's Photographic Unit in the period from 1935 to 1941. The country was still staggering from the economic collapse of 1929, and millions of people were destitute. Roy E. Stryker was asked to supervise the production of a photographic record of the misery of the farmers, who were exceptionally hard-hit, and their drought-ravaged lands.

The project was begun with twelve photographers, of whom Walker Evans, Dorothea Lange (Fig. 1.33), Carl Mydans (Fig. 1.34), Arthur Rothstein, Ben Shahn, and John Vachon are perhaps the best known. All of them were extremely competent and sensitive artists. In the six years of the project, they travelled the country from end to end, concentrating on the South, Midwest, and West, and produced a 270,000-negative record of the plight of the country's farm people. It was an inspired project which told the story of the Depression more powerfully and directly than words could possibly have done.

Photography played an important part in World War II

World War II caught the nation off its guard. It had still not recovered fully from the Depression and life was relatively leisurely, but the Japanese attack on Pearl Harbor galvanized industry into action. The part that photography played in the war cannot be detailed, but it was surely a most important one. There was a tremendous surge in optical research and development, and the so-called *rare earth* glasses which had just be-

Figure 1.33   Dorothea Lange (1895-1965), *Breadline* (Courtesy of the Art Institute of Chicago)

Figure 1.34   Carl Mydans (1907-   ), *Migrants camped on U.S. 70, Tenn.*, Mar. '36 (Library of Congress)

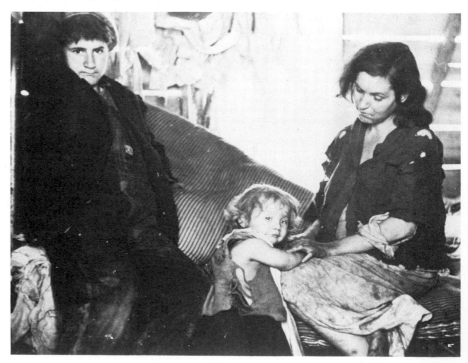

gun to be used before the war were put into mass production. There was a corresponding improvement in film materials, too.

The War's end brought sweeping social changes. With the new peace came a growing prosperity bringing with it a flood of consumer goods. With it also came the sobering realization that the world's last frontiers had been explored and, that for the first time in history, man had the physical capacity to exterminate himself with one grand gesture. To many young people in the '50s and '60s, these factors combined into a ghastly paradox. They saw ahead of them lives of comfort and material plenty but devoid of purpose, empty of human value, and ominous from the threat of atomic disaster, runaway population growth, and resource depletion. Some of them looked at this new, crazy world with suddenly sharpened perception, and, while many were caught up in waves of semiorganized protest and demonstration, a few expressed themselves through their art, including photography.

The War's end brought sweeping social changes

Robert Frank's book, *The Americans*, gave us a first shocked look at ourselves in 1959. The pictures seem quite ordinary now because Frank's work started a style which is still popular. In 1959, however, it was new and startling; direct, artless, often irritating. It confronted us with things we had trained ourselves not to see and we reacted with gut feelings of loneliness, dislocation, and a dismayed recognition of life's overwhelming trivia (refer to portfolio section, p. 291). Frank's work was a new, raw descendant of the social commentary approach to imagery, traceable through the F.S.A. documentary of the Depression, to Hine, Riis, and Thomson; but it had a new roughness of style which seemed to deny, or at least ignore, the older traditions of compositional elegance and the concept of the "fine print." *The Americans* leads more or less directly to the work of Lee Friedlander, Gary Winogrand, Danny Lyon, and others who have come to be known as the *Social Landscape* photographers.

Robert Frank's book, *The Americans*

While the Social Landscape style—if there really is such a thing— is characterized by a rather low-keyed, introspective observation of the strange aspects of familiar social situations, it parallels, and sometimes overlaps, the more recognizable approach of the photojournalists. Here the deliberate use of intelligible symbols is obvious, as is the intent to inform, comment upon, and persuade. An excellent example of this "editorial" style, relating to the turbulent years of protest in the 1960s, is the book, *America in Crisis*, featuring the photographs of the *Magnum* group and published by Holt, Rinehart and Winston in 1969.

The editorial style

Until about 1960 the photojournalists were major interpreters of the world's news and the photo-illustrators played a major part in moulding public taste and controlling buying habits. It was a serious blow to both groups when that lusty young medium, television, began to usurp their functions. *Look* magazine died rather quietly in 1971, a victim of increased costs and reduced advertising income; the same factors which had previously eliminated *Colliers, Saturday Evening Post*, and others. *Life* struggled gamely on but the handwriting was on the wall. In spite of a brave editorial policy of "more picture emphasis," economic pressures and waning public interest in the magazine picture-story concept finally took their toll; the magazine published its last regular issue in December 1972.

Photojournalism and illustration will never be the same again

As the flow of advertising money began to shift from magazine space to television, a similar, but less traumatic readjustment was forced on the illustrators. While some of the well-established photographers were relatively unaffected, a great many saw their profits dwindle. By 1970 it was clear that photographic journalism and illustration would never be the same again. Television has the public firmly in its grip and has become a frighteningly effective influence on our lives.

Photography in the schools —the SPE

By 1960 photography had begun to find rather widespread acceptance in the high schools, colleges, and universities. It spread rapidly, often being offered by departments of art or journalism, but also, occasionally, being located in such diverse areas as engineering, speech, graphics, or education. The content and direction of these courses has varied widely. In 1963 a group of teachers including Henry Holmes Smith, Aaron Siskin, Arthur Siegel, John Schulze, Art Sinsabaugh, Robert Heineken, Nathan Lyons, and others, founded the Society for Photographic Education (SPE) to establish formal lines of communication between teachers of photography, to encourage the growth of photography in the schools, and to cooperate with other organizations, such as the Professional Photographers of America (PP of A), also interested in education. The SPE has grown slowly but steadily and now has several hundred active members widely distributed over the United States, as well as a few members from foreign countries. A recent estimate places the number of photography students in colleges and universities at over 80,000.

Image styles have blended and merged

This relatively sudden and widespread education of photographers, especially in the historic and stylistic trends of the medium, together with photography's frequently close association with the other arts, has inspired great changes in imagery. Before World War II most photographers were content to work within rather stable, traditional styles. Postwar trends are less easily catalogued. Although the venerable tradition of "straight" photography is still healthy, many photographers have now abandoned the purity of the straight image in favor of various manipulated or mixed-media forms. Styles have blended and merged almost inseparably. The transition from straight documentary imagery to the extremes of symbolism, derivation, and manipulation is a continuous one without obvious boundaries. It seems significant, too, that while many photographers have been evolving away from the straight image concept, a few painters have been frankly imitating the snapshot. Thus it begins to appear that we have come full circle; the separations between photography, painting, and printmaking no longer seem clearly defined. Perhaps we have finally reached that stage of maturity and enlightenment which will allow us to call ourselves "artists" if we choose to, without having to define or defend the medium or media we choose to work in.

Japan and Germany recovered swiftly

World War II left Japan broken and Germany helpless and divided. Their photographic industries, which had been supreme before the war, were disrupted and inactive. Both countries recovered swiftly, however, and in a few years German cameras and lenses were again being produced. Japan, which before the war had never been thought of as a producer of quality goods, also began manufacture of cameras and lenses and in a very short time became a leader in the field. Today the American camera manufacturing industry is no longer competitive in the high-precision lines, and the vast majority of cameras on our market are Japanese-made.

In that market now, the 35-mm cameras outnumber all other types, and for several reasons. They are small and convenient to carry; film is cheap and of excellent quality; the cameras are extremely versatile in use; they are very widely available; and they are relatively inexpensive. The prism-reflex design has given them some of the viewing advantages of the much larger view camera, and extra lenses and accessories of all kinds are available.

35-mm cameras are now most popular

But much of their popularity has to be laid to the modern trends in imagery. To a generation of photographers weaned on television, bombarded from birth with magazine and newspaper photographs, and casually familiar with all sorts of cinematic images, the painstaking perfection of a single black-and-white *still* photograph seems anachronistic. The world is now a frantic, terrifying, and exhilarating place and much of modern photography expresses this clearly. This is the age of expression and protest, and technical niceties are generally considered to be irrelevant and unimportant. For work in this vein, the 35-mm camera, hand-held, is an excellent tool. It seems likely that the still smaller *half-frame* cameras will become increasingly more popular, too, for the same reasons.

Gradually over the years, the photograph, which began as a tantalizing and transient shadow and became a wonderful and treasured artifact, has lost its charm. Its novelty is long gone, its value cheapened by overuse; it has become an item of casual interest to be produced, consumed, and forgotten—or so it often seems.

But is this really true? Among the millions who click camera shutters every day, there are certainly a few individuals, as there have always been, who sense some personal significance in the making of a photograph. Photographers like Ansel Adams, Paul Strand, Imogen Cunnningham, Minor White, Henri Cartier-Bresson, Eugene Smith, Bruce Davidson, Diane Arbus, Jerry Uelsmann, and hundreds of others, have demonstrated clearly that photographic imagery can be more intense and meaningful than the mere picturing of things.

Is photography an art, a craft, a science, a hobby? Who really cares? It is, without any doubt at all, the most vital and significant visual force in the world today.

Photography is the most vital visual force in the world today

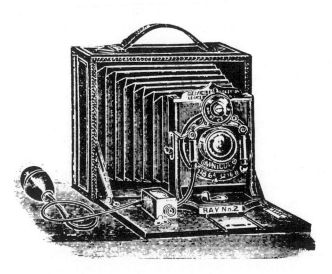

2

Photograms

Photography harnesses light to produce images

Photography harnesses light to produce images. It can do this because light is a form of energy which affects many substances in one way or another, and the effects are often visible. Freshly sawn pinewood, for example, will darken gradually in sunlight; so does human skin. Dyes bleach, plastics disintegrate, and plants turn green when exposed to light. Light energy can also be transformed into electrical energy by *photo cells*, and this phenomenon is used to count manufactured parts on production lines, to turn on streetlights, to produce the sound you hear in the motion picture theater, and to work that handy measuring device, the photographic exposure meter.

In almost every phase of photography, you will have to consider light in some way: by exposing things to it; protecting things from it; changing its color, or brightness, or direction; focusing it, or diffusing it. Light is the substance of photography. The sooner you become aware of its effects —physical, chemical, and artistic—the sooner you will become competent as a photographer.

The simplest photographic image is the photogram

The very simplest photographic image that can be formed is the *photogram*. It is easily demonstrated by partially shielding some light-sensitive surface and exposing the rest of the surface to light. You will see plenty of examples of this sort of *printed-out* photogram at any beach in early summer where bathing suit patterns show up clearly in white Caucasian skin against pink backgrounds of sunburn.

A photogram is a recorded shadow

A photogram is simply a recorded shadow. You can make one by placing an object of almost any sort on a sheet of photographic printing paper such as Kodak *Azo* or *Polycontrast* (or the equivalent product of any other manufacturer) and exposing the paper to very strong light, preferably daylight, for several seconds or minutes. The image is formed gradually as the light energy darkens the sensitive *emulsion* surface coating of the paper.

It is a negative image

The finished picture will show the object's shadow as a light tone against the darkened background. Since the image is pale where the light did not strike it and dark where the light was brightest, it reverses the normal tonal scale and is called a "negative" image.

Printing-out

A photogram made in this way is not generally satisfactory, since, unless it is somehow stabilized, the action of light will continue and darken the whole area in time. This technique is referred to as *printing-out* the image.

A more flexible and versatile technique for making photograms makes use of the *developing-out* process. Here the exposure to light is relatively brief, and only a *latent* (invisible) image is formed directly. The sensitized paper is then immersed in a *developer* solution which chemically reduces the latent image to a visible image composed of minute particles of metallic silver.

Developing-out

The developed image is not permanent or stable until the unused sensitized material has been removed, and this function is fulfilled by the *hypo* or *fixing bath*. This is followed by a prolonged wash in running water, and the finished print is dried. The image, white on a black background, is negative (Fig. 2.1). It is much more contrasty than the printed-out image and is stable and permanent. A printed-out photogram can also be fixed for permanence, but the image is usually an unpleasant yellowish-brown and lacking in brilliance.

Developing and fixing the image

An amusing variation of the standard photogram technique is the *cliché verre*. One of the very earliest forms of photographic printing, it is simply the reproduction of drawings done on glass (Fig. 2.2). Clichés can be made from drawings done on any transparent material, however, including cellophane, mylar film, and plexiglas. Very interesting patterns can be produced by scratching through the blackened emulsion of an old negative or by alternately drawing and scratching through ink or paint films on plastic.

Cliché verre images are interesting

Since, in the developing-out process, the image is formed gradually and progressively in the developer solution and can be arrested at any point by immersion in the *stop* bath, it is possible to paint an exposed sheet of paper with developer and control the darkness of the resulting pattern by alternate treatments with developer and stop bath (short-stop). Paper immersed in the hypo, however, will be *fixed* and will no longer react to the developer in a normal manner.

Figure 2.1

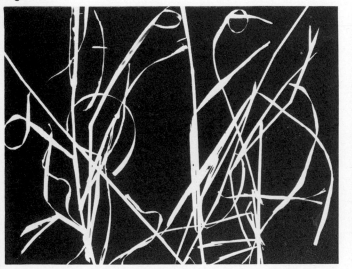

Figure 2.2

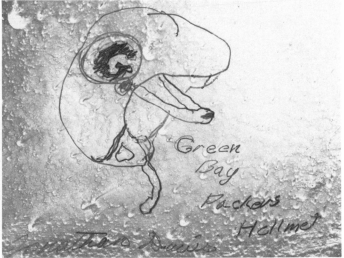

Stains can be produced

Interesting stain patterns can sometimes be produced by dirtying up the process, handling the developer-laden print with hypo-contaminated fingers, smearing the paper with other chemicals during development, or leaving a developer-soaked print out in the air for some time without fixing it.

Solutions once contaminated should be discarded

All of these stains result from generally undesirable darkroom practices, and they are likely to be impermanent; but for the purposes of experimentation, they may lead to interesting visual results. It is important to remember, however, that good, clean, controlled, and predictable photographic work cannot be done in this way; that chemical solutions, once contaminated by this sort of intermixing, should be discarded before serious printing is attempted.

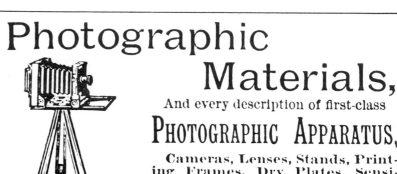

Introduction to Print Development

3

Producing photographic images, including photograms, on paper is called *printing* and it is one of the most entertaining aspects of the photographic process. Here the personal involvement of photographer with image is immediate and fascinating. Here the fruits of hours of planning and labor are suddenly realized. Here the final delicate control of tone, contrast, scale, and composition is brought to bear. Printing is fun. It is also demanding, and it is a skill which no good photographer ever seems to master to his complete satisfaction.

Printing seems simple at first glance—so simple that beginners tend to become careless after the first few sessions. Fight this tendency! Carelessness will certainly lead to poor print quality!

The photographic *enlarger* (Fig. 3.1) is a machine which can be used to project the magnified images of photographic negatives onto sensitized papers, and it can be used to project shadows of small objects as well. Two new considerations will enter into the planning of photograms made in this manner: the images can be varied in size with ease; and the shadows can be projected either in- or out-of-focus; that is, either sharp and well-defined or soft-edged and blurred (Fig. 3.2).

Producing photographic images on paper is called printing

Beginners tend to become careless; fight this tendency!

The enlarger can project images

Figure 3.1

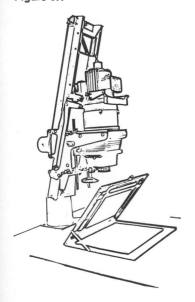

Figure 3.2

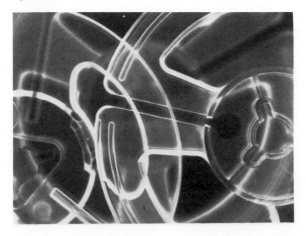

**After exposure,
the paper must be processed**

The projected image of a photogram subject can also be used as a light source for a conventional photogram; that is, objects can be placed on the paper surface at the same time that patterns are being projected onto it, to form combined images. It is also possible to make two or more photograms on the same paper, one after the other, if the patterns are carefully chosen to overlap favorably. There is danger here of obliterating one image by the subsequent ones if they are overdone.

After exposure to the printing light, the paper must be *processed* in chemical solutions to convert the invisible latent image into a visible one.

**Most of the chemicals are safe,
but ...**

Although most of the chemicals used in photography are "safe" in the sense that they are not violently poisonous, a few of them are dangerous. It is a good idea to treat them all with respect. None of the solutions which you will use for paper processing is normally harmful, but some individuals are allergic to one of the chemical ingredients of the developer solution and may get a rather serious skin rash from contact with it.

In addition to this, the developer solution will oxidize slowly in air to form a strong brown dye which is very difficult to remove from clothing; the fixer solution is a fairly effective bleach for some clothing dyes; and an old, used fixing bath may contain enough silver to stain clothing indelibly. The stop and fixing baths are both mildly acidic, and, while neither of them is at all dangerous to handle, they can cause considerable corrosion on some metal surfaces.

**Contamination of the baths
can cause staining**

It should be obvious, of course, that the various chemicals should never contact the paper surface except in the normal sequence of processing steps. Chemical contamination of the baths will at least degrade the quality of the finished print and may cause disastrous staining of the paper.

Here are some suggestions for avoiding darkroom problems.

1. Wear old clothes or a lab apron.
2. Be sure that all utensils are clean before and after use.
3. Keep all liquids—especially hypo—in the sink. Keep the worktables dry.
4. Wash up spilled chemicals with clean water.
5. Keep your hands clean while processing. Wash and dry your hands before leaving the sink area.
6. Follow instructions exactly.

**Chemicals are mixed
to form stock solutions**

If you have purchased your chemicals in powder form, they must be mixed with water to make the *stock solutions*. Follow the instructions given on the packages.

Arrange at least three clean trays in the darkroom sink (Fig. 3.3a). Working normally from left to right, the trays will contain—

Developer, D-72 or Dektol;
Stop bath, 1% acetic acid solution;
Fixing bath or hypo, F-6 or Rapid-Fix.

Figure 3.3

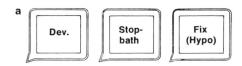

If sufficient sink space is available, it is convenient to use as many as six trays. The last three (Fig. 3.3*b*) can be used for—

> Water rinse;
> Hypo clearing agent;
> Water wash, running water.

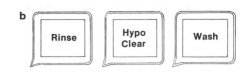

To prepare the *working solution* of developer (in this case Kodak's D-72 or Dektol) from the previously mixed *stock* (or storage) solution, dilute one part stock with two parts water. An 8″ × 10″ tray will require about a quart of solution to provide good working depth, so the developer proportions might be—

Preparing the working solutions; developer

> Dektol stock solution, 10 ounces;
> Water, 20 ounces.

The second tray should contain the stop bath, or *shortstop*. To make the shortstop working solution, add about 1½ ounces of 28% acetic acid to about 30 ounces of water. The 28% acetic acid shortstop stock should be kept in a labelled bottle. You can buy it already prepared or you can do it yourself by diluting *glacial* acetic acid. CAUTION: glacial acetic acid is highly concentrated, 99½%, and dangerous. Handle it with caution!

Shortstop

Figure 3.4   To make *Shortstop* Stock Solution

To prepare 28% acetic acid, add three parts of glacial acetic acid to eight parts of water (Fig. 3.4). It is wise to do this in a well-ventilated area. Glacial acetic acid fumes are extremely penetrating and unpleasant. Don't keep the glacial acid bottle in the darkroom; it might be confused with the 28% stock solution.

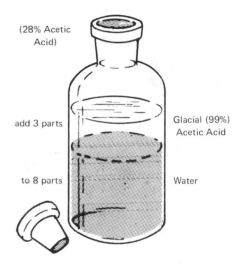

The 28% shortstop stock solution has a strong odor and may irritate sensitive skin, but it is not dangerous. The working solution is completely safe. It is only about 1% acetic acid, which is approximately one-fifth as strong as table vinegar.

The third tray should be filled to a good working depth with the fixing bath solution *without dilution*. In this case the stock and working solutions are the same.

The fixing bath

Having prepared the working solutions, adjust their temperatures; 21° C. (70° F.) is ideal, but the range from about 16° C. to 26° C. (60° F. to 80° F.), is workable. Since the chemical activity of the solutions is related to their temperature, it is a good idea to standardize on a temperature which can be repeated day after day so that the results can be predicted. Very high temperatures should be avoided, since the paper may be physically damaged by hot water. Whatever the temperature, all the baths should be about the same. Try to avoid extreme variations from bath to bath.

Photographic paper must be unwrapped and handled in total darkness or in the yellowish *safelight* in the darkroom. It must not be exposed to white light except while making the print exposure. The various chemical processing steps must be carried out in the safelight illumination only. Take only one sheet of paper out of the package at one time and close the

Photographic paper must be handled in safelight

package tightly to avoid *fogging* the remaining sheets. Even the safelight is not *safe* for prolonged exposure.

Developing the print

After making the exposure, develop one sheet at a time. Slip the exposed paper sheet into the developer solution as smoothly and quickly as possible and begin to agitate it by rocking the tray. The agitation need not be violent or fast, but the solution should be kept constantly moving across the paper emulsion. Occasionally, poke the corners down to keep the surface covered evenly with liquid. Vary the speed and direction of agitation to prevent streaking.

If you don't want to get your hands into the processing solutions, you can use *tongs* for handling the paper. It's a good idea to have two; one for the developer only and the other for use in the shortstop and the hypo. The use of tongs will save wear and tear on your hands (the developer is about as bad as soapy water) and will help to prevent stains; but there is real danger of cracking or bruising the print emulsion if you're not careful. You'll almost have to use your hands to process large prints and many photographers find tongs a nuisance even for small ones.

Don't touch the print surface unnecessarily and particularly avoid pressure on the emulsion or prolonged finger contact in one place; body heat may speed up the development and cause a dark spot, or a chemical stain may result.

Some authorities advise placing the paper in the developer facedown (while some caution against it). Either position is workable for the first few seconds, but the print should be turned faceup as soon as it is thoroughly and uniformly wet with developer and allowed to complete its development faceup. The important thing is to get the print into the developer and thoroughly wet as quickly, as uniformly, and with as little fuss as possible.

The image will begin to appear in about ten to thirty seconds and will build up fairly rapidly. It should be essentially complete in about forty-five seconds (for contact printing papers such as Azo) to a minute-and-a-half (for projection papers such as Polycontrast). Regardless of the appearance of the image, prints on contact papers should be developed for *one minute* and projection papers for *two minutes*. Then they should be removed from the developer, drained for a few seconds, and placed immediately in the stop bath.

Don't try to control image tone by varying developing time

It is a mistake (and one which most beginners make) to try to control the image tone by varying the print developing time. If the image is too dark, it can only be corrected satisfactorily by making another print and reducing the exposure time. If the print is too light in tone, make another and expose it to light for a longer time.

The exposure change may have to be rather considerable if the tone of the print is obviously bad. Doubling or halving the exposure time will probably not be too extreme. If the print is completely white, increase the next exposure by at least ten times. If completely black, cut the next exposure by the same amount. Several adjustments of this magnitude may have to be made if you are attempting to use a very sensitive paper in very strong light, or a relatively insensitive one in very dim light. Remember, though, the developing time should not be tampered with in an attempt to control image tone.

Agitate the print in the stop bath for about thirty seconds to a minute (*Resin-Coated*, or *RC*, papers need only about five to ten seconds). At this time, you may hear a high whining or whistling sound which is caused by tiny streams of gas bubbles, formed by the reaction of the acid with the developer alkali, being forced out through the paper fibers. You may also see them rising to the surface of the solution. This is usually of no consequence, but merely indicates that the stop bath is doing its job.

Agitate the print in the shortstop

If the sound occurs after the print has been placed in the hypo bath, it is an indication that the developer has not been neutralized and that longer immersion in the stop bath is advisable, or perhaps the stop bath has become weakened with use and should be replaced with fresh solution. Adequate treatment in an active stop bath is important both to avoid exhausting the acid in the hypo bath and to help prevent possible staining of the paper. You may not hear any whistling sound at all. Don't worry, it doesn't necessarily mean that you're doing something wrong. Let the print remain in the stop bath for at least thirty seconds with agitation and transfer it to the hypo.

The print should be agitated in the hypo for about a minute, then allowed to soak for another minute or two before it is safe to view in white light. If it is to be allowed to remain in the hypo with other prints be sure to agitate them all every few minutes, leaving a different one on top of the pile each time. RC papers should be removed from the fixer after about two or three minutes. Prolonged fixing of even normal paper prints is not a good idea since it may cause excessive hardening of the paper emulsion and bleaching of the image tones. It is best to remove prints from the hypo after five to ten minutes and hold them in a large tray of clean water for further treatment. The water should be changed from time to time. RC papers should not be allowed to soak for extended periods or their water-repellency will be lost. Process them straight through without delays if you wish to take full advantage of their chemical resistance and rapid drying characteristics.

Agitate the print in the hypo

Do not soak RC papers

The shortstop will effectively remove developer from the fingers, but it is not a good idea to rinse your hands in the shortstop after having them in the hypo bath. Keep a tray or graduate of water near the hypo tray and use it to rinse your fingers thoroughly before going from the hypo to any other solution or before drying your hands on a towel.

Rinse the hypo off your hands before touching anything

If you plan to carry the print out of the sink for inspection or any other purpose, rinse it for at least a minute in running water to remove all the surface hypo, and let it drip-drain in the sink. To be completely safe, wet prints should always be carried out of the sink area in a clean tray, perhaps containing a little clean water.

After a number of prints have accumulated in the holding tray they can be rinsed very briefly in running water and transferred, one by one, to a tray of hypo clearing bath, prepared according to the instructions on the package. RC paper prints do not require this step and, as a rule,

Treat the prints in hypo clearing solution

should not be treated in the clearing bath. Since hypo clearing baths vary in type and method of use, no specific instructions can be given here. Follow the manufacturer's instructions.

Wash the prints thoroughly

Following the hypo clearing bath, the prints should wash in running water for at least as long as recommended on the hypo clearing bath package, perhaps fifteen or twenty minutes after the last print is placed in the wash tray. If no hypo clearing bath is used, the washing time should not be less than one hour (RC prints need no more than about five minutes). Don't let the prints bunch together during washing. The running water must flow between and around them freely. Wash only a few prints at a time and use a large tray for best results. The wash must be timed from the moment the last print is placed into the water. An unwashed print added to a tray full of washed prints will contaminate them all and necessitate rewashing the whole batch. Insufficiently washed prints eventually discolor or fade, although this may not occur for years. Much more seriously, they may contaminate the dryer, the drying racks, or other prints.

Drying the prints on a drum dryer

After washing is completed, the prints may be dried in any of several ways. The easiest method of drying uncoated papers is *matte-drying* on a heated-drum type dryer. Turn on the dryer a half-hour or so before use and allow it to reach an operating temperature of about 121°C. to 135°C. (250°F. to 275°F.).

Figure 3.5

The washed prints are squeegeed individually on a glass or stainless steel plate to remove surface water, then placed on the dryer blanket *facedown*. The slowly moving belt will carry them around the heated drum surface, eventually dropping them, dry, into the receiving basket.

Glossy drying of suitable papers is similar, except that the washed prints are soaked in a *glossing* solution, such as Pakosol, squeegeed, then sponged with Pakosol on the emulsion side and placed *faceup* on the dryer blanket so that the print face will contact the polished drum surface as it dries. The wet emulsion is literally moulded to the drum surface and will dry with a mirrorlike gloss.

Only glossy papers can be ferrotyped

Only uncoated papers manufactured specifically for glossy drying can be glossed (sometimes called *ferrotyped*) in this way. Other papers, if dried faceup, will take an imperfect, blotchy, or mottled gloss which is unacceptable.

Papers can be resoaked and redried to change their surface if desired. Thus a matte-dried print can be changed to a glossy one, if it is a glossy paper, and a mottled gloss can usually be converted to an acceptable matte surface if the print is soaked until limp and dried *facedown*.

RC papers should be air-dried

RC papers must not be dried on the drum dryer. Simply sponge or blot them surface-dry and either hang them from a line with spring clothespins or lay them out, preferably facedown (although some authorities advise faceup) on special drying racks (Fig. 3.5) or on clean, uncolored cloth. Because they will have absorbed very little moisture during processing they will air-dry quickly without excessive warping or curling and the natural sheen of the paper surface will be retained. Warmed air can be circulated around the prints to speed drying but excessive heat (over 87.8°C. or 190°F.) should be avoided.

Partially washed prints of the ordinary variety can also be dried, if time is short, by simply laying them out on newspapers or towels, faceup, to air-dry. They will usually curl severely, but this does no harm. They can be resoaked as soon as it is convenient, washed as usual, and dried on the dryer. *Do not dry partially washed prints on the dryer.* If the dryer blanket becomes contaminated with hypo, it will, in turn, contaminate clean prints which touch it.

It is not necessary to have access to a heated dryer to dry prints well, although these machines are fast and convenient. Blotter books (Fig. 3.6*a*) and blotter rolls (Fig. 3.6*b*) are available for matte-drying, and ferrotype tins can be used for drying glossy prints. Drying time is extended, typically overnight, but the results can be as good as those obtained with the more elaborate and expensive drum dryers.

Drying prints in blotter books or rolls

After the printing session is over, close up your paper package and turn on the white lights. Discard the working solution of developer and rinse out the developer tray with the stop bath. Then rinse both developer and shortstop trays, inside and out, with clean water and stand them in the racks to dry. Pour the used fixing bath back into a storage jug and label it "Print Fixer." Wash out the fixer tray with several changes of water, paying particular attention to the rim where dried droplets of hypo will be likely to be found. Stand the tray to dry.

Cleaning up

Some varieties of hypo clearing bath may be saved but some do not keep well. Consult the manufacturer's recommendations and if they do not specifically suggest discarding the solution it can probably be saved and used again. Pour it into a clean bottle and label it "Hypo Clearing Bath." Discard both the fixer and the clearing bath when they have treated about fifteen 8″ × 10″ prints per quart of working solution. Rinse out the clearing bath tray and stand it to dry. Wash the other utensils you may have used, such as funnels, graduates, print paddles or tongs, etc., and put them away. Wipe up stains or spills and go over the spots with a wet towel to clean up any residual chemical. Discard excess test strips and spoiled prints, rinse out the sink, and wash and dry your hands. Straighten up the enlarger table. Be sure to take your negative out of the enlarger carrier.

Figure 3.6

Take a last look around to be sure the water is off and that everything is clean and in its place. Be sure to turn out the lights if you are the last to leave.

Figure 3.7

SUMMARY
No white light! Safelight color, yellow (series OC).

1. Developer: D-72 or Dektol, diluted 1:2 with water, volume sufficient in a tray to cover the prints comfortably. Use at about 21° C. (70° F.), with constant agitation. Develop enlarging papers for two minutes; contact printing papers for one minute. Discard developer after printing session is over, or after developing about fifteen to twenty 8″ × 10″ prints per quart of solution.
2. Stop bath: 1% acetic acid. Immerse print for about thirty seconds (RC papers, five seconds) with agitation. Discard after about fifteen prints have been treated per quart of solution.
3. Fixer: "Rapid Fix," prepared for prints (see instructions), or F-6 used without dilution. Fix for about five to ten minutes (RC papers two to five minutes) with occasional agitation. Save after use but discard after fixing sixty to eighty prints per gallon of solution.
4. Water rinse: to remove surface fixer (not required with RC papers but a brief rinse will do no harm). Rinse in running water for thirty seconds or so, or let soak in a tray of water for several minutes with occasional agitation. Extended soaking in a small volume of water may cause yellow stains.
5. Hypo clearing bath: dilute and use as directed on the package. Do not exceed the recommended maximum treatment time for prints, particularly in hot weather, as softening of the emulsion may result in some baths. Some varieties may be saved but do not treat more than about fifteen prints per quart of solution. This treatment is not recommended for RC papers.
6. Wash: in running water. RC papers, four to five minutes with frequent agitation and generous water flow, other papers as directed in the hypo clearing bath instructions. Keep prints well separated and assure adequate water flow around them. All the prints in the wash tray must be washed for the full recommended time **after the last print is placed in the wash water.**
7. Glossing-flattening solution: not recommended for RC papers; other well-washed prints should be treated according to package instructions. Bath may be reused but should be discarded when it becomes visibly cloudy or dirty or when it has treated about twenty 8″ × 10″ prints per quart.
8. Dry: sponge or blot RC papers surface-dry and hang them from a line with spring clothespins or lay out facedown on racks or clean cloth to dry. Squeegee ordinary paper prints to remove surface moisture and dry on a heated dryer or place them in a blotter book or roll. Glossing solution is only necessary if the prints are to be ferrotyped but can be used regardless of drying method.

Have you ever taken Photographs ?   Send for our catalogue and copy of "Modern Photography."

Using the Enlarger

4

An *enlarger* is a projection printing machine. It contains a light source consisting of a special opal bulb and some sort of system for directing the light through the negative which is held in place by the *negative carrier*. The illuminated negative image is focused by a lens onto the paper surface. The paper is held in place by the enlarging *easel* which rests on the enlarger *baseboard*. Figure 4.1 diagrams a typical enlarger with its parts labelled.

**An enlarger
is a projection printing machine**

The size of the projected image is controlled by the height of the enlarger above the paper. The entire body of the enlarger can be raised and lowered on the vertical column and locked in the selected position. After this adjustment has been made to get the image to approximate size, the image must be brought into sharp focus. This is done by adjusting the lens position with the focusing knob.

**Image size is controlled
by the enlarger height**

Focusing will change the image size somewhat, so that some further adjustments of the enlarger height may be necessary, followed in turn by a final focusing adjustment. This sequence of adjustments should be done with the enlarger lens set at its widest aperture, to make the image bright and the focusing adjustment as precise as possible.

**Focusing will change
the image size somewhat**

Figure 4.1

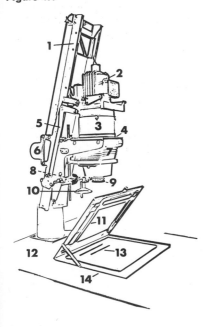

1. Upright or Column
2. Lamphousing
3. Condenser Assembly
4. Negative Carrier
5. Lever for Lifting #3
6. Counterbalance Spring
7. Bellows
8. Focusing Knob
9. Lens
10. Red Safelight Screen
11. Adjustable Border Masks
12. Baseboard
13. Paper Guides
14. Easel

47

**Controlling image brightness
with the iris diaphragm**

Figure 4.2

Paper held for printing by easel

Image brightness will be decreased as the enlarger is raised for the larger image sizes. Brightness can also be decreased by closing the iris diaphragm in the lens by turning a knurled ring on the lens barrel, a process which is called *stopping down* (Fig. 4.2).

Proper exposure of the printing paper must be determined by test. Exposure is controlled by varying either the light intensity on the paper surface, or the time of exposure, or both. Raising the enlarger, stopping down the lens, or using a dense negative will all necessitate longer-than-normal exposure times. The normal time range, using a moderately dense negative, medium enlargement size, and a fairly large lens aperture, will probably be between about five and thirty seconds.

The paper is held flat for printing by the easel masks. In some easel designs, the masks are thin metal strips which can be adjusted to provide various rectangular openings so that almost any picture shape can be obtained. Usually, the masks are adjusted to form narrow borders around the selected print area. Adjustable easels usually can accommodate several standard sizes of paper; for example, $5'' \times 7''$, $8'' \times 10''$, and $11'' \times 14''$.

If most of your pictures are of one size and do not vary from standard proportions, you will find nonadjustable easels convenient. They are available in most standard paper sizes. The printing paper is inserted from one end and slides along under marginal guides, until it is centered in the mask opening. These easels are normally made of heavy sheet metal, painted yellow, a color which is convenient for composing the image and which will not reflect dangerous white light through the paper.

Timers control print exposure time

Enlarger *timers* are used to control the time of print exposure. A typical timer will provide a range of from one second to one minute and will allow repeated exposures of the selected duration, once set. There is a manual light switch provided for focusing the image, and, on some models, a socket for the safelight which will switch off the safelight when the enlarger light is on. The timed interval is started by pushing a button on the timer face. The timer will automatically shut the enlarger light off when the interval is completed and reset itself for the next print.

Some types of timers are electronically operated and may provide a greater range of times as well as an exposure-cancelling switch and other features. Many timers provide for foot-switch control if desired.

**Using the enlarger light
to make photograms**

The enlarger is a convenient light source for making photograms or contact prints with a printing frame. For both these operations, you will need to use enlarging paper; contact printing paper is not sensitive enough to be useful in enlarger light.

For photogram use, set the enlarger body high enough to provide an ample circle of light to work in, and, temporarily inserting a scrap of paper or an old negative into the carrier, focus the enlarger lens. While this is not absolutely necessary, it will avoid the possibility that the lens may be accidentally focused on some piece of lint or other blemish up in the condenser system somewhere, thus keeping your working light "clean."

Control the illumination intensity with the lens diaphragm. For photogram exposures, it will usually be best to close the lens down to a fairly small opening, otherwise the exposure times may be inconveniently short.

Put a sheet of white paper, not sensitized, in the easel and adjust the easel masks to form an opening of the proper size and shape. Set up the photogram materials on the easel, watching the effect of the shadows in the enlarger light. When you have arrived at an interesting arrangement, memorize it and remove the objects from the paper. Turn off the enlarger light and replace the white paper sheet with a sheet of sensitized paper, emulsion (shiny) side up. Close the paper package to protect the remaining sheets during the photogram exposure. Replace the objects in their proper places on the sensitized paper surface and make an exposure of, say, twenty seconds.

If the image, after suitable development, is too dark, cut the exposure time in half and try again. If it is too light, double the exposure time for the next print.

If your enlarger has a red *safelight* screen (Fig. 4.3) which can be swung under the lens, you can make your photogram arrangements directly on the printing paper. It may be a little difficult to see the shadow patterns in the red light, but the paper will not be affected by it, and it has the advantage of immediacy. Be careful not to let stray white light reach the paper while you are making your arrangements. If the enlarger leaks white light in any quantity, you may have to work fast to avoid fog.

If you wish to use the enlarger as a light source for contact printing regular negatives, proceed as follows. Remove the spring back of the print-

Figure 4.3

Making contact prints with the enlarger light

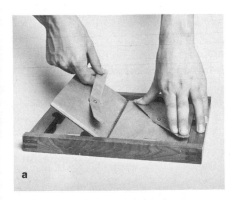

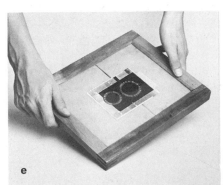

Figure 4.4

ing frame (Fig. 4.4*a*) and clean the glass (Fig. 4.4*b*). Place or tape the negative onto the glass, emulsion side up, that is, with the back of the negative against the glass (Fig. 4.4*c*). Place the sensitized paper (projection paper, such as Polycontrast, for use under the enlarger light) over the negative, emulsion down, that is, so that the emulsion of the paper is in contact with the emulsion of the negative (Fig. 4.4*d*). Close the frame. Place the frame on the enlarger baseboard, glass side up (Fig. 4.4*e*), and turn on the enlarger light to make the exposure. Process the paper and determine exposure corrections, if necessary, just as in making photograms.

Contact prints can also be made in daylight or regular artificial light, but projection paper will be found to be too sensitive for this purpose. Use a contact printing paper such as Azo.

Enlarger bulbs have limited life

A good enlarger is a precision machine which should last for years if well cared for. Replacing the bulb from time to time and keeping the optical system clean will usually be the only maintenance required. Bulb replacement will be required fairly frequently if you are not careful to turn off the light when it is not being used for actual printing activities. The bulbs are not designed for more than a few hours of continuous use but, if used for their intended purpose, should normally last for a year or more. Don't develop the habit of using the enlarger light as a work light for other tasks. In a school community darkroom this practice may inconvenience neighboring workers and can fog someone else's paper.

The height adjustment of the enlarger (unless it is motorized) will have some sort of locking device to keep it from slipping out of position during use. Be sure that the lock has been released before you try to raise or lower the enlarger head.

Brute force destroys

On some machines the operating gears are made of nylon, and they can be damaged by strong-arm tactics. As with all photographic equipment, a good slogan might be "don't force it." The adjustments are designed to work easily. If they don't, there is something wrong and it should be corrected, not just overpowered. Brute force destroys!

The Camera Image: The Pinhole Camera

5

In making photograms, you had to cope with and solve the problems of paper exposure and processing. You should now be aware of the fact that exposure can be controlled by varying either the light intensity or the time of exposure, and that different papers may require widely different exposures to yield usable images.

You should have discovered that a projected image can be focused, or made sharp by adjusting the spacing between the lens and the subject, or the lens and the image, or both. You may also have found out that the exposure for a greatly magnified image must be greater than for a slightly enlarged one, other things being equal. If these principles are clear in your mind, you should have no difficulty in understanding the way in which an image is formed in a simple camera.

A camera is like an enlarger or projector in reverse; the *subject* in the projector is inside the box, and the image is formed outside it. The projected image is usually larger than the subject. The camera subject is external, and its reflected light enters the box to form an image which is usually smaller than the subject. In either situation, the positions of subject and image can be reversed. If the subject replaces the image, the image will be formed where the subject was and at the same relative magnification. In both camera and projector, lenses are used to focus the images sharply.

A camera is an enlarger in reverse

The earliest ancestor of the camera did not use a lens of any sort to form its images. The camera obscura was a fairly popular fourteenth to eighteenth century curiosity. In its first form it was, as the name implies, a darkened room with a small hole in one wall. Observers sitting inside could see the rather blurry images of outside objects formed on the opposite white wall surface. Because light rays travel in essentially straight lines, light reflected from objects on the ground, slanted up to pass through the aperture in the wall and continued up to strike the wall at the top. Similarly, objects in the sky were imaged near the floor, and the image was reversed from right to left for the same reason.

The camera obscura

The camera obscura image was formed from unfocused light rays, and the sharpness of the image depended upon the size of the aperture and the distance from the aperture to the white screen. A relatively large aperture and great distance from aperture to screen were factors contributing to lack of sharpness of the image. Since a very small aperture produced a dim image, and a short image "throw" resulted in a small

51

Figure 5.1

**The pinhole camera image
does not require focusing**

Making a pinhole camera

Figure 5.2

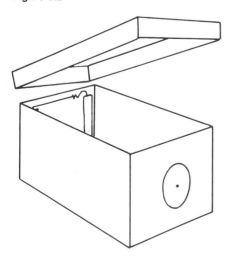

image, the camera obscura dimensions were necessarily a compromise between image sharpness, image brightness, image size, and crowd capacity. Even at best, the image sharpness would not be considered satisfactory for most photographic purposes today.

Portable models of the camera obscura equipped with simple lenses were popular with amateur artists who used them to form tracing images on a ground glass. From these instruments, the photographic camera was eventually derived.

A small model of the camera obscura, such as the pinhole camera, can be used to take pictures of fair quality and has certain advantages over even the best of modern cameras. A pinhole camera can be made in virtually any shape or size, and the image does not require focusing for optimum sharpness. The pinhole image, practically speaking, is uniformly sharp for all objects pictured, regardless of their position in space; and since no actual *refraction* or bending of light rays is involved in the image formation, the pinhole is free from a number of defects which are inherent in any lens system (although, to be sure, it has a few shortcomings of its own). Figure 5.1 is a typical pinhole photograph.

The pinhole camera can be simply a cardboard box (Fig. 5.2) big enough to contain a sheet of film, and provided with a pinhole in the side opposite the film. The box must be light-tight in all other respects to avoid fogging the film. A *shutter* flap to close the pinhole before and after the exposure interval is a desirable feature, and some method must be devised to insert and remove the film in a convenient manner.

A good method of making the pinhole is as follows. Select a piece of aluminum foil which is smooth and free from cracks or other blemishes, and about an inch across. Lay it on a flat, hard surface such as glass or smooth metal and press the point of a common pin straight down against its center. Tap the pin firmly with a light hammer or something similar, and check to see that a clean hole has resulted. The hole should be round and smooth-edged, and the foil should not be burred or pushed out on either side. The size of the hole will be hard to measure or estimate, but it should be easy to see, while still too small for the pin to slip into. A diameter of about .5 to .25 mm (1/50 to 1/100 inch) will do nicely.

The side of the aluminum foil which will face the film should be blackened to prevent reflections. A candle flame can be used to smoke the foil. Some types of lighter flames will work too. Be careful to avoid either melting the foil or closing up the pinhole with too much soot. The finished pinhole foil can be taped over a larger hole cut in the side of the box. Paint the box interior surfaces black.

The back of the box can be hinged with opaque tape so that the film can be taped into place. Loading the film must be done in total darkness, and the camera must be completely sealed with opaque tape before bringing it out into the light.

To take a picture with the pinhole camera, simply place it on a firm support, facing the subject, and open the shutter flap. Both the camera and the subject must remain motionless during the exposure if a sharp image is desired.

Pinhole camera exposures can be determined best by trial. Times may run from a minimum of a second or two (for a small box used in brilliant sunlight) to an almost infinite maximum. Intervals of a minute or so are typical in normal bright daylight conditions, while studio conditions may demand an exposure time of an hour or more. There are several variables which will affect the exposure time. Short times will result if:

1. Fast (sensitive) film is used, such as Tri-X.
2. The pinhole is large.
3. The pinhole-to-film distance is short.
4. The subject is in brilliant light.

If you are an igenious designer, you may be able to make a camera which can be compressed or extended in length to yield *wide-angle* or *telephoto* effects with the same pinhole. A camera whose pinhole-to-film distance is substantially less than the film diagonal measurement will produce pictures in which the details are small in scale but which include a wide panorama. If the camera length is much greater than the film diagonal, the image will be unusually large in scale but will not include a very large field of view. Naturally, the longer box will require longer exposure times than the short one will.

A little thought may lead you to the conclusion that a very small pinhole will yield sharper results than a larger one, but this is not entirely true. While sharpness increases to some extent as the hole size is decreased, the effect of *diffraction* limits the sharpness which is attainable. Diffraction refers to a scattering of light rays as they pass close to any edge. As the hole size is reduced, the proportion of scattered to unscattered rays which can pass through to the film increases, and definition is reduced. At extremely tiny apertures, the image is considerably degraded. Thus it is possible to define an optimum size for the pinhole as "small enough to prevent excessive spreading of the image points (due to the divergence of the light rays) but large enough to prevent excessive diffraction." In practice the best compromise seems to be a camera proportioned so that the distance from pinhole to film is about 250 to 400 times the diameter of the pinhole. If we use the letter f to stand for the pinhole-to-film distance, the above relationship can be expressed as:

Optimum aperture $= f/250$ (for example).

An opening so described is sometimes called the *relative aperture* because it relates two important variables of the system, the pinhole size and the length of light travel inside the box. The term "relative aperture" will assume more importance in discussions of lens systems and practical cameras later on.

Using the pinhole camera

Wide-angle or telephoto effects

Diffraction limits sharpness

Optimum size for the pinhole

Relative aperture

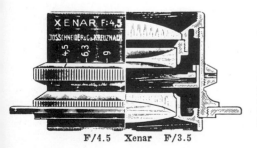

6

Sheet Film Handling and Development

Films should be handled in total darkness

Most films are considerably more sensitive to light than papers are. Many films are also sensitive to light of all colors, so that no *safelight* can be used with them with complete safety. They should, therefore, be handled in total darkness.

The emulsion faces you when the notches are in the upper right-hand corner

The emulsion side of a film sheet can be identified by code notches (Fig. 6.1) which are cut into one of the short sides of the sheet. When you hold the sheet with the long sides vertical and the notches are found in either the upper right or the lower left corner, the emulsion side is facing you. For simplicity, remember: hold the film vertically; the emulsion faces you when the notches are in the upper right-hand corner.

Figure 6.1

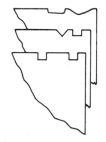

The number and shape of the notches are a clue to the identity of the film. For example, Tri-X pan film sheets can be identified by three closely spaced V-shaped notches. Plus-X film sheets are marked with one V-shaped notch, a space, then two closely spaced nearly square notches, reading from left to right. These notching codes are printed on the bottom of the film boxes and on the information sheets which are included in the film boxes. Save the sheets for reference. You must know who made the film before it can be identified by the notches, but the position of the notches does identify the emulsion side of the sheet, regardless of the manufacturer.

The notches also identify the film type

Sheet film holders for camera use

For use in a camera other than a pinhole camera, sheet films are loaded into *sheet film holders* (Fig. 6.2). Holders are designed to contain two sheets of film at a time—one on each side—in separate light-tight compartments. The film sheets are inserted from one end so that the edges of the sheets slip under narrow metal guides at the sides of the compartment (Fig. 6.3a). When the sheet is pushed all the way in, the entering end slips under a similar guide, and the trailing end of the film is held in place by a hinged flap which closes the end of the holder and seals it against light leakage (Fig. 6.3b). Then a *dark slide*, held in slots just above the film surface, is slid closed, and as it interlocks with the end flap, the film chamber is made light-tight (Fig. 6.3c).

Holders must be loaded in total darkness. It is good practice to load the film into the holder so that the notches on the short edge of the film sheet lie under the holder flap. If this is done, it is easy to check the notches without unloading the film if the emulsion type must be identified.

Figure 6.2

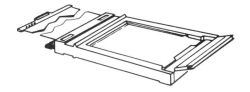

Figure 6.3

  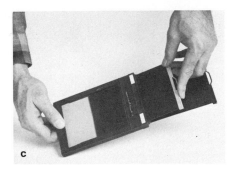

It is conventional to insert the slides into the holder when loading the film in such a way that the silver-colored, or shiny, top margin of the slide faces out. The other side of the holder clip is painted black. The shiny side is also identified by a deep notch or a row of embossed dots or lumps, a feature which makes it possible to tell which side is which in the dark (Fig. 6.4). As a general rule, a closed holder with the shiny side of its slide showing should contain fresh, unexposed film. If the dull or black side of the slide shows, the holder may contain exposed film or it may be empty.

Film holders are equipped with simple latches which can be swung over the closed slides to keep them in place. Some photographers consider a holder empty if its latches are open, regardless of the color of its slide clips. This is a more elegant code, and entirely feasible if you pay attention to detail. If there is any doubt in your mind, it is prudent to check the contents of a holder in the darkroom.

Sheet films can be developed in trays, like paper, or in special tanks. It is usually convenient to do small batches of film (up to perhaps six sheets) in a tray, while larger numbers of sheets can be handled more easily and rapidly in tank-and-hanger equipment (Fig. 6.5).

Regardless of the method of handling used, the film must be treated somewhat differently from paper if the process is to be controlled. Paper is usually processed *by inspection* under safelight conditions. The darkness, or *density*, of the print image is controlled by the length of the exposure time, and the developing time is not usually varied. Print images are usually developed to *completion*, that is, the image is fully formed during the two minute developing time and will not change much if development is prolonged.

Films, on the other hand, are rarely developed to completion. Development is normally stopped long before the image has reached maximum density, and the degree of development is controlled by careful regulation of the developer temperature and the time of development. Uniform agitation of the films in the solution is very important for good results. The procedure is complicated by the fact that it must be done in total darkness from the time the film is unloaded to the time it has been fixed in the hypo bath.

Film developer is usually less vigorous than paper developer, but the solutions are very similar in other respects. Film can be developed in paper

**The shiny side
of the slide indicates fresh film**

**The black side
of the slide indicates exposed film**

Figure 6.4

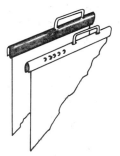

**Sheet film can be developed
in trays or tanks**

Figure 6.5

**Film development is controlled
by time and temperature**

developer, but the results would be rather harsh and contrasty. Similarly, papers will develop in film developers, but the image on the print will appear weak, and gray or brownish in tone, and the developing time would be excessive.

Film processing is similar to paper processing

The other chemical baths are very similar. It is good practice to use separate hypo baths for film and paper. In some cases, the film fixer is made stronger than the recommended paper dilution. Because films absorb less liquid than papers do, the washing time for films is less than for prints. Drying the finished negatives is different too; they are simply rinsed in a wetting agent after the wash and hung to dry in a drying cabinet or in a dust free area. Films should never be put on the print dryer.

Developing a few sheets of film in a tray

The easiest and quickest method of processing a few sheets of film is to do them in trays. There is some knack to it, but a little practice will make you proficient and the results can be excellent. The main danger in tray processing is the possibility of scratching or gouging the emulsion with the fingernails or with the corners of other films. To avoid this problem, handle the sheets with the balls of the fingertips, not the nails; never *slide* the films together in a stack, lay them together; and never allow the films to swirl rapidly in the wash tray. Keep the water running fast enough to move the sheets, but slowly.

Arrange three trays in the sink

Arrange three clean 8″ × 10″ trays in the sink (Fig. 6.6). From left to right fill the trays to a workable depth with developer, shortstop, and hypo. The other solutions required—hypo clearing bath, wash water, and wetting agent—can be provided later after the lights are turned on.

Adjust all solutions to 20°C.

Adjust the temperatures of all solutions to 20°C. (68°F.) before proceeding. Be careful to avoid contamination of the solutions and be sure that the table surface next to the sink is kept clean and dry. Wipe your hands thoroughly before handling the film. Set a timer for the desired interval or arrange for someone outside the darkroom to keep time for you. **Turn out all the lights before unloading the film.**

Turn out the lights before unloading the film holders

Figure 6.6

Agitate the film gently

Place the films smoothly, emulsion side up, onto the surface of the developer solution and pat each one under in quick succession (Fig. 6.7a, b, c). Do not put them all in at once. Tray agitation is continuous but need not be rapid. The films should be gently nudged into one corner of the tray and held there lightly while extracting the bottom sheet (Fig. 6.7d and e). Lift the sheet out of the solution and place it flat on the top of the pile (Fig. 6.7f). Press it down gently with the fingertips. Similarly, extract the bottom sheet by lifting the pile with one hand and slipping the sheet out with the other. Place it on top of the pile and pat it down. Continue this procedure throughout the developing period.

While they are wet, the films can be scratched quite easily. The gelatin coating will absorb water and swell up, first becoming rather sticky and then slippery. Touch the emulsion side as little and as gently as possible and avoid pressure. Be very careful not to cut the emulsion with either your fingernails or the corners of the other film sheets. Never try to develop sheet film with print tongs.

When the developing time is over, tranfer the sheets to the shortstop one by one and agitate as above for about thirty seconds. Then move the

Figure   6.7

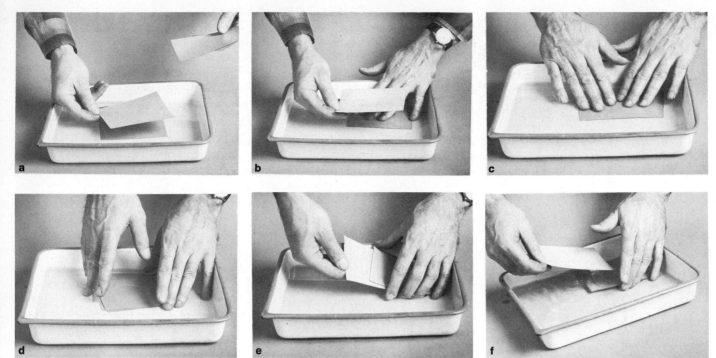

films to the hypo bath and agitate for about one minute. *Wash your hands before touching anything after using the hypo.* Leave the films soaking in the hypo and turn on the lights.

Agitate the film in the shortstop

At this point, the films should have a blackish visible negative image on the emulsion side. The backs may appear to be solidly covered or streaked with a milky coating. This coating is really the unused sensitive portion of the emulsion which was neither exposed nor developed, and which the hypo is in the process of dissolving. It will gradually disappear as you watch it, and when it is no longer visible, the negatives are said to be *clear*.

Put the films in the hypo; wash your hands

The clearing time of film depends on the kind of film it is and the strength or freshness of the hypo bath. For this reason no time is specified for the hypo treatment, but the films should be left in the hypo solution for *twice as much time as it takes them to clear*. In other words, if the films apparently clear in one minute, they should remain in the hypo for two minutes. If clearing time is ten minutes, total time should be twenty minutes. If clearing takes longer than ten minutes, it probably indicates that your hypo is exhausted. Discard it and use a fresh solution.

Hypo the films twice as long as they take to clear

Fixing is followed by a rinse in water, then place the films in hypo clearing bath with occasional agitation for the time recommended for that product. Wash as recommended, and follow with a brief soaking (a minute or so) in a wetting agent solution such as *Photoflo*, prepared according to the label instructions. Hang to dry in a dust-free environment. Special stainless steel film clips are made for this purpose, but ordinary wooden spring clothespins can be used if necessary. Clip each of the film sheets by one corner, and be sure that they will not contact each other while they are drying.

Hypo clearing bath, wash, and wetting agent

Hang the films to dry

Figure 6.8

SUMMARY

Total darkness.

1. Developer: Kodak HC-110, dilution B, 20°C. (68°F.). Use no less than 4 oz. of solution for each 4″ × 5″ sheet of film, a minimum of 8 oz. total. Agitate continuously. Discard after use. Developing time as recommended. Other developers may be used; follow the instructions supplied.

2. Shortstop: 1% acetic acid, as for printing, 20°C. (68°F.). Agitate continuously for about 30 seconds. Discard after use.

3. Fixing bath: Rapid fix, prepare as recommended for films, or use Kodak F-6 solution at regular strength, 20°C. (68°F.) for twice the clearing time. Agitate at intervals. Save after use. Discard when clearing time reaches about 10 minutes.

4. Water rinse: 16°C. to 24°C. (65°F. to 75°F.) for 30 seconds or more with continuous agitation. Discard.

5. Hypo clearing bath: about 21°C. (70°F.), dilution, time, and agitation as recommended. Save if desired. Discard when hypo is discarded (unless the manufacturer gives other instructions).

6. Wash: running water, with occasional agitation, at about 21°C. (70°F.), for time as specified on hypo clearing bath package. If hypo clearing bath is not used, wash must be for at least 30 minutes.

7. Wetting agent: Photoflo solution at about 21°C. (70°F.), prepared according to package instructions. Soak for about 1 minute. Distilled water may be advisable if tap water is "hard."

8. Dry: suspend each film sheet by one corner using film clips or wooden spring clothespins. Hang in a dust-free place or in a film drying cabinet, if available.

Keep the dry negatives in negative envelopes for protection from dust and fingerprints.

Calculating Exposure

7

When a lens is focused on an object at infinity the distance from the lens to the film plane is called the *focal length* of the lens. Small cameras, obviously, use normal lenses of fairly short focal length; the normal lenses for large cameras are correspondingly longer. Because the farther light travels from the lens to the film the dimmer it becomes, it would seem probable that small cameras would provide greater film illumination than large cameras do. But large camera lenses are often larger and open to wider diameters than small camera lenses and, clearly, the wider diameter will admit more light than will a smaller one. Actually, lens *speed* (light transmitted to the film) depends upon **both** the focal length and the aperture size of the lens. A large-aperture lens will expose film more quickly than will a small one if the focal length is held constant; if their apertures are the same diameter, the shorter focal length lens will provide more film illumination than the longer one will.

The focal length of a lens

Lens speed depends upon both focal length and aperture

In practice lens speed is indicated by *f/ numbers* which are the numbers found on the lens mount, calibrating the aperture scale (Fig. 7.1). There is a standard series of these numbers. Your camera will undoubtedly have at least some of these, indicating the various settings of its iris diaphragm:

Lens speed is indicated by "f/numbers"

f/ . . . 1.4   2   2.8   4   5.6   8   11   16   22   32 . . .

Notice that every second number in the ascending series is doubled. Each of these numbers expresses the relationship of lens aperture diameter to focal length, for example, f/2 means that the lens focal length is twice as great as its diameter; f/5.6 means the focal length is 5.6 times the diameter, etc. Because they express this relationship the numbers are called *relative apertures*.

They are sometimes called "relative apertures"

In the series above, f/1.4 stands for the largest opening and f/32 stands for the smallest (Fig. 7.2). Each number in the series will transmit twice as much light to the film as the next higher number; for example, f/2 gives the film twice as much light as does f/2.8, while f/2.8 transmits twice as much as f/4, etc. This is another way of saying that a one-second exposure at an aperture of f/2 is the same as a four-second exposure at an aperture of f/4, or a half-second exposure at f/1.4. As a further example, if it were true that an exposure of 1/125 second at f/1.4 was correct for some situation, each of the other aperture numbers in the sequence would also be usable with the exposure times indicated below.

Figure 7.1

Aperture:	f/1.4	2	2.8	4	5.6	8	11	16	22	32
Time, Secs:	1/125	1/60	1/30	1/15	1/8	1/4	1/2	1	2	4

Figure 7.2 Focal length

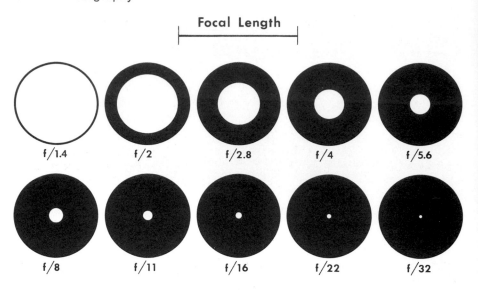

Time exposures of more than a few seconds are quite unusual in ordinary photography. Most pictures are taken at exposure times measured in fractions of a second. The camera shutter is designed to open and close in a precisely regulated manner to provide these brief exposure intervals and these times, or *speeds*, are marked on the shutter dial on the camera body (Fig. 7.3) or sometimes on the lens mount. The shutter speeds are written as whole numbers but they mean fractions of a second. For example, in the normal sequence of shutter speed numbers found on most modern shutters:

Shutter speeds are marked in whole numbers

(B)   1   2   4   8   15   30   60   125   250   500   1000

But they refer to fractions of a second

the number "1" stands for "1 second" while "2," "4," and "60" stand for "½ second," "¼ second," and "1/60 second," respectively. The setting, "B," stands for "bulb." It provides for manually timed exposure intervals longer than one second. Some older shutters are numbered like this:

(B)   1   2   5   10   25   50   100   250   500   1000

Figure 7.3

These numbers have the same meaning; "10" means "1/10 second," "250" means "1/250 second."

The aperture and shutter speed settings work together to provide the film with the amount of light energy it needs to form its image properly. More exposure can be supplied to the film by using a larger lens opening or a longer time of exposure, or both. Exposure is reduced if the lens opening is made smaller or the shutter is set at a higher speed, or both. For example, if you have set the camera for an exposure of 1/30 second at f/8 and decide that you want to change it to provide only half as much exposure, you could use either of these settings:

> 1/60 at f/8 or
> 1/30 at f/11

other possible settings, giving the same exposure as these, but changing both values, are:

> 1/500 at f/2.8
> 1/250 at f/4
> 1/125 at f/5.6
> 1/15 at f/16
> 1/8   at f/22
> 1/4   at f/32

Although all these combinations provide the same effective film exposure they affect the image itself in different ways. The higher shutter speeds will stop subject motion, for example, reducing or eliminating blurring of rapidly moving objects (Fig. 7.4). The lower shutter speeds will allow blurring to occur (Fig. 7.5) and, for some sorts of photographs, this may be a highly desirable effect. Large lens openings will isolate the object focused on, producing a shallow *depth of field* which blurs both back-

f/numbers and shutter speeds work together

Figure 7.4   A relatively high shutter speed has stopped this action. The long lens also allowed the picture to be made from a safe distance. (Courtesy of the University of Michigan Press)

Figure 7.5   A slow film and small aperture permitted a shutter speed of one second in this picture. During the exposure the camera was "panned" to follow the moving car, thereby blurring the background beyond recognition and suggesting speed. (Courtesy of the University of Michigan Press)

Figure 7.6 The conditions here—dim light and the possibility of subject motion—dictated a large lens aperture in spite of the fast film used. The picture was planned to make the best of the shallow depth of field. (Courtesy of the University of Michigan Press)

Figure 7.7 This subject needed to be sharp from foreground to background so a small aperture was required. Even with fast film the light was too dim to allow a high shutter speed. A "Time" exposure of several seconds was used. (Courtesy of the University of Michigan Press)

ground and foreground objects (Fig. 7.6). Small lens openings will tend to give greater depth of field, extending the range of sharp focus to include more of the background and foreground space (Fig. 7.7). The choice of lens opening and shutter speed from all the possible combinations normally available, is almost always a compromise between motion blur and adequate depth of field.

The ASA film speeds

The choice is less difficult if the film in use can produce a good image with very little light, but some films need more light than others. A film which is highly sensitive to light will require relatively little exposure and is said to be a *fast* film. A *slow* film needs more light for adequate image formation. The relative *speed* of films is indicated by numbers assigned to them by the manufacturer. They are called *film speeds*, *ASA exposure index* numbers or, simply *ASA* numbers. There is also a standard sequence of these numbers. Here are some of them.

. . . 20 25 32 40 50 64 80 100 125 160 200 250 320 400 500 . . .

The list can be extended in both directions as far as necessary (notice that every third number in the ascending sequence is doubled).

The slowest film commonly available in camera stores is Kodachrome 25, a color slide film. It has an ASA speed of 25. A very fast 35-mm film available in cartridges for camera use is Kodak's type 2475 Recording Film. Its speed is listed as 1000. Since a film's sensitivity is directly proportional to its film speed value, you can determine the relative speed of Kodachrome and type 2475 films by dividing 1000 by 25, which is 40. This means that Kodachrome needs 40 times more light to form an image than 2475 does. In other words, if an exposure of 1/10 second at f/8 were found to be correct for a Kodachrome 25 picture situation, it would be possible to photograph the same situation on type 2475 at an exposure of only 1/400 at f/8.

We have now identified three factors which affect film exposure: lens opening, shutter speed, and film speed. The fourth factor is light itself, specifically the amount of light available at the subject position. Subject light is measured with an exposure meter and when the meter has been set to work with the proper film speed number (Fig. 7.8) it will provide a series of pairs of lens openings and shutter speeds, any pair of which will provide sufficient exposure to make the picture possible. If the light is intense it will permit the use of slow film or high shutter speeds or small lens openings, or some combination of these. If the light is dim, you may have to resort to fast film or use slow shutter speeds or large apertures in some combination.

The four factors which affect film exposure

Figure 7.8

In the normal sequence of picture-taking, the film speed is usually fixed by the fact that you will have a roll in the camera and it is inconvenient to replace it until it is used up. The subject light condition is also a fixed condition, generally, so the adjustments are typically restricted to lens and shutter settings. Fortunately there are usually several usable combinations to choose from and it is normally possible to pick one which will produce a satisfactorily exposed negative which is also reasonably free from subject or camera movement blur and which has adequate depth of field.

How they relate to each other

You can see, then, the relationship of the four elements of the exposure problem: film speed, light intensity, lens aperture, and shutter speed. The film speed will dictate the amount of light you need to provide inside the camera; the exposure meter will measure the amount of light available outside the camera and advise you how to use it; the aperture and shutter settings, together, can be adjusted to provide a suitable proportion of the available light energy for the film to use.

As was stated earlier, it is a confusing characteristic of the f/numbers that the largest numbers identify the smallest holes. An aperture of f/2.0, therefore, is larger and transmits more light to the film than an aperture of f/4.0, for example. Furthermore, because the f/numbers are derived from the **linear** measurements of diameter and focal length, but refer to the **area** of the lens opening, f/2.0 does not transmit merely **twice** as much light as does f/4.0, it transmits **four times** as much. From this we can derive the following rule:

Large numbers identify small holes

Lens speed varies inversely with the square of its f/number.

Thus, the comparative speed of two lens openings can be found by squaring their f/numbers and dividing the result. Which is faster and how much, f/2.0 or f/8.0?

Comparing lens speeds

First square both numbers:

$$2 \times 2 = 4 \quad \text{and} \quad 8 \times 8 = 64$$

Then divide the larger by the smaller:

$$64 \div 4 = 16$$

Therefore, the f/2.0 lens is faster (it is the lower number and stands for the larger opening) by 16 times. It is also possible, of course, to divide the f/numbers themselves and then square the results:

$$8 \div 2 = 4 \quad \text{then} \quad 4^2 = 16 \text{ as above.}$$

Exposure meters: photovoltiac type

Exposure meters have taken many forms in the past, but the most common ones available today are photoelectric devices of two types, photovoltaic (Fig. 7.9a) and photoconductive (Fig. 7.9b). The voltaic type consists simply of a light sensitive selenium cell, which is capable of converting light energy into electrical power, and a sensitive indicating meter. Light striking the cell produces a voltage proportional to the light intensity. The voltage, in turn, forces electrical current through the sensitive galvanometer coil, causing the indicating needle or pointer to swing across a calibrated scale. The degree of needle deflection is related directly, therefore, to the intensity of light. In this type of meter no external power source is required. The meter is truly operated by light power alone.

Photoconductive type

The photoconductive meter differs in one fundamental respect. Power is provided by a tiny battery. Battery voltage attempts to force current through the meter coil but is hindered by the extremely high electrical resistance of the light-sensitive cadmium sulfide (CdS) cell. However, the cell resistance is reduced when light strikes it, and the current which is allowed to flow to the meter movement is proportional to the light intensity on the cell surface. In some of the newer meters the familiar galvonometer needle has been replaced as an indicator by tiny glow lamps or light emitting diodes (LEDs) thus eliminating the delicate mechanical structure of the microammeter movement and providing a type of meter which combines high sensitivity with very small size and almost total immunity to damage from the normal jolts and shocks of rough handling.

Figure 7.9

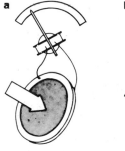 

a   b

Each type has advantages

Each meter type has its advantages and limitations. The photovoltaic types are generally simpler and more stable under extremes of temperature. They also respond to colors more uniformly and more in the manner that the film will respond to them than the CdS cells sometimes do. On the other hand, the selenium meters are more delicate and susceptible to physical damage and are not as sensitive to dim light. CdS meters are very sensitive and durable and can be made very small for incorporation into camera viewing systems. Their major shortcomings are a slight, but undesirable, sensitivity to infrared light, slow response time in dim light, some temperature sensitivity, and a characteristic called "memory" which describes the cell's inability to measure dim light accurately after having been exposed to brilliant light, an effect which can influence low range readings for minutes or even hours. The recently introduced *silicon blue* cells are said to combine the good qualities of both older types; good color response, good stability under all conditions of use, small size and physical ruggedness, fast response under all light conditions, freedom from memory effects, and good sensitivity to dim light.

The Reciprocity Law of exposure

In normal conditions it is true that exposure will vary uniformly with changes in either light intensity or exposure time and there is a statement to that effect called the *reciprocity law* of exposure. However, if film is exceptionally dimly or brilliantly illuminated, its sensitivity diminishes; the exposure time must be disproportionately increased to compensate; and the reciprocity law is said to fail. Since these unusual illumination levels are necessarily accompanied by unusual exposure times, it has become commonplace to blame reciprocity failure on the exceptional exposure intervals themselves, rather than on the film illumination level which is mostly responsible. For most purposes this is an insignificant distinction but in some cases reciprocity failure can occur during exposures of "normal" length. For example, a film exposed to a very wide range of luminances for a "normal" time may exhibit less sensitivity in the shadow areas than the reciprocity law would predict while, at the same time, obeying the law in the image highlight areas. The effect is underexposure of the shadows and a consequent increase in contrast. The opposite case is also true. Very brief exposure time (very intense exposing light) appears to reduce film sensitivity in the highlight areas more than in the dimmer shadows, resulting both in a general loss in apparent film speed and a decrease in contrast.

And its famous failure

The useful exposure range of the film obviously lies between its sensitivity threshold and its saturation point, and it is within this range that *proper exposure* of the subject will place all the tones of black, white, and gray that identify the subject areas. This can be accomplished in at least three ways. You can determine the average luminance of all the subject areas, and, using this as a basis, calculate the exposure which will cause the film to render that one luminance as an average density of middle gray. Or, you can determine the luminance of the lightest object in the scene and set the meter in such a way that the film records that luminance as "white" (white on the negative, of course, is a heavy density). Or, you can determine the luminance of the darkest object, and set the meter so that it records it as "black" (low density on the negative). In all three cases, you have to assume that placing one subject value in its proper place in the film range will cause all the other tones to fall into their proper places, too. They usually will.

Determining exposure

Figure 7.10

It's quite likely that the three exposures just determined will not be the same, in fact they may differ rather considerably. Yet, for practical purposes, all are *correct exposures* in that they reproduce the subject tonal scale in a recognizable manner. The negatives will exhibit an overall difference in density, with the shadow-based exposure resulting in the thinnest (least dense) negative, the average-based exposure somewhat more dense, area for area, and the highlight-based exposure producing a fairly heavy density overall. In general, thin negatives are best. They require minimum printing times, and the image quality is usually superior to heavily dense images in several respects. Bear in mind that a *thin* negative, to be useful, must contain all the necessary image densities in their proper relationships. If exposure of the film is insufficient, the negative will lose shadow detail and will cease to be merely thin and become underexposed.

Meter scales are usually designed to work easily with the *average* luminance method of exposure calculation. When the film's exposure index number has been set into the calculator dial, it is only necessary to adjust the dial to the average luminance reading of the subject to display the desired exposure information; the lens opening and shutter speed which will result in "proper" exposure of the scene (Fig. 7.10).

Meters read average luminance

Figure 7.11

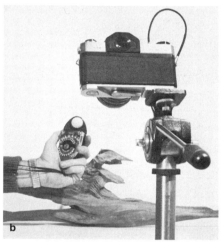

Reflected versus incident light

Point the luminance meter at the subject; point the incident meter at the camera

Figure 7.12

The mechanical operation of the meter is simple and generally foolproof. Most exposure errors are the result of the photographer's clumsiness in *taking the reading* of the subject luminance or of his failure to interpret the reading correctly. Including even the so-called *spot meters* which are designed to read very small areas of the subject and which often incorporate lens systems to focus image light on the photocell, almost all meters think they are giving you an average reading regardless of what you think they are doing. This is true simply because the meter sees no shapes or tones in the subject as separate areas. The light which it reads is all the light from all the subject areas within its field of view, randomly reflected to form a single, blended, truly "average" tone. As far as the meter is concerned, its whole field of vision is uniform in tone; sometimes bright, sometimes dark, but never mottled.

This meter characteristic may lead to substantial errors in exposure in cases where the subject is small in relation to a background of contrasting value. Consider the case of a black kitten in a field of snow or a nightclub singer in a white dress, spotlighted on the darkened stage. In both cases the desired image detail lies near one end of the film range and leaves little room for error. In both cases a meter reading taken from some little distance away from the subject will be largely influenced by the background tone, and the average luminance of the meter's field of view will not represent the average luminance of the subject itself. Consequently, the kitten will look like a hole in the snow, and the singer will resemble a snowman if the meter readings are used as given.

So far we have been considering meters which read light reflected from the subject toward the camera, and they are called *reflected* light or luminance meters. In an attempt to reduce the possibility of error from situations such as described above, someone conceived the idea of taking *incident* light or illuminance readings. Incident light meters read light falling upon the subject rather than light reflected from the subject. An incident light reading, therefore, ignores the color or value of the subject entirely and assumes that whatever the subject may be, it is of average reflectance. The incident light meter will give the same reading for a black subject that it gives for a white one in the same light condition, and it may not agree with reflected light readings taken in the same situation.

The two meter types require different handling. The luminance meter (Fig. 7.11a) must be pointed at the subject, along the camera line-of-sight or from the actual camera position. The incident meter (Fig. 7.11b) is pointed at the camera lens from the subject direction or position. Incident type readings can be taken with a luminance meter if an ideal subject is substituted for the real one while measuring the light. Prepared gray cards are sold for this purpose. Reflecting 18 percent of the incident light, such a card represents an average of all luminances that an ideal subject would contain, and will lead to good exposure in most cases.

Adapters are available for most luminance meters which convert them into incident meters (Fig. 7.12). In effect, the conversion attachment amounts to building into the meter a standard gray card to substitute for the subject. It is usually a translucent plastic hemisphere attached over the photocell, designed to transmit about 18 percent of the incident light to the cell surface. The cell, in other words, sees the inside of a luminous hemisphere instead of the subject. An incident meter is really just a luminance meter taking readings of its own private little world.

Reflectance readings of middle gray subjects, or subjects containing an equal distribution of black and white, such as a checkerboard, will probably agree closely with incident readings taken in the same light condition. When the two meters disagree, the incident reading is probably the safer of the two to use, since it tends to place the subject luminance range, whatever its extent, squarely in the middle of the film's best range. The luminance meter in skilled hands may produce more precisely controlled exposures, particularly if the subject is unusual in luminance range or tonal distribution. In unskilled hands under the same conditions, the errors may be serious. Incident readings are generally more suitable for use with color film than are reflected readings because of their greater consistency. Both meters have difficulty with certain subjects. The luminance meter with the black-cat-in-the-snow situations mentioned previously and with very small objects where the shadow of the meter itself might affect the readings. The incident meter will have trouble with subjects which are physically remote or inaccessible and in light conditions which cannot be simulated, and with subjects which are transmitting or producing light, such as stained glass windows or neon signs.

The meters may agree or disagree

Both have trouble with certain subjects

The present trend in exposure determination is toward the use of meters built into the camera body itself, often incorporated in some way with the camera viewfinder (Fig. 7.13). In the *prism-reflex* 35-mm cameras, these meters have become highly developed and are both accurate and convenient. In general, they are arranged to read the light intensity of the image itself, and this principle offers real advantages over the conventional, separate meter. In the first place, the boundaries of the meter's field of view are clearly marked in the finder, so that the photographer can see specifically which tones are being included in the reading. Second, because the reading is taken inside the camera, any effect that the lens itself, or lens attachments might have upon image intensity are automatically taken into account (with most cameras, but not all). Third, these meters are typically "coupled" with the camera shutter and aperture adjustments so that setting the meter controls to determine exposure also adjusts the camera itself to the proper settings.

Built-in meters are convenient

Within the last few years a number of fully automatic cameras have been introduced, the most recent of which are single-lens-reflexes featuring fully interchangeable lenses and accepting all the accessories available for the semiautomatic and manual models. While some of these cameras offer *shutter priority* systems, which means that the photographer selects the shutter speed he wishes to use and the camera automatically adjusts itself to the appropriate lens opening, other models employ *aperture priority*. In this system the photographer selects the desired aperture and the shutter speed follows it automatically.

Shutter priority; aperture priority

Figure 7.13

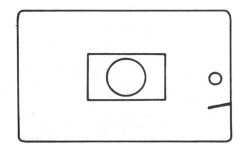

Shutter priority systems sometimes involve a *trapped needle* mechanism in which finger pressure on the shutter release locks the meter pointer and thereby limits the maximum opening of the diaphragm. This system is widely employed in small range-finder-type cameras and has the advantages of being relatively simple, cheap to manufacture, and surprisingly effective. The only major drawback is the rather unusually long travel and firm resistance of the shutter release button.

Aperture priority systems are necessarily much more sophisticated. The infinitely variable shutter speeds required are set electronically and, in one camera at least, ingenious circuitry in the meter system "remembers" the light reading taken through the lens even after the reflex mirror has flipped up for the exposure and allows accurate automatic exposures of several seconds without any further reference to the subject light condition. This method is probably more useful for general purposes since the preselected aperture assures control of depth of field. Shutter speed variations are not usually important to the pictorial quality of the photograph unless subject or camera motion gets out of hand but depth of field is often critical, especially in close-up work.

Automatic exposure control can usually be overriden

Almost without exception the automatic exposure control systems can be disconnected or overridden so that the photographer can take full command of the picture variables if he wishes to. This sort of automation is a great convenience, relieving the photographer of all duties except focusing, and, of course, finding something to photograph.

Built-in meters are luminance meters and are still subject to some errors in interpretation but camera manufacturers are hard at work on that problem, too. Various systems in existence attempt to compensate for the inherent limitations of the luminance meter by restricting the field of view for "semispot" readings, or by including several cells in the field of view for more accurate averaging of the area, or by "weighting" the reading of the bottom or center of the field so that light in those areas has more effect on the reading than does light from the rest of the field. While these attempts are interesting and make good advertising copy, it is still possible to make mistakes in exposure with the most advanced cameras. Ultimately, the photographer has to decide what he's trying to do before he can expect the machine to do it.

The View Camera, Lens and Shutter

8

The view camera is a considerably refined version of the pinhole camera. Instead of a pinhole, a lens is provided to admit light to the film and form the image. A shutter mechanism provides for accurately timed exposure intervals of very short duration, and a *diaphragm* or *iris diaphragm* mechanism is incorporated in the shutter housing to permit adjustment of the light intensity at the film plane. A focusing adjustment is also necessary, and the view camera permits a greater adjustment of focus than any other camera type.

A view camera is an extremely versatile machine (Fig. 8.1). It can be converted for almost any photographic purpose by interchanging its various parts or attaching accessories, but this very flexibility makes it a cumbersome camera to handle. It must be used on a tripod, and operation of the controls is slow because almost no automatic features are included in its design. These facts, coupled with the fact that it produces a larger image than most hand cameras do, indicate that the view camera is most useful for methodical work of high precision, where speed of operation is unimportant—or at least less important than complete control of the image quality.

View cameras are made in several sizes which are indicated by the dimensions of the film that they are intended to use. Thus, an "eight-by-ten" camera will accept 8″ × 10″ sheets of film; a "four-by-five" requires 4″ × 5″ film.

View camera lenses are usually mounted in *between-the-lens* shutters, or, as they are sometimes called, *leaf* shutters. These terms are descriptive. The shutter is constructed of overlapping leaves or blades of thin metal arranged concentrically around the lens axis, and pivoted in such a way, that they can either block all light from entering the lens or be swung away to form a circular opening through which light can pass to the film. The shutter mechanism is located "between-the-lens" elements, hence its name (Fig. 8.2).

Good shutters of this type have very light-weight leaves and other moving parts. The bearings are low-friction, and the leverage on the leaves is considerable. A strong mainspring can snap the blades open or closed in as little as a few thousandths of a second.

The purpose of the shutter is to allow light to enter the camera for brief periods of time and to provide automatic and repeatable timing of these

**The view camera
is a refined version
of the pinhole camera**

Figure 8.1

Between-the-lens or leaf shutters

Figure 8.2

The shutter controls the interval of exposure

intervals. A setting or two is also provided which permits manual timing of relatively long intervals. The exposure intervals are called *shutter speeds* (Fig. 8.3a). View camera shutters often provide speeds of from one second to 1/200 second, or so, in one of the following sequences:

1,   2,   4,   8,   15,   30,   60,   125,   250   or,
1,   2,   5,   10,   25,   50,   100,   200.

Exposure intervals are called speeds

In both cases above as explained in the previous chapter, the numbers indicate the denominators of fractions of which 1 is the numerator. For example, the number 2 does not mean two seconds, it means one-half second. Similarly, 8, 25, and 250 mean respectively, ⅛ second, 1/25 second, and 1/250 second.

The time and bulb settings permit manual control

The two other speeds often provided are *Time* and *Bulb*, marked *T* and *B*. The Time setting will open the shutter for an indefinite period which will continue until it is manually closed. The setting is intended for very long exposure times during which the camera may be left alone. The Bulb setting also permits long exposure intervals, but the shutter must be held open by finger pressure on the release lever. The shutter will close when the pressure is removed.

Bulb takes its name from the rubber squeeze bulb which photographers used to actuate their pneumatic shutters in the good old days. Air pressure forced the blades open, where they stayed as long as the pressure was maintained. When the bulb was released, the blades fell shut. Some shutters of this type still exist, and pneumatic shutter release devices which can be used with almost any camera are widely available today.

Most shutters must be cocked before they will operate

All shutters which provide for high speeds (short intervals) must be *cocked* like a gun before they will operate. A prominent lever protruding from the shutter body makes this possible (Fig. 8.3b). Cocking or *setting* the shutter puts the mainspring of the mechanism under tension, ready to actuate the leaves. The shutter is set into operation by a lever which releases the catch holding the mainspring taut, allowing the spring to move the mechanism. This lever, reasonably enough, is called the *shutter release* (Fig. 8.3c).

The self-timer, the synchronizer, and the press-focus lever

Three more devices are sometimes included in a view camera shutter. A separate spring and gear train, the self-timer, provides for delayed action of the shutter—up to ten or twelve seconds after the release is pushed—to allow the photographer to get into his own picture or (a much more practical use) to allow the camera to settle down, if it is precariously balanced on a flimsy tripod, before the exposure is made (Fig. 8.3d).

A switch is usually built into the shutter to permit the firing of flash-bulbs or electronic flash units during the brief interval that the shutter blades are open. Such switching action is called *flash synchronization*. Adjustment is provided to allow precise timing of the firing point (Fig. 8.3e).

Figure 8.3

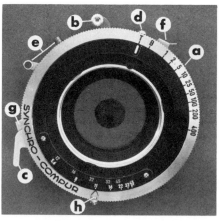

A third device, especially useful on the view camera, is the *press-focus* lever or button (Fig. 8.3f). This device allows the shutter to be opened, and remain open, at the movement of a lever, regardless of the setting of the shutter speed scale. Since this can be accomplished by touch alone when one is familiar with the shutter, it is a convenient method for checking the image without disturbing any of the shutter settings and without the necessity of peering at the scales.

While the shutter can be made to operate by pressing the release lever (which may cause vibration of the camera during the exposure) or by using the delayed action device (which may not be convenient), most view camera pictures are taken with an accessory called the *cable release*. Essentially a long and flexible plunger, the *cable* screws into a special socket (Fig. 8.3*g*) on the shutter body. Its use will prevent hand movements from jarring the camera during the release (refer to Fig. 8.1).

The cable release prevents hand movements from jarring the camera

Not a part of the shutter mechanism, but included in the assembly, is the iris diaphragm, whose purpose is to regulate the intensity of light on the film plane by varying the size of the lens opening. Like the shutter, the diaphragm is composed of thin metal leaves overlapped to form a circular opening concentric with the lens axis. The size of the opening is adjusted by means of a lever on the shutter body which moves across a calibrated scale (Fig. 8.3*h*).

The iris diaphragm regulates light intensity

In the early days of photography, before adjustable diaphragms were generally available, it was common practice to change the size of the lens opening by inserting into the lens barrel, through a slot in one side, a thin metal plate called a *stop plate* or simply a *stop*. A set of stop plates, each with a hole of different size, provided for a wide range of aperture adjustment. The stops were marked with a number indicating the relative light intensity each would provide at the film surface.

When metal stop plates were in use (they are still used in certain special cameras), it was customary to adjust the size of their holes so that each, in sequence, passed half or twice as much light as the preceding one. Thus, if a stop which required an exposure time of one second were replaced with the next smaller one, the exposure would have to be increased to two seconds to produce the same image density. Replacing a large stop with a smaller one was, and still is, called *stopping down*. Going the other way is called *opening up*. The term "stopping up" is never used.

Gradually, the term *stop* has come to mean a number of things. It is still used in reference to a specific lens opening, as "What stop are you using?" It is often used to mean a change in the lens opening which produces a doubling or halving of the previous exposure, as "open up one stop," meaning "double the exposure," or "cut it a couple of stops," meaning "reduce the exposure by four times."

By extension of this last meaning the term "stop" is also used to describe a change in exposure from any cause or by any means, as when the sun goes under a cloud, "The light has dropped a couple of stops," or "Tri-X is a couple of stops more sensitive than. . . ."

The markings on the iris diaphragm scale are the f/numbers discussed in the previous chapter. On many cameras the maximum aperture is not in the standard sequence and does not represent a *full stop* change in exposure from the next marked opening. Numbers like f/4.5, f/6.3, and

The diaphragm markings are f/numbers

Figure 8.4

Figure 8.5

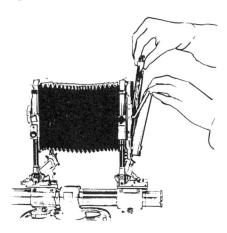

Figure 8.6

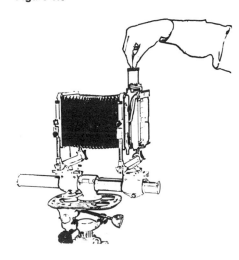

f/7.7 are common first markings and would fall between the normal markings in the scale. Some lenses are equipped with *click stops*, a feature which permits blind adjustments of the diaphragm. Clicks indicating the half-stop positions are common, too, but usually on smaller cameras.

The markings on the front retaining ring of a typical view camera lens are as follows: "Schneider-Kreuznach (the manufacturer), Symmar (the name of the lens design), 1:5.6/180 (the relative aperture and /the focal length in millimeters), 8496515 (the lens serial number)." This lens would be commonly identified as "a 180 mm, f/5.6 Schneider Symmar."

If its various specialized adjustments are set at the neutral position, the view camera is a relatively simple machine to operate. For ordinary work the lens board and the camera back should be centered and parallel to each other, and the unused adjustments should be locked. The camera must be used on a tripod, and it should be mounted straight on the tripod head so that tilting the head forward and backward will not deflect the image horizon. Both front and back standards of most view cameras are equipped with focusing knobs, and they should both be adjusted if necessary to balance the camera on the tripod. Be sure to lock all adjustments securely, but not so tightly that they bind.

Adjust the tripod height by lengthening or shortening the legs. A minor change in height may be made with the tripod central column, but it is risky to operate a view camera on a column extended more than just a few inches because of probable vibration.

Point the camera in the general direction of the subject. Open the shutter by using the Time setting, or the press-focus lever, and open the diaphragm fully. Cover your head and the camera back with a black *focusing cloth* and look at—not through—the ground glass (Fig. 8.4). The image will appear on the ground glass upside down, backwards, and in full color.

Loosen the tripod head controls slightly and move the camera as necessary, while watching the image on the ground glass, to adjust the composition. Image size can be adjusted by moving the camera toward, or away from the subject. When the composition is satisfactory, lock the tripod head controls firmly.

Adjust either the front or back focusing controls until the image is in focus, or sharp. You may find that it is not possible to get all of the image in focus at one setting. If this is the case, focus the most important area. Lock the focusing controls.

Close the shutter and set it on the desired speed. Cock the shutter if necessary. Set the diaphragm pointer on the selected aperture number. Insert the film holder in the camera back being careful not to move the camera out of position (Fig. 8.5). Pull out the front dark slide (Fig. 8.6). Press the cable release to make the exposure. Insert the dark slide, with the black side showing to indicate exposed film. Remove the holder from the camera.

An ordinary camera sees objects in perspective just as the eye does. It will record the sharp convergence of railroad tracks receding into the distance, and it will picture tall buildings as tapering into the sky. In pictures of this kind the depth of field of the lens is sometimes inadequate to cover the subject area because the subject cuts through it at an angle rather than lying parallel (Fig. 8.7).

A camera sees objects in perspective just as the eye does

A view camera has adjustments designed to help solve these problems. They are called the *shifts* and *swings*, and refer to movements of the front and rear standards of the camera which make it possible to change the normal alignment of the lens and film (Fig. 8.8). The *shifts* are movements of either standard which keep the lens board and film plane parallel to each other but decenter the lens with respect to the film, either vertically or laterally (the vertical shift of the lens board is referred to specifically as the *rising front*). The *swings* allow the standards to pivot around either a vertical or horizontal axis. The rotation around the horizontal axis is often referred to as a *tilt*.

A view camera has adjustments to help solve these problems

The shifts are usually used to reduce or eliminate the normal effect of converging lines in perspective and are particularly effective in architectural photography. The shift adjustments are also valuable for making slight changes in composition of the ground-glass image, eliminating the need to move the entire camera. Both of these uses are feasible because the image formed by the lens at the film plane covers a much larger area than the film itself (Fig. 8.9), and the film can be positioned to record any portion of it.

Use of the shifts

The perspective convergence of a building, for example, is caused by the fact that the building top is farther from the camera than the building foundation is, and since distant objects are normally seen as smaller than close objects, the top must appear smaller than the bottom. But this is true only when the camera is tilted back to look up at the building (Fig. 8.10*a*). If the camera is pointed horizontally so as to look perpendicularly at the building front, there is no convergence, but the top of the building is out of the picture (Fig. 8.10*b*).

To maintain the parallelism of the verticals—but include the top of the building too—the camera is adjusted to face the building squarely, specifically so that the *camera back is parallel to the subject plane*, which insures against perspective convergence, and the rising front is raised until the building is composed on the ground glass as desired (Fig. 8.10*c*). As

When camera back and subject plane are parallel perspective is eliminated

Figure 8.7

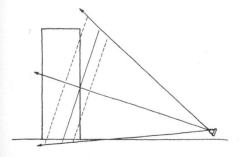

Figure 8.8

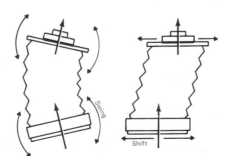

Figure 8.9

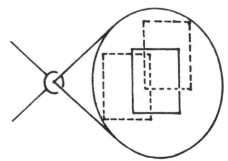

Figure 8.10

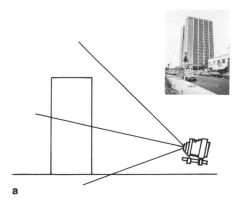

a

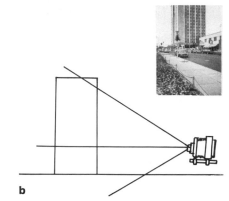

b

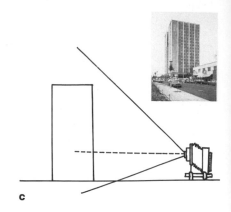

c

Swings can improve depth of field coverage

Figure 8.11

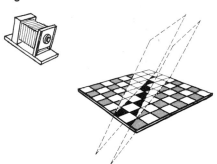

Figure 8.12 No swings used, lens wide open; depth of field is very shallow.

Have your cake and eat it too

long as the camera back and subject plane are parallel, the subject will be devoid of perspective convergence. If the lens board is also parallel, the depth of field will cover the subject plane most efficiently.

If reduction of perspective effects is not of primary importance, it is sometimes possible to use the swings to make better-than-normal use of the available depth of field. For example, suppose you are trying to photograph a chess game from an angle of about forty-five degrees and at fairly close range. You will probably find that with the camera in its neutral position the depth of field will be inadequate to cover the width of the board even with the lens stopped all the way down (Figs. 8.11 and 8.12).

Now consider the position of the board image in space near the film plane. The near point of the board must be imaged behind the film and above film center, while the far point of the board must be imaged in front of the film and below center.

By swinging the film plane to coincide with the plane of the image in space, you can get the entire board into sharp focus without having to stop down at all, but the effect of perspective distortion (convergence) will be emphasized (Fig. 8.13).

If perspective must remain nearly normal, it may be possible to tilt the lens board forward far enough to include the subject in the depth of field without adjusting the back, but the image will then be formed on the very edge of the lens field and sharpness and illumination of the image may not be adequate. The best procedure is to swing the back first to coincide with the image in space, accepting the distortion, then adjust the lens board for best sharpness by observing the ground-glass image with a magnifier. Then stop the lens down a little farther than seems to be required for excellent depth of field coverage. The resulting negative will be sharp, and the distortion can be compensated for (restituted) by adjusting the enlarger during printing. The final print will be both undistorted and sharp if all is done well—a clear case of "having your cake and eating it too" (Fig. 8.14).

Most efficient use of the lens field in this application will be achieved when the respective planes of the subject, camera back, and camera lens board—suitably extended—meet at a common point in space (Fig. 8.15).

Figure 8.13 Back swung to coincide with image plane in space; lens stopped down only one stop for adequate depth of field, but image is strongly foreshortened.

Figure 8.14 The original perspective can be closely approximated by "swinging" the enlarger easel and negative carrier.

Figure 8.15

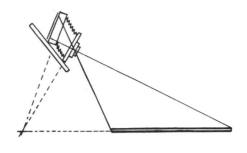

In practice it will be found that there is more than one way to adjust the camera to achieve the various results described above. For example, it is possible to correct for building convergence by tilting the camera up to cover the subject first, then tilting the back and lens board forward until they parallel the subject plane (Fig. 8.16). The ultimate effect is identical to that attained with the rising front; that is, the lens and back are parallel to the subject but vertically decentered. Either method of adjustment is effective and proper. They are not different adjustments, merely different methods of arriving at the same end.

In setting up the view camera to deal with problems which are not as obvious in their solution as those above, much fumbling with the controls can be avoided if you will remember the simple rule: "Adjust the camera **back** first, then adjust the lens board." All significant control of perspective is accomplished with the back shifts and swings, as are some gross adjustments of the depth of field coverage. Save the lens shifts and swings for relatively minor refinements of the image.

It should be obvious that the lens used for the adjustments described above should be capable of forming an extensive image area on an essentially flat plane in space, and that the sharpness of the image should be adequate out to its edges. The lens, in short, should be very well corrected for the various aberrations, and should, in addition, cover a fairly wide field even at maximum aperture.

Although good lenses of four-element Tessar-type construction (Fig. 8.17a) are suitable for view camera use in normal focal lengths and at

Figure 8.16

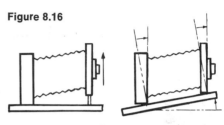

There is more than one way to adjust the camera

Adjust the back first

The lens must be well corrected and cover a wide field

Figure 8.17

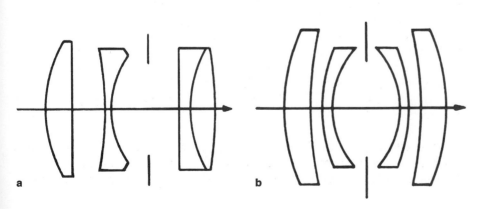

a   b

Figure 8.18

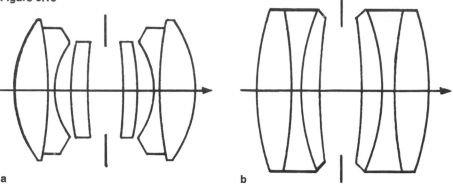

a   b

moderate apertures, they do not, as a rule, provide sufficient coverage to permit more than modest adjustments without some loss of image quality. Lenses of more nearly symmetrical construction (Fig. 8.17b) are probably preferable, since they are likely to provide better coverage, and are more likely to maintain their correction at close subject distances.

Two of the better lenses available today, the Schneider Symmar (Fig. 8.18a) and Goerz Dagor (Fig. 8.18b), combine good correction, wide coverage, and moderate speed with the added virtue of being convertible; that is, the rear component can be used alone as a long focal length lens of fairly good quality, satisfactory for many purposes when stopped down. This feature has been eliminated from the newest Symmar-S design, however, in the interests of better correction and enhanced performance for the complete lens.

Swings will be limited with wide-angle and telephoto lenses

The swings possible with wide-angle lenses will be limited by the inflexibility of the compressed camera bellows as well as the restricted image area available. Some cameras provide recessed lens boards or special bellows units for use with short lenses to allow for some bellows movement, but the swings and shifts should be used with caution with wide-angle lenses. Even in "neutral," the lens field is likely to be only slightly larger than the film area, and deterioration of image quality near the edges of the field will be rapid and extreme. For the same reason long lenses of telephoto construction will permit only moderate swings, since their image circle is deliberately restricted. Long lenses of conventional construction will permit extreme adjustment without much loss of quality.

The Hand-held Camera

9

If we define a *hand-held* camera as one which does not require a tripod or other mechanical support for its normal operation, the category becomes a very extensive and varied one. It would include some sheet-film cameras such as the old 4″ × 5″ Speed Graphics as well as the more recent and popular Instamatics which use special cartridge-loading roll films to make negatives and transparencies less than an inch square. It also includes the "ideal format" rangefinder cameras; the "2¼″ square" and the 6″ × 7″ reflexes, both single-and twin-lens; and a great variety of 35-mm and subminiature cameras, reflex and rangefinder, manual to fully automatic. There is one type, however, which is so widely used that it is familiar to almost everyone who has ever taken a picture. It is, of course, the 35-mm single-lens prism reflex (SLR) of which the Nikon, Leicaflex, Pentax, and Canon are perhaps the best-known examples (Fig. 9.1).

The hand camera and the view camera are opposites. Each has been designed for a particular kind of picture-making and both have become highly specialized. The view camera has sacrificed or compromised ease and speed of handling, physical size and weight, to gain almost unlimited interchangeability of parts, greater control over image perspective, extreme accuracy of framing and composition, and very high image quality. Its design encourages slow, careful work directed toward the perfection of a single image. The hand camera, in contrast, has evolved in the direction of speed and convenience of handling. Remarkable refinement of design and precision of manufacture have kept image quality high in spite of the fact that the useful image area is relatively small in relation to the total mass of the camera itself. The size, weight, cost, and mechanical complexity of the SLRs result from the many automated and convenience features built into them. They are incredibly adaptable cameras; capable, with additional or interchangeable accessories, of making pictures under almost any conditions. They will do almost anything pretty well, except provide view camera image quality, which of course they are not intended to do.

The unique feature of the SLR is its viewfinding-focusing system. Unlike most other cameras the SLR employs the same lens for viewing the image that is used in making the film exposure. The viewing image and the film image are, therefore, not merely similar to each other but are virtually identical. In the words of a popular TV comedian, "What you see is what you get."

Everyone knows the SLR

Figure 9.1

The hand camera and the view camera are opposites

The SLR viewfinder is unique

Figure 9.2

Figure 9.3

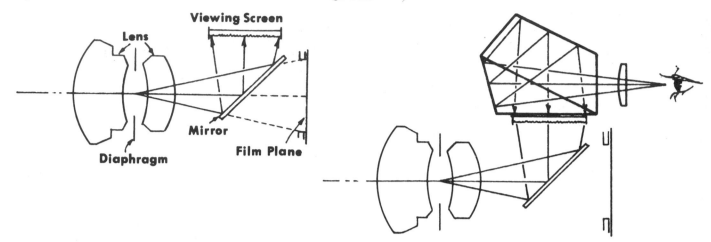

A roof prism corrects the image

Figure 9.4

Focusing aids: the rangefinder prism

The single-lens reflex design is diagrammed in Figure 9.2. Light entering the lens is reflected upward from the inclined mirror so that the image is formed on a ground-glass screen mounted in the top of the camera body. If viewed directly in this position the image will be seen upright but reversed from left to right because of the mirror reflection. Almost all reflex cameras nowadays correct this lateral reversal of the image by adding a "roof prism" to the ground-glass viewing system (Fig. 9.3). Sometimes called a "penta-prism" because it has five active faces, this precisely polished block of optical glass, plus a small ocular lens, presents to the eye a correct image only slightly reduced from apparent life size. In most prism SLRs the viewing image area is a little smaller than the actual film image dimensions. This is usually no great disadvantage since it allows for slight inaccuracy in framing and, more importantly, coincides very closely with the actual useful image area of the conventional color slide mounts.

Focusing 35-mm cameras is generally accomplished by turning a large collar or ring on the lens mount (Fig. 9.4). A double helical thread assembly serves to move the lens toward or away from the film surface, the range of adjustment of most normal lenses being sufficient to allow focusing on any subject from about two feet in front of the camera to infinity. The distance from the lens to the ground-glass focusing screen is identical to the lens-to-film distance. When the image appears sharp, therefore, the film image will be sharp, too. Almost all SLRs employ focusing aid devices, though, because visual focus on the ground-glass surface is difficult to appraise with real precision, especially in dim light.

One such device, the so-called *rangefinder prism* consists of two shallow wedges of glass or plastic laid side by side but pointing in opposite directions. They are generally circular in outline and cemented in the center of the ground glass. Because of their prismatic form, the wedges refract light and are so placed that each sees only the light which reaches it from one half of the marginal area of the lens opening. These, of course, are the light rays which are bent most sharply in focusing so the image which they form appears to go in and out of focus very abruptly. Because the wedges point in opposite directions they fracture the out-of-focus image

Figure 9.5

Figure 9.6

at their line of intersection (Fig. 9.5). When the camera is accurately focused the image appears unbroken (Fig. 9.6).

A more common focusing aid is the *micro-prism grid*, usually a small circular area in the center of the ground glass consisting of dozens of minute pyramids of plastic. The pyramid faces, individually, act like the range-finder prisms described above but the cumulative effect is to disperse the out-of-focus image in several directions rather than simply bisecting it (Fig. 9.7). A slightly out-of-focus image appears to shimmer but the focused image seems quite normal, much as it would appear on an ordinary coarse ground glass (Fig. 9.8).

Neither of the two devices is as effective as it might appear to be, for two reasons. In the first place, the angle of the prism faces determines the direction from which they will accept light. If the prisms are designed to work well with a lens of normal focal length they cannot as easily accept the more steeply angled rays from a shorter focal length nor the near-parallel rays from a longer lens. With unsuitable focal lengths, one half

The micro-prism grid

Figure 9.7

Figure 9.8

or both halves of the rangefinder prism assembly may simply appear black. Moving your eye slightly may cause the black to lighten but the other half will then appear dark. An idea of the point of focus can be obtained by moving the eye rapidly back and forth, comparing the image in the two sections as they alternately lighten, but it is a haphazard method and no real improvement over the conventional ground-glass focusing procedure. Under the same conditions the micro-prism grid simply ceases to function and begins to resemble a dark and granular ground glass.

Parallax focusing

A third focusing aid allows *parallax focusing*. A special unground viewing screen is required. These parallax screens can be installed in some cameras on special order, while, for those cameras which feature user-interchangeable screens, they are usually available as accessories. Parallax focusing screens are usually marked with a fine cross or other reference point in the center of the viewing field. The reference mark lies precisely in the focal plane. An image, accurately focused, must also lie in the focal plane whereas an out-of-focus image will lie either before or behind the plane.

In using parallax focusing you should fix your eye on the reference mark while remaining conscious of the aerial image which will appear to float in the viewing space. If the image is out of focus, moving the eye slightly from side to side will cause the image to shift laterally with respect to the reference mark. When the camera is properly focused, the image and the mark will occupy the same spatial position and no shift will be apparent as the eye is moved. It is important to realize that the aerial image will probably *appear sharp* whether it is properly focused or not. Improper focal adjustment can only be detected by image movement relative to the fixed reference mark. This sort of focusing is inconvenient for everyday picture-taking but is useful for such special purposes as some sorts of close-up work.

When you press the button, the mirror flips up

During viewing and focusing the reflecting mirror angles down behind the lens, directing the image light upward to the ground glass. It obviously can't remain there during the exposure of the film. When you press the shutter release button, therefore, the first effect is to release the mirror lock so that springs can flip the mirror up out of the way, permitting image light to flow back into the camera. As the mirror comes to rest it seals off the ground glass so as to prevent light from the viewing prism eyepiece from entering the film chamber and possibly fogging the film. At virtually the same time the lens diaphragm closes down to its preselected aperture setting and then the shutter mechanism is activated to make the actual exposure.

Most SLRs use focal plane shutters

Almost all interchangeable-lens-type SLRs are equipped with *focal plane* shutters. The mechanical linkage required to provide interchangeable through-the-lens viewing with between-the-lens shutters has generally been considered too complicated, too restrictive in design, or too expensive to make it worthwhile. Although between-the-lens shutters have certain desirable characteristics they are quite rare in SLR design.

How focal plane shutters work

Focal plane shutters, as generally installed in 35-mm cameras, lie just in front of the film surface and consist of two separate cloth or metal-foil curtains attached to rollers at opposite ends of the camera body, a little like two opposing window shades. When the shutter is "cocked" or "wound" the shutter curtains, closed tightly together, are pulled across the film gate against strong spring tension and held in place until released. When the shutter release is pressed the shutter curtains are allowed to separate; the leading curtain snaps across the film gate allowing the exposing light to reach the film, then, after a preselected interval, the second curtain follows, closing off the film gate and terminating the exposure.

For shutter speeds of up to about 1/60 second (higher in some cameras) the action proceeds as described above. The film is completely uncovered by the first curtain's passage before the second curtain begins its motion. At some critical speed, however, the curtain transit time equals the effective exposure time, in other words, the second curtain must begin to close at the instant the first curtain has reached the fully open position. For higher speeds, since the curtains can't be made to move faster, the second curtain must start sooner and the full area of the film is never completely uncovered at any given instant during the exposure interval.

Obviously the accuracy and satisfactory operation of a focal plane shutter depend upon a lot of variables. A very serious problem to be solved in the design of these shutters is unevenness of exposure across the film width. One cause of this problem is the fact that the curtains must accelerate from rest to full speed in just a millimeter or two of travel and their speed must be immediately stabilized and unvarying for the rest of the distance across the film plane. In practice this is impossible. Acceleration is rapid but not instantaneous and it does not cease at the moment the curtain starts to open but continues, with the result that curtain travel at the end of the film gate is faster than at the beginning and effective exposure time is progressively reduced. One solution to this problem is to make the second curtain travel a little slower than the first so that the curtain aperture gets progressively larger as its speed increases.

Some focal plane shutters expose film unevenly

Another serious difficulty which afflicts almost all focal plane equipped cameras to some degree, is an unevenness of curtain operation which shows up as stripes of varied densities in the developed negatives (Fig. 9.9). The cause is apparently an uncontrolled oscillation of the shutter curtains which causes the curtain slit width or its velocity to vary randomly as it moves. This annoying problem is acceptably slight in most expensive cameras and some less expensive ones, but serious enough in some to make ruinous marks on the negatives. It is much more of a problem with large shutters than with small ones and it is usually most obvious at the higher shutter speeds, although some evidence of marking may be

Some mark the film

Figure 9.9 Although the contrast of these images has been emphasized in printing the patterns are clearly visible on the negatives and in ordinary prints. This is the way four different cameras' focal plane shutters expose film at 1/1000 second. Watch for this unevenness in pictures of clear skies or other large areas of uniform tone. Large shutters are likely to be worse than this.

a   b   c   d

found at speeds as low as 1/125 second in some cameras. Watch out for this defect in landscape skies or other large areas of uniform subject tone.

All may distort moving images

Because a curtain shutter tends to "wipe" the image onto the film like a paint roller, some rather bizarre image distortions can occasionally occur. Portions of a moving image which happen to follow the curtain slit across the film will be rendered as streaks while image details which move rapidly against the direction of shutter travel may appear compressed or even disappear entirely. Similarly, image details moving at right angles to the shutter travel sometimes appear strangely warped. In the old days of large, slow-moving curtain shutters these effects were common, often dramatic. They are much less so now but still show up from time to time.

Flash synchronization

Most cameras come equipped with built-in synchronization for both electronic flash and conventional flashbulbs. This mechanism simply switches firing current to the flash unit at the instant required to assure complete illumination of the film during the shutter opening. Some camera designs make flash operation relatively foolproof; with others it is possible to mix up the operations and fire a flashbulb at the electronic flash synchronization setting and vice versa. In general this is disastrous. Flashbulbs fired at the *strobe* setting may synchronize satisfactorily at the lower shutter speeds but not at the higher ones while electronic flash triggered at the flashbulb setting will fire prematurely and probably not illuminate the film at all during the shutter operation. Because of its extremely short duration, electronic flash will not synchronize satisfactorily at any setting with those focal plane shutter speeds which restrict the shutter curtain opening. At these higher speeds the flash will simply print the image of the shutter curtain slit somewhere on the film leaving the rest of the frame area blank. The maximum "full-curtain-opening" speed is usually 1/60 to 1/125 second for small cameras but may not be more than 1/25 second for the larger shutters used in 120 film size cameras. It is usually printed in color on the camera shutter speed dial or marked with a prominent symbol of some sort.

Quite a number of SLRs are now equipped with *Copal Square* shutters. This shutter type operates just ahead of the film like a conventional focal plane shutter but employs rigid metal leaves travelling vertically instead of the usual curtains. Electronic flash synchronization is possible at speeds up to 1/125 second due to the shorter travel of the shutter leaves. In other respects image results are similar to those obtained with curtain shutters.

Built-in meters

Most SLRs now have built-in exposure meters which are operated by adjustment of the camera lens and shutter controls. A dial somewhere on the camera body can be set at the appropriate ASA index for the film in use. Correct exposure setting of the controls is indicated in the camera viewfinder by the position of the meter needle or, in some newer designs, by some combination of glowing indicator lights or light-emitting diodes. In most cameras either the shutter speed setting or the aperture setting or both are also displayed so that there is no need to remove the camera from your eye to consult the scales.

Full-field meters

Most SLR metering systems are *full-field* or *averaging* types, which means that they are affected by light from the same area of the subject that is seen in the camera viewfinder. Most, in fact, actually read the light intensity of the finder image itself rather than the subject luminance so that the meter reading will tend to compensate for filters used over the lens or for the light loss caused by unusual extension of the lens focal distance in close-up photography. Obviously, since the meter field coincides with the lens field, the finder image indicates quite precisely the subject area which the meter is "seeing," regardless of the lens in use. This one feature makes the built-in meter considerably easier to use and more reliable in use than an ordinary hand-held meter reading reflected light.

In some cameras the meter field is *weighted;* that is, it gives greater emphasis to some area of the image than to the remainder of the field. *Center-weighting* is used in a number of camera types, while at least one variety features a *bottom-weighted* design. In some cases it is possible to switch from average to weighted readings at will. A relatively few designs employ "semispot" readings. While some of these camera types meter a specifically delimited area of the finder image (Fig. 9.10) just as in the full-field designs, other types measure the light before it reaches the ground glass by using a sensitized area of the mirror itself as the light receptor, or by swinging a photocell into the light path on a hinged or pivoted arm which flips out of the way before the exposure. None of these methods is clearly superior of inferior to the others. Good results can be obtained with any of them.

Weighted meters

Figure 9.10

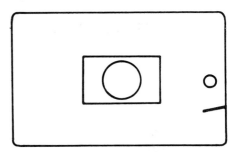

Although meters which read the finder image brightness can be influenced by light from the finder eyepiece the effect is seldom serious. The photographer's eye and head usually shade the finder sufficiently to keep the light intensity low and the meter cells are arranged and baffled so as to minimize their sensitivity to light from this source. Still, it is a good idea to remember the possibility of this error and to shield the finder eyepiece as effectively as possible, both during the meter reading and also during the actual exposure. The mirror is supposed to seal the film chamber against light from the ground glass during exposure but there is always the possibility of a leak.

Because small camera images must be enlarged rather considerably to be useful it is important that the negatives be very sharp. Assuming that the camera is equipped with a good lens, the two most common causes of unsharp pictures are improper focus and camera movement. Of these two evils camera movement is probably the most difficult to avoid consistently, but avoid it you must if you hope to make good pictures.

Negatives must be sharp to enlarge well

You should probably practice various methods of holding and operating your camera to find the one that is most comfortable and gives you the best control. Most people eventually settle on some variation of the grips illustrated in Figure 9.11. The important aspects of the grip are balanced support, lack of muscular tension, and freedom of movement for the focusing and shutter release fingers. Practice pressing the shutter release until you can do it rapidly but so smoothly that there is no perceptible movement or vibration of the camera body.

Find a comfortable grip

Students sometimes ask "what's the slowest shutter speed that's safe to hand-hold?" There isn't any definitive answer to that question. Some people are steadier than others; some images don't have to be enlarged much; short lenses are easier to hold than long ones, etc. Although a lot of photographers seem to take pride in their ability to hand-hold ex-

What's the slowest speed to hand-hold?

Figure 9.11

posures of 1/15 or even ⅛ second, it's a wise person who looks for support before that. As a rule of thumb, it's probably a good idea not to count on sharp results, hand-held, if the shutter speed is longer than the reciprocal of the lens focal length in millimeters. In other words, if you're using a 50-mm focal length lens, don't hand-hold exposures of longer than 1/50 second; 1/25 second is probably safe for 25-mm lenses and if you can hold a 250-mm lens consistently at 1/250 second you're doing pretty well.

Brace the camera, but avoid tension   At slower shutter speeds it becomes increasingly important to brace the camera against the face, and the arms against the body to insure against vibration (Fig. 9.12). Don't overdo this, however. Excessive pressure may cause muscle tension and trembling. Avoid resting your arms on the center of your chest or you may see the camera jumping up and down in time with your heartbeat. Avoid straining to hold your breath during

Figure 9.12

Figure 9.13   **Figure 9.14**

the exposure for the same reason. You'll be steadier if you take a deep breath and exhale slowly as you press the shutter release. By all means take advantage of any available support (Fig. 9.13). Lean, or rest the camera against a door casing, street lamp post or whatever is handy and, if the subject permits, make several exposures; one may be much sharper than the others.

If you do a lot of shooting at slow shutter speeds you may want to consider using a *chest-pod*. Although there have been camera support gadgets designed expressly for wearing on the chest, a regular tabletop tripod will serve the purpose admirably. Figure 9.14 shows how the little tripod can be adjusted to hold the camera comfortably at near-eye-level. Again, be careful not to position the tripod legs where they will be affected by your heartbeat. These little tripods are also very useful for bracing the camera against a variety of surfaces, as shown in Figure 9.15. With some care it is possible to make short time exposures in this manner, using a cable release, of course, to release the shutter.

For reliable insurance against camera movement, at least with lenses of moderate focal length, you should use a good tripod. Although the idea of putting a "hand" camera on a tripod seems incongruous, it is better than throwing unsharp negatives away, unprinted. You must also take some other precautions, however. Never extend the tripod center column farther than necessary. Always use a cable release or the camera's self-timer to trip the shutter and (if possible) always raise the camera mirror manually to avoid the inevitable lurch (however slight) at its release. If the exposure is long enough to be timed manually it's a good idea to employ the old "lens cap" exposure technique. Hold a black card in front of the lens; release the shutter on "Bulb" and hold it open with the cable release; remove the card after the vibration has ceased and make the exposure. You can let the shutter close to terminate it or cover the lens first if you prefer.

For lenses of more than, say, 250-mm focal length, it may be necessary to provide extra support. Strangely enough, resting your hand on the camera or on the lens barrel close to the tripod head may actually improve sharpness to some extent by damping the vibrations of the shutter and mirror. The mass of the lens and the normal elasticity of the tripod can combine to act like a tuning fork, sustaining vibrations for a considerable

Consider a chest-pod

Use a tripod

Figure 9.15

Brace long lenses carefully

Figure 9.16

Figure 9.17

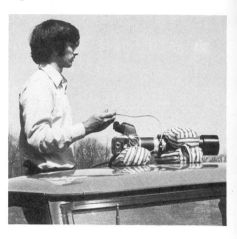

period of time. A good way to eliminate vibration is to support the front of the lens in some way. A second tripod can be used but it is very inconvenient. A relatively easy and effective method is illustrated in Figure 9.16. A couple of half-inch dowels or similar wooden sticks are taped firmly to the tripod legs and to the lens barrel after the camera position has been finalized. Minor vertical adjustments can still be made by using the tripod center column. If picture conditions permit it's a good idea to raise the mirror manually when shooting with long lenses on a tripod.

Shot bags are excellent support

If the camera can be placed or rested on some surface you can positively insure against movement by bedding it firmly on shot bags or bean bags (not sand bags as they may leak abrasive dust onto your camera) and laying another one or two across the top of the lens barrel. For very long lenses this is by far the best method (Fig. 9.17). Although shot bags are heavy and awkward to carry around they are invaluable for purposes like this. Use them also to brace against the legs of the tripod or to anchor it when working in the wind (Fig. 9.18).

The gyro-stabilizer— expensive but effective

If you want the freedom to hand-hold the camera but need extra support, you can buy a battery-powered gyro-stabilizer unit (Fig. 9.19). These neat and expensive little gadgets attach to the tripod socket of the lens or camera body and add only about a pound or two of weight to the outfit. When the gyros reach full speed, however, the camera is eerily suspended on a miniature space platform which will squirm in your hands like a live thing when you try to move it. Movement in all directions is still possible, of course, and the camera will still hit the ground if you let go of it, but the gyros resist sudden movement or vibrations, particularly in a vertical plane, effectively subduing your normal muscular twitches and tremors. After some practice you will find it possible to shoot at moderate speeds with surprisingly good results while walking or riding in a car, boat, or plane; while with a comfortable stance and the gyro support, exposure times of $\frac{1}{8}$ or 1/15 second with lenses of up to 100-mm or so, are quite practical.

Figure 9.18   **Figure 9.19**

Most hand cameras yield fairly small negatives which require at least moderate degrees of enlargement for comfortable viewing. It's obvious, therefore, that the negative image quality should be as high as possible. Extra care in processing and printing is certainly in order and cleanliness at every stage of the processing is imperative if good prints are desired. Beyond these precautions, however, there is one simple rule which, if followed, will improve most students' beginning work immediately and dramatically: **USE THE WHOLE NEGATIVE AREA!** While this is good advice to follow in using any film size it is especially important for 35-mm and smaller negatives. Not only will tight and careful framing improve sharpness, reduce grain, and help subdue dust and lint spots, but it will also force you to pay attention to the picture itself—and that's good!

USE THE WHOLE NEGATIVE

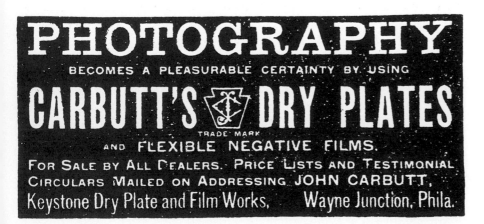

10 Developing Roll Film in a Tank

Roll films are processed in small tanks

Roll and 35-mm films are usually processed in small cylindrical metal or plastic tanks. The film is loaded in total darkness onto the tank reel, where it is guided into a long spiral by the grooves or wires of the reel flanges. Some skill and practice is required to load the reels efficiently, but instructions are supplied with the tanks and it is generally wise to follow them. The pictures accompanying this discussion show the various operations involved in loading the two most popular reel sizes in the familiar stainless steel tanks (Fig. 10.1).

The difficulties which most beginners encounter can be traced to faulty insertion of the film end into the reel core clip or slot. If the film is not started perfectly straight and centered (Fig. 10.1 *h, i, r,* and *s*) between the flanges, it will almost certainly jump a groove and the adjacent layers of film will touch.

Loading difficulties, blotches, and fingernail marks

The most obvious result of this problem will be blotches of undeveloped emulsion on the finished negative strip, corresponding to the areas of contact where the developer solution was not active. A secondary result is the formation of "fingernail marks"—little soft-edged black crescents occurring wherever the film kinked or was folded. These are caused by pressure on the emulsion which exposes it almost as if light had struck it. The marks are developed images and cannot be removed (Fig. 10.2).

Aside from the difficulties which you can expect to run into while you are learning to load the reels, tank development is very convenient and effective. The procedure and the chemicals for tank processing are very similar to those used in tray processing, with the major exception of the agitation procedure.

Intermittent agitation is employed in tank development

Tray development demands constant agitation of the film for good results, and this speeds the process up because of the relatively efficient circulation of fresh developer over the film surface. The condition of *constant agitation* is often specified in developing time tables and is almost invariably shorter than the times given for *intermittent agitation* which is employed in tank development.

Constant agitation is not practical with small tanks because the restricted channels formed by the film layers and the reel flanges are very likely to cause turbulence patterns in the developer, which in turn cause localized areas of overdevelopment. To avoid these effects, most authorities recommend relatively gentle agitation for brief intervals during the development period separated by much longer intervals of rest.

As a rule of thumb, any film in any developer should receive no fewer than six periods of agitation during development, and the agitation periods should total no more than about one-sixth the total time of development. A typical recommendation might specify an agitation period of five seconds every thirty seconds during a total development time of five minutes.

The agitation should be gentle, and in the stainless steel canister-type tanks, it is accomplished by simply turning the tank over and back two or three times during the five second period. (The tank must be capped, of course, to prevent leakage.) The only exception to this rule is the initial period of agitation which must be performed immediately after the developer is poured over the film or the film placed into the developer if you are working with an open tank in the dark. It is generally recommended that this agitation be fairly vigorous, and that it be punctuated by a couple of sharp raps of the tank against the sink side or bottom; the purpose of this procedure being to dislodge any air bells which might otherwise cling to the emulsion, preventing the action of the developer, and causing *pinholes* in the image.

The agitation should be gentle

Development streaks are also possible if agitation is not performed at all but for a different reason. In this case the oxidation products of development remain next to the film emulsion, instead of being flushed away, and inhibit the development process. These inhibiting chemicals are apparently heavier than the other ingredients of the solution, and in their leisurely flow down the film surfaces, they leave underdeveloped streaks which, very typically, run across the film width. This pattern of underdeveloped streaks serves to distinguish insufficient agitation from overagitation which is typified by relatively irregular and nondirectional areas of heavy density concentrated mainly around the edges of the film near the reel flanges where developer velocity is highest.

Development streaks are possible

Film tanks must be loaded in total darkness, of course, but after the cover is placed on the tank the lights can be turned on for the actual processing. All of the solutions can be poured in and out of the tank through a lightproof aperture in the lid.

Tanks must be loaded in total darkness

Any general purpose film developer will be reasonably satisfactory for use with roll or 35-mm films but for best results these films should be processed in fairly gentle developers and handled with great care. It is important that the film's inherent granularity not be emphasized more than is necessary and that no physical damage to the delicate gelatin layers occurs. It is also important, especially with the smaller roll and 35-mm film sizes, that the maximum image sharpness be produced and preserved.

Almost any developer will do, but be gentle

There is a great deal of mystique surrounding roll film developers and developing techniques. Some of it is probably founded in fact and some, no doubt, is nonsense. Regardless of the claims of manufacturers of exotic proprietary developers, there is no magic potion on the market. In any

There is no magic potion on the market

35-mm film

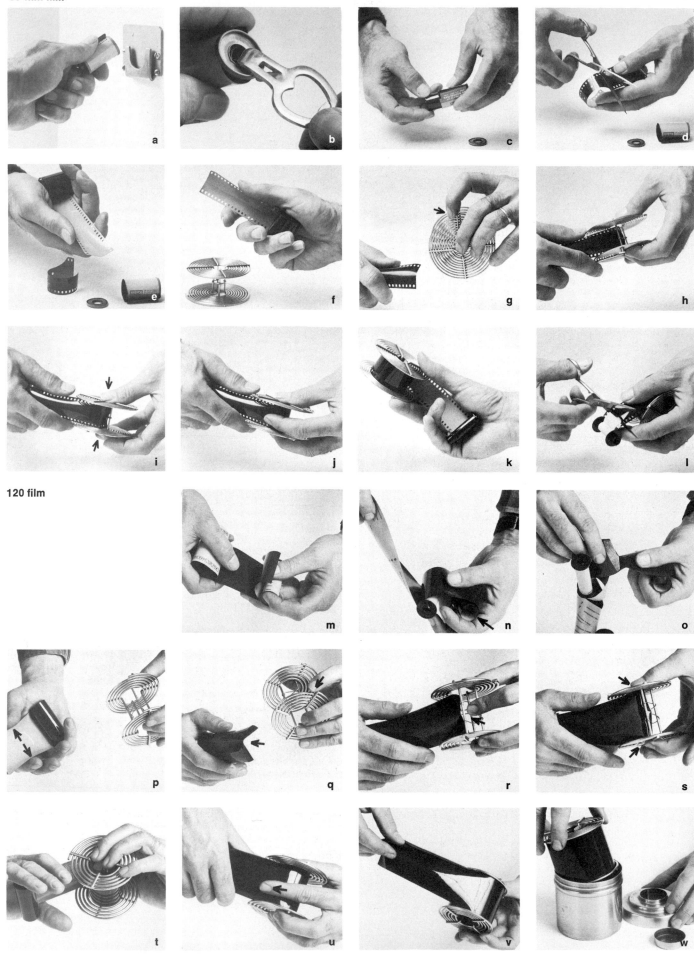

120 film

Figure 10.1

a. Open the film cartridge by inserting the flat end into the special tool shown and prying off the end cap.

b. An alternative method: use a regular beer can opener.

c. Remove the film spool from the metal shell. The film is not backed with paper so use care in handling.

d. Cut off the loading tongue cleanly. Some films will tear satisfactorily, but scissors are recommended. You must cut mylar-based films, they will not tear.

e. "Palm" the film spool letting the film strip lie in your hand, emulsion side up. Squeeze it slightly between thumb and fingers to keep it from rolling back up into a tight curl.

f. Another view of the "palmed" film.

g. Holding the film reel as shown, be sure the end of the spiral wire points toward the film. Check it with your finger tip to make sure.

h. Locate the opening or clip in the reel hub and insert the film end.

i. Center the film between the reel flanges with thumb and fingers and, holding it there, pull lightly and bend the film sharply into the first groove of the spiral track. Practice this in the light, with scrap film, until it is easy to do.

j. Keeping the film under light tension, feed it onto the reel by rotating the reel, a half turn or so at a time, with the left hand. Use your left forefinger to feel for possible wrinkles.

k. A twenty-exposure roll almost loaded.

l. When the entire strip has been loaded, cut off the spool with scissors and tuck the free end of the film strip into position on the reel. A thirty-six-exposure roll of film will fill the reel completely and may even protrude an inch or two. Don't worry about it; just put the reel into the tank, put the cover on, and proceed to step x.

Loading 35-mm film onto tank reel (total darkness)

m. Unroll film roll, film end appears.

n. Film rolling up in left hand.

o. Tear paper backing away from film.

p. "Palming" film; thumb and finger hold film tongue straight.

q. Right hand holds film, left hand positions reel, left forefinger locates reel spiral end.

r. Left forefinger depresses reel film clip; film tongue inserted.

s. Left middle finger and thumb center film between reel flanges. A very important step.

t. Left hand rotates reel, right hand feeds film.

u. Left forefinger rides lightly on film back to feel for unevenness.

v. Reel nearly loaded, right hand finishes last turn.

w. Insert loaded reel into tank.

Loading 120 film onto tank reel (total darkness)

x. Pour developer into tank through light trap in top. Tilting avoids "airlock."

y. Agitate. Turn film tank over and back.

z. "See-saw" film through wetting agent solution.

aa. Drain wetting solution. Film held in horizontal position a moment drains clean.

Normal room light

Figure 10.2   If you don't load the tank properly or if you handle the film roughly your negatives and prints may suffer, as shown here. On the negative strip (seen from the emulsion side) the irregular black blob resulted from improper loading; adjacent layers of film touched, preventing the processing liquids from doing their work. The raw emulsion material, neither developed nor fixed in this case, appears on the negative as milky-gray area which is virtually opaque to transmitted light. It prints as a totally white shape. The little black crescent shapes I call "fingernail marks" because they resemble nail trimmings. They result from kinking the film; they print white or light gray.

really objective test of developers it would be very difficult to prove any developer normally used for roll film to be clearly superior to any other. A solution outstanding in one respect will probably be inferior in some other respect and you must simply decide which characteristics are important to you. Actually, the mystique is part of the fun. If you really think your developer is superior to all others it makes you feel a little superior yourself.

D-76 is satisfactory

For general use a simple MQ-borax formula such as Kodak's D-76 (see pages 109–111), DuPont's 6D, or Ilford's ID-11 will be found to be perfectly satisfactory. Image sharpness and graininess are both acceptable; developing conditions can be varied widely for good image contrast control and the solution is cheap, keeps well, and is clean and easy to use.

One-shots

If maximum sharpness is desired a good *one shot* developer will probably be a good choice, especially one of the several concentrated liquid formulas on the market like *Rodinal* or *Ethol TEC*. These developers typically produce exceptionally "crisp" images of smooth tonal gradation and enhanced edge contrast. As a rule, they work well at normal film speeds but may require rather long developing times. They will almost certainly emphasize the inherent grainy structure of the film, producing a characteristic pepper-and-salt texture which is obvious, but sometimes decorative and seldom objectionable.

Minimum wet time is desirable

There seems to be general agreement that the processing time of roll and 35-mm films should be kept as short as possible. The advantages of "minimum wet-time" processing are said to include improved sharpness, minimum grain, and minimum danger of physical damage to the emulsion.

There is certainly a valid reason for not prolonging the wet time unduly but its significance should not be overemphasized. Reducing a thirty-minute wet time to twenty-eight minutes, for example, will not change the printing characteristics of your negatives significantly. There is, in fact, considerable danger that using warm solutions, strong developer concentrations, abbreviated washing times, or forced negative drying procedures, simply for the purpose of reducing wet time, will damage your negatives rather than improve them. Try for "minimum wet time" certainly, but don't get hysterical about it. Cleanliness, consistency, and control are much more important concerns. If you simply practice good, efficient working habits you'll get good results. You can worry about "minimum wet time" after you've solved all the major problems and are producing otherwise perfect pictures.

There is disagreement among some experts about the use of an acid stop bath after roll film development. Again, let's consider the facts soberly. Years ago when emulsions were thick and soft and when they were developed in developers activated by sodium carbonate, the reaction between the carbonate and an acid bath occasionally caused the formation of bubbles of carbon dioxide gas within the emulsion. This sometimes resulted in little blisters or pits being formed in the gelatin. Nowadays films are thinner and tougher and the developers for roll film, at least, contain only small amounts of carbonate or none at all. Blistering or pitting of the emulsion is almost unknown and acid shortstop baths seem not only harmless, but advisable.

**The stop bath—
to use or not to use?**

The fallacy of avoiding the acid bath and replacing it with plain water or, as some authorities recommend, taking the film out of the developer and putting it directly into the hypo, is apparent when you consider the fact that all normal fixing baths contain substantial amounts of acid or an acid salt. This acid, which will neutralize the developer alkali if the stop bath does not, is included to insure adequate hardening of the film emulsion since the usual hardeners are not effective in alkaline solution. Substituting plain water for the acid shortstop bath, therefore, not only permits the developing action to continue for a while after the film is removed from the developer, but, more seriously, hastens the neutralization of the fixer acidity, thus destroying its hardening action. Additionally, the fixer acid is just as likely to cause pits and blisters in the emulsion as is the shortstop bath since the two baths contain the same acid in practically the same concentration and the same reaction will take place in each. It seems rather obvious, therefore, that the shortstop bath is beneficial since its use will prolong the useful life of the fixer and, unless it is made excessively strong, is no threat whatever to good negative quality.

There is one more possible reason why the use of an acid stop bath may be preferable to water alone. Admittedly this is a special circumstance, but it is possible that in areas of the country where the mineral content of the water is very high, the water may be relatively strongly alkaline. Under these circumstances it will probably be necessary to prepare film developers with distilled water. If such a developer is followed by an alkaline water rinse, the developing action will certainly be sustained and may even be accelerated. A mildly acidic rinse is certainly to be preferred to an alkaline one, and, in my opinion, to a neutral one as well.

**A mildly acid stop bath
is probably best**

Development should be timed

Film development should be timed either from the moment the **developer** is poured into the tank until the moment the **shortstop** bath is poured into the tank, or from the moment the tank is full of developer until it is full of shortstop. Give the film about thirty seconds in the shortstop, with agitation. After the shortstop bath, pour in the fixer and agitate briefly. The tank cover can be removed to check the film clearing time after a minute or so. Total fixing time should be twice the clearing time, just as with sheet film. Rinse the film in the tank briefly and treat it with hypo clearing agent for the recommended time. Then wash for the recommended time.

Film can be washed while on the reel

The film can be washed while on the reel by removing the tank lid and allowing a gentle stream of water to flow into the open reel hub. It is a good idea to empty the tank completely two or three times during washing to assure complete water changes and to eliminate the milky coating of tiny air bubbles which is likely to form on the film surfaces.

Drying procedure to avoid dirt and water spots

Following the wash, roll films and short lengths of 35-mm film should be removed from the reel, a clip attached to each end, and the film strip held by the clips, suspended in a narrow loop so that the looped end is immersed in a tray or tank of wetting agent solution. Raise and lower the clips alternately so as to run the film loop through the solution rather briskly, being careful not to let it rub on the bottom or sides of the container any more than necessary. After three or four passes through the wetting agent, stretch the film strip out nearly horizontally with one edge down and allow the liquid to drain across the film width. Lower one hand a little so that the water finds its way to one end of the strip and drips off. When dripping has nearly ceased, lower the end of the film slowly until it hangs straight down and carefully hang it to dry in a dust-free place.

The purpose of this rather elaborate procedure is to remove from the film surface any particles of pipe scale, dust, dirt, or lint which might be adhering to its surface, or which might be floating in the wetting bath. The vigorous agitation will tend to rinse off surface particles. The horizontal draining position allows loosened particles to take the shortest possible path out of the image area, and the gradual straightening of the film strip to the vertical position tends to prevent the draining water at the film edge from spreading back over the film surface with its collected dirt and lint particles.

Wiping the film should be the last desperate resort

If these procedures do not result in *clean* negatives, check your drying location for airborne dust, and if that is satisfactory, try mixing the wetting agent with distilled water instead of tap water. Wipe the film surfaces gently *under water* before placing the film in the wetting bath, if necessary, but wiping the wet film strip with a damp chamois or viscose sponge to remove surface moisture should be a last desperate resort. The probable hazards outweigh the possible benefits.

If your arms are too short

You may find it impossible to run a full 36-exposure roll of 35-mm film through a tank of wetting agent solution. Even if your arms are long enough to handle it the film may spring into a tangled mass as soon as you attempt to form it into the necessary loop. If this happens coax the film back into the tank or into a trayful of weak wetting agent solution, prepared with distilled water. Let it soak for thirty seconds or so, then attach film clips to each end of the strip and hang it up to dry letting it drain naturally. With luck you will have no drying streaks but if some should occur, the film can be resoaked in distilled water for a few minutes, wiped gently in the water, retreated with weak wetting agent, and dried again. If the scums persist use a still weaker wetting agent or omit it entirely. If the wetting agent is omitted, wipe the film surfaces after removal from the distilled water and immediately after hanging them to dry with a "photograde" chamois skin, thoroughly soaked in distilled water and squeezed as dry as possible.

Roll films will rarely have to be wiped. For some reason they are seldom affected by hard water scums if reasonable care is taken in washing and rinsing them. Scums are common on 35-mm films but normally only on the film back, rarely on the emulsion side. Do not wipe the emulsion side unless it is absolutely necessary.

Silly as it seems there are good and bad procedures even for wiping film with a chamois. You can get good results if you follow this procedure (Fig. 10.3). First, be sure the chamois is of "photo" quality, clean, free from dust and dirt particles, and thoroughly saturated with distilled water. Second, **squeeze** it just as dry as you can, but **don't** wring it dry. Wringing chamois leather will certainly stretch it severely, may tear it, or may cause the surface fibers to detach themselves. If this occurs you may find your negatives covered with tiny furry specks after they dry. Third, fold the damp-dry chamois neatly into a flat pad, several layers thick and a little wider than the film width. Fourth, hang the wet film strip from a clip and hold it fairly taut by light tension on the lower end; then, applying very light, but even pressure, make one slow pass down the length of the film strip with the chamois pad. If the chamois is dry

Figure 10.3

a. Saturate the chamois thoroughly. Ideally it should be stored in a weak solution of sodium bicarbonate (baking soda) which will keep it soft and prevent spoilage. Allowing it to air-dry between uses will tend to make it shed fibers when it is resoaked.

b. Squeeze it dry, but don't wring it.

c. Spread it out smoothly. It should appear to be dry; if damp spots are visible squeeze it some more.

d. Fold it into a neat flat pad with the edges concealed.

e. This is the way the pad looks when folded. Wrapping the leather around a pencil will serve the same purpose and will make it easier to wipe the wider 120 roll films.

f. Holding the film under some tension against the top clip, wipe the back of the film from top to bottom in one smooth motion. Don't wipe the emulsion side unless absolutely necessary.

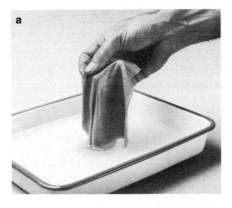

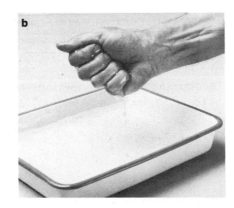

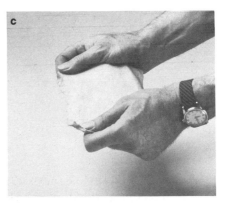

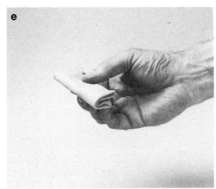

enough and if enough layers have been folded the chamois will absorb all the surface moisture from the film and leave it spotless. If water droplets or visible hazy streaks are left on the film surface, resqueeze the chamois, refold it, and repeat the operation, **gently!**

If this procedure or an equally good one is followed, the film should dry free from blemishes. Wiping the film is certainly advantageous in reducing "wet time" but this must be weighed against the possibility of scratching the emulsion. In general, following the principle that "if you don't touch it you can't scratch it," I'd advise wiping only after normal drip-drying has been tried and found unsatisfactory for some reason.

Drying the film   Films should be allowed to dry in a dust-free place. If heat is used to hasten drying it should be mild. Heat lamps directed at the wet film may cause damage to the emulsion or even permanent warping of the film base. Warming the air in the film chamber is a preferable procedure but be sure to avoid excessive heat. The best method is to dry the air with a dehumidifier. Gentle forced air circulation is helpful in speeding drying but be sure the air is filtered to remove all dust.

Storing the negatives   After the films are dry, remove them from the dryer and, handling them carefully by the edges, cut them into convenient strips. It is customary to cut 120 roll film negatives into strips of from two to four exposures depending upon the actual image dimensions. Cut 35-mm negatives into strips of six to fit the standard envelopes or the notebook-punched plastic envelopes which are designed to hold a full 36-exposure roll. It is best not to put more than one strip of negatives into each envelope sleeve. Don't roll up the negative strips for storage unless the layers are interleaved with clean paper or plastic. Store the negatives in a clean, dry place, away from excessive heat.

SUMMARY

Total darkness
1. Load the film onto the appropriate tank reel and place in tank. Put cover on tank. Turn on the lights.

Figure 10.4

Normal Room Light
2. In three beakers or graduates prepare appropriate volumes of developer (D-76, HC-11OB, Rodinal, Ethol TEC, or other), stop bath (1% acetic acid), and fixing bath (Rapidfix, or equivalent, diluted for use with film). Adjust them all to 20°C. (68°F.). Set an interval timer for the desired developing time.
3. Developer: pour developer into tank until it starts to overflow. Start the timer, replace top cap on tank, and agitate vigorously for 10 to 15 seconds. Thereafter, agitate by turning tank over and back twice at intervals of 30 seconds. Let tank rest between agitation periods; don't hold it or carry it around. About 30 seconds before the end of the development time pour developer out.
4. Stop bath: immediately pour stop bath into tank so that tank overflows just as the developing time is up. Agitate the stop bath continuously for 30 seconds and pour out.
5. Fixer: set timer running and note time. Pour fixer into tank and agitate for 10 to 15 seconds. While tank is resting wash up and replace utensils. Remove tank cover and wash it thoroughly. Inspect

film. If film is not clear, replace it in fixer and check it at 30 second intervals until it clears, then replace it in fixer and leave it for another interval equal to the total clearing time. Then pour fixer back into storage jug.

6. Water rinse: fill open tank with clean water, agitate briefly, and empty three or four times.

7. Hypo clearing bath: pour clearing bath into tank and agitate it by lifting reel out of solution and replacing it two or three times. Repeat at frequent intervals during clearing time recommended by manufacturer.

8. Wash: allow slowly running water to flow into the center of the open tank for time recommended by manufacturer of hypo clearing bath. At frequent intervals empty tank and allow it to refill to insure complete water changes.

9. Wetting: fill tank with wetting agent solution prepared with distilled water. Use absolute minimum of wetting agent necessary to insure clean drainage. In very hard water areas precede this bath with two or three thorough rinses in clean volumes of distilled water.

10. Dry: agitate films in wetting agent as described in text, then hang to dry in a dust-free place. Gentle drafts of filtered air, dehumidified, or slightly warmed, will speed drying. Avoid violent air movement or excessive heat. Wipe film surfaces only if absolutely necessary to avoid surface scums; however, careful wiping with a clean, soft chamois, thoroughly soaked and squeezed very dry, is advisable if wetting agent is not used.

Store the negatives in negative envelopes or sleeves to preserve them from dust and fingerprints.

11 Photographic Emulsions, Films and Papers

Gelatin, a remarkable material

At present, photography depends almost entirely upon the light-sensitive properties of the silver halides, notably chloride, bromide, and iodide, suspended in a gelatin emulsion. Gelatin is superior to all other known materials for this purpose for several reasons. It holds the sensitive ingredients in very uniform suspension. It melts easily for mixing and coating and sets readily when cooled. It adheres well to a variety of materials; it is tough and flexible. It absorbs water solutions of processing chemicals readily without being dissolved, and it is not adversely affected by any of the normal chemicals used in processing. It is transparent for efficient exposure but can be dyed very easily if desired, either to control exposure or to produce actual colored images. It also enhances the sensitivity of the silver halide crystals and contributes materially to the selective action of the developer, helping to prevent the unexposed halides from being attacked and developed by the reducing agents in the solution. It is, all in all, a very remarkable material.

The silver halides are sensitive to light

The silver halides in the pure state are only weakly sensitive to light. They are relatively very sensitive to ultraviolet "light" which is invisible to the human eye and quite sensitive to visible blue light, but the rest of the spectrum barely affects them at all. For all practical purposes, they can be considered blind to green, yellow, orange, and red. Their overall sensitivity is such that they can be used to make slow printing papers, such as contact printing papers, without much modification; but for use in film emulsions, their general sensitivity to light has to be increased greatly, and their range of sensitivity extended to include all of the visible spectrum, or more, in the case of infrared-sensitive films.

Simple emulsions are color-blind

Emulsions can be modified for almost any degree of sensitivity or color response

The specific techniques by which these speed increases are obtained are well-kept secrets, but the general methods are known. Emulsion sensitivity can be enhanced by mixing bromide and iodide, for example, by washing the emulsion during manufacture, and by "ripening" it with heat, or by treating it with certain chemicals such as ammonia. Color sensitivity is controlled by certain sensitizing dyes incorporated into the emulsion. By these and other means, the basic emulsion ingredients can be modified for almost any degree of sensitivity, for color response, and for control of such characteristics as contrast, grain size, and gradation.

Ordinary, orthochromatic, and panchromatic sensitivity

It has been general practice to classify emulsions by color sensitivity into three general groups: *ordinary*, noncolor sensitized or blue-sensitive; *orthochromatic*, or blue- and green-sensitive; and *panchromatic*, meaning sensitive to all visible colors.

98

Panchromatic films are sometimes further divided into three groups: *type A*, or slightly red-sensitive; *type B*, or normally red-sensitive, matching approximately the sensitivity of the human eye; and *type C*, or abnormally sensitive to red. In recent years these categories have become somewhat blurred, but *Pan* films generally are sensitive to all colors, *Ortho* films are blind to red, and the *Ordinary* films are essentially blind to all colors but blue (Fig. 11.1).

Several printing papers are available with panchromatic and orthochromatic sensitivity, too. The majority of papers can be classed as "ordinary," however.

Because most printing papers for black-and-white work are only sensitive to blue, it is possible to use them in red or yellow light without exposing them. Thus we are able to illuminate the printing area of a darkroom with enough light to see by without endangering the paper. Such safelights are available for use with virtually all sensitized materials, but their utility is limited in the case of panchromatic emulsions, because the film is really sensitive to the safelight color, green, and will be affected by it if the light is too bright or is used for too long a period.

The green color is chosen for use with pan films because the eye is most sensitive to it (not because the film is least sensitive to it) and less green light intensity will be required. Even so, it is not truly "safe" and should only be used with very slow materials or in case of some emergency.

Most printing papers are blue-sensitive

Figure 11.1   Following the rule that colors to which the film is very sensitive will appear in the print as light tones, and colors to whcih the film is not very sensitive will appear dark in the print, see if you can determine the colors of the plastic chips and the rooster in these photographs. You can check your decisions by consulting the full-color illustration on p. 353 of this book. Figure *a* was taken on an "ordinary" blue-sensitive film, Figure *b* was an orthochromatic film, and Figure *c* was made on a popular panchromatic film of type "B" sensitivity. The fourth picture, Figure *d* was made on Polaroid film, type 52. Its color response verges on type "C" panchromatic balance.

Safelights may not be entirely safe

Some caution should be exercised in the use of any safelight to avoid fogging the emulsion, since with one exception, safelights do actually transmit a significant amount of radiation to which the emulsion is sensitive. The exception is a safelight for papers which uses a sodium vapor lamp whose radiation consists entirely of strong yellow light confined to a region of the spectrum which is essentially outside the sensitivity range of a blue-sensitive emulsion. It can be used at fairly high intensities without danger and makes the "darkroom" a very light room indeed.

Contact papers are slow and produce images of highest quality

Printing papers are available in two general use categories, those intended for contact printing (negative in contact with the paper surface) and those intended for use in projection printers or with conventional enlargers. The contact papers are typically very slow and produce images of delicate gradation to yield the highest possible photographic quality. The image color is subject to some variation depending upon the conditions of development, but it is typically brownish or greenish, tending toward more neutral tones and higher contrast as the developer strength is increased. Some papers are designed to produce obviously warm tones and some are inherently cold-toned in any developer. Special developer formulas are available to enhance these tendencies.

Enlarging papers are more sensitive

By comparison, projection or enlarging papers are much more sensitive to light, although there is a considerable variation in speed among various papers in this category. The image quality seems somewhat less delicate, particularly in the highlights and shadow areas; but this may be an illusion related to the coarsening of the image details because of enlargement and the slight fogging which results from projection. Projection papers provide the same variety of image color but are generally somewhat less affected in this respect by the developer composition and strength. Typical general purpose papers exhibit a slightly warm, black image tone which tends toward neutrality if development is prolonged.

All papers are supplied in a variety of sizes and weights

All papers are supplied in a variety of sizes, ranging from about $2\frac{1}{2}'' \times 3\frac{1}{2}''$ to about $20'' \times 24''$ in cut sheets and also in rolls of $20''$ and $40''$ width and several yards in length. The paper stock also varies in weight or thickness, from light-weight, or "document stock" through single-weight, medium-weight, double-weight, and heavy-weight. Single-weight and double-weight are the most common varieties.

And stock color

The paper stock color is usually specified, too. Here the various manufacturers use their own terminology, but typical descriptions are: "white," "natural white," "brilliant white," "snow white," "cream," "ivory," and "buff." The stock color may or may not relate to the ultimate image tone, but in general a warm-toned stock is coated with a warm-toned emulsion, and cold-toned emulsions will be supplied on neutral or blue-white papers.

And surface texture

The paper surface is another important characteristic to consider. Again the manufacturers' terms and surfaces vary, but most papers are available in "glossy" which will produce a mirrorlike surface if ferrotyped, or a highly lustrous, smooth surface if dried naturally. Many other surfaces are also supplied. Typical names are "smooth," "smooth luster," "rough luster," "fine-grained luster," "tweed luster," "silk," "semimatte," and "suede matte."

Resin-Coated (RC) papers are becoming more popular and are now available in several varieties. Featuring a special water-resistant base, these papers are especially valuable for reducing printing time since they can be processed very rapidly and, because they absorb very little water, dry quickly without forced air or heat. In most respects they can be handled about like ordinary papers but they should not be subjected to temperatures over about 88°C. (190°F.) either in drying or mounting. The RC "glossy" surface is unique, too. It will air-dry to a high gloss finish without any special treatment at all, and, in fact, should *not* be ferrotyped.

RC papers are becoming popular

The contrast of films is generally controlled by conditions of development, but most papers are supplied in specific contrast grades, designated by a number from 0 to perhaps 6 or by descriptive names such as "soft," "hard," "ultra hard," etc. (Fig. 11.2). For "normal" negatives you should choose grade 2 in most papers, while if the negative is unusually contrasty, it can be printed more satisfactorily on a "soft" paper such as 1 or 0. Low contrast negatives will print best on a "hard" paper such as 3 or more. While varying development is not a universally useful method of controlling paper contrast, it is partially effective with some types, and these papers may be supplied in only two or three grades. Extreme variations in developing time will be unsatisfactory with any paper, as there is much danger of color change, fog, weak or mottled blacks, and staining.

Some papers are supplied in specific contrast grades

If your negatives vary in contrast, it may be convenient to use one of the variable contrast papers on the market. Rather than being supplied in a specific contrast grade, these papers are capable of producing any reasonable degree of contrast at the whim of the photographer (Fig. 11.3). The papers are coated with a mixture of emulsions, one component being

Variable contrast papers are also available

Figure 11.2 Printing paper contrast is indicated by number. The low numbers indicate low contrast; high numbers indicate high contrast. These prints, all made from the same negative show the range of a typical enlarging paper.

Figure 11.3 Pictures which must have detailed blacks and whites require careful control of contrast and here the flexibility of variable-contrast papers is useful. This picture printed best on Polycontrast, through a PC 2½ filter. (Courtesy of the University of Michigan Press)

primarily sensitive to yellowish light, the other responding mostly to purplish light. If the paper is exposed to yellowish light (it requires a special brownish-orange safelight), the low-contrast emulsion is affected and the resulting print image will be "flat." Purple light will cause the paper to produce a high-contrast image, and white light, or some blend of purple and yellow light, will produce an intermediate degree of contrast. One brand of paper, Ilford *Multigrade*, is an exception; it produces a high-contrast image in yellow light.

The light color, and therefore the contrast, is controlled by filters which are inserted into the light path of the enlarger. The filters are numbered to correspond to normal paper contrast grades; that is, the normal contrast filter color is usually designated number 2 while filters which will produce higher contrast are numbered 3, 4, and in one case, 5. The lowest contrast is provided by a yellow filter, number 1. In some filter sets there are filters of intermediate colors, such as 1½, 2½, and 3½. In the Ilford set, numbered from 1 to 5, the number 3 is considered "normal." An older series, introduced many years ago by DuPont, contained filters numbered from 1 to 10. In this series the number 5 was considered "normal."

The range of contrast attainable on variable contrast papers corresponds approximately to regular paper grades from about 1 to about 4. Variable contrast emulsions are very convenient and economical to use and have almost no serious limitations. Some photographers maintain that they do not yield as clean whites or as rich blacks as do graded papers, and others complain that the filters introduce diffusion, thereby reducing both image sharpness and contrast. These claims are probably at least partially valid; but practically speaking, the papers are capable of producing excellent results, and they are so convenient that their minor shortcomings can be overlooked.

Filters are used to vary contrast

It is true that the filters used with these papers can be a source of trouble if they are used under the enlarger lens; that is, if they are filtering the image light. Even in this position, they will be harmless if they are kept clean and if they are not moved during the exposure, assuming that they are of good quality in the first place. It is safer, however, to use the acetate sheet filters sold for use above the condenser system of the enlarger where the light is still unfocused. Here the filters cannot disrupt the image sharpness or contrast, and they can be removed and replaced for multiple exposure techniques without causing any image shift.

The filters may cause difficulty, but it can usually be avoided

There are a few special purpose papers which may be of some interest. At least two manufacturers offer a water-resistant paper which does not absorb liquids and therefore speeds the washing and drying operations.

Special purpose papers

There are several papers on the market, too, that are exceptionally thin and do not crack when folded. They are useful for greeting cards, back-to-back mounting of prints, etc. For pictures requiring exceptionally high contrast, there are special papers, not usually in stock in the amateur photographic supply stores, but sometimes available on special order. Information on these papers can be found in the graphic arts or industrial arts sections of photographic materials catalogs.

Most papers are non-color sensitized, but a few are orthochromatic, and at least one variety is panchromatic. This is Kodak's Panalure, intended for making black-and-white enlargements from color negatives. It must be handled in total darkness for complete safety, but brief exposure to a dark brown safelight is permissible.

The so-called stabilization process is convenient for fast production of prints for immediate use. It is an automatic developing process, accomplished by feeding the exposed paper into a small machine which rolls an activator solution across the emulsion for almost instantaneous development, then applies a coat of stabilizing solution which renders the image semipermanent. The entire procedure takes only a few seconds, and the print is delivered damp-dry and ready for use in a few minutes.

Stabilized prints are heavily contaminated with the processing chemicals and should not be stored with conventional, well-washed prints or negatives. If a permanent image is required, a stabilized print can be fixed and washed in the conventional manner. The exposed paper can also be processed completely in normal printing chemicals if desired, but ordinary printing paper cannot be used successfully in a stabilization processing machine.

Most modern films are coated on an acetate base. For conditions requiring extreme dimensional stability, a polyester base material is used (typical trade names are Gafstar, Estar, and Cronar). Films coated on polyesters are characterized by virtual immunity to shrinking and stretching, reduced tendency to curl (when suitably coated on both sides) springiness and extreme toughness. When the situation demands complete flatness and stability, glass plates are still used. A surprising variety of emulsion types can be supplied on glass, and for many technical and scientific purposes, it is the only satisfactory material.

Beginners are sometimes surprised to discover that most films are strongly colored on one side. Some films, too, have a tinted base, usually bluish or grayish. These colors are intended to reduce light conduction (light piping) within the film base material or reflections from the back surface of the base material back into the emulsion. Such reflection, if unsuppressed, would cause a spreading or *irradiation* (Fig. 11.4) of the more heavily exposed areas of the image and reduce definition. In extreme cases, the light around a point image may be reflected back and forth between the film surfaces several times causing a bright ring or halo around the image. This phenomenon is called *halation*, and the colored film back-coating which is designed to prevent it is called the *anti-halation backing*.

Sheet films for view camera use are available in a variety of sizes from about $2\frac{1}{4}'' \times 3\frac{1}{4}''$ to as much as $30'' \times 40''$ in some types. They are coated on a fairly thick base material for stiffness and flatness, since in popular cameras, the film is held in place in the holder only by its edges. In large specialized cameras, the film sheets are sometimes held flat in the image plane by vacuum.

Now relatively rare are *film packs* for use in view and press-type cameras, up to $5'' \times 7''$ in size. Film packs consist of twelve or sixteen sheets of very thin-base film packaged in a disposable metal box, and arranged in such a way that the films can be pulled into position for exposure one by one by means of paper tabs which protrude from one end of the container. When loaded into a *film pack adapter* and installed on

Figure 11.4 The high-speed recording film used here has no antihalation backing or base dye and permits the extreme highlight irradiation shown around the figures. Bleached lips and skin tones result from film's extreme red sensitivity. (Courtesy of the University of Michigan Press)

Film emulsions are coated on acetate or mylar

Most films have a colored backing or a tinted base

It helps prevent halation

Sheet film comes in a variety of sizes

Film packs are now relatively rare

the camera, the pack is light-tight. Ordinary film packs have now been replaced in popularity by the smaller roll film sizes. Polaroid film packs, on the other hand, have replaced the older rolls.

Roll film and cartridges

The term *roll film* is generally understood to include the paper-wrapped rolls such as 120, 127, 116, etc., but to exclude the popular cartridge-loaded 35-mm size. Both types are *roll* film in the sense that both consist of strips of film wound around spools, and the distinction is a rather arbitrary one. To further confuse the issue, there are at least three other sizes which are thought of as "roll film" but which are cartridge loaded—the very popular amateur film sizes 126 and 110 in so-called Kodapak cartridges, and the professional 70-mm film which comes either in bulk rolls of 100 feet or in cartridges of 15 feet, perforated on both edges just like 35-mm film.

By far the most common roll film, however, is the paper-wrapped 120 size. These rolls are made light-tight for handling before and after exposure by an opaque paper backing strip which is longer than the film strip itself and to which the film is attached, at one point only, by a strip of tape. The paper is also slightly wider than the film and seals the film edges from light, theoretically, at least, by close contact with the spool flanges.

Practically all modern cameras include automatic frame-spacing mechanism

A little length of paper preceding the film can be unrolled safely to thread into the camera. It is called the *leader*. The individual exposure frames can be spaced along the length of the film strip by centering the *frame numbers* on the paper backing strip in a little window in the camera back on older cameras. Practically all modern cameras include automatic frame-spacing mechanisms in their design.

One film size, 220, is not backed with paper but is simply taped to the paper leader and *trailer* strips. Twice as much film can be loaded into a standard 120 size roll by this expedient, but it cannot be used in cameras which rely on frame numbers for frame spacing.

Roll films, paper backed, are pulled through the camera by the simple procedure of threading the paper leader into an empty film spool in the camera and winding it up by means of a winding knob or crank. In cameras which space the frames automatically, the spaces are determined by either measuring the film as it passes through the exposure *gate* by means of a toothed wheel pressing on the film edge, or by sensing and compensating for the increasing diameter of the film roll on the take-up spool. The latter method is satisfactory if it is well adjusted, but the former is more positive. In some cameras the frame spacing changes progressively as the film is used, but this is not a serious problem if the frames remain separate from each other.

35-mm film is perforated on both edges

The 35-mm films, and some other sizes, rely on a sprocket wheel in the camera to count the frames and control spacing; therefore they are perforated on both edges, and are loaded "raw" into metal cartridges or cassettes for daylight handling. The leader is simply the end of the film itself, usually cut into a *tongue* for easy loading. The film in the cartridge is protected from light by a plush light-trapped slit in the cartridge through which the leader protrudes. Before the film can be removed from the camera after exposure, it must be rewound back into the metal cartridge, since there is no paper backing to protect it from light. By comparison, paper backed roll film can be removed safely from the camera after it has been wound onto the take-up spool because the roll is sealed by the paper trailer strip.

A different concept in film cartridges is the Eastman Kodapak, a completely sealed unit designed for use in Instamatic and similar cameras. Kodapaks contain either twelve or twenty exposures and are available in either color or black-and-white. For the present, at least, the use of Kodapak type cartridges is essentially limited to the amateur market.

One special film variety merits special mention, the picture-in-a-minute Polaroid film which combines in one operation the making of a negative and a print. In most instances the negative is formed on paper and is thrown away as soon as the print is obtained. One type, now available in two sizes, provides a very high quality film negative as well as a paper print.

This film is very convenient for use in situations requiring precise control of exposure, since it provides a reference print within about twenty seconds after exposure. If the print indicates that the picture is properly exposed and that the composition is satisfactory, it is only necessary to fix and harden the film negative for future printing by conventional methods. If the reference print is not satisfactory, the picture can be re-done immediately and changed as necessary.

The quality of the finished negatives is extraordinarily good. They are extremely fine-grained, very sharp, and possess a very satisfactory gray scale. At present this material is available in boxes of individual packets (55 P/N) for 4″ × 5″ cameras and in the more familiar metal packs (Type 105) for the popular "amateur" cameras.

Other Polaroid films are supplied in packs, and in boxes of individual film units, all of which must be used in the company's own cameras, or camera back units which are available for some other cameras. The black-and-white film, in whatever form, consists of two parts: the light-sensitive sheet, usually paper, on which the camera exposure is made; and a separate sheet of printing paper, not light-sensitive, which receives its image from the negative by silver-diffusion.

After exposure, the "film" and paper are pressed firmly together, face-to-face, and run through steel rollers in the camera back. A pod of developer gel is burst by the pressure and the chemicals spread evenly between the two surfaces to effect development and fixation in one operation. The action is virtually instantaneous for black-and-white films, being complete in about ten seconds (twenty seconds for the type P/N) during which the negative image is formed and the remaining positive is then transferred through the gel layer to the paper surface where it forms the final image.

A relatively recent Polaroid camera design produces images which develop themselves without any externally applied chemicals. It is a totally dry process and there is no waste paper to be discharged. So far, only color prints can be produced.

Most black-and-white Polaroid films have high sensitivity to light. ASA ratings of 400 and 3,000 are common and special purpose emulsions are available at speeds of up to 10,000. A high contrast emulsion and films which produce slides for projection are also manufactured.

The Polaroid films

12 Developers

The reducing agent changes the latent image into a visible one

When an exposed film is immersed in a developer solution, one of the developer ingredients, the *reducing agent* or developing agent, begins to change the latent image to a visible one. It accomplishes this by converting (*reducing*) the exposed silver halide crystals to metallic silver particles. There are many compounds capable of reducing silver halides, but only a few are practical for use as photographic developers. The two most common ones, usually used in combination, are p-methylaminophenol sulfate, commonly known as *metol*, and p-dihydroxybenzene, or *hydroquinone*.

Metol is fast, soft-working, and toxic to some people

Metol (also called Elon, Pictol, Rhodol, etc.) is a white powdery material which dissolves fairly easily in plain water but reluctantly in a strong solution of sodium sulfite. It keeps well in dry form but oxidizes slowly in solution unless preserved. It is an active, fast-working developing agent which tends to produce images of low contrast and, when suitably restrained, low fog density. It is toxic to some people, causing a very severe skin rash. It was first proposed as a developer in about 1891.

Hydroquinone starts slowly, but builds high contrast

Hydroquinone crystals are white, glossy, and needlelike in form. They dissolve readily in hot water but with difficulty in cold. Hydroquinone oxidizes fairly rapidly in either dry form or solution. It is very slow in starting development; but once under way, it acts rapidly and builds high contrast. Hydroquinone is very sensitive to the restraining action of bromide in solution and becomes practically inert at low temperatures. With a caustic accelerator, it is noted for extremely high contrast results with films, and, when used in low-sulfite solutions, will also "tan" or harden the gelatin emulsion as it produces the silver image. Hydroquinone and metol used together produce a solution which not only possesses the best characteristics of both agents, but is longer-lived and generally more useful than either one used separately. Hydroquinone has been in use since about 1880. It is nontoxic.

Pyro produces a stain image and tans the gelatin

Pyrogallic acid (pyrogallol) is called *pyro* for short but is officially known as 1, 2, 3, trihydroxybenzene. It is a very old organic developer, having been first used in 1851 by Frederick Scott Archer. It is generally supplied in crystalline form and is very soluble in water. It is one of the least stable of the developing agents; some of its working solutions will oxidize in a few minutes whether they are used or not. Pyro is a vigorous, soft-working developer. In low-sulfite solutions it tans the gelatin image and produces a strong yellow-brown stain image along with the normal silver one. It is also notorious for staining skin, fingernails, and utensils but is not considered to be toxic.

First proposed in 1888, p-aminophenol hydrochloride is a fine developing agent which produces neutral black images, free from fog even without restrainers. It is a white crystalline material, freely soluble in water, which can be mixed in very concentrated form with a strong accelerator to make a long-lived stock solution. The popular developer concentrate, Rodinal, is made in this way with a variety of p-aminophenol. When diluted with as much as 50 to 100 parts of water it makes an excellent solution for one-time use. Sometimes classed as toxic, p-aminophenol hydrochloride has been recommended for use by individuals sensitive to metol. Once marketed by Kodak as Kodelon, p-aminophenol hydrochloride is now available from Eastman's Organic Chemicals Division under its chemical name.

p-aminophenol can be mixed in very concentrated form

Phenidone is a developing agent (1-phenyl 3-pyrozolidone) introduced and named by Ilford Limited and used mainly by that company in prepared developers. It is a white crystalline powder, slightly soluble in cold water and quite similar to metol in action. It is almost always used in combination with some other developing agent. It is very active, keeps well, and is not very sensitive to the restraining action of bromide. It is not considered toxic and can generally be used without difficulty by persons allergic to metol.

Phenidone can replace Metol and is not toxic

There are several other reducing agents which are useful, but they are less well known and seldom used except by enthusiastic experimenters. Amidol is one which makes a fine print developer but which spoils rapidly and is toxic. Glycin is occasionally used in fine-grain film developers and is noted for its neutral gray-black image tone, its very low fogging tendency, and excellent keeping qualities. Adurol, or chlor-hydroquinone, was once popular for paper developers in which its action approximates a mixture of metol and hydroquinone. It is now rare. Pyrocatechol is somewhat similar to pyro in action but is less active. Accelerated with a caustic and in high dilution, it makes a very fine "compensating" developer for modern thin-emulsion films. Paraphenylene diamine (base) is a fine-grain developer which reduces film speed in most formulas and is toxic.

Amidol, Glycin, and Pyrocatechol

Most of these developers will produce good results with the right films and may even be found to be better for some purposes than more conventional chemicals. If you have mastered the basics of photography and want to try some old-fashioned or exotic solutions, you will find experimenting with these chemicals rewarding. It's unlikely, though, that you'll notice much improvement or even much difference in your results unless you are already skilled and know the characteristics of your usual developers very well indeed.

The reducing agent alone is not a satisfactory developer for several reasons. It is not active in plain water solution (except amidol), but must be alkalized. It oxidizes readily and so spoils quickly, and it has a tendency to reduce unexposed silver halide as well as the latent image itself, causing "fog." To overcome these deficiencies, other chemicals are included in practical developer solutions.

Most reducing agents must be alkalized or accelerated

The *accelerator* or *activator* is the chemical ingredient which stimulates the reducing agent. Almost any alkali will serve, but some are more suitable than others. In paper developers the accelerator is usually sodium carbonate (pure washing soda) and its reaction with the acid in the short-stop bath causes the tiny streams of gas (carbon dioxide) bubbles which

Sodium carbonate is commonly used in paper developers

you sometimes hear and see rising from the edges of a print in the short-stop. This reaction is harmless to papers as a rule, but it can cause blistering and pitting of film emulsions. For this reason carbonate is not generally used in developers intended primarily for roll films, although its use in sheet-film developers is not uncommon.

**Borax and Kodalk
are often used in film developers**

Many ordinary film developers are accelerated with sodium borate, (borax) or sodium metaborate (Kodak's *Kodalk* is said to be a metaborate compound) both of which are relatively mild alkalis. Developers intended for onetime use (*one-shots*) may employ more vigorous accelerators such as sodium hydroxide (lye) or potassium hydroxide (caustic potash). In general the activity of the developing solution is directly related to its alkalinity, so that a high concentration of a strong alkali will normally indicate a vigorous, contrasty, fast-working developer. It is also generally true that a highly alkaline developer will soften and swell the emulsion more than a milder one will, and this can cause problems in handling the films during processing.

**Reducing agents must be
preserved or they will oxidize**

Most reducing agents are so easily oxidized that their active life in solution is quite short unless they are somehow protected, so practical developing solutions usually contain an ingredient which serves as a *preservative*. The most common preservative is sodium sulfite, but sodium bisulfite or potassium metabisulfite are occasionally used, generally in addition to some sodium sulfite.

**The usual preservative
is sodium sulfite**

Sodium sulfite sometimes serves as more than a simple preservative. It is slightly alkaline, so that it can accelerate some developing agents, notably amidol and metol, satisfactorily. In high concentration it also exerts some solvent action on the silver halides, and thus tends to reduce grain size to some extent, a trait which was more useful before the advent of thin emulsion films than it is now. Sulfite also reduces the gelatin tanning effect of pyro and hydroquinone and inhibits the formation of the pyro stain image.

**Proper mixing of the developer
is important**

In mixing developing solutions from bulk chemicals, it is good practice to start with the preservative and add the reducing agents to that solution. This insures the minimum oxidation of the developer. Metol is an exception to this general rule. It dissolves quite easily in sulfite solutions of up to about 5 percent concentration but becomes virtually insoluble in stronger solutions. Because of this, and since it is a relatively stable agent anyway, it is customary to dissolve the metol first in plain water, then add the sulfite and the other ingredients in order. Glycin, on the other hand, is essentially insoluble in plain water but dissolves readily in a sulfite solution. Most of the other agents will dissolve satisfactorily in either water or sulfite solution.

**Potassium bromide
is used to restrain the developer**

All developers have a tendency to attack the unexposed silver halides to some extent, producing an overall silver deposit unrelated to the image and known as *fog*. To reduce this tendency most developing solutions contain an ingredient called the *restrainer*. It is generally potassium bromide.

Reducing agents vary in their susceptibility to the restraining action of bromide. Hydroquinone is much affected by relatively minor changes in bromide concentration while, on the other extreme, phenidone is hardly affected at all by reasonable amounts of bromide and must be restrained by some other chemical, usually benzotriazole.

Restrainers slow down developing action and also affect image color in some cases. Increasing the bromide content of a developer will usually make it produce brownish or greenish image tones, while benzotriazole in any excess tends to shift the image tone toward blue-black. It is generally desirable to use as little of the restrainer in a fresh developer solution as is required to inhibit fog, since the bromide content of most developers will increase automatically with use as the silver bromide of the latent image is reduced to metallic silver.

Restrainers may influence the image color

Developers may not always contain specific chemical ingredients for each of the functions just described. Amidol, for example, is both preserved and accelerated by sodium sulfite so that a useful developer can be made using only amidol, sulfite, and benzotriazole. Kodak's D-23 developer formula contains only metol (the Kodak brand is called *Elon*) and sulfite. Metol is a powerful, long-lived reducer with fairly low fogging tendencies, so the sulfite can both preserve and accelerate it and no restrainer is needed. Another successful two-chemical developer is one (attributed to Windisch) which contains the reducing agent *pyrocatechol* accelerated by sodium hydroxide. This solution must be mixed just before use since it is not preserved and it causes some (usually acceptable) fog, but it is uniquely suited for use with modern thin-emulsion films, producing a long-scale image with exceptional edge-sharpness.

Some developers contain fewer than the four basic ingredients

Some formulas may contain more than the basic four ingredients and include chemicals which have unusual functions. Alcohol is sometimes specified to increase the solubility of the reducing agents. Citric acid is used as a clarifier in some paper developers to help maintain clean whites. Sodium sulfate (not sulfite) is occasionally used to prevent excessive swelling of the gelatin at high temperatures, and there are many other such special-purpose chemicals.

While some contain more than four

There are a very great many prepared developers and published formulas, and the majority of them are intended for more or less "normal" processing. If you are a beginner it will be wise for you to pick one which is cheap, available, and convenient for you to use, and get to know it thoroughly. Until you become quite expert, one "normal" developer is very much like any other, and cost alone is no indication of effectiveness.

Pick a developer and get to know it thoroughly

A good film developer for general use is the old standby, Kodak D-76. It is recommended for low contrast and good shadow detail and can be used as is or diluted with equal parts of water if the time of development is appropriately adjusted. This formula contains a rather high concentration of sulfite and no restrainer, but it is a fine performer and will give good results with most films under average conditions. Chemicals should be dissolved in the order given.

Kodak's D-76 developer

Water 52° C. (125° F.)	750 cc
Elon	2 grams
Sodium sulfite(dessicated)	100 grams
Hydroquinone	5 grams
Borax, granular	2 grams
Cold water to make	1 liter

Kodak's D-72 paper developer

A good general purpose developer is Kodak's D-72. It is a fast working developer, suitable for prints on all types of papers and also useful for rapid processing of films when high contrast is desired and some coarsening of image texture is not objectionable. The following formula is a stock solution which should be diluted with two parts of water for general use.

Elon (metol)	3.0 grams
Sodium sulfite (dessicated)	45.0 grams
Hydroquinone	12.0 grams
Sodium carbonate (monohydrated).......	80.0 grams
Potassium bromide	2.0 grams
Water	1.0 liter

Dissolve chemicals in the order given. Developing time ranges from about one to two minutes for papers and from about three and one-half to five minutes for films. Dilution of 1:1 with water gives greater contrast on films and faster developing times. This is, however, primarily a print developer.

One-shot developers are intended for one-time use

Some developers for films are intended for only onetime use. They are called *one-shot* developers. More commonly the developer is saved after use and reconditioned by the addition of a *replenisher* which is formulated to replace the exhausted chemicals and maintain the solution at a more or less uniform strength. The replenisher is usually similar in composition to the developer itself (in fact some developers are replenished by addition of a small volume of their own stock solutions), but the replenisher is likely to contain proportionately more reducing agent and accelerator than the normal developer, since these are the ingredients which are used up or neutralized in use. Many replenishers contain no restrainer because bromide is a by-product of the development process and tends to increase in concentration as the developer is used. This gradual increase in the bromide concentration is one of the factors which limits the life of a replenished developer.

Developers which are reused are usually replenished

Commercial processors use deep tanks and replenish

Commercial processing labs use *deep tank* processing techniques, involving substantial volumes of solutions, and replenish in proportion to the area of film processed. Their chemicals are exhausted by use rather than by age, and replenishment is rather accurately controlled. For this purpose the use of a replenisher is eminently practical and economical.

The individual user, however, is more apt to run into trouble with a replenished solution. His use of the solution is likely to be intermittent and infrequent so that considerable weakening of the chemicals will result from the effects of age. He uses a very small volume of developer—seldom more than a gallon, and usually only a quart—so that there is little reserve strength. His agitation procedures mix a great deal of oxygen (a developer's greatest enemy) with the solution, compared to the commercial lab where *nitrogen burst* agitation uses a harmless, inert gas.

Replenishment may not work so well for the individual user

Also, driven by the urge to economize, he may try to process more film in the solution volume than it can stand. As a result, he is likely to discover that his negatives are exceptionally dense and contrasty when done in a fresh solution, compared to thin, weak results in the old. This is clearly false economy.

From time to time two-solution developers appear on the market, and their characteristics are attractive. The first solution contains the reducing agents, the second the accelerator, and they are intended to be used in sequence. Typically the film is immersed in the first bath for something like two or three minutes, then transferred to the second for a similar period. Developing action takes place when the absorbed reducing agents are acted on by the accelerator, and the action is self-limiting.

Two-solution developers are attractive

Although commercial versions of two-bath developers are said not to need replenishment it is advisable to maintain the volume of the baths by addition of fresh solution as necessary. It is also possible, although not recommended generally, to increase the contrast of the negatives by extending developing time in either or both of the solutions. These developers tend to be strongly compensating in action, that is, they work vigorously in the areas of low density but weaken rapidly as negative density builds up. This action tends to limit contrast and provide relatively high effective film speed making two-bath developers especially suitable for films which must be developed to very low contrast but which must, at the same time, exhibit well-detailed shadow areas.

But contrast control is limited

A compensating two-bath developer based on Kodak's D-23 formula has been popular for years. It is recommended for use with both roll and sheet films and is a favorite with "Zone System" workers (see Chapter 24). Films are developed in the standard D-23 formula for a period of two or three minutes with constant agitation, then placed directly into a 1% solution of Kodalk and agitated for another three minutes. Both density and contrast will be affected to some degree by changes in temperature, agitation or time of immersion in either or both baths. Very small volumes of the solutions can be used and it is a good idea to discard the developer after use. Here is the D-23 formula, one of the simplest developers ever compounded but a very effective one.

A compensating version of D-23

Elon	7.5 grams
Sodium Sulfite, dessicated	100.0 grams
Water	1.0 liter

Make the Kodalk solution as follows:

Kodalk	10.0 grams
Water	1.0 liter

Another novel developing system which periodically appears on the market is the so-called *mono-bath* developer. Also a self-limiting developer, this one combines a more or less normal developer with the fixing bath, all in one solution. Its claimed advantages are not unlike the two-bath type; uniformity of processing results, wide latitude of time, temperature, and agitation.

The mono-bath is another novel system, but difficult to control

In spite of its appealing simplicity, the mono-bath has never been very popular. Like the two-bath, its main charm is its main fault. The fact that development and fixation of the image are proceeding simultaneously simply means that the latent image is being built up and eaten away at the same time and maximum potential image density can never be achieved.

The bath is also subject to chemical imbalance which makes results somewhat uncertain after a little use. The lack of effective control of image contrast is also a serious drawback.

Some years ago, before the advent of the so-called *thin-emulsion* films, one of the major considerations in selection of a developer was its grain characteristic.

Grain is the visible texture of the image

Grain or (more properly) "graininess" is the visible and sometimes obvious pepper-and-salt texture of the image. It results not from the individually developed silver particles, which are too small to be visible under normal magnification, but from clumps of the particles which are seen as units. To understand the formation of grain, it may be helpful to visualize the emulsion as a transparent layer of some thickness which contains randomly dispersed particles of silver halide in crystalline form. The emulsion is many crystals deep and they appear in overlapping array like the leaves of a tree.

The crystals vary somewhat in sensitivity and also in size; so that after development and after the fixer has dissolved the undeveloped crystals, the image consists of a visually porous mass of silver particles with random spaces left between them. Again like very distant tree foliage, the visual effect is one of masses of particles seen more or less as units, separated by irregular areas of light.

Many factors affect the appearance of grain

There is probably more mystique surrounding the characteristics and control of grain than in any other single area of photography. Almost every photographer will have firm opinions about which film and which developer will produce the most desirable grain pattern. There are, in fact, many factors which affect the subjective appearance of graininess in the finished print, and the film developer, these days, is one of the least significant of the several influences.

Studies of the formation of the silver image during development have shown that there is little difference in the appearance of the individual particles produced by the various reducing agents. In general the particles, which resemble little tufts of steel wool, are finer in texture when developed in metol, for example, than when developed in hydroquinone, and the actual size of the individual particles relates somewhat to the energy of the developer; but there is not much to indicate that, *if the image is developed to a given density*, any one of the common reducing agents is substantially finer grained than any other.

One exception is a seldom-encountered reducing agent, paraphenylene diamine, which, in addition to being extremely low in reduction potential, seems to exert some solvent action on the silver halide crystals as it develops. Its undeniably fine grain characteristic is gained at the expense of a substantial loss in effective film speed, and some loss of image edge-sharpness.

Modern film manufacturing techniques have as much influence on the image grain size as any other single factor. Emulsions are generally thinner than they were years ago, and the halide crystals are more uniform in size and sensitivity than was previously the case. It is also probable that the dispersion of the crystals is more uniform, and that other factors have been incorporated in film manufacture which help to control grain irregularities. Films are certainly better than they used to be; faster, sharper, finer grained, and more consistent, and developers have much less to do with the improved results than their various manufacturers would have you believe.

In the old days fine grain was obtained by the use of low energy developers and by the use of silver halide solvents in the developer solution. Developing times in these developers were excessive—often a matter of half-an-hour or more. The use of these weak, high-solvent formulas led inevitably to loss of film speed, soft edge definition, and increased fog level, as well as the physical softening of the emulsion and attendant problems in handling. Overexposure of the film was a necessity, causing problems of flare, halation, and irradiation, all of which tend to reduce contrast and definition of the image.

Fine grain used to be obtained with weak, high-solvent developers

The resulting grain structure was unquestionably fine, virtually nonexistent in fact, in the hands of an expert, but the price was too much to pay. We now prefer edge sharpness, tonal brilliance, full film speed, and short developing times and are generally willing to accept the grain structure that accompanies these qualities.

We now prefer sharpness, tonal brilliance, and full film speed

One of the many things which sometimes contributes to the effect of grain in the image is not really grain at all but simply slight *reticulation*. In its usual form, reticulation is an obvious wrinkling or cracking of the gelatin of the emulsion. It occurs when the emulsion swells to the point where it is torn loose from the film base or is deformed into ridges and furrows. In extreme cases patches of the emulsion may simply detach themselves and float away or remain attached at some point as flaps. Reticulation is likely to occur as a result of sudden or extreme changes of temperature during processing. It can also result from prolonged soaking, or from any other condition which tends to swell the gelatin excessively.

Some grain may be reticulation

It appears that prolonged soaking of the film permits the silver particles to "clump" by some sort of physical attraction for each other. Whether any actual "migration" of the particles takes place or not, granularity does seem to increase if films are resoaked after processing, as in postdevelopment treatment of density or contrast, or simply in rewashing.

Prolonged soaking or resoaking increases grain size

Modern techniques lean toward the use of inherently fine-structured emulsions, developed in highly energetic but highly diluted developers. There are several advantages in the use of such a developer. In the first place, high-energy developers can be highly concentrated because relatively small amounts of very powerful chemicals are used. As stock solutions these formulas keep extremely well. As very diluted working solutions, they are reliably uniform (if used immediately after dilution) and can be discarded after one use. Their high dilution tends to make them "compensating" in action, that is they tend to work more slowly in areas of high image density than in areas of low density, thus preventing excessive contrast while extending shadow detail. This same tendency causes the *adjacency effect* of enhanced edge separation and contrast, giving an

One-shot and compensating developers

illusion of sharpness and crisp definition to the image forms and textures. One-shots can be made very clean-working, producing almost no fog or stain, and very important to the busy photographer, they are fairly fast working.

Printing conditions can affect grain

The quality of the printing illumination has a great deal to do with the appearance of image sharpness and negative grain. Diffused light makes the structure relatively indistinct, while a directed beam, such as illuminates the negative in a condenser enlarger, will tend to emphasize and sharpen both the image edges and the grain pattern. "Mushy" grain in the print will be more likely, in most cases, to result from inaccurate focusing of the enlarger, or from the use of a poorly corrected enlarger lens, or from the questionable practice of stopping down the enlarger lens excessively, than from the actual structure of the negative image.

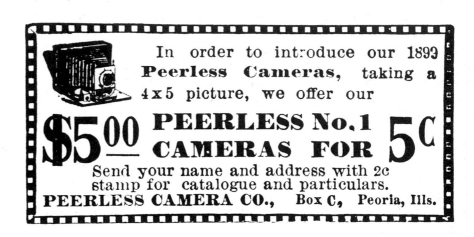

The Stop and Fixing Baths

13

When a film is removed from the developer, the chemicals absorbed into the gelatin emulsion layer continue to function for a little while; and the image continues to build up to some extent, increasing in both density and contrast. If the film is held in the air for any length of time, the developer may oxidize to a colored compound which will stain the emulsion. We generally try to avoid these two problems by rinsing the film immediately after its removal from the developer in an acid solution called the *stop* bath or *shortstop*.

After the developer, rinse the film in an acid stop bath

The shortstop is normally a 1% solution of acetic acid. It acts by neutralizing the accelerator which is alkaline, thereby halting development almost instantly, since most developing agents are inert in acid solution. It also tends to prevent staining by rinsing the surface developing chemicals off the film, by stopping the chemical action, and by shielding the film emulsion from exposure to air.

Shortstop is usually a weak solution of acetic acid

A plain water bath is better than nothing for this purpose, but the acid solution has obvious advantages. It also has at least one disadvantage. When used with developers which contain a carbonate salt as the accelerator, the acid-carbonate reaction releases carbon dioxide gas within the emulsion layer. If this occurs suddenly or excessively, the gas bubbles may rupture the gelatin layer causing blisters or pits, and the image is marred.

Gas bubbles may rupture the gelatin layer

Fortunately, the reaction is not often this dramatic, and its effects can be minimized by a few simple precautions. First, when using a strongly alkaline carbonate developer, be sure that the shortstop bath is not stronger than about $1\frac{1}{2}$% acetic acid. Second, give the film a brief rinse, ten seconds or so, in plain water before placing it in the shortstop. This will dilute the carbonate and remove some of it from the film emulsion. Third, and very important, agitate the film constantly for at least the first thirty seconds after it goes into the shortstop bath. Fourth, never work with high-carbonate developers and acid shortstops at high temperatures. Keep the processing temperature below 21° C. (70° F.), but not *too* much below. Hydroquinone, which is a normal ingredient in developers of this kind, becomes inactive at about 13° C. (55° F.).

Don't feel that you can avoid this problem by eliminating the shortstop bath. Dropping a carbonate-loaded film into the fixing bath will not only cause the same gas reaction but will also tend to upset the acid balance of the fixing bath. This will hasten the destruction of the fixer and may cause stains on the film as well.

The stop bath protects the hypo

115

While any acid properly diluted will serve as a shortstop, acetic acid is the best because it is compatible with the fixing bath. The acid salt, sodium bisulfite, can also be used safely, but many other acids tend to cause decomposition of the hypo (sodium thiosulfate) or have other disadvantages. The stronger, inorganic acids such as hydrochloric or sulfuric are difficult to maintain at the proper diluted strength, and their working life is brief. All in all there seems to be no good alternative to acetic acid, nor is one needed, for general use.

Preparing the stop bath from 28% acetic acid

Acetic acid is available in at least two strengths. The so-called *commercial* strength, or what will probably be recognized in the photography stores as *shortstop stock solution*, is 28% acid and is not dangerous to handle. A normal-strength shortstop bath can be prepared from this stock as follows:

Acetic acid, 28% . . . . 50 cc
Water . . . . 1 liter

Glacial acetic acid should be treated with respect

The most concentrated grade of acetic acid is *glacial*. It is 99½% pure. In this concentration the acid should be treated with respect. It is not as violently dangerous as sulfuric acid, for example, but it is still capable of causing painful burns. Its most striking characteristic, though, is its odor. It is simply overwhelming, sharp, penetrating, and suffocating. A good whiff of it will send you gasping for fresh air.

In addition to this, the vapors are said to be inflammable, and the acid itself is a powerful solvent for some common plastics—like watch crystals, for example. Glacial acetic acid should not be stored in a cold place. It freezes at about 17° C. (62° F.), and the resulting ice chunks may break the bottle.

To prepare 28% acetic acid add 3 parts glacial to 8 parts water

It is not a good plan to prepare a shortstop bath directly from glacial acid. The dilution is excessive, and the risks of handling the concentrated acid are too great. Although it is certainly economical to buy the acid in glacial form, it should be diluted to 28% for stock use. To prepare a 28% solution from glacial acetic acid, add:

Acetic acid, glacial . . . . 3 parts
to Water . . . . 8 parts

Figure 13.1   To make *Shortstop* solution

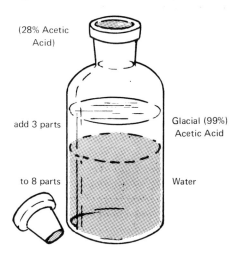

(28% Acetic Acid)

add 3 parts

Glacial (99%) Acetic Acid

to 8 parts

Water

To find the actual volumes of liquids required to make a certain quantity of stock solution, divide the desired volume by 11 to find the volume of each "part," then multiply by 3 to find the acid volume and by 8 to find the water volume required. For example, to find the volume of glacial acid required to make about one quart of 28% stock solution, divide 32 ounces (one quart) by 11. Call it roughly 3, the number of ounces in each "part." Then, 3 parts of 3 ounces each make 9 ounces, the glacial acid volume. Eight parts times 3 ounces equals 24 ounces of water. Add 9 ounces of glacial acid to 24 ounces of water and fill the quart bottle. If you have to waste a part of one ounce, the loss is not a great one.

Mark the liquid levels on the storage bottle

You may find it convenient to mark these liquid levels, once determined, on the storage bottle (Fig. 13.1). Then it is a simple matter to mix the stock solution the next time you need it without recalculating the proportion.

In the event that you need to use the glacial acid, undiluted, to prepare the shortstop bath, measure out 15 cc of glacial acid and add it to a liter of water. This will result in a solution of approximately 1½% acid. Using the more familiar U. S. system of liquid measure, about one-half fluid ounce of acid per quart of water will give about the same strength bath.

If you must make a working shortstop solution from glacial acid . . .

Occasionally, it is desirable to use a *hardening* shortstop bath; that is, one which will toughen and shrink the gelatin, so that it will be less susceptible to physical damage in later processes. There are several chemicals which can be used for this purpose, but the one generally used as a shortstop ingredient is potassium chrome alum. A suitable formula is:

A hardening shortstop bath

Potassium chrome alum . . . . 30 grams
Water, not above 32°C. (90°F.) . . . . 1 liter

It is especially important, when using a shortstop bath containing chrome alum, to agitate the film immediately when it is placed in the bath and to continue the agitation for a minute or so. If this is not done, a surface scum may form on the film. It is easier to avoid the scum than to remove it. Films should be treated in the bath for about three minutes, total, with frequent agitation after the initial period.

It is important to agitate the film immediately

Chrome alum is a purplish crystalline material which dissolves well, but slowly, in warm water to make a rich purple-blue solution. Its life in solution is quite short, and since there is no easy way to tell when it is wearing out (unless you want to monitor its acidity), it is best to mix it in small volumes as needed and simply discard it after use. It is not expensive. With age and use it will usually turn from purple to green, but by the time the color has shifted noticeably, it has probably long since worn out. Chrome alum baths are not usually recommended for use with printing papers.

Mix the chrome alum shortstop fresh for each use

Although the film image is temporarily stable while it is in the shortstop bath, it is by no means permanent. Development has ceased, but the developing agents may still be present in the emulsion in small amounts. The undeveloped silver halides are also present and still light-sensitive, although their sensitivity will have been diminished by being wet. Exposure to moderately bright artificial light at this point will not harm the image, provided the process is continued normally, and the film is moved on to the fixing bath on schedule. There is seldom any need for light at this time, however, and it is generally a good idea to wait until the film has been in the fixing bath for a minute or two at least before turning on any white lights.

The film image is temporarily stable in the shortstop bath

The primary function of the fixing bath is to remove the undeveloped silver halides, thus desensitizing the film so that it can be exposed to strong light without further effect. There are only a few materials which can be used for this purpose, and not all of them are entirely satisfactory. Ammonia is a solvent for silver chloride (and silver bromide), but it is unpleasant to use because of its suffocating odor and its strong alkalinity. The cyanides of potassium and sodium are effective solvents for all the halides, but they also attack the image to some extent and are deadly poisons. The thiocyanates of sodium and potassium have considerable sol-

The fixing bath removes undeveloped silver halides

Only a few chemicals are satisfactory halide solvents

Sodium thiosulfate, hypo, is the most common

vent action on the normally used halides, but the most practical and useful fixing agents are the thiosulfates of sodium and ammonium. Both of these chemicals are sometimes referred to familiarly and inaccurately as "hypo," but the term really belongs to sodium thiosulfate. It derives from Herschel's name for this chemical, which he discovered in 1819. He called it sodium hyposulfite.

Sodium thiosulfate is usually supplied either as irregular crystalline chunks, whitish-transparent and dusty, or as oblong particles about the size and shape of cooked rice grains. It is, in fact, sometimes sold as *hypo rice.*

The two forms are identical chemically, but the "rice" is preferable because it is a little easier to measure and dissolve. In any form, hypo is extremely soluble in water. It is best to dissolve it in warm water, about 52°C. (125°F.), because the solution will be cooled considerably by the mixing reaction.

Hypo is not poisonous, but handle it carefully

Hypo is not poisonous, but it is so destructive to the latent image and to the unexposed and undeveloped halides that it has to be considered a dangerous chemical in the darkroom. It should be handled with care for this reason and kept safely in the "wet" area of the workspace. Many of the streaks, stains, and spots that beginners find appearing on their prints can be traced to hypo contamination of the developer, the various processing tools and utensils, the "dry" work area, or the photographer's fingers. Learn to treat this chemical with respect or prepare yourself for considerable darkroom frustration.

Hypo and water alone are not satisfactory for general use

Hypo and water alone will dissolve the silver halides, but that simple solution is not a satisfactory bath for general use. In the first place, the hypo will not neutralize the developer, so if films or papers are placed directly into a plain hypo solution without an intervening acid shortstop, the development will continue for a little while during the fixing process. There is danger of staining, too, as the developer oxidizes. This is particularly serious with papers.

Even when acid shortstop is used, the plain hypo bath is not entirely desirable because the acetic acid carried into the hypo with the film or print will tend to decompose the hypo, causing the bath to *sulfurize* or form a milky precipitate of sulfur. This not only destroys the hypo itself but also tends to make the image unstable, so that in time it will fade or stain. Immediate staining of papers is possible, usually in the form of an overall "sallowness" or yellowing of the whites.

Sodium sulfite will prevent sulfurization

The addition of sodium sulfite will cure these problems. It functions as a preservative for the hypo just as it does for the reducing agents in the developer. In fact it also preserves the developer which is carried into the hypo bath, thus preventing oxidation stains.

A useful bath must contain a solvent, a preservative, and an acid

A useful fixing bath must contain at least a halide solvent, a preservative, and an acid. It is possible to provide these functions with only two chemicals if an acid sulfite salt such as sodium bisulfite or potassium metabisulfite is used instead of the sodium sulfite and acetic acid combination. A suitable formula is DuPont's number 8-F.

Water, 52°C. (125°F.)	750 cc
Sodium thiosulfate	240 grams
Potassium metabisulfite	24 grams
Cold water to make	1 liter

Dissolve the hypo completely before adding the metabisulfite. Fix prints for at least five minutes and wash thoroughly. This bath is not usually recommended for use with film.

This can be done with two ingredients: DuPont's 8-F

This bath or a solution of hypo, sulfite, and acetic acid will make a satisfactory fixer, but it has no hardening effect on the gelatin, and the emulsion may soften or even float off the film stock if the temperature is too high. To prevent this, and for film use generally, a hardener, usually potassium alum, is included. The life and efficiency of the hardening-fixer is increased with the addition of boric acid which postpones sludging as the bath ages and helps to maintain the hardening action at a more constant level throughout the life of the solution. In some formulas, the boric acid is replaced with a metaborate which serves much the same purpose but reduces the sulfurous odor of the normal bath.

Usually a hardener is also desirable

The nonhardening baths are used primarily for prints which are going to be *toned* in subsequent solutions. They should be used with great care in warm weather, when the processing solutions are warm, or when the processing time has been abnormally long. They are not usually recommended for films, but you may find them useful if you are trying to reticulate film deliberately.

Nonhardening baths are usually used for prints to be toned

For most purposes, especially in warm weather, it is desirable to use a hardening fixing bath. A simple formula, suitable for both films and papers, is GAF's 201.

For most uses a hardening bath is preferable: GAF's 201

Solution A

Water, 52°C. (125°F.)	500 cc
Sodium thiosulfate	240 grams

Solution B

Water, 52°C. (125°F.)	150 cc
Sodium sulfite, dessicated	15 grams
Acetic acid, 28%	45 cc
Potassium alum	15 grams

Add solution A to solution B, then add:

Water to make	1 liter

In baths of this kind, the alum and the acid (at least) are sometimes mixed separately from the thiosulfate to avoid possible sulfurization. It is a good idea to allow the solutions to cool before mixing them together (this will be no problem with the thiosulfate solution), and it is important to stir them vigorously when adding solution A to solution B. Normal fixing time is from five to ten minutes at 20°C. (68°F.).

The addition of 7.5 grams of boric acid (crystals) to the formula above, dissolved after the acetic acid in solution B, will make a more stable solution with longer life. Kodak's odorless formula, F-6, is essentially similar (it contains a little more acetic acid) but replaces the boric acid with 15

Kodalk makes the bath long-lived, odorless, and sludge-free

grams of Kodalk, a proprietary alkali. These solutions are all satisfactory for use with either films or papers, and are long-lived and relatively sludge-free, especially the latter two.

The so-called rapid fixers are similar, but include an ammonium salt

The so-called "rapid" fixers are quite similar to the formulas just described but may include an ammonium salt such as the chloride or sulfate in addition to the normal hypo, or they may replace the hypo itself with ammonium thiosulfate. At least one manufacturer recommends the use of potassium thiocyanate (DuPont formula 9-F) as a rapid fixer for paper, but this is unusual.

They should be used cautiously with papers

The rapid fixers are very convenient, since they are much more active and have a greater working life, but they should be used cautiously with papers as a rule. Contact papers in particular are likely to be bleached if they are not watched carefully and removed promptly from the bath when fixed, and the image color of any paper type is likely to be altered somewhat if fixing is prolonged.

But they are excellent for film

Rapid-fix solutions are much more useful for films since the halides used in film emulsions are less soluble, film emulsions are thicker and richer in silver, and they are generally more difficult to fix than papers. This is particularly true of the very high speed *recording films* which can hardly be fixed at all in a normal hypo bath which has been partially exhausted.

This is not to say that the rapid baths should not be used for general purpose fixing. They are completely practical for both films and papers, but since they are so highly active, and since they have more tendency to attack the silver image (particularly the delicate tones of contact papers) than regular hypo has, they must be used with some discretion. Most manufacturers who sell prepared stock solutions of rapid fixer specify different dilutions for use with films and papers. These recommendations should be followed.

Dried rapid-fix is difficult to dissolve

Ammonium thiosulfate has one characteristic which you may not like, but which is a blessing in disguise. Its solutions dry to an almost insoluble white powdery stain which is difficult to remove even from glass surfaces. While this is a nuisance in one way, it at least prevents the dried fixer from being spread around the darkroom by the normal handling of the stained utensils and surfaces. Hypo, on the other hand, is almost instantly dissolved by the touch of a damp finger and can be transferred from place to place almost indefinitely by a sloppy worker—to the considerable detriment of his pictures. Neatness and cleanliness in the darkroom will avoid this problem with any fixer.

The fixing bath must be in good condition for image permanence

When a fixing bath is fresh, it will work rapidly, and the compounds it forms in the emulsion are quite readily soluble in water. As the bath ages, however, the residual compounds are more complex and some are almost insoluble. Even prolonged washing in running water will not remove these salts from the emulsion to a satisfactory degree, and the image will surely fade or discolor eventually as they gradually react with the silver image and decompose it. It is important that the fixing bath be maintained in good condition to insure reasonable image stability and permanence.

Silver can be recovered from used hypo

Commercial photo-finishers can afford to extend the life of their fixing baths by maintaining a constant acidity and by removing the dissolved silver from the solution. Silver recovery is more trouble than it's worth for the average photographer, although it is worth considering if you use as much as a few gallons of hypo a week. The recovery units can be purchased or leased, and the saving in fixing chemicals plus the money received from the sale of the silver may pay for the recovery and provide a little profit besides.

Most of us are not volume users of photographic materials, and since hypo is relatively inexpensive material, we generally use it up and throw it away. Here the problem becomes one of determining when to discard the bath. There are several signs which indicate that the fixer is worn out. If it begins to appear sludgy or milky after some use, it is almost certainly spoiled. It may also begin to look slightly slimy and froth easily when stirred, a sure sign of an old, exhausted bath. None of these signs of deterioration is sufficiently sensitive to be useful. By the time they appear you have already doomed some of your pictures to a short lifespan.

Several signs indicate the fixer is worn out, but . . .

A better check on the condition of the fixer is to determine the time it takes the fresh bath to "clear" a scrap of film. Then, during use, check the bath from time to time with a piece of the same film to see how much the clearing time has increased. When the time is twice as great as it was when the bath was fresh, you can consider the bath exhausted and discard it. Another good method is to add a few drops of one of the commercial *hypo test* solutions to a small volume of the bath and observe the reaction. The formation of a milky precipitate of sulfur is an indication of exhaustion.

It is safer to test it

A simple and useful solution for this purpose can be made as follows:

A simple hypo-test solution

> Potassium iodide . . . . 5 grams
> Water, preferably distilled . . . . 100 cc

Mix and store in a small bottle with a dropper top. To test for hypo condition add five drops test solution to 5 cc of the fixing bath in a small test tube and shake. A noticeable milkiness or cloudiness in the solution indicates exhaustion.

The life of the hypo bath can be extended and the fixation of your prints improved if you use two fixing baths instead of one. Prints should be treated for a minute or two in the first bath, then transferred to the second. The bulk of the work is done by the first bath and it will wear out first. Check it with film scraps or the test solution and discard it when it is exhausted. Then replace it with the second bath and mix a fresh batch of hypo for the second tray. By this technique, the prints are always well fixed in a relatively fresh solution, and the formation of insoluble salts in the emulsion is minimized.

Two-bath fixing is efficient

Hypo is not removed from the emulsion easily by plain water washing. In the process of fixing the emulsion, hypo has permeated it and also soaked into the paper fibers so that getting it out is more a matter of soaking than rinsing it off the surface. Films and Resin Coated (RC) papers are easier to wash effectively because they are not as absorbent, but even films will have to be washed for at least a half hour in running water to reduce the residual hypo level to a safe value. Resin Coated papers normally require only about five minutes washing. Prints on light-weight papers should be washed for an hour or more, and double-weight and

Hypo is not removed easily by plain washing

heavy-weight papers should have a couple of hours at least. These recommendations assume that the emulsions have been well fixed in fresh fixer. If the bath was old, and if the insoluble complex salts have been formed in the emulsion, no amount of simple washing will be sufficient for image permanence.

Hypo clearing agents can reduce washing times greatly

The use of a hypo clearing agent or a hypo eliminator can reduce these washing times greatly and add to the life of the images as well. A number of them are on the market, and they should be used as directed. They are not required for use with RC papers.

In the absence of a commercial product, you can make an effective hypo clearing bath as follows:

Sodium sulfite serves as a washing aid

Sodium sulfite . . . . 20 grams
Water . . . . 1 liter

Soak the films or prints for five minutes in this solution, then wash films for ten to fifteen minutes and ordinary paper prints for twenty to thirty minutes in running water, with occasional thorough agitation. If water is scarce, films can be washed, following the clearing bath, by soaking them for at least a minute in each of ten separate volumes of water in a tank or tray. Uncoated paper prints should soak for two or three minutes in each of the ten changes of water (RC paper prints should soak for one minute in each of five baths), and you should be sure that they are separated and interleaved in each bath.

Making Prints by Projection

14

Setting up the enlarger for projection printing of negatives is similar to the procedure used in making photograms with one major exception. You must adjust the optical system to match the negative size you are using. If you are going to print a 4″ × 5″ negative, you will need a 4″ × 5″ negative carrier, a lens of from about 135-mm to 160-mm focal length, and condensers to match the lens focal length. Negatives which are 2¼″ × 2¼″ require a lens of about 75-mm focal length and condensers to match. Thirty-five-mm negatives take a 50-mm lens and appropriate condensers. If the enlarger you are using has adjustable condensers be sure they are set properly before proceeding.

Adjust the enlarger optical system to match the negative area

If the lens focal length is too short for the negative size, you will not get full *coverage;* that is, the picture corners may be cut off or be badly out of focus. If the lens is too long for the negative, it is not so serious; it merely means that the enlarger will have to be raised higher than normal for the enlargement size you want.

If the lens is too short it will not cover

If too long the enlarger will have to be higher than normal

Condenser mismatch is more troublesome. Condensers must usually be selected to match the lens, not the negative. If the condensers are too long in focal length for the lens in use, the image may be cut off at the corners; the illumination of the image will be uneven—usually a hot spot in the center with dark edges—or the image may be restricted to a circle with rainbow fringes. If the condensers are a little too short, the result is sometimes not unworkable; but if the mismatch is extreme, the illumination of the image area may be uneven and the corners will be masked off. Don't take chances with these variables. Use the right equipment for the job you want to do and you will avoid a lot of trouble and disappointment (Fig. 14.1).

Condensers must usually match the lens, not the nominal negative size

Enlarging lenses are properly matched to the condensers when they are placed at, or near, the focal point of the condenser system (Fig. 14.2*a*). Thus a condenser designed to work with a 6″ lens, for example, wastes a great deal of its light when used with a 2″ lens for normal enlarging (Fig. 14.2*b*) and a small condenser system (short focal length) does not properly illuminate a long lens and will cause a *hot spot* in the image (Fig. 14.2*c*).

Under some conditions, condensers may not match their normal lenses and must be deliberately mismatched for best results. A familiar example is the setup for projecting reduced images instead of enlarged ones. Here the lens must be *racked out* a considerable distance in order to focus the

Sometimes they must be deliberately mismatched

Figure 14.1   If you have good negatives to print but the prints come out looking like this, it may be the fault of your enlarger. If it's a condenser model check to be sure you have the right condensers installed and that they are positioned correctly for the lens in use. A somewhat similar effect can occur if the enlarger lens is too short to cover the entire negative area.

Figure 14.2

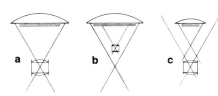

Figure 14.3

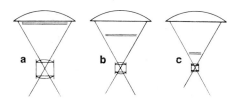

small image, and the easel may have to be propped up on boxes to get it close enough to the lens. A lens of short focal length must be used, but it is used at a great focal distance (see the chapter on "Close-up Photography"). Under these conditions, the short lens is in the same position relative to the condensers that the longer lens would normally occupy, and is fully illuminated.

To repeat, the best results are obtained when the distance from the enlarger lens to the condenser surface, regardless of the nominal focal length of the lens, is very nearly equal to the focal length of the condenser. Some manufacturers take advantage of this fact by making the negative carrier position adjustable, thereby managing to match all the usual lenses under all conditions of magnification with only one condenser system (Fig. 14.3).

Another sort of enlarger light system, the *diffusion* source, which was popular years ago, is making a strong comeback. Diffusion sources used to feature large matte-surfaced reflectors above the enlarger bulb and a layer, or layers, of frosted or opal glass above the negative carrier to spread the light out as evenly as possible over the negative area. Enlargers of this design were generally inefficient, providing a relatively dim printing light even with high-wattage bulbs. They were very likely to run hot, often buckling the negative in the carrier and sometimes even damaging it if the exposure was prolonged. Modern versions of the diffusion enlarger are quite a different story. Now the light is more typically diffused by multiple reflection in an integrating sphere (a much more efficient method) and the negative is as well protected from heat as is typical in condenser enlargers. In some cases small fans are incorporated in the design for extra insurance against heat damage.

Diffusion enlargers

Modern diffusion enlargers are particularly adapted to color printing since the lamphouse design makes filter insertion or adjustment a relatively simple procedure. In the more expensive models the filters are an integral part of the housing and their insertion into the light path is controlled by externally calibrated dials or knobs.

Diffusion enlargers typically produce prints of somewhat lower contrast than do condenser types but this is easily compensated for by developing the negatives for slightly longer times or by employing a more constrasty grade of printing paper. In return for this trivial inconvenience the diffusion system will tend to de-emphasize minor dirt specks and blemishes on the negative, minimizing the need for print spotting and tending to reduce the prominence of the image grain structure as well. In other respects the two enlarger types are essentially similar. Either will produce excellent prints when it is properly manipulated and coupled with an appropriate negative.

They produce slightly lower contrast

The lens you use should be selected to "cover" the area of the negative you are interested in printing, not necessarily the nominal negative size. Thus, if you plan to enlarge the complete image area of a 4" × 5" negative, you must use a 135-mm lens or longer. If, however, you are only interested in the central area of the negative, the lens can be shorter. For example, if the area is, say 1½" square, pick a focal length of 50 to 75 mm and condensers to match. Be sure to center the desired image area directly over the lens. If you cannot center the image, you must select a longer focal length lens to be sure of adequate coverage.

Lens selection

Negatives should be cleaned carefully before enlarging to avoid dirty prints. It will help considerably if you have processed the negatives carefully and stored them in clean negative envelopes, but some dust is inevitable.

Negatives must be cleaned carefully before enlarging

Dust the negative on both sides with a soft brush to remove the worst of the dirt, then put the negative in the carrier so that the emulsion side of the negative will face down (toward the paper surface) when the carrier is inserted into the enlarger. It is convenient to keep the top of the negative toward you in the carrier, since (because the lens will invert the image) it will then be right-side-up on the easel.

Figure 14.4

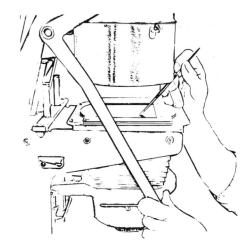

The negative will accumulate some dust on its way into the enlarger. If you want clean prints you must dust it again, in place. If you are using an enlarger which permits it, lift the condensers as far off the carrier as possible and reach in with a small sable brush to get at the negative surfaces (Fig. 14.4).

Turn the enlarger light on and the dust spots will show up in the beam like stars. Remove them one by one with the brush tip. If you encounter one which sticks, poke at it gently with the pointed end of the brush handle. If you sharpen the brush handle with a knife, removing the paint to form a tapered wooden point, you will have a fine tool for "dust nudging," and one which is not likely to damage the negative.

Make a tool for dust nudging

Moistening the brush tip slightly by wiping it on your forehead or nose will help, both to dispel static electricity which makes the dust cling, and to hold the particles once they are off the negative surface. "Nose oil"

Nose oil works; don't use too much

sounds unsanitary, but it works. Use a heavier application to smooth out greasy fingerprints and some types of water scums that occur on negatives. Nose oil will also help eliminate hairline scratches that show up usually on the backs of negatives that have been handled a little too roughly. Don't use too much or it will show in the image. Rub it on with your fingertip and blend it smoothly with another clean finger. If the scratch normally prints white, it can usually be repaired—at least partially—with the nose oil treatment. Scratches which print black are too deep to repair this way.

For the squeamish there are commerical scratch removers on the market which will work as well or perhaps a little better in some cases, but nose oil is always handy and much cheaper to use.

Projecting the image

Once the negative is clean and in the enlarger be sure that the condenser assembly sits down snugly on the carrier to seal in the light. There should be no appreciable leakage at this point. Turn on the enlarger light and raise the head until the image is close to the desired size. Focus. Readjust the size if necessary. Refocus. Compose the image on the easel, adjusting the masks for the desired shape, then remove the white focusing paper from the easel. Turn out the light. Stop the lens down a stop or two.

The proper exposure must be discovered by trial, as follows . . .

The proper exposure must be discovered by trial and a good method is as follows. Cut a sheet of printing paper 8″ × 10″ size into about five or six *test strips*, each eight inches long. Put all but one back into the package for future use. Place the strip across the image area on the easel (the light should be out, or the red "safe" screen in place) so that it crosses the most important area of the image. Set the timer for some very short time interval like, say, two seconds, and punch the button to make the exposure.

Figure 14.5

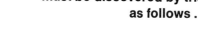

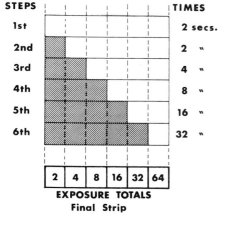

EXPOSURE TOTALS
Final Strip

Now cover about one-sixth of the strip and give the remainder another two-second exposure, or the same as the first exposure, whatever it was. Now set the timer for twice the original time, in this case, four seconds. Cover another sixth of the strip and make the exposure. Cover another sixth and double the last time, to make eight seconds. Continue this routine, doubling the previous time for each step, until the strip is completely covered. It should now contain six separate exposure steps, resulting from individual exposures of 2, 2, 4, 8, 16, and 32 seconds. The accumulated total exposures will be: 2, 4, 8, 16, 32, and 64 seconds (Fig. 14.5).

A test strip made in this way will cover a wide range of possible exposures, but more importantly, the density interval between the steps will be uniform along the entire strip. While it may seem that the exposure interval between thirty-two and sixty-four seconds is ridiculously long for testing purposes, it is no more significant than the interval between two and four seconds. The exposure is simply doubled in each case.

A test strip covers a wide range of possible exposures

The testing procedure, which many photographers use, of starting with some small value like, say, four seconds and adding some fixed time increment to it repeatedly (e.g., 4 plus 2 plus 2 plus 2 plus 2, etc.) seems more reasonable at first glance, but is really less so. In the first place, in six steps, which are about all a single strip will allow, the fixed-increment strip covers a very limited total range of possible exposure times. Starting with ten seconds, for example, and adding increments of two seconds, you will cover the range from ten to twenty seconds, and, unless you are quite sure of the approximate exposure required, this strip may not include it. Even starting with two seconds and adding increments of two seconds, you will reach only twelve seconds in six steps, for a range of 1:6. In many situations this range will not be adequate, either.

In the second place, the density difference between adjacent steps becomes less apparent as the total exposure increases, thus, while the difference between the first step, say two seconds, and the second, two plus two, is 1:2—a useful and clearly visible difference—the difference between the next-to-last step, ten seconds, and the last, twelve seconds, is almost negligible and may not even be visible at all.

You will probably find, with experience, that the first method (geometric) is best for finding unusual exposures such as might result from abnormal enlargement ratios, unfamiliar printing papers, and exceptionally dense negatives (Fig. 14.6). The second method (fixed increment) will be useful in correcting "almost right" first guesses in familiar circumstances (Fig. 14.7).

The geometric versus the fixed increment test strip

Figure 14.6

Figure 14.7

Processing must be controlled

Don't try to save the test strip by varying development

Don't overlook the fact that the value of the test strip depends upon control of the processing (developing conditions) as well as exposure. Develop the test strip for the recommended time, regardless of its appearance. Don't try to "save" it by removing it from the developer prematurely, or by extending the developing time, or you will invalidate the test. (Review the print processing instructions in Chapter 3.)

After the hypo bath, rinse the test strip thoroughly in water and inspect it in white light. If the range of test exposures has included the proper time, one or two of the sections of the test strip should appear to be nearly normal in tone. Make a full print using the exposure time which produced the best looking test strip, or an average of the best two if you can't decide between them. Process this print just as you did the test strip, without regard for its appearance, for the proper recommended time. Then rinse the hypo off the print in running water for a minute or two and inspect it in white light.

Density is controlled by exposure

If you are fortunate, the print may appear normal and acceptable, but the chances are that it will indicate a need for some further tonal adjustment. Overall changes in *density*, or darkness, can be effected by simply adjusting the exposure time. Increasing the time will darken the print, decreasing it will make the image lighter in tone.

Contrast is controlled by the paper grade

Overall changes in *contrast* can be accomplished by changing the paper contrast grade, or, if you are using a variable-contrast paper, by changing the color of the enlarging light by suitable filtration. If the print appears flat, or too low in contrast, change to a higher-numbered grade of paper. If the print is too contrasty, make the next one on a "softer" paper; that is, one with a lower number. On variable contrast paper, these same changes are accomplished by selecting filters of the appropriate number, since they correspond closely to numbered papers in effective contrast.

Figure 14.8

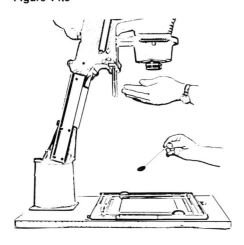

If the print is almost satisfactory but seems to need local changes in either density or contrast, more heroic measures will have to be taken. Image areas can be lightened or darkened selectively by *dodging* or *burning*. Dodging refers to the technique of shading part of the print area with your hand, a card, or a wire-handled *dodging tool* (Fig. 14.8) during a portion of the exposure so that it receives less light than the rest of the image. A dodged area will, therefore, be rendered lighter in tone than the rest of the image.

Burning or "burning-in" refers to the technique of adding light by giving extra exposure time to a relatively small area of the image to make it print darker in tone than it normally would. The two terms are almost interchangeable in the sense that dodging an area really results in burning-in the rest of the print and vice versa.

Local changes can be made by dodging or burning

Local tonal adjustment will have to be made if the test image shows lack of detail in either highlights or shadows or if the overall tonal distribution appears "unbalanced" in the format. If any of these flaws are apparent, the first step in correcting them is to determine, by further testing, the exposure times which will be required to produce the desired densities in each of the offending areas. If there are several areas to be treated, it may be helpful to outline them in a simple sketch or tracing of the image, jotting down in each area the time which it will require.

For purposes of illustration let's assume that you have produced the print shown in Figure 14.9 with an overall exposure of, say, twenty seconds. Appraisal of the composition is a subjective matter, but let's pretend that the cropping is satisfactory. You feel, however, that the picture does not work well for several reasons. First, the distribution of dark tones is "spotty." There is a visual lump of dark in the center of the format, with a rather unpleasant division of light-toned areas in the foreground and behind the central figure. Second, the figures on the left need strengthening. Third, the overhead canopy is too attractive to the eye. It should be darkened and subdued. Fourth, the central figure should be slightly separated from the group behind it, and the sleeve and eyeglasses accented for visual effect.

Make a sketch of the composition, indicating these desired changes, and, after testing the exposures which will be required for each area, indicate the exposure times on the sketch as in Figure 14.10. The normal exposure which will render the central figure and its immediate surroundings is twenty seconds. Details in the coat and eyeglasses will require less than this—you decide to dodge the three areas for a total of eighteen seconds, dividing the time more or less evenly among them.

The perimeter of the composition, including the left-hand figures and the canopy overhead, require double the normal exposure, or twenty extra seconds, while the lower left corner which contains distracting out-of-focus highlight patterns must be subdued even more strongly. Burning-in alone will not suffice here. The highlights must be darkened with the rest of the area so you must also *flash* this area with raw white light.

Flashing

Armed with this information, you set the timer for twenty seconds, pick up your dodging tool, and start the exposure (Fig. 14.11).

Hold the dodging tool high enough above the print surface so that its shadow covers the required area and keep it moving to avoid an obvious shadow edge. While counting eighteen seconds, dodge the three areas which you wish to lighten, being careful to confine the path of the shadow to the areas to be treated as nearly as possible. Twist or tilt the tool as required to make the shadow conform in shape to the image area. In this case, you may wish to make a special tool to match the long, thin contour of the coat highlight. A piece of pipe cleaner bent to match the highlight area and suspended on the end of a thin music wire handle would make a good tool for this purpose.

When the light goes off, put down the dodging tool and punch the timer for the second exposure. During this interval, you must shield the central area from light, and since this is a large area of simple shape you can use your hand as a tool. Keep it moving, adjusting the shape by maneuvering your fingers into an extended fist, and turning the hand as required. Change hands frequently to avoid casting an obvious shadow of your wrist and move the wrist as far as possible back and forth during the exposure to keep the edge exposure uniform. You may, of course, if you prefer, make a large dodging tool for this purpose.

Figure 14.9

Figure 14.10

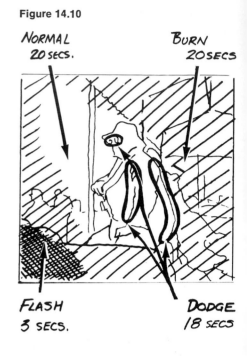

Figure 14.11

The next exposure, flashing the corner for three seconds, can be done by using the enlarger light, with the negative removed, but this is a risky procedure because of the brightness of the light and the area which it covers. A safer method, and one providing much more control, is to use a small penlight flashlight. Prepare it for the purpose by taping a cone of black paper over the lens so that a controlled spot of light is produced. If the light seems bright it will be safest to muffle it somewhat by tucking a little tuft of absorbent cotton into the open cone end. The ideal light beam will be quite dim, confined to a definite and rather small area, but soft-edged.

Make the flash exposure by handling the hooded penlight as you might use a spray can. "Brush" the area to be flashed being very careful not to allow the light to spill over into other areas of the picture. You will have to remember where the areas are because the image will not be visible when the enlarger light is out. If your enlarger is equipped with a red safe-light screen, it is convenient to work in the red image light, but it will still be difficult to see the image clearly as a rule.

The use of these techniques will make it possible for you to improve most of your pictures, since it is a very rare negative which contains perfectly balanced tones. Be careful and use discretion. It is easy to get carried away and produce an image which is obviously false, or one which has distressing extremes of tone or loss of detail.

You will find as you gain experience in dodging and burning that some control of print contrast can be achieved in this way, but there will be situations which cannot be improved by simple local variations of exposure.

Some control of local contrast is possible

An underexposed negative, for example, will normally print with unpleasantly dark and murky shadows and you may feel that they should be dodged to improve the picture. It's unlikely that simple dodging will help much, because lightening the area will only change murky black to murky gray without any improvement in contrast. In fact, the contrast may appear to have been reduced.

Any real improvement must not simply lighten the area, but must enhance the lighter tones while maintaining the blacks which provide a reference for and emphasize the grays. This can sometimes be accomplished by using a variable contrast paper and printing the shadows through a high contrast filter.

Use the filters carefully

This is a fairly tricky procedure, but it is worth trying. Generally it is advisable to start with the high contrast filter and burn in the offending shadows. Then change to the normal filter and expose the rest of the picture while dodging the shadow areas. If you are using under-the-lens filters be sure that they are placed in identical positions in the holder and that they lie flat, otherwise they may deflect the image enough to produce double edge lines. Be sure, too, that you do not combine a filtered image with an unfiltered image, for the same reason. Even though you don't need to use the "normal" filter to achieve "normal" contrast on these papers, you should use the filter in combination printing to preserve the image size, position, and focus.

Figure 14.12

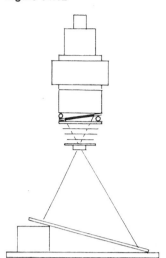

It is sometimes necessary to correct, or emphasize, image distortion during projection. Distortion usually implies that one side of the image is smaller than it should be in relation to the other side, and correction requires that the smaller side be magnified enough more than the larger during projection so that the two sides match. Accomplishing this is fairly easy. Since it is apparent that the farther the image is projected the larger it becomes, it is only necessary to tip the easel so that the small edge of the image is projected farther, to restore the proper size relationship.

There are, of course, the usual problems to face. Tilting the easel will throw the image out of focus on one or both edges, and to correct this condition, it will be necessary in most cases to tilt the negative in the opposite direction. In other words, lowering the right edge of the easel, as you face the enlarger, will require raising the right edge of the negative, and vice versa. Make this adjustment while watching the projected image closely, and adjust the focus of the enlarger frequently so that it remains best in the center of the easel.

With care you will be able to tilt the negative to just the right angle (usually a fairly slight one—less than the easel angle as a rule) so that the image plane lies perfectly on the tilted paper surface and the resulting print will be as sharp as a conventionally projected one. Strips of cardboard or in extreme cases, a pair of pencils will hold the negative in the desired position of tilt (Fig. 14.12), one wedged between the negative carrier and the condensers on the low side of the negative, and one between the carrier and the bellows frame on the negative high side. Be sure that the light leaking out from under the condensers does not reflect back onto the paper surface. It may be necessary to seal the gap with black paper or tape.

The principle here is the same as the one involved in distortion control with the view camera which is explained in greater detail in a later chapter. When this technique is used in printing negatives produced by a properly handled view camera, a very considerable amount of image distortion and perspective control is possible.

Print Finishing

15

For many photographers, the excitement of making pictures seems to reach a climax during the act of printing and with certain justification. This is when the image is seen for the first time as a real, recognizable thing. It is the moment of triumph or despair. Disappointing images get no further than the wash, sometimes no further than the shortstop, but even the good ones seem to lose their appeal during the fixing, washing, drying, and mounting steps that follow that first heady moment of appearance in the developer. It isn't any wonder, then, that very few prints ever seem to reach the stage of completion that makes them look like the products of a craftsman.

**Printing is a time
of triumph or despair**

This attitude of casual disrespect for a created product has almost no parallel among artists in other media, and probably stems, in part, from the fact that photographs are inherently "cheap." There is no precious original. Identical copies can be produced endlessly if desired, and, superficially at least, every photograph looks like every other photograph. With these strikes against it, the photograph which appears before the public with tattered corners and mottled finish, fingerprinted and covered with dust spots, simply represents effort wasted. Good craftsmanship can't save a bad picture, but it can certainly enhance a good one.

**A photograph poorly finished
represents effort wasted**

Assuming that the composition and tonal gradation of the picture are good, there are still certain things which must be attended to before the picture can be called *finished*. It must have a good surface; it must be free from image blemishes like dust marks and scratches; it should be mounted on some firm, smooth surface such as mounting board or masonite; it should be trimmed to size neatly; and, if the image is to be left unmatted, the print edges should be finished in some way to avoid a rough feeling in the hand and a raw appearance.

**Certain things must be done
before the picture is finished**

First things first. Any print which is going to be shown will almost always have to be *spotted;* that is, the little flaws and spots and lint marks and scratches which have printed along with the image will have to be eliminated.

**Any print to be shown
will have to be spotted**

Check the print as soon as it has been hypoed and washed to see if there are any black spots to be taken care of. You may be lucky, but more likely than not there will be one or two somewhere. The most effective way to deal with them is to bleach them chemically, and this can be done with any of several formulas.

Black spots will have to be bleached or reduced

If the spot is not entirely black and if it is fairly large and soft-edged, it may be possible to merely lighten it somewhat, enough to make it match its background tone. This can be done with a mild solution called *Farmer's reducer* which can be made up as follows:

Solution A
Potassium ferricyanide . . . .   2 grams
Water . . . . 100 cc

Solution B
Sodium thiosulfate (hypo) . . . .   25 grams
Water . . . . 100 cc

For use, take one part A and one part B and add to six parts of water. For faster action, use less water, for milder action use more water.

Farmer's reducer must be used fresh

Farmer's reducer must be used fresh. The chemicals lose strength rapidly after being mixed together, although they will keep for some time in separate containers as individual stock solutions.

Before treatment in any sort of bleach or other postdevelopment chemical solution, the print should be well washed, both to prevent possible stains and to assure proper chemical activity.

Work on the damp emulsion

Have running water handy

Apply the reducer with a small brush and keep it moving

The print need not be dried, however; in fact, if the spots are indefinite in outline or if the area is fairly large, it is advantageous to work on the damp emulsion. Lay the print on a smooth surface such as a sheet of glass and incline it slightly so that it can be flushed with water, letting it drain into a large tray or sink. A source of running water or a couple of quarts of water in a convenient container should be handy. Blot the print surface dry and apply the diluted Farmer's reducer with a small pointed brush, being careful to stay within the boundaries of the spot and to keep the brush tip moving. It is a good idea to keep the brush fairly dry (certainly not dripping wet) and to recharge it frequently with fresh reducer. Flush the print surface frequently with plenty of water and again blot it dry before going on. The action will be gradual and can be halted by a flood of water. Be very careful not to drip reducer on the print surface and avoid letting the solution drain downhill from the treated area.

Some staining may occur

You may occasionally have difficulty with staining of the surface. A very slight yellowing of light grays and whites may occur normally, due to the color of the ferricyanide. This will probably wash out in the running water, or it may require immersion in the fixing bath or a special clearing bath. A 5% solution of sodium bisulfite is usually effective. If more severe staining is encountered, it is probably due to chemical contamination. Perhaps the print was not washed sufficiently (seldom serious with Farmer's reducer) or perhaps the mixing containers or the brush contained chemical traces.

It is safest to use quill or plastic ferruled brushes

Sometimes if a small blotter is used to sponge up the reducer before it is rinsed off, the blotter itself may cause bleaching of the print surface as it is applied repeatedly to the emulsion. Be sure to touch the surface only with a clean area of the blotter, or use a fresh one each time, or rinse the surface thoroughly with running water before blotting. Strong blue stains can occur on the print if the ferricyanide encounters particles of rust in the water or if the ferrule of the brush is rusty. It is safest to use quill or plastic ferruled brushes for all print bleaching formulas.

If the area to be reduced is large and soft-edged, you may be able to treat it with a cotton swab. This requires an expert's touch, but it is not impossible to get good results. Dilute the reducer somewhat more than usual and work with the print nearly flat. Keep a hose with running water in one hand and flood the print surface every few seconds. It will not be necessary to blot the print. Simply wipe it as dry as possible with a quick stroke of your hand and apply the reducer-soaked swab, squeezed almost dry. The swab should be somewhat less than half the diameter of the area to be reduced and it should be moved rapidly over the area in a random pattern. Don't allow a puddle of reducer to remain quiet for even an instant; it is likely to leave an outline. Keep the swab dry and flush the area frequently using lots of water and varying the direction of flow to avoid directional streaks.

Treat larger areas with a cotton swab

Be especially careful if the area is light in tone or if it must be reduced to a near-white tone. The action will seem to accelerate as the image thins out and the last gray tint will disappear with disconcerting rapidity. It will also be very apt to mottle, and it is characteristic of the reduced image that its last visible trace is grainy and yellowish. If you want to save the print, you'd better stop before the gray approaches white, unless, of course, you deliberately want to remove all traces of the image from the area.

Completely black spots, particularly if they are tiny and sharp-edged, will probably have to be bleached out totally, since gradual reduction of tone is almost impossible when the area is not appreciably larger than the brush tip. For this purpose a stronger solution must be used. Concentrated Farmer's reducer will remove these black spots quickly enough, but it is likely to leave a brown stain. The same criticism is valid for the dichromate bleaches.

Small black spots will usually have to be bleached

An effective and easy-to-use solution is ordinary tincture of iodine, available at any drug store. Apply the tincture with a fine brush, depositing a heaping drop on the spot to be removed, and wait for a few seconds. The spot will be seen to lighten, but may not appear completely white. If the first application does not do the job, pick it up carefully with the corner of a moistened blotter to avoid smearing and repeat. The spot will appear pinkish or brownish when all silver is converted. As long as it appears gray, there is some silver left. When bleaching seems complete, the remaining brown stain can usually be removed by washing the area with a brush-load of fresh fixing bath. Old or contaminated fixer may leave a permanent stain. The print must now be treated in hypo clearing agent and washed as if it had just been processed.

Tincture of iodine is an effective bleach

If the iodine solution seems ineffective, it may be because it is old, but more likely it's because there is residual hypo in the emulsion. Hypo deactivates iodine instantly. Occasionally, the iodine will strike through the emulsion into the paper and react with starch in its fibers to form a bright blue dye. This is no cause for alarm; hypo or, preferably, a simple non-

Hypo will remove the stain

hardening fixer will usually remove the blue stain without difficulty. The hypo-metabisulfite fixer formula, which is given in the chapter on "The Stop and Fixing Baths," is recommended as a clearing bath for iodine and many other similar stains.

Permanganate is a better bleach for large areas

Most bleaches will remove the silver image with satisfactory efficiency, but very few will leave the bleached area of a print completely white and stain-free. The iodine bleach will be satisfactory for small areas, but if you must remove large areas of dark gray or black from a print a better bleach solution can be made as follows:

Solution A

Potassium permanganate . . . .   2 grams

Water, 52°C. (125°F.) . . . .   1 liter

Solution B

Hydrochloric acid. . . . . 50 cc

Water, cool . . . . 1 liter

Store the solutions separately and mix the working solution just before use. It should be discarded when a visible scum appears on the surface or when any trace of brown, grainy precipitate shows on the prints. It will not last for more than half an hour or so whether used or not. To prepare the working solution, mix equal parts of *A* and *B* and apply with a brush or a cotton swab (avoid metal ferrules). Dilution will slow the bleaching action and reduce staining.

Clear the permanganate stain with 5% bisulfite solution

After bleaching is complete, rinse in running water for two or three minutes, or until the print drippings are no longer tinted, then soak in the nonhardening fixing bath, referred to above, for several minutes to remove the brown permanganate stain. Use fresh fixer; old or used fixer may not remove the stain entirely. If some stain does remain after the fixer, it can sometimes be eliminated by soaking the print for several minutes in a 5% sodium bisulfite, or potassium metabisulfite, solution, but if all the chemicals are used fresh and the trays and utensils are clean, you should have no difficulty with staining. Treat the print in hypo clearing agent solution and wash as usual.

It is not easy to achieve a clean, sharp edge around the image with brush-applied bleach. If the image is large or complicated in outline, it may be advisable to *mask* the image itself with some waterproof material and simply soak the print in bleach to remove the background. An excellent masking fluid called "Maskoid" it specially formulated for this purpose. Use it if it is available.

Resists for print bleaching

Slightly thinned rubber cement is sometimes recommended as a suitable coating material, but it is difficult to keep at the proper consistency and messy to handle. Also, when used thick enough to be really effective as a *resist*, it does not brush out well and you may have trouble following the image outline cleanly.

Lacquers such as the familiar model airplane dope can also be used, but they may not stick to the emulsion tightly enough to prevent the bleach from seeping under the edge of the coating. They are also difficult to remove cleanly when the bleaching is finished. There are prepared resist materials for sale for making electronic printed-circuit boards, and these fluids work fairly well. They are not easy to find, however, and you will probably have to use more common material. A fairly satisfactory resist can be made by dissolving paraffin or candle wax in turpentine. Use only a little turpentine and a lot of wax to make a slightly thick solution but one which is fluid enough to brush easily. Apply it fairly thick, and be sure the areas covered do not have bubbles or pinholes in them. The turpentine will dry fairly slowly, and it is advisable to let it dry naturally and completely before immersing the print in water. Don't let the mixture soak into the print edges, or it will make the paper translucent (this is a good way to prepare *paper negatives*, but it's not desirable for regular prints).

The print will warp severely when it is immersed in the bleach solution because the paper will expand where it is not coated with resist. There is danger that the wax may lift off the surface and allow the bleach to penetrate the image areas if the warping is extreme. Fortunately, the bleach, if used full strength, is very rapid, and if you get the print completely covered and agitate the solution vigorously, the image will be completely bleached before the paper has had a chance to expand to its fullest extent. Get it into the water rinse as soon as bleaching is complete. If the wax comes off in the water, no harm is done. Complete the fixing and washing as outlined above.

Wax resist may lift in water

The resist material should be removed from the print before it goes into the hypo if possible. The "Maskoid" film can be pealed away easily. Rubber cement can be removed by gently rubbing it off with the finger tips; benzene will remove any traces that remain. Acetone will dissolve most lacquers. Turpentine will remove any bits of wax that cannot be flaked off the surface of the print. None of these solvents will harm the emulsion but be careful not to rub the gelatin surface too hard or you may abrade the water-soaked areas. Use several changes of solvent with clean cotton, and when you are sure the resist has been removed completely, let the print soak in plain water for a few minutes to flatten out and become uniformly wet. Then complete the fixing, hypo-clearing, and washing steps as usual.

It is not unusual for print papers, particularly thin ones, to become mottled with translucent areas during chemical treatment. This condition is called *water-soak*. It may occur in the shortstop with some papers, especially if the bath is unusually strong or if it is prolonged. It is also apt to show up when papers are soaked in the hypo. Prints seem to be especially susceptible to water-soak if they have been dried and are then resoaked for some reason, and bleach baths are notorious offenders in this respect, probably because of their strength and acid content.

Papers often water-soak

Water-soak is unsightly while the print is wet, and it may still be visible as a faint grayish pattern after the print is dry, but usually it disappears during drying. If it is visible in the dry print, it can sometimes be eliminated or at least reduced, by resoaking the print thoroughly and redrying. If plain water is not effective, try soaking in a strong shortstop solution or a solution of wetting agent before rewashing.

It can sometimes be eliminated by resoaking and redrying

Figure 15.1

**Prints dried in blotters
are generally flat**

After the chemical treatment is done, the print must be thoroughly washed. If it is to be dried with a nonglossy surface—that is, without ferrotyping—it can be placed in a blotter book or roll and allowed to dry naturally (Fig. 15.1a, b). This may take a day or two or three, depending upon the humidity, but the results are generally good; prints usually come out of the blotters flat and unwrinkled.

**Dry RC prints on screens
or hang them**

Figure 15.2

One of the best ways of drying ordinary prints, and the recommended procedure for Resin-Coated prints, is to blot them surface-dry and lay them out on screens to dry naturally in the air. The screens are simple to construct from wood and plastic fly-screen material (Fig.15.2). It is convenient to make them large enough to accommodate several prints and to stack several frames in a drying rack. Leave several inches between them for good air circulation. Ordinary paper prints should be dried facedown to prevent or minimize curling. RC prints can be dried either side up but it is safer, perhaps, to lay them out faceup unless airborne dust is likely to be a problem. **If space is at a premium, RC prints can be dried very satisfactorily by hanging them from a line with spring clothespins.**

**Prints should emerge
from a heated dryer
a little leathery**

Ordinary uncoated prints can also be dried on a heated dryer which will speed up the process but is somewhat more likely to warp the paper. Deformation can be kept to a minimum if the prints are soaked for a minute or two in a glossing or flattening solution, then squeegeed surface dry, blotted on both sides, and placed on the dryer blanket facedown. The dryer should be just hot enough to leave the paper a little "leathery" as the prints emerge. If the temperature is too high, the prints will be apt to shrink unevenly and become crisp; a condition which will gradually disappear as the emulsion absorbs moisture from the air but which makes the prints immediately susceptible to cracking if they are not handled with care.

**Light-weight papers
may dry with rippled edges**

Large prints, and especially prints on light-weight papers are likely to warp and become rippled along the edges when heat dried. This tendency can be reduced if you are especially careful to blot the prints thoroughly before placing them in the dryer and if the dryer heat is kept low and the belt speed slow. Prints warp when they dry unevenly. Anything you can do to make the drying process even and gentle will help to prevent deformed prints.

They can sometimes be flattened

If the prints do warp in spite of your best efforts to prevent it, they can sometimes be flattened, if they have not been too badly overdried, by weighting them down under clean, flat boards and allowing them to stand for a day or two. If this treatment doesn't work, try dampening the backs of the prints (not RC prints) with a slightly moistened sponge and press them between cardboards in a dry-mounting press at about 93.3° C. (200° F.). Be sure to dry out the press pad thoroughly before using the press for dry-mounting.

Drying glossy prints

RC paper prints will dry to a high gloss without ferrotyping or other special treatment. If a glossy surface is desired on regular papers be sure you have used the proper paper surface. Prints which have been made on any surface other than one specifically named "glossy" cannot be ferro-typed successfully. Be sure the prints are thoroughly washed, then soak them in a glossing solution for a few minutes. Remove them from the bath, face-to-face, two at a time (Fig. 15.3a), and lay them against a sheet of plate glass, or something similar, which has been propped up almost vertically and placed so the prints can drain into the glossing solution tray. Squeegee each pair of prints carefully (Fig. 15.3b), then place them between blotters and go over them with a print roller to dry the paper backs as thoroughly as possible (Fig. 15.3c).

If all goes well, the surface will be flawless

Then peel them apart and place them, one at a time, on the dryer blanket, faceup, so that the emulsion side will contact the metal drum surface. Immediately wipe each print surface carefully with a small, clean sponge (lintless!) wet with the glossing solution, so that as the emulsion makes contact with the hot drum it is flooded with liquid (Fig. 15.3d). The dryer should be hot enough so that the prints are thoroughly dry as they emerge. They should drop off the drum without any tendency to stick, and, if all has gone well, the surface will be mirror-smooth and flaw-less.

There are at least three potential difficulties

This rather elaborate ritual will help to avoid at least three potential difficulties. First, thoroughly drying the print backs speeds drying time and helps to avoid uneven drying and possible sticking. One form of

Figure 15.3

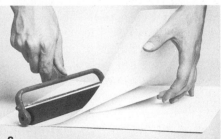
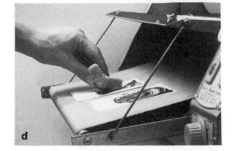

Oyster shelling

uneven drying called *oyster-shelling,* can occur when the perimeter of the print dries before the center does. The dry edges lift off the drum surface and shrink while the damp center section remains firmly stuck to the drum, and the print emulsion is strained or sometimes even torn at the line of contact. Then another narrow band of emulsion lifts, dries, and shrinks, leaving another ridge of strained gelatin, etc. When the print finally drops off the drum, the surface is marked by a series of roughly concentric ridges resembling an archery target in relief, or, as the name suggests, an oyster shell. The print, of course, is ruined.

Oyster shelling is seldom encountered if the print is blotted dry, so that the paper back is uniformly damp, and then flooded with glossing solution on its face only, just as it enters the dryer. The print center remains relatively dry while the excess fluid squeezed out around the edges by the drum pressure will dampen the blanket and tend to retard drying of the print perimeter. (If this is overdone or if the dryer blanket is soiled, brown stains may form on the print backs). Second, wiping the emulsion with a sponge will remove particles of scale or lint that may have been picked up in the glossing tray. Third, the last-minute flooding of the surface with glossing solution will assure that the drum and the print will make a good "wet" contact.

Dirt particles

Some of the time at least, glossy prints will be flawed in one way or another, and the causes and cures are sometimes hard to discover. The most common difficulty is an imperfect gloss due to dirt particles which will cause little circular dull spots, obviously indented into the gelatin surface. The particles often remain stuck to the emulsion. Lint and hair are occasionally found stuck to the surface too, leaving their images in the gelatin as dull lines. Wiping the wet print surface as previously described will minimize these defects. It should be obvious that the dryer drum must be clean and dust-free. If the machine has not been used for some time, it will be wise to wash the drum surface with clean water and vacuum-clean the blanket before drying valuable glossy prints.

Air bubbles are fairly common

Air bubbles between the print and the drum are also fairly common. They rarely are larger than mere flecks on the print surface, but occasionally you may see a relatively large one. If the spot is essentially circular and clean-edged and if the rest of the surface is well glossed, the problem may be due to insufficient squeegeeing pressure between the dryer roller and the drum. This can only occur on those dryers whose rollers use spring pressure. When drum weight supplies the pressure, this flaw is rare.

Freckling of the surface may result

More or less uniform *freckling* of the surface may result if nonglossy paper is ferrotyped. The relatively rough surface simply will not conform to the smooth drum surface. A similar effect will often occur if glossy paper is not flooded with liquid as it meets the drum, but in this case, the freckling is often in stripes with fairly good gloss in between.

Freckling will also occur if the dryer drum is so hot that the print sizzles when it touches the drum surface. The cure is obvious—cool the drum a little, resoak the print, and try again. Another common cause of overall freckling is overhardening of the print in the hypo bath, either by using a bath containing too much hardener or by prolonging the treatment in the bath beyond a reasonable length of time. The cure for this latter problem is not always effective but is worth trying. Resoak the print in warm water for several hours to soften the emulsion and dry it again. Even overnight soaking may be necessary, but if overdone, the gelatin may swell to the point of disintegration. Prevention of overhardening is simpler. Don't allow prints to remain in the hypo bath longer than is necessary to fix them thoroughly. Most papers will be well fixed in two or three minutes, with agitation, in fresh hypo. To leave them soaking for more than ten or fifteen minutes is to ask for glossing troubles.

Another more serious problem is *sticking*. In dry weather it is not at all unusual for thoroughly dry, glossed prints to cling to the drum by static electricity, but they can be peeled off easily without damage to either print or drum. Under some conditions, however, some prints will actually adhere to the drum surface so that they cannot be removed without being literally torn off. This is a rather mysterious condition which may suddenly manifest itself, harass you for a few days or weeks, and just as suddenly cease.

A more serious problem is sticking

Sticking is usually aggravated by an almost invisible film of dirt—and perhaps gelatin—which will gradually accumulate on the drum surface with much use. Sometimes the problem will disappear if you simply wash the drum surface thoroughly with a very mild cleaning powder such as Bon Ami and rinse it clean. Do this as gently as possible. The drum surface will scratch very easily, and the scratches will appear forevermore on the surface of your glossy prints.

The real cause of sticking is probably excessive softening of the print emulsion. This can occur if the fixing bath does not contain any hardener at all or if the bath has been weakened by much use. It can also result if the prints have soaked in water for a considerable time before ferrotyping or if the water has been excessively warm or soft. Prolonged treatment in the hypo clearing bath may also add to the difficulty. Some brands of printing papers seem more apt to be affected by these influences than do others, but all papers will stick if sufficiently provoked.

It is probably caused by excessive softening of the emulsion

If sticking becomes a sudden problem, try washing the dryer drum first. If that fails to stop it, check out your chemicals. Use fresh hypo with adequate agitation, and for at least ten minutes, but not much longer, as there is danger of bleaching the prints. Limit your hypo-clearing treatment to the minimum recommended time; don't let the prints accumulate in the bath. Wash in cool water, not less than about 18°C. (65°F.) for reasonably good washing efficiency, and for no longer than necessary to assure reasonable permanence. Use the minimum drum heat which will dry the paper adequately, and compensate by slowing the drum speed of rotation. If all these measures fail, clean up the drum again and try treating the prints in a separate hardening bath after the fixer. This will almost certainly prevent sticking, but may cause a freckled gloss.

How to avoid sticking

Don't confuse this condition with the normal sticking which will occur if the print is not fully dry as it appears. Raising the drum temperature or slowing its rotation will cure this simple problem.

Prints can also be ferrotyped without a heated drum dryer by rolling them, facedown, onto a polished chrome-plated ferrotype tin. Blot the print backs dry and let them dry naturally in a draft-free location. Oyster-

Ferrotyping prints without a heated dryer

Plastic sheets are good; don't use glass

shelling, which is much more common with air-dried prints than with those dried on a drum dryer, can be avoided, at least some of the time, by covering the prints on the ferrotype tins with blotters and towels under moderate pressure. The drying time will be prolonged considerably, but results are usually good. Acrylic plastic sheets (Lucite or Plexiglas) will serve as excellent ferrotype plates but don't try to use plate glass. The print emulsion is very likely to stick firmly to glass, ruining the print. Again, RC papers air-dry to a high gloss without ferrotyping or special handling of any sort.

After drying, the print should be mounted on some sort of board to keep it flat for comfortable viewing and to protect it from being folded or creased in handling. Cardboard, mat board, or illustration board are the usual materials, but the foam-core plastic boards are useful if a very light-weight mount is required.

There are a number of methods for mounting prints

There are a number of methods of attaching the print to the mount. Specially formulated rubber cements are sometimes recommended, but they are not really permanent. Ordinary rubber cement is likely to discolor the print in time and should not be used except for work which will not be preserved. Some people like to *wet-mount* their prints on wood or masonite panels. This is a particularly good method of mounting very large prints. Ordinary wallpaper paste will suffice for this purpose as will Elmer's white plastic resin glue, but neither can be considered a permanent adhesive. Paste will dry out and disintegrate in time, and the plastic resins sometimes contain ingredients which will affect the photographic image. This deterioration is a slow process, however, and prints mounted with these adhesives may last for years without serious fading or staining.

Wet-mounting is good for very large prints

A print to be wet-mounted should be soaked, then blotted dry on both sides. The glue is applied to the mounting board surface with a serrated-edge spreader, such as is used by floor tile installers (an old comb can also be used) and the damp print is rolled from one end to avoid trapping air bubbles. Very large prints can be handled most easily by two persons. Each takes an end, suspending the print in a *U* shape over the glue-covered board. The center of the print is then lowered to the mount board and the ends are carefully laid down.

Be sure to leave a wide margin around the image area

Small air bubbles can be squeegeed or rolled out, starting from the print center and working toward the edges. Use firm pressure but don't try to squeeze out all the glue. The prints will dry satisfactorily if they are laid facedown on clean sheets or towels and lightly weighted. Be sure to leave enough margin around the image when making the print so that the print edges can be folded around the mount. If the print is smaller than the mount board, the extruded glue will make a terrible mess and the print edges will be likely to lift as they dry.

Wet-mounting is not usually worth the trouble for small prints, but they can be stuck down successfully with either Elmer's or ordinary gelatin, softened, then melted in warm water. The gelatin should be mixed rather thick, and since it has no adhesive quality until it is almost dry, the prints will have to be held flat on the mount during drying with a weighted board or something similar.

By all odds the easiest, neatest, and quickest method of mounting photographs is *dry-mounting* in a heated mounting press. A shellac-impregnated tissue sheet is placed between the print back and the mount board, and the sandwich is pressed together at a fairly high temperature until the shellac melts and bonds the print and the board together. A satisfactory way to accomplish this is as follows.

Turn on the mounting press. Set temperature to about 135° C. (275° F.)—not more than 88° C. (190° F.) for RC prints. Leave press closed but not clamped shut, so that the rubber base pad can warm up. At intervals, while you are preparing your prints for mounting, open the press and remove the pad to cool briefly in open air (Fig. 15.4). This procedure will assure a dry pad, and helps prevent moisture problems during the mounting process.

Check your mounting board for absorbed moisture by placing a sheet of it in the press for a few seconds, then feeling its surface for dampness when it is first removed. If it feels damp or steamy, it should be dried out, sheet by sheet, by several cycles of heating in the press and cooling in air. This, of course, will steam up the press pad again, and it will have to be dried out before it will be safe to use for the actual mounting.

Check the prints to be mounted to see if they are reasonably flat and free from edge ripples. Prints which cannot be pressed absolutely flat between two cardboards without buckling or wrinkling will have to be soaked and redried or steamed flat in the press. Moisten their backs with a slightly damp sponge, and heat them between cardboards, following the same procedure outlined for drying the boards themselves. Dry the pad again.

Place the print to be mounted facedown on a clean, smooth paper surface, lay a sheet of mounting tissue on it, aligning at least two edges, and stick the tissue down with a light stroke of the tacking iron (Fig. 15.5a). Tack the tissue to the print in only one spot, preferably near center. Use light pressure; a heavy touch will leave an irremovable mark on the print face.

If the print is to be mounted in the center of a large board for eventual matting, it is only necessary to trim the excess tissue so that it does not

The best method is dry-mounting

Figure 15.4

**Warm up the press,
dry out the pad**

Flatten the prints if necessary

**Tack the dry-mount tissue
to the print with a tacking iron**

Figure 15.5

a

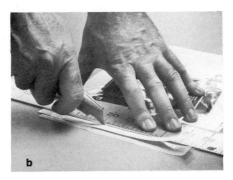

b

c

extend beyond the print edges. If the tissue is not trimmed flush with the print, it will stick to the cover sheet in the press.

If the print is to be presented without borders of any kind so that the image "bleeds" all around, it should now be trimmed to approximate size, cutting both print and tissue together to leave about quarter-inch borders on all sides.

It is best to trim the print with a knife and straight-edge

If the print is to be presented in position on a larger mounting board, unmatted, it must be trimmed to exact size. It is best to do this with a mat knife and metal straight-edge. Print trimming boards are likely to leave a slightly rough edge, especially on heavy-weight papers. Keep the print under fairly heavy pressure during trimming to prevent the tissue from slipping (Fig. 15.5b). It will have a tendency to pull a little during trimming and may protrude enough to stick to the cover sheet.

Tack the tissue to the mount board

Place the trimmed print, faceup, in position on the mounting board and, holding it firmly in place, lift a corner and stick the tissue to the board with the tip of the tacking iron (Fig. 15.5c). Be sure you have not lifted the tissue with the print.

Cover the print and put it into the press

Now, if the press has reached operating temperature, place the board, print side up, on the press pad. Cover the face of the print with a large clean sheet of paper and close the press firmly. The time required to effect a good bond will depend upon the temperature of the press, the thickness of the cover sheet, and the weight of the mounting board, among other things, so you will have to experiment a little. A good first try might be fifteen seconds.

If it is not well fastened down . . .

When the print comes out of the press, it should be firmly stuck to the mount and can be handled immediately. If it is not well fastened down, lift up a corner and investigate. If the print is stuck more or less firmly to the tissue, but the tissue is not adhering to the mount board, and if the tissue still looks quite lustrous or shiny, it may be an indication that the time was too short. Put it back in the press and double the time.

If the print is loose from the tissue but the tissue is stuck to the mount, and especially if the tissue looks dull, it indicates that too much heat or too much time have been used. You may not be able to restick this print. Heat it again, very thoroughly. It may stick or it may come off entirely. If it comes off, take another piece of tissue and start over.

You may be able to get it off with a household iron

In dire emergency (if it's the only print you have, and it won't come off the mount or stick down either) you may be able to get it off with a regular household iron. Lay the print down on a flat surface, faceup, and cover it with a sheet of thin paper. Reach under the cover sheet and pick up a corner of the print, then place the iron (not over about 121° C. [250° F.]) as close to your fingers as is comfortable and move it slowly back and forth across the corner. As you lift up on the print, you should be able to feel the melting adhesive giving away.

Be careful not to crease the print against the edge of the iron but keep some tension on it. With practice, you will be able to strip the print from the board, moving the iron slowly across the print as you pick up the print behind it. Dry-mounted prints can also be soaked off their mounts with alcohol, or any of several other solvents; but since these liquids are all either inflammable or toxic, they should be used with extreme caution.

Occasionally, you will find a print which appears blistered. This indicates a trapped air bubble and may result from any of several causes. The print may have been warped into a bowl-shaped plane so that the edges were sealed down before the center could be flattened out. You may have sealed an air bubble under the tissue with the tacking iron. But the cause is most likely to be moisture, either in the board or the press pad, vaporized by the heat before the tissue could adhere to the board.

Air bubbles under the print

It is sometimes beneficial to reheat the print, and weight it down quickly after removal from the press so that it cools flat and under considerable pressure. Occasionally the bubbles can be flattened by reheating the print and letting it cool while holding it bent backward, but this is not always effective.

In stubborn cases, if anything can be done at all, it may be possible to puncture the bubble with a pin—preferably through the mount board—and reheat. Sometimes the air can be worked out to the edge of the print by pressing on the bubble as you lead it along with the hot tacking iron (use a cover sheet, of course). It will then have to be reheated in the press.

Dirt particles trapped under the print will show up as little sharp-pointed lumps which are extraordinarily visible. They can be camouflaged somewhat by pressing them down gently with the flat side of a fingernail or other smooth object. Be careful not to press too hard or you will simply make a dimple out of the peak. Sometimes, too, if the press has been allowed to get dirty, the rough press surface may emboss the print, or melted shellac may be smeared on the print surface. Nothing can be done about dents in the emulsion, but shellac smears can be removed with alcohol.

Dirt particles trapped under the print will show

Although some photographers prefer to "spot" prints before they are mounted (for fear of ruining a mounted print) it is easier to work on prints when they are fastened down on a flat, firm surface. There is also the remote possibility that dye-spotting done on an unmounted print may shift in color perceptibly, due to the heat of the mounting press, and become visible, especially if the areas are very light-toned or if the spotted area itself is large. This, therefore, is the time to take care of the white spots on the print. On certain papers, such as the very dull-surfaced "suede" finishes, it may be possible to spot out white blemishes with an ordinary pencil, but this is not the best method. Pencil, if it can be made to stick to the print emulsion at all, will certainly cause a surface shine, and may also cause indentations in the surface. It may, however, be satisfactory for minor spotting, particularly if the print is to be coated for presentation with wax or plastic spray.

Now take care of the white spots

Another method seldom used for prints to be exhibited, involves painting out the white spots with special tempera paints, called *spotting colors*. These paints are water-soluble and cover the spots well but leave an obvious deposit on the print surface which is unsightly. Prints which are to be used for reproduction are often retouched this way since the surface texture does not affect the image seen by the copy camera.

If the surface is not important, tempera retouching is probably the best method, since it allows extensive corrections to be made with the airbrush as well as by hand, and a full range of tones from black to white is readily obtained. Beware, though, tempera retouching will darken perceptibly when coated with plastic sprays or varnishes.

Display prints should be dye-retouched

For prints which will be displayed only dye retouching will be satisfactory and it is limited in tonal range. Dark grays and black cannot be matched. The lighter tones, however, can be handled with complete effectiveness, and the print surface of even glossy prints is unchanged. Dye is fairly easy to work with too, but you will have to practice a little to become expert.

Beginners get into trouble with dyes

Most beginners get into trouble with dye spotting because they try to use the dye like paint. You cannot do this. The dye doesn't cover the light area, it merely tones the gelatin; the tone is absorbed, it does not lie on the surface. The process is not instantaneous either. The dye absorption takes a little time and is progressive. For this reason a brush charged with dye will make a relatively light mark if it is moved rapidly across the print surface but will produce a much darker tone if moved slowly or allowed to rest in one place for a few seconds.

Here is an approach . . .

Here is an approach to dye retouching that should give you good results. First, provide yourself with a bottle of dye of the appropriate color to match your prints. Prints on ordinary papers will normally require a "neutral" black dye tone such as "Spotone" #3. If the image has been printed on "warm" or "cold" papers, or if the development has been unusual, or if the image has been chemically toned after development, you may have to use a warm (brownish) or cold (bluish) dye color, "Spotone" #2 and #1 respectively. Several dye colors are available, and they can be blended together to match just about any image color that can be produced on black-and-white papers.

Assemble these materials

You will also need a small container of water; a clean metal, glass, porcelain, or plastic surface to mix dyes on (a saucer is fine for this purpose); a good quality red sable water color brush, about #4; some scraps of blotter, paper towels, or tissues to wipe the brush on; and a couple of old prints to practice on. Assemble these materials conveniently on a well-lighted table surface, and you are ready to begin.

Prop the print up so that you can see clearly without any interfering surface glare. Dip a brushful of dye out of the bottle and spread it on the saucer. Dip the brush in the water and transfer a brushful to the saucer near the dye puddle. The brush should now contain a very light-toned dye and water mixture.

Point the brush, dry it on a blotter

Holding the brush almost parallel to the tissue or blotter surface, stroke it lightly so as to bring the hairs to a fine point. Do this repeatedly, turning the handle in your fingers, until the brush is perfectly pointed and until it no longer leaves an obvious mark on the tissue. It should be almost surface-dry but should contain a little moisture inside.

Holding the brush quite vertically, touch the point lightly to the old print margin and draw a slow, fine line. The areas of the image which match this line tone, or are a little darker, are the places to start with. Find a light-toned blemish on the spoiled print and practice your brush-work.

The easiest areas to work on are relatively soft-edged spots in light or medium gray backgrounds and in a textured area of the image. It is better still if the image grain is prominent. Don't try to obliterate the spot, just camouflage it. If the background is textured, match the texture with your brushstrokes. Work carefully as you approach the edges of the spot. If you are not careful, you can paint a dark ring around it without being aware that you are doing so.

Don't try to obliterate the spot, just camouflage it

As you proceed, the moisture in the brush will gradually be used up, and the dye will tend to get darker. Start out with very slightly "dirty" water in the brush and work on the lightest areas. You will find that only a trace of dye in the water will be plenty for the near-whites. Blend the dye and water in the saucer as you need it.

Most authorities suggest a very small brush such as a #0 or #00 but I can't agree. The larger brush will allow more uniform control of dye tone, will require less frequent replenishment, and, if it points well, will make just as fine a line as will the smaller brush.

Don't try to pick up just a little of the dye mixture on the brush tip. Soak the brush in it, then stroke dry on the tissues. If it leaves any sign of moisture on the print emulsion as you work, it is too wet. Work with just the tip of the brush, and with very light pressure build up the desired tone with a series of stippling strokes which match the image or grain texture.

White spots in very dark areas cannot be completely hidden with dye, but they can be subdued. Use a slightly wetter brush and leave it in contact with the emulsion for a few seconds at a time. Use the dye full-strength and take your time. You will find that you can get a darker tone by working intermittently. The emulsion seems to take the dye better when it is fairly dry and will accept only so much at any one time. Let it rest a few minutes and go at it again with a fresh brush-load. Above all, take it easy.

Dye retouching is not a one-stroke technique. Best results will come from a gradual building up of tones with repeated light strokes of the brush tip.

Dye retouching is not a one-stroke technique

Generally it is preferable to work with the dyes on a dry print, but there are some types of spots which are easier to handle if the emulsion is damp. Work on a dry print if the areas to be touched up are small in size, sharp-edged or crisply textured, or on a medium to dark background. Work on the damp print, squeegeed dry, just as it would normally go into the dryer, if the areas are large, soft-edged, or on very light backgrounds.

In general, wet-print work will require slightly darker dye mixtures, for the same tone, than will be needed on the dry emulsion, and the dye

Wet-print work will require darker dye mixtures

will form a naturally softer outline. There is some danger, however, that the dye color will change a little as the print dries and for this reason wet-print work, especially in large areas, must be considered risky.

Prints are often presented without borders

Photographic prints are often presented trimmed without any borders, or matted, or mounted on a large board so that the print image is seen against a plain background. The easiest method is the first. Simply mount the print on some sort of board to stiffen it and hold it flat, and trim print and board to exact image dimensions. It is best to use a mat knife and metal straight-edge for trimming and to make the cut with a series of light strokes rather than attempting to go through both print and mount board with one mighty effort.

Trim with a knife; sand off the wire edge

Keep firm pressure on the straight-edge and press lightly with the knife. Always cut on the side of the straight-edge away from the center of the print, that is, keep the straight-edge over the picture area so that if the knife slips, it will not ruin the image. Be careful to keep the corners square and the image edges parallel.

Then sand the edges with fine sandpaper, rounding the edges slightly and stroking away from the emulsion to avoid fraying the edge of the image (Fig. 15.6). The knife blade will have raised a sharp "wire-edge" on the emulsion side and the sanding should remove this. When the edges feel smooth to the touch, blacken them with smooth strokes of a china-marking pencil or a litho crayon and then rub them thoroughly with tissues to remove the excess and polish the edges slightly. You can also use white crayons or even paraffin if you prefer light-toned or untinted edges.

Treat the edges anyway you like, but treat them somehow

Some photographers prefer white edges, some leave them plain, and some bind the edges with tape. An elegant edge finish, but one which requires careful glue-mounting, involves cutting the mounting board to exact size first, then mounting the over-size print on it, and folding the print margins back over the board so that the image literally wraps around the edges. Treat the edges any way that you like but treat them somehow.

Mounting with borders

Mounting a photograph in some selected position on a large board will require careful measurement, but it is not particularly difficult. First trim the photograph and its attached dry-mounting tissue to the exact shape and size desired, using a print trimming board or, preferably, a mat knife and straight-edge. Inspect the trimmed print carefully to see that the

Figure 15.6

tissue is not showing outside the print edges (it sometimes pulls during trimming); if it is visible, trim it again so that it is even with the print perimeter. If this is not done, the tissue will show as a thin, glossy outline around the mounted print and may even stick to the cover sheet if enough of it is exposed.

Lay the trimmed print on the mount board and decide where you want it to be placed and how wide the borders should be. Trim the board if necessary to adjust the borders and the overall size of the mount for best visual effect.

Mount the print for best visual effect

It is usual, but by no means mandatory, to position a print on a mount so that the side borders are equal in width and so that the bottom border is somewhat wider than the top border. The top border is generally as wide as, or slightly wider than the side borders. Measure the width of the print and subtract it from the width of the mount. Divide this number by two to find the width of each side border. Mark the border widths on the board very lightly with soft pencil so that the marks can be erased later. It is usually best to adjust the top and bottom border widths by placing the print on the board and moving it up and down in the space until it looks right. Mark the vertical position in pencil with light, unobtrusive dots or short lines. It is not necessary to draw lines completely around the print position.

Now position the print within the guide marks and hold it down firmly. Lift one corner, being careful not to lift the tissue with the print, and tack the tissue to the mount with a light stroke of the tacking iron. This will keep the print from slipping out of position while it is being placed into the dry-mounting press. Heat the print in the press, using a cover sheet to protect its surface. Erase the position marks carefully with a soft eraser.

Prints mounted on a plain board, as just described, may look a little "bald" or unfinished, and many photographers prefer to *mat* the print images; that is, to place the print behind a cut out opening in a piece of fine cardboard or mat board so that the image is set back behind the board surface and is outlined by a thin shadow edge. The procedure is similar to the one just described, but there are a few differences in detail.

Many photographers prefer to mat their prints

A print to be matted should not be trimmed to exact size before mounting, but the precise final image dimensions must be known. You can find them most easily by *cropping* the image with strips of black or white paper or cardboard laid over its surface and adjusted for the best compositional effect. *Cropping L's* (L-shaped cardboard strips) are handy for this purpose (Fig. 15.7a). When you have decided upon the composition shape and size, measure the image dimensions and jot them down.

Cropping L's are handy

Tack a piece of dry-mounting tissue to the back of the print and trim print and tissue only enough to remove any overhang. Leave at least a quarter-inch margin around the image dimensions. Select a piece of mat board, cut it to the appropriate size and shape, and determine the position of the mat opening by measurement. Mark the positions of the corners of the image opening with very light pencilled dots or short lines, being very careful not to indent the board surface (Fig. 15.7b). Use a knife and straight-edge to cut the indicated opening (Fig. 15.7c).

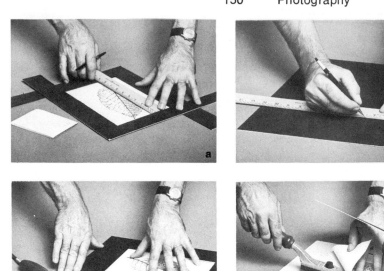

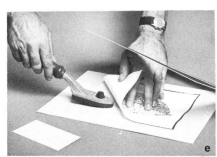

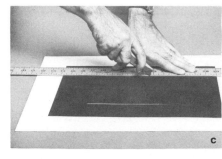

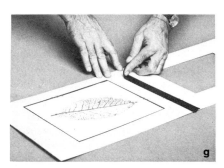

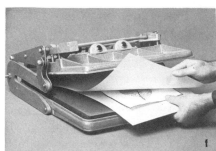

Figure 15.7

Center the image in the mat opening

Now cut a sheet of mounting board to the same dimensions as the mat and, placing the print on it, lay the mat over the print and center the image carefully in the mat opening (Fig. 15.7*d*). When the image is precisely composed in the opening and the mount and mat boards are exactly aligned, remove the mat, lift one edge of the print and tack it to the mount board (Fig. 15.7*e*). Cover the print face with a clean cover sheet and put it in the mounting press (Fig. 15.7*f*). When the print is mounted and when the mat board is placed over it and aligned exactly with the edges of the mount board, the print image should be correctly outlined by the mat opening. The two boards may now be glued together or bound together by neatly taping the edges. Some photographers prefer to tape the mount to the mat only at the top (Fig. 15.7*g*). Hinge mounting may help to avoid buckling of the boards if they are subjected to changes in humidity, but cementing the two together firmly, with all edges flush, will also make a neat unit which can be handled easily and is attractive (Fig. 15.7*h*).

Cutting a mat requires some skill. The cuts must be clean and straight and the corners should be square and free from tufts of uncut fibers. Most people find it easiest to make vertical cuts and to use several light strokes rather than one heavy one to penetrate the board. Be sure to keep the knife from wavering so as to avoid fraying the edge of the board, and cut

Figure 15.8

a. Use "cropping L's" to establish composition; measure the image dimensions and make a little diagram of the mat proportions.

b. Cut mount and mat boards to proper size. The mount board may be fractionally smaller. Be sure both boards are absolutely square-cornered and have parallel sides.

c. Draw the outlines of the mat opening on the BACK of the mat board.

d. You can use a metal straight-edge for a cutting guide but a T-square is better. Press the T-square against the table edge to brace it firmly and align the mat board with it carefully. Use a sheet of cheap illustration board or poster board under the mat to protect the tabletop and to provide a smooth, firm cutting surface. Replace this board when it becomes roughened; you cannot make smooth, clean cuts on an uneven surface. Corrugated cardboard can be used, but is not recommended.

e. Position the mat cutter so that its edge is parallel to the guide line and place the blade tip just behind the cross-line, as shown. The blade length should be adjusted so that it will cut completely through the mat board but only slightly into the cutting board surface.

f. Holding the board firmly in position press the blade tip through it. Be sure that the edge of the mat cutter is parallel to the guideline.

g. The Dexter mat cutter is for right-handed people. Slide the T-square over to the cutter to guide it, bear down on the cutter and push with the heel of your hand. It should cut cleanly and easily.

h. Keep firm pressure on the T-square as it guides the cutter. Cut just a little past the corner marks to avoid tufts of uncut fibers in the finished mat corners.

i. The finished mat should have straight, clean edges and neat corners. Wavy edges result from letting the cutter wander away from the T-square; imprecise corners can be caused if the cutter is not parallel to the guidelines when it is first positioned; tufted corners indicate that you are not cutting far enough past the corner guidelines and rough or ragged edges can be caused by an uneven or soft surface under the mat board or by a dull blade.

Put a piece of old cardboard under the matte while cutting

just a little way past the corners so that they will be clean and precise. It is safest to place the straight-edge over the mat margins, rather than the center, and cut toward the opening; so that if the knife slips, it will not damage the mat itself. Be sure to put a piece of old cardboard under the mat board while cutting, both to avoid damaging the table surface and to insure a good edge. You will not be able to make a clean cut if the surface under the board is rough or uneven.

After you have gained some skill in mat cutting, you may want to try "bevelling" the mat opening edges. You can cut bevelled edges by hand by simply holding the knife at a slant against the straight-edge, but it is not easy to keep the blade at a constant angle and the cut edge may look wavy. Don't try too steep an angle at first. Practice holding the knife about fifteen degrees from vertical until you gain confidence. Bevelled mats can be cut easily with one of the patented mat cutters which hold the blade rigidly at a selected angle. Figure 15.8 illustrates the procedure for cutting a bevelled mat using the popular "Dexter" mat cutter.

Ordinary inexpensive mat boards will be quite satisfactory for square-cut mats, but bevelled mats will look better if they are cut from high quality stock. Cheap board usually consists of a thin facing of paper glued to a coarse, pulpy cardboard center. This coarse, dark colored center is usually not evident in square cuts but is distinctly visible and ugly in a bevelled edge. For bevel-cutting, select a board which has a fine-textured, light colored paperboard center. It will be more expensive but much more attractive when finished.

You can choose the board you like, but most photographers seem to select either black or white boards in preference to colored ones. If you use black mat board consider blackening the cut edges of the mat opening. It will be one more evidence of your care and craftsmanship.

A picture that's worth finishing at all is worth finishing well

This may seem like a lot of trouble to go to just for one photograph, but presentation is at least half the battle, and any picture that's worth finishing at all is worth finishing well.

Characteristics of the Photographic Lens System

16

When a ray of light travelling through air encounters a denser medium such as glass, several things may happen to it. If the glass is a window with polished parallel surfaces, uncolored, and transparent, and if the light rays strike the surface perpendicularly, they will pass through essentially unscathed (Fig. 16.1*a*). Some of the light energy will be lost by reflections from the surface as the ray enters the glass and again from the air surface as the ray leaves the glass. Some energy will be absorbed by the glass itself, and there will no doubt be some minute loss caused by diffusion or scattering, but the total loss from all causes will be negligible.

When a ray of light encounters glass several things may happen

If the glass is translucent, the greatest loss of intensity will be from the effect of diffusion or scattering of the light rays (Fig. 16.1*b*). If the glass is opaque, it will simply absorb the light energy and refuse to transmit it (Fig. 16.1*c*). If the glass is colored, the absorption of light energy will be selective, certain wavelengths of the light will be absorbed while others are transmitted (Fig. 16.1*d*).

It may be transmitted, reflected, diffused or absorbed

If the light ray strikes the window at an angle other than perpendicular to the surface, the loss of energy from surface reflection will increase as the angle becomes more acute and another important effect occurs, that of *refraction*, or bending, of the light ray (Fig. 16.1*e*). Refraction will

It may be refracted

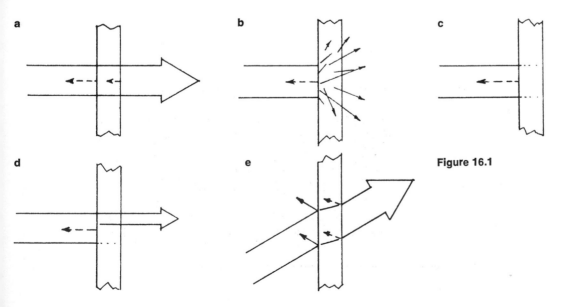

a   b   c

d   e   **Figure 16.1**

Figure 16.2   The watery effect of objects near the ground line is due to the refraction of light by heat waves rising from the black asphalt surface.

occur whenever light passes from a medium of one density to a medium of different density if its angle to the surface is other than perpendicular. Refraction is responsible for the "wet pavement" mirage, for the distortion of the shape of the sun as it approaches the horizon at sunset, and for the wavery quality of things seen through a jet engine exhaust or through binoculars on a hot summer day (Fig. 16.2).

In all these cases the effect is due to differences in the density of air itself as it is locally or unevenly heated. Similar effects can be observed in liquids, as when mixing hypo concentrate with water, pouring hot water into cold, or allowing an ice cube to melt in still water. In every case the effect observed results from the deflection of the light rays in their passage from the subject to your eye and the consequent distortion of the image.

Refraction is influenced by color

Refraction of light is influenced by its color. The longer wavelengths of light, which we perceive as oranges and reds, are bent less sharply by a change in medium than are the shorter bluish waves. The classic demonstration of this effect involves passing a white light ray through a glass prism (Fig. 16.3). The ray is bent twice in the same direction as it passes through the prism's two air-glass interfaces so that the ray is deviated from its original direction of travel. White light contains all the spectrum colors, and since the cool colors are bent more sharply than the warm ones, the colors tend to separate, forming a rainbow pattern. In nature the rainbow itself results from the refraction of sunlight and the consequent dispersion of the colors by water droplets in the atmosphere.

The rainbow results from dispersion of colors

If two similar prisms are placed base-to-base, and parallel light beams are allowed to strike their adjacent faces, the emerging light will converge, or focus at some position in space (Fig. 16.4). The zone of focus is not a point because each of the beams is deflected in only one plane and the intersecting planes form a line.

Figure 16.3

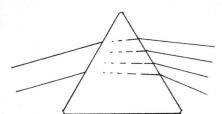

Figure 16.4

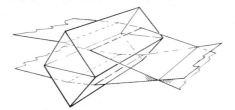

Figure 16.5

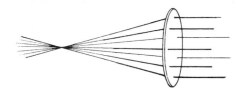

Focus at a point can be achieved by rounding the prism faces into spherical curves, and when this process is carried out to its logical extreme, a lens is formed (Fig. 16.5).

Focus at a point can be achieved by a lens

Simple lenses may be designed to converge light to a *real* image or to diverge, or spread, light rays. The familiar reading glass, or burning glass, is a good example of the converging, or *positive* lens. The artists' reducing glass is about the only well-known example of the simple *negative* lens. The image seen in the negative lens, reduced in size but brilliant, is called a *virtual* image. It appears to be floating in space and cannot be made to focus on a screen.

Real and virtual images

Positive lenses are thicker in the middle than at their edges; negative lenses are thin in the center with thicker edges. Both types are made in several forms: positive lenses (Fig. 16.6a,) with one face flat and one face bulging out (plano-convex); both faces convex (Fig. 16.6b), or one convex and the other weakly hollowed (convex-concave, Fig. 16.6c). Negative lenses may have one plane and one concave face (plano-concave, Fig. 16.6d); both faces concave (Fig. 16.6e); or one face concave and the other weakly convex (concave-convex, Fig. 16.6f).

Positive lenses are thick in the middle; negative lenses are thin

Lenses in which both faces curve the same way (Figs. 16.6c, f) are called *meniscus* lenses.

Meniscus lenses

Lenses of different types may be combined to form a *lens system*. The individual pieces of glass, singly or arranged in unified groups, are often called *elements* of the lens. In some technical literature, they are also sometimes called *glasses*, and the term "element" may be used to describe a group of two or more glasses mounted as a unit. More commonly a unit of this kind is called a *group*, and a major assembly of the completed lens which can be removed as a unit is called a *component*. The terms, as you can see, are used rather loosely and interchangeably.

Elements, glasses, groups, and components

Figure 16.6

a   b   c   d   e   f

Figure 16.7

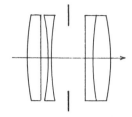

Lens groups which are composed of glasses whose faces are glued together by some sort of transparent bonding material are called *cemented* groups or elements. Uncemented elements, mounted together, make an *air-spaced* group. A complete lens may consist of, for example, four elements, or glasses, arranged in three groups, in two components (Fig. 16.7). The front component of this lens (a Tessar-type arrangement) is airspaced. The rear component is cemented. When one component of the lens can be used alone, the lens is called a *convertible* lens.

Simple lenses are unsatisfactory because of aberrations

Simple lenses can be used in photography, but the images which they can form are not very satisfactory because of inherent defects called *aberrations.*

One of the most common is spherical aberration

One of the most common and troublesome is *spherical aberration* (Figs. 16.8, 16.9) which causes the light rays passing through the margins of the lens to be refracted more sharply than they should be to converge with the central rays. The result is a diffused zone of focus rather than a well-defined plane. No possible focusing adjustment can produce a sharp image of all these rays on the film surface. Since the effect is more pronounced

Figure 16.8

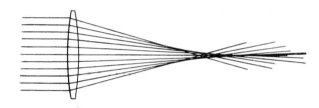

Figure 16.9 Spherical aberration is responsible for the soft-sharp quality of this photograph. This picture was made at the lens' maximum aperture (f/2.9). When stopped down to f/4, or farther, it is quite sharp.

Figure 16.10

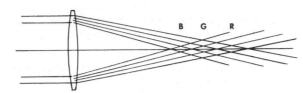

 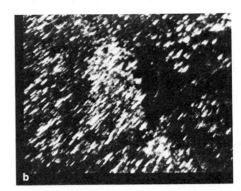

Figure 16.11 These enlarged details from the corners of a transparency show how the lens focused red light (*a*) and blue light (*b*). Some of the blue streaking is probably due to ultraviolet light and could have been reduced somewhat by using a "skylight" (Wratten 1A) filter over the camera lens. In the color transparency, and prints made from it, the streaks show as red-yellow blobs with sharp blue tails (see back colorplate, p. 354).

near the margins of the lens where the glass curvature is greatest, it often can be overcome to a satisfactory degree by stopping the lens down, thus excluding the marginal rays. Some loss of image light results.

The *chromatic aberrations* (Figs. 16.10, 16.11 and see back colorplate, p. 354) cause blurring of the image in black-and-white photography and color fringing in color photography. Due to the dispersion of the spectrum colors during white light refraction, the defect is inherent in the design and construction of the lens and cannot be cured by stopping down, although the increased *depth of focus* thus obtained may improve the apparent image sharpness. Lenses in which color correction has been carried out for two colors are adequate for general work and are called *achromats*. Lenses with full three-color correction for exacting work are called *apochromats*.

The chromatic aberrations cause blurring and color fringing

Astigmatism afflicts lenses as well as the human eye and may not be eliminated by stopping down, although the blurring of the image is reduced at small apertures. An astigmatic lens distinguishes between lines radiating from the image center and lines perpendicular to them and will not form them both sharply on a single plane. A classic example is the image of a wagon wheel in the exact center of the lens field. An astigmatic lens, if focused on the wheel spokes, will blur the circle of the tire (Fig. 16.12*a*). If focused on the tire, the image of the spokes will be blurred (Fig. 16.12*b*). The lens cannot be adjusted to focus sharply and simultaneously on both radial and tangential lines. The effect of astigmatism, and most of the other aberrations, is most severe near the edges of the lens field.

Astigmatism afflicts lenses as well as the human eye

Figure 16.12

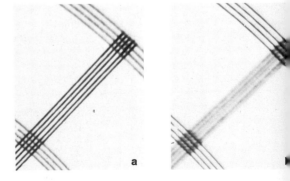

Distortion, sometimes referred to as *linear distortion* or *curvelinear distortion*, takes two forms, *pincushion* and *barrel*. The image of a window frame, as it might be affected by these aberrations, is shown in Figure 16.13. Distortion is seldom noticeable in "normal" lenses of moderate aperture unless they are used for extreme closeups. Telephoto and wide-

Distortion; pincushion and barrel

Figure 16.13

a   b

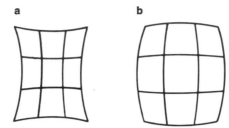

Figure 16.14   Distortion is a design feature of "fish-eye" lenses. This is what extreme barrel distortion does to a casement window.

angle lenses, zoom lenses, and normal lenses of extreme speed will usually show some signs of distortion. The effect is most noticeable in lines which lie parallel to and close to the picture edges. Lenses of nearly symmetrical construction are likely to be relatively free from distortion, or *rectilinear*. Distortion is deliberately emphasized in "fish-eye" lenses for effects typified by Figure 16.14.

Coma does not affect the axial rays

Coma is somewhat like spherical aberration but affects light rays passing diagonally through the lens margins. It does not affect the lens *axial* rays. While it does cause a general blurring of the image, the image details appear to be more smeared than diffused, and the image may have a kind of exploding-from-the-center appearance. Bright image highlights may appear comet-shaped (Fig. 16.15) with the size and length of the comet tail depending upon the severity of the aberration, the accuracy of image focus, the aperture size, and the position of the highlight in the lens field (the effect is much more pronounced near the edges of the field). Coma is common in speed lenses but can usually be effectively subdued by stopping down.

All lenses are afflicted by field curvature

All lenses are afflicted to some degree by the problem of *field curvature*. In simplest form this means that the image is formed on a bowl-shaped plane rather than a flat plane (Fig. 16.16). Pictures taken with such a lens can never be uniformly sharp all over, and the usual effect is a relatively sharp center area and blurred corners and edges. If the focus is adjusted, it is possible to bring the corners into focus, but then the center will be found to be soft. Stopping down to quite small apertures may mask this effect by increasing the *depth of focus* but at the expense of lost lens speed.

It may become a problem at close-range

Most good lenses have been designed to produce a reasonably flat field, but curvature may become a problem if a lens designed for general purpose work is used for close-up photography, particularly if the subject is a flat plane and the lens must be used relatively wide open. For this reason, enlarger lenses which must project a flat negative onto the flat paper surface, are particularly well corrected for field curvature and are designed for use under rather specific limits of magnification.

Figure 16.15 Here coma is used purposely to form these decorative candle "flames."

Figure 16.16

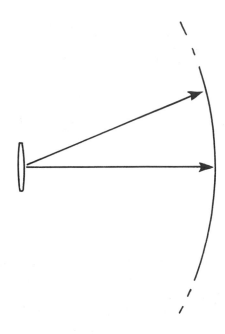

Field curvature, and some of the other aberrations as well, might be objectionable if an enlarger lens were used for normal photography at infinity; and for the same reason, the use of a camera lens in an enlarger is a risky procedure. It is best to use the lenses for their intended purposes if optimum image quality is required.

While it is not properly called an aberration, *flare* is a serious problem in some lenses. Flare refers to stray light, not part of the focused image, which reaches the film and fogs it. Probably most of the flare in a typical lens results from reflections which occur at each lens element surface. Some flare light results from dust or greasy films on the lens surfaces, and chipped, cracked, or scratched lens elements are also likely causes (Fig. 16.17).

Flare is serious in some lenses

Figure 16.17 You have to try hard to produce this kind of flare with modern coated lenses, but it's possible. The smaller spots, spaced randomly around the flare pattern, are caused by dust spots on the front surface of the lens, glowing in the sunlight. To avoid problems like this keep the lens free from dust particles and always keep the lens shaded so that direct light cannot strike it.

It can be reduced by using a lens shade

Practically, flare can be reduced substantially if light from outside the subject area can be prevented from entering the lens. *Lens hoods* or *sunshades* are intended to accomplish this. A very considerable reduction in flare, and a consequent increase in light transmission, image contrast, and color purity can be achieved if the air-to-glass surfaces of the various lens elements are coated with a very thin film of certain metallic salts. The coating is transparent but appears colored in reflected light for the same reason that an oil film on water appears colored; it is less than a wavelength of light thick, and therefore absorbs certain colors by internal reflection and cancellation.

Coating increases contrast and color purity

It was a major breakthrough in lens technology

Uncoated lenses are supposed to waste about 5 percent of their incident light per air-to-glass surface. When you consider the fact that a modern *zoom* lens may contain fifteen or more elements, most of them uncemented, it is obvious that lens coating techniques represented a major breakthrough in lens technology when they were first introduced in the 1930s. Previous to this the most successful high quality lenses were either composed of few elements and were therefore necessarily very slow, or they were assembled from cemented elements which minimized flare by reducing the number of the air-to-glass surfaces.

Multiple-coating layers can be tuned

In recent years a technique for applying multiple coatings to instrument lens surfaces has been adapted for use on camera lenses. Since each coating layer can only suppress a relatively narrow band of light color with real efficiency a conventionally coated lens may still produce objectionable flare patterns of colored light. Multiple-coating layers, each "tuned" to control a specific band of the spectrum, can reduce total flare dramatically with no apparent ill effects on the image. When "multicoating" was first announced it was easy to infer from the glowing test reports and from advertising claims, that the more coating layers a lens possessed the better was its performance. It is now apparent that not every surface of every lens needs to be multiple-coated. Virtually all manufacturers are now applying multiple layers of coating to some surfaces of most of their lenses; the number, shape, refractive index, and arrangement of the glass lens elements determining the coating requirements. The improvement in contrast and color purity that multiple coating brings out is startling in some lenses, the only apparent penalty being their moderate increase in cost.

Diffraction limits sharpness

Another phenomenon which limits the sharpness of the photographic image, but is not an aberration of the lens, is the effect of *diffraction*. Also related to the wave-nature of light, diffraction produces a kind of scattering of light rays as they pass through an aperture or close to an edge. At normal photographic lens apertures diffracted light is so small a proportion of the total film illumination that it is negligible, but as the aperture is reduced in size, diffraction becomes more and more troublesome and causes a general diffusion of the image by enlarging the image points into blurry concentric circles.

In theory at least, the sharpest image which any lens can form is produced at its widest aperture. In practice the best image sharpness results when the lens is stopped down far enough so that the reduced aperture size and increased depth of focus reduce the effect of the various aberrations, but not so far that diffraction becomes a problem. In general purpose lenses, this seems to be about two or three stops down from maximum aperture.

When a lens of normal construction is focused on a very distant object, considered to be at *infinity* for practical purposes, the *focal length* of the lens can be found approximately by measuring the distance from the aperture (iris diaphragm) to the image plane (Fig. 16.18). Photographers use the focal length designation of a lens more for identification than anything else, in somewhat the same way that a realtor might mention "eight room" or "six room" in describing a house; some implication of the size and the potential use is conveyed.

A so-called normal lens sees or will cover everything within about 25° of its axis or a field of perhaps 50° total. This establishes the "normal" relationship between image size and focal length. In general "normal" lenses will cover a film size whose diagonal measurement is from about 90 percent to 100 percent of the focal length (Fig. 16.19a). If the lens is designed to cover a much larger field than normal, it is called a *wide-field* or *wide-angle* lens (Fig. 16.19b).

Wide-angle lenses are sometimes referred to as *short* lenses because their focal lengths are shorter than normal. *Long* lenses are those whose focal lengths are greater than normal (Fig. 16.19c). A long lens may simply be an ordinary lens being used to cover a smaller-than-usual film size, or it may be of special *telephoto* construction, which means that the lens is physically rather short but its focal length is magnified by its unique optical construction.

A telephoto lens is designed to cover a relatively narrow angle, in some cases just a few degrees, so that it can never be used for "normal" coverage on any film size. A large "normal" lens will serve as a long lens on a small camera but cannot be used for wide-angle or wide-field work because of its limited coverage.

A large wide-angle lens, however, can be used as normal on a slightly smaller camera than it was designed for and will serve as a long lens for a small camera, but this is not desirable. Wide-angle construction is expensive, and the use of such a lens for other than its intended purpose is not only wasteful, but will compromise both lens speed and image quality to some degree.

Best sharpness is generally attained at about two or three stops down from maximum aperture

Figure 16.18

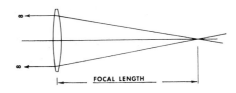

FOCAL LENGTH

Normal lenses cover about a 50° field

Wide-angle lenses are short lenses; telephotos are long lenses

It is best to use a lens for its intended purpose

Figure 16.19

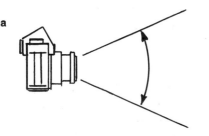
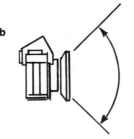
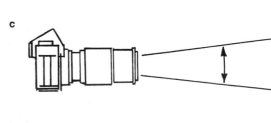

17

Depth of Field and Depth of Focus

The zone of sharpness including the subject is called the depth of field

Figure 17.1

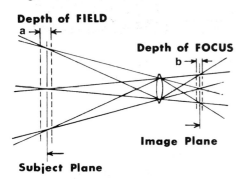

Depth of FIELD

Depth of FOCUS

Image Plane

Subject Plane

When a lens is focused on an object, there is some distance in front of the object and some behind which will also be acceptably sharp. This zone of sharpness which includes the subject is called the *depth of field* (Fig. 17.1a). Since the image is a three-dimensional replica of the subject, the subject depth of field is recreated at the image plane. In this position it is referred to as the *depth of focus* (Fig. 17.1b) because it represents a little distance through which the film can be moved without affecting the apparent sharpness of the image.

The *apparent sharpness* is the determining factor in establishing the limits of depth of field. You might compare focusing a lens to climbing a hill with the position of ultimate image sharpness analogous to the summit. If the hilltop is smooth and broadly rounded, it will be difficult to determine the exact summit as it is difficult to determine exact focus, and the definition of hilltop as distinguished from hillside may be debatable.

If you focus a view camera on some very distant point of light such as a streetlight at night or a bright metallic reflection in daylight, the focused image will appear to be a point, too small to have shape or dimension (Fig. 17.2a). Now defocus the image considerably and the point will grow into a circular blob of light called a *circle of confusion* (Fig. 17.2b). As long as the circle of confusion is visible as a circular blob, we identify it as unsharp; but when the image is focused so that the circle is too small to identify as a blob, we accept it as a point and call it *sharp*.

A defocused point will grow into a circle of confusion

The extent of the useful depth of field depends on the size of the circle of confusion which we will tolerate. If, in the demonstration above, we move the subject toward the camera until the image becomes an obvious blob, we will have established one limit of the depth of field. If we repeat the experiment, this time examining the ground-glass image with a magnifier, we will see the deterioration of the image point into a visible circle of confusion much more readily, and the limits of acceptable sharpness, the depth of field, will be found to be much closer to the central point of "perfect" focus.

Three conditions of use affect sharpness

There are at least three conditions of use which will affect the degree of sharpness necessary in the final print image. *First* is the visual acuity of the observer, and his tolerance for lack of sharpness. He may not notice or be offended by some lack of precision in the image edges. *Second*, the viewing distance of the print. Lack of sharpness will be apparent at close range but may be unobjectionable or invisible at greater viewing

Figure 17.2

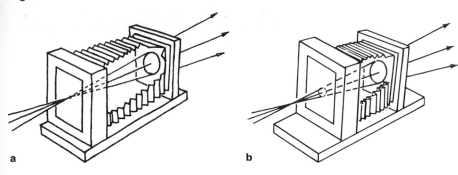

a   b

c. The out-of-focus sparkles from the surface of a sunlit pond form these decorative circles of confusion.

distances. *Third*, the magnification of the print. Image sharpness decreases as magnification increases, so a large print will appear less sharp than a small one, from any given distance.

There are two general methods of predicting the extent of the depth of field. One, useful with the view camera (and with SLRs), is visual inspection of the ground-glass image with a suitable magnifier (Fig. 17.3). The other is the use of prepared tables of depth of field or the use of the camera's own depth of field scale if one is included (Fig. 17.4). These guides will be based on some arbitrarily selected circle of confusion size and must be modified if the picture is to be viewed in some unusual way or is to be made exceptionally large or small.

Remember, however, that the transition from sharp to unsharp is a gradual one, and the boundaries of the depth of field will not be well defined. Most of your concern with depth of field will involve being sure that some object is safely included in the depth, usually with plenty of leeway, or being sure that some object or area is definitely out of focus.

**There are two methods
of predicting depth of field**

**There are three methods
for controlling depth of field**

Figure 17.3   For "grab shots" like this, depth of field tables are useless. You can judge the depth of field and the visual effect of the background blur on the ground glass of a single-lens reflex. This picture was made with a 105-mm lens on a Nikon. (Courtesy of the University of Michigan Press)

Figure 17.4

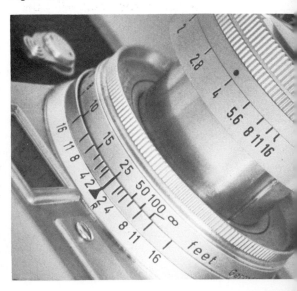

More subtle control than this will be difficult. There are three methods for controlling the extent of the depth of field. They are adjustment of the subject-to-camera-distance, selection of lens focal length, and adjustment of the camera aperture.

Distance   The depth of field of a lens focused on infinity (for objects very far away from the camera) is, by definition, infinitely great since it extends "beyond" infinity. The depth of field for objects much closer than infinity is reduced because the depth limits no longer reach infinity but become measurable. When the object approaches very close to the camera, the depth is severely restricted because the dimensions of the image itself become large relative to the acceptable circle of confusion diameter and the fixed limits of the depth of focus.

Focal length   Short lenses are said to produce greater depth of field than long ones (because long lenses produce larger images [Fig. 17.5]). Since the limits of depth of focus are fixed by the size of the acceptable circle of confusion, it is apparent that less of a large image than of a small one can be included in the satisfactorily sharp zone. Remember, however, that if the small image is enlarged to the same size as the larger one, its circles of confusion are also enlarged and effective depth of field is reduced proportionally.

Aperture   Since the circle of confusion size depends upon the angle of the converging light rays (other things being equal), and since the angle depends upon the diameter of the lens opening, it follows that reducing the aperture will reduce the size of the circle of confusion. This is why stopping down the lens of a camera will increase depth of field (Fig. 17.6). Image

Figure 17.5   The wide-angle (short focal length) lens used here provided adequate depth of field at a fairly wide relative aperture and allowed a hand-held shot in spite of poor light conditions. (Courtesy of the University of Michigan Press)

Figure 17.6   Because the subject was very close to the camera this picture was taken with a wide-angle lens and the composition planned accordingly. The camera was zone-focussed using the lens depth of field scale so that the near plane would include the foreground objects and the far plane just reached the window. A fairly small aperture (f/16) was used at a shutter speed of one second. (Courtesy of the University of Michigan Press)

circles too large to be seen as sharp at the larger aperture are reduced when the lens opening is reduced and the subject points that they represent are then seen to be in focus.

Analysis of the depth of field variables indicates that the critical factors in determining depth are the lens diameter (*linear* aperture, not *relative* aperture or f/number), focal length, subject distance, and, of course, print magnification. It is also apparent that these factors are not equally effective in controlling depth of field. Furthermore, the relationships are not simple ones; substantial changes occur at very short and very long subject distances. In general it is safe to say that, over a subject range of from **about** five focal lengths to about 500 focal lengths (about ten inches to eighty feet for the typical 35-mm camera normal lens) the relationships are quite stable and, depth of field will vary uniformly as follows:

Their basic relationships

1. Depth varies *inversely* with lens diameter
2. Depth varies *inversely* with focal length
3. Depth varies *directly* with the *square* of the distance
4. Depth varies *inversely* with print magnification
5. Depth varies *directly* with print viewing distance

Depth advantage comparison

Rephrasing the statements above to be a little more specific, we might say, for example, that "doubling lens diameter halves depth," "doubling focal length halves depth," "doubling distance quadruples depth," "doubling print size halves depth," and "doubling viewing distance doubles depth." Since these factors may either aid or oppose each other in determining the ultimate effective depth in the print it is convenient to examine their effects by giving them *depth advantage* numbers. For example, since a 50-mm lens will give twice as much depth as a 100-mm lens (all other things equal, of course) let's rate the 50-mm lens at "2" and the 100-mm lens at "1." Similarly, an aperture diameter of 30-mm would rate "2" compared to a 60-mm aperture ("1") and, by the same standard, an aperture of 15-mm diameter would rate "4."

The example in Figures 17.7*a*, *b*, and *c* may help to clarify this concept. Here the same lens was used at a fixed distance but the aperture was varied. Which setting should provide the greatest depth?

Focal length and distance constant; aperture varied

	Figure 17.7a	Figure 17.7b	Figure 17.7c
F.L.	125 mm	125 mm	125 mm
Diam.	15.6 mm	7.8 mm	3.9 mm
Dist.	4 ft	4 ft	4 ft
Mag.	4 x	4 x	4 x
Focal length advantage	1	1	1
Diameter advantage	1	2	4
Distance advantage	1	1	1
Magnification advantage	1	1	1

(Multiplying) Totals: $1 \times 1 \times 1 \times 1 = 1$ $1 \times 2 \times 1 \times 1 = 2$ $1 \times 4 \times 1 \times 1 = 4$

Figure 17.7

a. Focal length: 125 mm. Aperture diameter: 15.6 mm. Subject distance: 4 feet. Print magnification: 4 diameters.

b. Focal length: 125 mm. Aperture diameter: 7.8 mm. Subject distance: 4 feet. Print magnification: 4 diameters.

c. Focal length: 125 mm. Aperture diameter: 3.9 mm. Subject distance: 4 feet. Print magnification: 4 diameters.

d. Focal length: 125 mm. Aperture diameter: 15.6 mm. Subject distance: 8 feet. Print magnification: 8 diameters.

According to our calculations Figure 17.7c should show the greatest depth and visual inspection of the prints bears this out.

The effect of image magnification

Figure 17.7d illustrates the same lens, working at an aperture diameter of 15.6 mm, at a distance of 8 ft, with 8× magnification (to keep the image details similar in scale). How does its depth compare with the other examples? Again using Figure 17.7a as a standard of comparison, the "advantages" of Figure 17.7d look like this:

Focal Length Advantage	(125mm)	1
Diameter Advantage	(15.6mm)	1
Distance Advantage	(8 ft)	4
Magnification Advantage	(8×)	.5

Multiplying, 1×1×4×.5 = 2, so we would expect Figure 17.7d to exhibit depth similar to Figure 17.7b. In spite of the fact that the position of the plane of sharpest focus is not quite the same in the two prints it is apparent that their depths are essentially identical.

If the aperture diameters of two lenses are the same and if they are used at the same distance from the subject and if the resulting negative images are enlarged to provide prints of identical scale, the depths of field will be the same. This is illustrated, in an extreme example, in Figures 17.8a and 17.8b. A 500-mm lens and a 50-mm lens, each working with an aperture diameter of about 11 mm (f/45 and f/4.5, respectively) were used at a subject distance of 32 feet. The 50-mm image is enlarged ten diameters more than the 500-mm image so that the image scale is the same in both photographs.

Figure 17.8
a. Focal length: 500 mm.
   Aperture diameter: 11
   mm. (f/45). Enlargement:
   4×. Time: 20 secs.
   Subject distance: 32 feet.
b. Focal length: 50 mm.
   Aperture diameter: 11
   mm. (f/4.5) Enlargement:
   40×. Time 1/5 sec.
   Subject distance: 32 feet.

In this situation the depth of field advantages work out like this:

	Figure 17.8a	*Figure 17.8b*
F.L.	500 mm	50 mm
Diam.	11 mm	11 mm
Dist.	32 ft	32 ft
Mag.	4×	40×
Focal length advantage	1	10
Diameter advantage	1	1
Distance advantage	1	1
Magnification advantage	10	1
(Multiplying) Totals:	1×1×1×10 = 10	10×1×1×1 = 10

Aperture and distance constant; focal length and magnification varied

The depths of field are obviously similar but the enlarged image is so degraded by its greater magnification and the texture of the film grain that it is difficult to appraise it for sharpness. In spite of the fact that the

Figure 17.9
a. 90-mm lens, 16″, f/11, 8 mm.
b. 180-mm lens, 32″, f/11, 16 mm.
c. 360-mm lens, 64″, f/11, 33 mm.

shorter lens, working at f/4.5, permitted a considerable speed advantage (⅕ second compared to 20 seconds for the long lens at f/45), it is only a technical victory, the image is worthless for any purpose other than demonstration. Thus, while short lenses do indeed provide greater depth at higher speed than long lenses do, this "advantage" must be weighed against image quality; in some cases the short lens will be preferable, in some cases it will not be usable.

Figures 17.9 a, b, and c show identical depths of field produced by three different focal lengths, three different aperture diameters (although the f/numbers are the same), and three different subject distances. Here are the depth advantages that each situation provides:

Other variations and how they effect depth

	Figure 17.9a	*Figure 17.9b*	*Figure 17.9c*
F.L.	90 mm	180 mm	360 mm
Diam.	8 mm	16 mm	33 mm
Dist.	16 in.	32 in.	64 in.
F.L. advantage	4	2	1
Diam. advantage	4	2	1
Dist. advantage	1	4	16
(Multiplying) Totals:	$4\times4\times1 = 16$	$2\times2\times4 = 16$	$1\times1\times16 = 16$

The depths of field as computed and confirmed by inspection of the images, are essentially identical.

SUMMARY

For minimum depth of field	For maximum depth of field
Get close to subject	Back away from subject
Use a long lens	Use a short focal length lens
Shoot wide open	Stop lens all the way down
Enlarge to giant size	Make a contact print
View print at close range	View print at a distance
Be critical of sharpness	Accept slight softness of detail

From the discussion above, it can be concluded that there are two general considerations in controlling depth of field: (1) aperture diameter, and (2) any factor which affects the image size as it is ultimately viewed, such as, lens focal length, subject distance, print magnification, and print viewing distance. Of these last factors, the most effective is the subject distance. Varying it will give you the most dramatic single control that is available.

The hyperfocal distance is of some interest

Although the mathematical calculation of depth of field is not important to the average photographer, one of the constants involved is of some interest. It is the hyperfocal distance, and it is expressed as follows:

$$\text{Hyperfocal distance (h)} = \frac{F^2}{fc} \text{ or } \frac{Fd}{c}$$

where F = focal length, f = relative aperture, d = aperture diameter, and c = the circle of confusion diameter, expressed as a fraction of the focal length, as, for example: F/2000.

The hyperfocal distance can be defined as the distance to the nearest plane of the depth of field when the lens is focused at infinity. Also, when the lens is focused on the hyperfocal distance, the depth of field extends from half the hyperfocal distance to infinity.

A fairly simple method of computing the hyperfocal distance is to multiply the lens aperture diameter by the denominator of the circle of confusion fraction (c in the expressions above). For example, if the circle of confusion selected is 1/1000 of the focal length, or F/1000, and aperture diameter is ¼″, the hyperfocal distance is ¼″ × 1000, or 250″ or about 21 feet.

Charts and tables are of questionable usefulness

Depth of field tables and charts are interesting to look at but their usefulness is questionable. In the first place, as mentioned before, depth of field depends upon the tolerance of the photographer for lack of sharpness. It is impossible to point to a particular line in the subject position and say "up to this line the subject is not acceptably sharp; beyond this line it is acceptably sharp," because the transition from "soft" to "sharp" is so gradual. Depth of field is also dependent upon the enlargement of the image and upon the conditions of print viewing. At the moment of film exposure these factors are intangibles.

Depth of field scales are purposely made rather vague

For these reasons, and others like them, depth of field tables are seldom consulted for normal work. They are sometimes valuable for work involving extreme close-up photography or other unusual situations. Most cameras are now equipped with depth of field scales integral with the focusing rings of the lens. Although they are purposely made rather vague to avoid implying that real precision is possible they are helpful in many instances, especially if the camera is not designed to permit inspection of the focused image directly.

Zone focusing is a useful technique

Perhaps the most useful application of the scales is in *zone focusing*. Zone focusing is a technique resorted to when the subject's position cannot be predicted with precision, and when it is necessary to shoot very rapidly. In most situations of this kind, it is possible to estimate the general area in which the subject will appear, and the camera can be set, by consulting the depth of field scale, to cover the desired range (Fig. 17.10). Suppose, for example, that you are photographing an automobile road race and have planted yourself at a difficult corner in anticipation of a spectacular skid or spin. You can't know for sure just where the action will occur, or even if it will occur, but you can select a general area of the road shoulder and the field outside where a spinning car is likely to go.

Let's assume that you are using a Hasselblad camera, and that the lens you select to cover the action area is the 150-mm telephoto. The film you are using, the light conditions at the corner, and the shutter speed you will need dictate a camera setting of 1/250 second at f/16.

First, focus the camera at some detail in the road which you consider to represent the nearest point of possible action and make a note of the distance indicated on the focusing scale (assume it to be thirty feet for purposes of illustration). Now focus on the farthest point of interest, and let's suppose it to be 100 feet. Now simply place the two distances astrad-

Figure 17.10   This picture was made with a 35-mm lens used at f/11 and "zone focused" at the hyperfocal distance—in this case, about 11 feet. The depth of field, from about 5 1/2 feet to infinity, easily includes this old couple and the entire length of the stadium without further adjustment. (Courtesy of the University of Michigan Press)

dle the focusing mark on the lens mount so that they are equally spaced between the depth of field indicating pointers (Fig. 17.11), and the camera is set to record a usefully sharp image of anything that happens between the two extremes. The position of sharpest focus happens to occur at about forty-six feet in this case, but this fact is of no real significance.

Scales and tables may not agree

If this same problem were to be solved with the aid of the charts which follow (Figs. 17.12a, b), the depth of field would seem to be substantially greater because the charts are based on a larger circle of confusion size than the lens calibrations are, and the necessary enlargement of the 2¼-

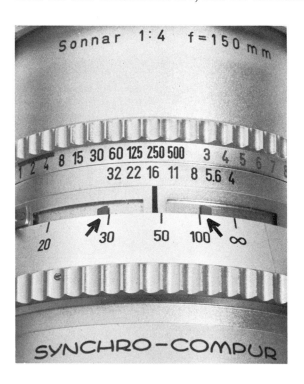

Figure 17.11

Figure 17.12

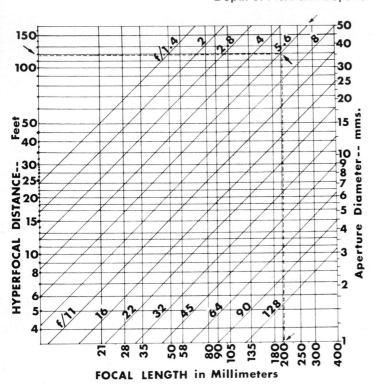

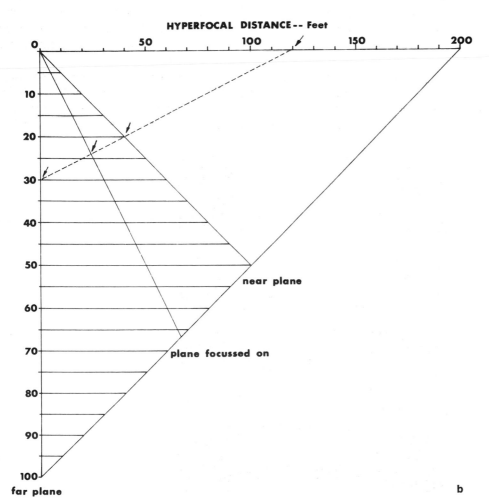

inch square negative requires an increase in the hyperfocal distance as well. This dissimilarity in results is not at all uncommon, and simply points out the general unreliability of depth of field calibrations taken from different sources or out of specific context. Take tables of this kind with a grain of salt, and when the tables and the lens mount calibrations differ, it is usually best to believe the lens markings, but not without some reservations.

With this warning, here are some charts

With this warning the preceding tables are printed to demonstrate the relationships of the focal length, aperture, hyperfocal distance, and the planes of the depth of field. These charts will provide useful depth information for any lens if used intelligently.

First, find the hyperfocal distance of your lens on chart (Fig. 17.12a) as follows:

1. Locate the lens focal length in millimeters on the bottom line. (One inch equals approximately twenty-five millimeters.)
2. Read straight up until you come to the diagonal line which corresponds to the aperture you plan to use.
3. Then read to the left to find the hyperfocal distance on the left margin. The dotted line example on the chart shows a lens of 200-mm focal length being used at an aperture of f/5.6 and indicates a hyperfocal distance of 120 feet.

Now, referring to chart (Fig. 17.12b), locate the hyperfocal distance of the lens on the top line, then connect this point with the distance focused on, extending the line to cross the "far plane" line of the chart. The limits of the effective depth of field are now indicated on the "near plane" and "far plane" lines.

The example shows that a lens whose hyperfocal distance is 120 feet, if focused at twenty-four feet, will provide a depth of field of from twenty to thirty feet.

These charts are based on a circle of confusion of F/1000 and will give useful information for lenses of normal focal length when the full length (longest dimension) of the negative is printed to approximately 8 inches, by enlargement or reduction if necessary. Wide-angle and long focus or telephoto lenses will not work reliably with this chart information as given. To use them determine the ratio of their focal lengths to the camera "normal" focal length and multiply the given hyperfocal distance by that factor.

For example, if the 200-mm lens in the illustration given above were not a "normal" lens (as it would be for a 5″ × 7″ view camera, for instance) but was used on a 35-mm camera, it would be considered a 5× telephoto, and its hyperfocal distance would have to be multiplied by at least 5×. The reason for this is, as mentioned above, the assumption that the finished image will measure 8 inches along its longest dimension. Thus a picture taken with a 200-mm "normal" lens would need little or no enlargement, since the negative would be 5″ × 7″, and its circle of confusion would be very nearly 1/100-inch on the negative. The 200-mm lens for a

35-mm camera, however, would cover a format of only about $1'' \times 1\frac{1}{2}''$ and would have to be enlarged at least five times to reach the "standard" print size. It would, therefore, require a much smaller circle of confusion size to withstand the greater magnification. Since the normal focal length of a 35-mm camera is about 40 to 50 mm (50 mm is actually slightly "long" for 35-mm film), the focal length ratio is roughly proportional to the print magnification.

If you intend to use this chart information for pictures to be printed larger than $6'' \times 8''$ increase the hyperfocal distance in proportion to the enlargement increase. Thus, an $11'' \times 14''$ enlargement, approximately twice the standard size, would require doubling the hyperfocal distance.

When there is no chance to get it again, get it right the first time with a **GOERZ DAGOR**

18

You may feel restricted by the normal lens on your camera

As you gain proficiency in photography, you may begin to feel restricted by the normal lens on your camera. You may wish you could select a relatively small area of the subject and fill your whole negative with it or take a full 90° sweep of landscape in one exposure. You may admire the dramatically emphasized perspective "distortions" or the flattened-out plane-on-plane effects which are commonly displayed in the popular magazines. These are effects which can only be achieved satisfactorily with lenses other than normal.

Changing film size will alter the effective angular coverage of the lens

To be useful any lens must form an image circle of good quality large enough to cover the film; but even if the image circle is considerably larger than necessary, the effective image area is only as great as the film area, and the lens effective angular coverage is determined by the film diagonal. Changing film sizes with a given lens, therefore, will alter the effective angular coverage of the lens. Thus, substituting a 35-mm film for the normal 4″ × 5″ film in a view camera will reduce the effective angular coverage of the normal 6″ lens from about 55° to about 15°, and the picture will be identical to one taken with a 35-mm camera equipped with a 150-mm telephoto lens.

The same effective angular coverage and perspective effect will result if you simply print a small portion of an existing negative. For example, printing the central 1″ × 1½″ area of a 4″ × 5″ negative taken with a 6″ lens will again duplicate the results obtainable with a 35-mm camera using a telephoto of the same focal length.

Any camera lens will produce the same perspective, as long as . . .

In fact any camera lens except the *fisheye* will produce the same perspective effect as any other, as long as they are all used from the same position and their images are enlarged or reduced to the same scale. The only major differences will be in the total area covered and the variations in sharpness due to the greater enlargement of some of the images.

For example, suppose some subject is photographed from the same spot with a 24″ telephoto for 4″ × 5″ film and a 19-mm wide-angle for 35-mm. The telephoto covers a field of about 14°; the wide-angle covers almost 100°. Naturally, the telephoto image will show only a small part of the subject area (Fig. 18.1a); the wide-angle image will be minute but will represent a very large area (Fig. 18.1b). In order to bring the two images to the same scale, it will be necessary to enlarge the small negative to about 32″ × 48″ or about 32 diameters (equal to the ratio of the focal lengths, 19 mm to 600 mm, approximately).

Figure 18.1

a. The 24″ lens covers a subject field of about 14° and renders details sharply. The exposure was 1/25 second at f/22.

b. The 19-mm lens covers a subject field of almost 100°, but the 14° field of the longer lens is rendered invisibly small (inside black outline). When this area is enlarged to match the 4″ × 5″ contact print it is apparent that the perspective is identical but the detail rendering is very poor. The exposure was 1/250 second at f/8.

c. The 19-mm lens image enlarged. This section of its image represents about 14° of the subject field.

Now the central 4″ × 5″ area of the enlarged wide-angle print will be identical in perspective to the 4″ × 5″ contact print from the longer lens image (Fig. 18.1c), and if both prints are viewed from a distance of twenty-four inches, both will appear normal and undistorted, because from this viewing distance the eye occupies the same position relative to the image that the lens occupied relative to the subject in taking the picture.

Figure 18.2 An example of perspective "distortion" which results from viewing a photograph from the "wrong" distance. Because the lens was placed close to Charlie's head to make this picture it must be viewed similarly to appear normal. Put your eye about an inch away from this picture to see Charlie as he really is.

Figure 18.3 The wide-angle lens used to make this picture emphasizes the size of the foreground figure and increases the apparent size of the room by "forcing" the perspective. (Courtesy of the University of Michigan Press)

2.5

Note: Correct viewing distance for normal perspective in Figures 18.3 through 18.7 is given in inches in a lower corner of each picture.

The so-called *distortion* of perspective will become apparent in both images if they are viewed from other distances. Realistic perspective will result only when the viewing distance equals the product of the lens focal length and the print magnification ratio. Thus, a picture taken with a 2″ lens and enlarged 10 diameters should be viewed from a distance of 20″; a picture taken with a 12″ lens and enlarged 4 diameters should be seen from 48″.

If unreal perspective is desired . . .

Figure 18.4 The apparent compression of subject space by lenses of long focal length is well illustrated here. Although these football players seem to be running over each other, they were actually well spread out over the practice field. (Courtesy of the University of Michigan Press)

If dramatically unreal perspective is desired, these relationships should be varied rather drastically, a slight change will simply make the picture look awkward. If you want the emphasized perspective effect of deep space, sharply converging perspective lines, and unusually large foreground objects, commonly called "wide-angle distortion," present a wide-angle image to the viewer so that he must see it from three or four times the "correct" viewing distance (Fig. 18.2). This will place him in an impossible position relative to the image perspective, and he will be strongly conscious of the visual contradiction (Fig. 18.3).

60

40   **3**

Figure 18.5 If you move up close to some object with a short lens and back away with a long lens you can make the object appear the same size in both pictures, as the tree trunk does here. The relative sizes of other objects in the picture space will not be the same, however, because size relationships and perspective effects are solely a function of camera-to-subject distance. Although these variations in size relationship are often called "distortion" they are no such thing. Each picture here represents accurately the view you would see if you were to stand where the camera was held in making the pictures.

To dramatize the *telephoto effect* show the viewer a narrow-field picture at very close range, perhaps one-third or one-fourth the "proper" distance (Fig. 18.4). From this position relative to the picture, he will be impressed by the unnaturally shallow space, the diminution of the perspective convergence, and the relatively enormous size of distant objects (Fig. 18.5).

There is nothing magic, therefore, about the image perspective formed by any given lens type. Any lens which forms an image field of adequate extent can be used for wide-angle work (Fig. 18.6), just as any lens of great enough focal length can be used for telephoto pictures. In practice, however, it is unlikely that any lens not specifically designed for wide-

Figure 18.7 This view of the runner could only be seen from the grandstand. The long telephoto lens used here produced a large, well-detailed picture of the runner himself and calls attention to a striking arrangement of lines which would have been insignificant in a normal-lens photograph from the same position. (Courtesy of the University of Michigan Press)

Figure 18.6 Another example of foreground emphasis by the wide-angle lens. In using telephoto lenses, it is convenient to separate forms by selective focusing—isolating a plane of sharp focus between areas of soft focus. The great depth of field provided by wide-angle lenses, on the other hand, demands other compositional devices. This vertical arrangement of forms in the picture space is one such device. (Courtesy of the University of Michigan Press)

2   **30**

angle photography would be very satisfactory for that use, and it is also true that real telephoto lenses have certain advantages over long lenses of ordinary construction for telephoto work (Fig. 18.7).

The term telephoto is correctly applied only to certain lenses

Although the term *telephoto* is often used to describe any lens of longer-than-normal focal length, it is correctly applied only to certain types of long lenses. A true telephoto lens functions somewhat like a telescope or a pair of binoculars, effectively magnifying the image. It consists of two groups of elements, widely separated—the front component positive and the rear component negative. The light path through a typical telephoto is shown in Figure 18.8b. Figure 18.8a diagrams the action of a lens of normal construction of the same relative aperture and focal length.

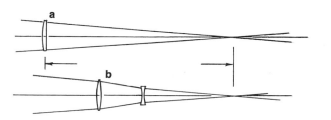

Figure 18.8

Telephoto construction gives certain advantages

Telephoto construction gives certain advantages over long normal construction. One advantage is the telephotos' smaller size. They are usually about three-fourths the length of a comparable normal lens and may be even less. For 35-mm cameras this short length is a particular benefit. The camera remains relatively compact, balances well, and can be hand-held with reasonable ease.

The inherently restricted field of the telephoto is also considered to be an advantage. A long lens of normal construction admits a great deal of light which is not part of the useful image. In spite of internal light traps and the matte black interior finish of the lens barrel, this excess light must certainly contribute to flare and resultant low contrast. The telephoto design restricts much of this side light and is said to produce images of superior contrast, when well designed. Whether this is true in practice is debatable but there is no doubt that excluding extraneous light is, in itself, desirable.

Telephotos also have inherent disadvantages

Telephotos also have their inherent disadvantages. They are not necessarily lighter in weight than normal lenses of the same focal length and aperture; in fact, they sometimes contain very thick glass elements and are distinctly heavy. But their greatest drawback is in their optical quality. They seem to be especially likely to suffer from certain of the aberrations, particularly distortion and the chromatic aberrations. This problem is not as serious as it would be if they were required to cover a wide field, but it is a limiting factor.

Telephoto lenses of moderate speed can be corrected very adequately and are generally completely satisfactory, but wide aperture telephotos are both rare and expensive. In general, the image circle formed by one of these lenses is only slightly larger than the intended film size, and its quality deteriorates rapidly past that edge. It is unwise, therefore, to use a telephoto (on a view camera) with any of the shifts and swings.

The long lenses for 35-mm cameras are generally of normal construction up to about 90 mm. From 90 mm on up to 500 mm or so, telephoto construction is the rule, but some of the longer lenses are simple achromatic doublets—two glasses, one positive, one negative; sometimes cemented, sometimes air-spaced. These simple lenses function very satisfactorily in this application because of their very narrow angular coverage and their moderate maximum aperture (rarely faster than f/5.6 or f/8.0). They are very light in weight, of course, but as bulky as a normally constructed lens, and the name brands are surprisingly expensive. A typical doublet is shown in Figure 18.9.

Very long lenses may be simple achromatic doublets

Figure 18.9

In recent years the *mirror* telephotos have become quite popular. Mirror systems can be designed to converge light just as a lens does except that the convergence results from reflection from a concave surface rather than refraction through a convex lens. Because it does not refract light, a mirror is inherently free from the chromatic aberrations. Mirrors are lighter and more compact than refracting lenses of the same speed, and their accuracy can be excellent, as evidenced by the fact that they are widely used in astronomical telescopes.

Mirror telephotos have become quite popular

A typical mirror telephoto system is diagrammed in Figure 18.10. Light enters the system through a large front lens which corrects spherical aberration and helps to flatten the image field. It is then reflected from the main concave mirror, and the beam is converged onto a smaller mirror cemented to the back of the corrector lens. The beam then passes through a baffled opening to the camera body. In some designs another lens is incorporated into the rear opening. A system of lenses and mirrors such as this is sometimes referred to as a *catadioptric* system.

Figure 18.10

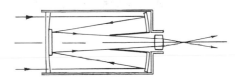

Mirrors have some interesting characteristics. They cannot be stopped down in the conventional manner because there is no practical place to put the diaphragm. Although it is possible to restrict the light intensity by simply covering part of the front glass, mirror lenses are usually used wide open, and the exposure is controlled with the shutter adjustment or with neutral density filters. Depth of field is, of course, shallow at close range, but this is often an advantage.

They cannot be stopped down in the conventional manner

It is characteristic of mirror lenses that their out-of-focus images dissolve into circles of confusion which have black centers (Fig. 18.11). These light doughnuts are blurred images of the front element with its opaque mirror insert. Precisely the same effect can be achieved with a conventional lens if a circle of black paper is stuck to the center of the front element and the lens is not stopped down.

Their out-of-focus images dissolve into light doughnuts

Wide-angle lenses are even more difficult to correct than are telephotos because all the aberrations become more severe and more difficult to deal with away from the center of the image, and it is obvious that increasing the angular coverage of the lens very greatly must necessarily cause vexing problems for the designer.

Wide-angle lenses are even more difficult to correct

Wide-angle lenses of only moderately wide coverage and relatively slow speed (small maximum aperture) are apparently no great problem. There are many excellent lenses in various focal lengths covering from 60° to perhaps 80° at apertures of from about f/3.5 to f/6.3 or so, and they are

Figure 18.11 The light "doughnuts" shown here are the circles of confusion formed by a mirror telephoto lens. They were caused by out-of-focus highlights on a distant object.

not particularly expensive. Such lenses are usually relatively simply constructed of from four to six glasses and are generally symmetrical, or nearly so, in arrangement. A few representative types are diagrammed in Figure 18.12.

If either a wider field or greater speed is necessary, the designer faces more serious problems and the lenses either become very expensive, if well corrected, or some performance compromise results. The nature of wide-angle coverage demands that the lens elements be deeply curved, and the front and rear elements are often made unusually large in diameter to avoid "vignetting" or reduction of image brightness in the corners. Both of these characteristics require expensive manufacturing techniques and complicate assembly. As a rule, therefore, very wide-angle lenses are relatively slow, less likely to be well corrected than are normal lenses of the same aperture, and relatively expensive. These characteristics become more pronounced as the angular coverage increases.

The mushrooming popularity of the single-lens reflex camera has complicated the wide-angle problem still further. Because simple very wide-angle lenses must be placed relatively close to the film surface, due to their short focal length, they cannot be used in the single-lens reflex cameras because they would interfere with the movement of the mirror during exposure. The only workable alternative is to reverse the principle of the telephoto lens; instead of building a lens system which is physically shorter than its effective focal length, as is done in telephoto lens design, it is necessary to construct one whose effective focal length is shorter than its physical length. The difference in construction and *back focus* (distance from the rear lens element to the image plane) of two representative lenses is diagrammed in Figures 18.13*a* and *b*. Figure 18.13*a* approximates closely the glass arrangement and back focus of the Leica wide-angle for the "M" series cameras, the f/3.4 21-mm Super Angulon. The Super Angulon f/4.0, 21-mm wide-angle for the Leicaflex is shown in Figure 18.13*b* in approximate scale.

Figure 18.12

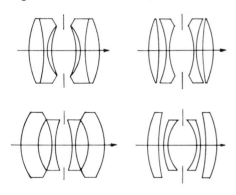

They are apt to be slow and expensive

Simple very-wide-angle lenses cannot be used in single-lens reflex cameras

Figure 18.13

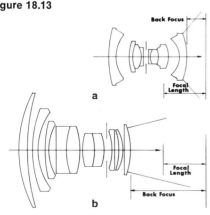

The regular Super Angulon is a lens of straightforward design while the Leicaflex lens is an *inverted telephoto* type sometimes referred to as *retro-focus* design. The principle, illustrated typically by this lens, provides an effective focal length actually shorter than the back focus of the lens.

The advantages of the retro-focus design are not obtained without penalty. The lenses combine the design problems of wide-angle and telephoto construction. As a result they are apt to be more expensive, less well corrected, bulkier, and somewhat more subject to flare than are comparable wide lenses of conventional construction. Also, because they require relatively enormous front elements to insure even illumination of the film plane, they will typically require extralarge and expensive filters. All this is not intended to imply that retro-focus lenses are impractical and inefficient. On the contrary, some of them are excellent. But you should be aware of the fact that they are unusually complex and precise, and, perhaps more than simple lenses, subject to individual variation in quality. One inherent advantage in retro-focus construction is that illumination of the margins of the image field can be made better than is possible in conventional construction.

Retro-focus advantages are not without penalty

Within the last few years some designers have attempted to improve lens quality and performance by incorporating one or more *floating* elements into certain designs. Shifting position automatically as the lens is focused, these elements optimize the design under all useful conditions. When the systems are well designed and precisely assembled they are quite remarkable and permit better image quality at wider aperture, over a wider field, and for a greater range of subject distances, than was previously possible.

Floating elements improve correction

Lens evolution has been rapid since the general availability of computers and one of the more conspicuous products of this new technology is the so-called *fish-eye* lens. While lens designers go to heroic lengths in normal lens designs to correct for linear distortion, insuring that straight lines in the subject will be similarly straight in the image, it becomes clearly impractical, if not impossible, to do this when the angular coverage becomes much greater than 120° or so.

In fish-eye designs, which typically cover angles of 150° or more, curvelinear distortion is allowed to run rampant and the only lines in the image which are straight are those passing through the exact center of the field. The image is circular, and in the case of the more extreme examples of this type, covers at least 180° (Fig. 18.14). In other words, a camera equipped with such a lens could, if placed on the floor and pointed straight up, photograph an entire room, including all the baseboards. So-called *fish-eye attachments* are also available which, when fixed over a normal lens, will produce a similar wide-angle circular image of generally adequate quality.

In fish-eye designs, distortion runs rampant

The optical quality of fish-eye lenses, and especially the supplementary attachments, is not comparable to normal lens quality, but the image is so unreal and dramatic that the fish-eye enjoys a continuing modest popularity. The lenses are naturally quite slow and have a limited range of aperture adjustment, sometimes using a *stop disc* rather than a conven-

Their optical quality is not comparable to normal lenses

Figure 18.14 The hemispherical field of the fish-eye lens makes an incredible jungle out of an ordinary cluster of mandrake plants. The front surface of the lens was only inches away from the plant stem in the foreground.

tional diaphragm. They are sometimes provided with a focusing adjustment, but hardly need it since, due to their very short focal length, the depth of field extends from just a few inches to infinity at the smaller stops.

Zoom lenses are remarkable

One of the most remarkable products of computerized lens design is the *zoom lens*. Essentially a telephoto lens design with movable elements, the zoom lens can provide a continuously variable range of focal lengths, within its design limits, while maintaining a focused image and a constant relative aperture. The difficulties in designing and constructing a lens system of this sort are obviously formidable, and it would be remarkable if they merely worked at all. In fact some of them are very good indeed and their obvious advantages have made them practically standard equipment on television cameras and professional movie cameras.

Figure 18.15

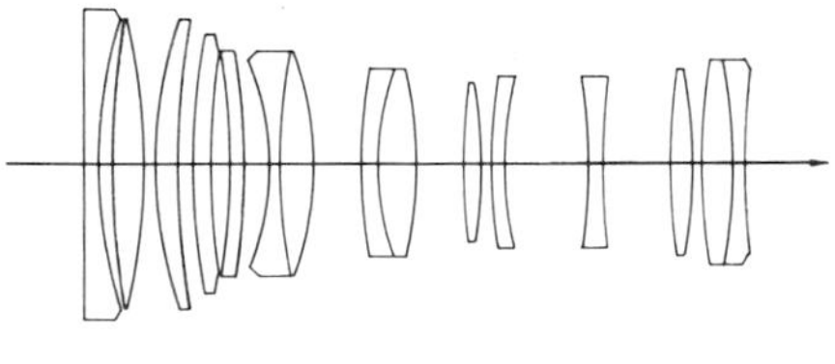

It is considerably easier to construct small lenses than large ones, and no lens type demonstrates this principle more obviously than the zoom. While zoom lenses for 35-mm still cameras rarely cover a focal length range of greater than about three or four to one, and are usually no faster than about f/2.8 to f/3.5, 16-mm movie zooms are available with focal length ranges of greater than ten to one, with maximum apertures approaching f/2.0. Also, many inexpensive 8-mm movie cameras are available with f/2.0 and faster lenses which can zoom over a range of 5 to 1 or more. Zoom lenses for cameras larger than 35 mm are practically nonexistent. The 45→90 mm f/2.8 Angenieux lens for the Leicaflex is shown in Figure 18.15.

Zoom lenses are more useful for movie cameras than for still cameras

Image quality is better in the movie zooms than in those designed for still cameras, at least they are more satisfactory in that application. The fact that the movie image is replaced on the screen at least sixteen times a second relieves any single frame of the responsibility of being critically sharp. In addition to this, movie cameras generally do not require as wide a field as do still cameras, so that a zoom movie lens is relatively easy to design and construct.

There is another advantage, too. Movie cameras are quite often used on a tripod, so that the unusual bulk of a zoom lens is no great problem. Thirty-five-mm camera zoom lenses are so cumbersome that hand-holding any but the smallest of them is very difficult.

All things considered, it seems likely that zoom lenses will continue to be very popular in film and television work and will probably replace fixed-focal-length lenses entirely. Except for certain specialized applications and their novelty value, zoom lenses are not apt to take over still photography until they become more compact, lighter, sharper, faster, cheaper, and cover a more extensive range of focal lengths than they now can.

There are a couple of special-purpose lenses, both more or less normal in design and construction, which may be of some interest. One of these is the so-called *process* lens which is intended for use in precision copying, engraving, color separation, and similar activities which demand the ultimate in image accuracy and color correction. The other is the *portrait* lens.

Process lenses achieve a very high standard of image perfection

Almost without exception process lenses are simple four-element designs (Fig. 18.16) which achieve their high performance by virtue of the facts that they cover only a moderate field, work at small aperture, and are specifically corrected for the kind of work they do. The very high standard of image perfection which they exhibit at their normal working distances (object and image distances nearly equal) is not as evident if they are used for infinity focus, although, because of their small maximum apertures and precise construction, they can be made to perform very well at any distance.

Lenses of similar correction for close-up photography are now supplied by a number of manufacturers for use on 35-mm and $2\frac{1}{4}'' \times 2\frac{1}{4}''$ cameras. Sometimes called *macro*-lenses, they are moderately fast (f/3.5 is typical) and can be used as general purpose lenses, but their best image quality is obtained at very close range.

Most lenses available today, especially the process lenses, are intended to produce the sharpest possible image, but there are a few which are intentionally made soft. They are usually referred to as soft-focus lenses or portrait lenses because they were popular in portrait studios for many years. Their advantages in portraiture were fairly obvious; they tend to minimize minor skin blemishes and they clothe the subject with a kind of ethereal haze which is generally considered attractive (Fig. 18.17). They are not nearly as common as they were before mid-century.

Portrait lenses employ severe spherical aberration

Figure 18.16

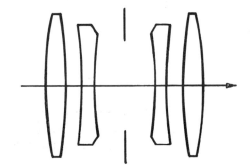

Their soft effect is somewhat different from that obtained by putting fog filters or diffusion screens over a normal sharp lens. The portrait lens achieves its effect by utilizing severe spherical aberration and, because of this, provides both a diffused (out-of-focus) image and a sharp one superimposed. It is the sharp image bleeding into a soft haze which dis-

Figure 18.17

tinguishes this kind of softness from that produced by simple diffusion or lack of proper focus, neither of which provides any sharp image at all.

Spherical aberration is one of the lens defects which is reduced by stopping down, and portrait lenses are likely to be fairly fast lenses used at maximum or near-maximum aperture. Some of them at least, are well corrected except for the spherical aberration and produce fairly normal, sharp images when used at apertures of f/16 or so.

Some use perforated plates instead of conventional diaphragms

Because it is sometimes desirable to retain the characteristic softness of the image but restrict the film illumination, or to vary the degree of softness without affecting exposure, some portrait lenses do not use conventional diaphragms but instead provide perforated plates to be placed over the lens for light control. The perforations are distributed over the whole lens surface thus admitting marginal as well as axial light rays to the camera, so as to retain the aberration. The size and number of the holes regulates the light brightness for exposure control.

A similar concept was employed years ago by Leitz with a lens called the Thambar. Designed for portraiture, this lens had a focal length of 90 mm, an aperture of f/2.2, and came equipped with a center-spot disc of glass which could be screwed into the front of the mount. The opaque center spot, by excluding the relatively sharp central rays, allowed the image to be formed entirely from the marginal rays. A considerable amount of residual spherical aberration in the design insured pleasantly soft image quality.

Spherical aberration has one virtue

Aside from the debatable esthetic value of spherical aberration, it does have one virtue. Every image *point* is extended into a *zone* of focus by the gradual variation in focal length of the lens regions from center to margin. For this reason, objects which might otherwise not be included in the depth of field of the lens at any given stop and distance may form focus zones which overlap at the film plane and be rendered equally sharp. The effect is to increase the useful depth of field while losing some of the overall sharpness, and especially contrast, which a more accurate lens would provide.

A similar effect can be produced by a conventional lens if its focus is changed during exposure or if a series of cumulative exposures are made, each at a slightly different focus. It is apparent that an abnormally great depth of field will result, but that both sharp and soft focus must exist at every focused point simultaneously.

A type of lens seldom seen by amateurs is the *anamorphic* lens used for wide-screen motion picture photography. Lenses of this type work like semicylindrical lenses, in that they compress one image dimension, usually the width, leaving the other normal. The resulting image covers a much wider field of the subject than normal but is significantly distorted. During projection through a similar lens oriented so as to compress the image vertically, or stretch it horizontally, if you prefer, the picture is restored to normal proportions but covers a much wider screen than usual.

Anamorphic and stretch lenses elongate the image

A similar result is obtained with the so-called *stretch* lens attachment sometimes used by photo-illustrators. In this device, movable prisms are adjusted in front of the camera lens to elongate the image in any direction desired. Usually the adjustment can be made for either side of the image area separately, or both can be stretched away from center. There is some loss in sharpness and color correction, and at some settings of the prisms rainbow flare spots may be formed within the image area.

All lenses are designed for light control and most of them do a very good job when they are new. They will continue to work well almost indefinitely if they are well cared for, but careless handling can reduce a fine lens to the quality of the proverbial pop-bottle-bottom in a matter of seconds.

Careless handling can ruin a lens in seconds

There are two general ways in which a lens can be damaged. The alignment of the elements can be disturbed, and the surface polish of the elements can be scratched, chipped, or dulled. No photographer in his right mind would ever deliberately throw a lens out of alignment. It would take a sharp jolt, dropping the camera, for example; or it could be done by taking the lens apart and reassembling it clumsily, which is to say without the proper tools and measuring equipment. But there is hardly anyone who can resist cleaning a lens, and improper cleaning can remove the lens coating or ruin the surface, or both.

Improper cleaning can remove the lens coating and ruin the surface

Some types of optical glass are soft, some are even slightly soluble in water, and all can be scratched. The moral is clear: *Don't touch* the surface with anything unless you have to. Pretend it's your eyeball.

Obviously, the best way to avoid having to clean a lens is to avoid getting it dirty. Make it a practice to keep your lens capped when it is not actually being used to expose film; cap it even between pictures if there is any delay at all. If you remove the lens from the camera, cap the back surface immediately and carry the lens in some sort of protective case or pouch, both to protect it from jolts and to exclude dust and moisture.

To avoid having to clean a lens, avoid getting it dirty

Dust on the surface is not a serious matter

Dust on the lens surface is not a serious matter. It can be removed safely and effectively with a soft brush wielded gently (Fig. 18.18a). A better method (and the only safe way to clean the mirror surface of your single-lens reflex camera) is to blow the dust off with gentle blasts from a squeeze-bulb (a soft rubber or plastic aspirator or "ear syringe" from the drug store is ideal; Fig. 18.18b) or one of the special aerosol cans of inert gas sold for photographic use. A periodic dusting of this sort is all the routine maintenance most lenses need if they are properly protected when not in actual use.

When and how to clean a lens

Sooner or later, however, a film will form on the lens surface. This is probably due to the gradual condensation of atmospheric contaminants and seems to be unavoidable. This must be removed as soon as it becomes apparent and certainly before it is obvious as a coating. A thorough cleaning is also indicated if the lens surfaces are excessively exposed to chemical fumes or smoke, or if they are spotted by dirty water or greasy deposits, including fingerprints.

First, dust the surfaces carefully

Then wipe gently with a moistened lens tissue

Polish gently with a clean, crumpled tissue

First, dust the surfaces carefully to remove any gritty particles which might scratch the glass during cleaning (see Figs. 18.18a and b). Then moisten a wadded piece of *lens tissue* with *lens cleaner* solution (Fig. 18.18d) and wipe the lens surface gently in a circular motion until the solution has been well distributed (Fig. 18.18e). Follow this with a gentle polishing using another piece of clean lens tissue gathered into a soft, crumpled pad. Be careful not to touch the portion of the tissue which will contact the lens to avoid transferring finger oils to the surface (Fig. 18.18c). If there is any sign of streaking or film remaining, repeat the procedure with clean tissues and fresh solution.

Lens tissues are specially made for this purpose and are supposed to be free from harsh fibers or particles which might cause scratches on the lens surfaces. Some seem to be harsher than others, however, and using lens tissue, per se, is no guarantee of scratch-free cleaning.

Other materials can be used if necessary, but be careful

If you do not have lens tissues available, other materials can be used. Some authorities have recommended well-washed linen or cotton handkerchief material, or even silk. Whatever you have at hand must be used if the job has to be done, but remember that the point is to avoid scratching the surface of the lens. A common material which seems to be both safe and very effective is surgical (long staple) cotton. It has advantages of being absorbent, clean, cheap, and convenient to use.

If lens cleaning fluid is not available, some other substance must be found since it is generally not a good idea to wipe a dry lens with a dry cloth. Clean water will do if nothing else is available; but it should be used sparingly, just enough to dampen and soften the cleaning cloth. A trace of liquid detergent or wetting agent can be added if a greasy film must be dissolved. Alcohol may also be used but other solvents are not advisable.

Minute scratches are relatively enormous compared to light waves

While it may seem that these elaborate precautions are unnecessary, remember that the minute scratches which result from careless or excessive cleaning are relatively enormous compared to a typical wavelength of light, and that they are as effective in diffusing and scattering light rays

Figure 18.18

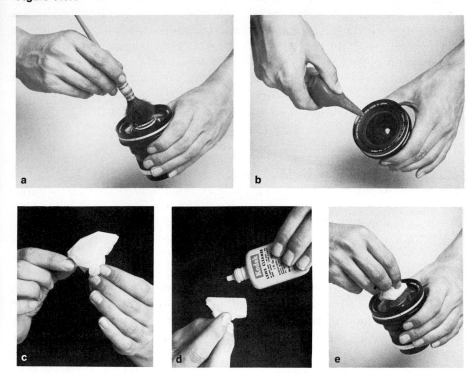

as any other prismatic form. Lens surface blemishes will reduce image contrast significantly long before the glass appears obviously dulled and the effect is so gradual that it goes almost unrecognized.

It simply does not make good sense to spend a lot of money for an excellent lens and then convert it to a merely good or adequate one through careless and compulsive cleaning. Give your lens a break—keep it clean and leave it alone.

**Back surfaces
are sometimes especially delicate**

The inner surfaces of a lens will probably not need to be cleaned at all unless the lens is stored and used in a particularly bad atmosphere for a very long time. All the precautions used in cleaning outside surfaces of the lens should be observed doubly when the back surfaces of the major components are treated. The lens coatings used on inside surfaces are sometimes more fragile than the exterior coating materials and can be destroyed by clumsy scrubbing.

Don't try to clean interior surfaces

If a film is visible on some interior surface of a lens cell, it is best to ignore it as long as possible. If it becomes serious enough to affect the image visibly, it will have to be removed, but *don't try to do it yourself.* Send the lens back to the manufacturer or to a competent lens repair shop.

19 Close-up Photography

For large film images, special techniques may be required

When it is necessary to produce an image on film, larger than about one-tenth the subject size, special equipment or techniques may be required.

Most small cameras will not focus close enough to allow for greater image size than this without special lenses or accessories, and some are not particularly satisfactory for close-up photography even when modified. Single-lens reflex cameras can usually be adapted rather easily and are generally excellent for the purpose if the relatively small image is not a

Figure 19.1
a. Medical illustrators often use photographs like this for reference in drawing. This close-up of the longitudinal section through the head of a human femur displays the architecture of the bone. It is shown here approximately life-sized. (Photograph by Mr. Wm. Brudon, Department of Anatomy, University of Michigan)
b. The electron microscope is capable of greater magnification and finer resolution of detail than is an optical microscope. This handsome design results from photographing Parenchymal and Kuppfer cells (rat liver) at a magnification, in this illustration, of about 2800×. (E.M. photograph by Dr. Wm. Burkel, Department of Anatomy, University of Michigan)
c. The muscle and peripheral nerve structure (rat) shown here at a magnification of about 40,000× demonstrate the remarkable resolution of the electron microscope. (E.M. photograph by Dr. Wm. Burkel, Department of Anatomy, University of Michigan)
d. The "scanning electron microscope" reveals surface details at high magnification, producing about 200 times greater depth of field than conventional optical microscopes can. These exotic forms are Otoconia crystals in the human inner ear, shown here about 1900×. (Scanning E.M. photograph by Dr. Muriel Ross, Department of Anatomy, University of Michigan)

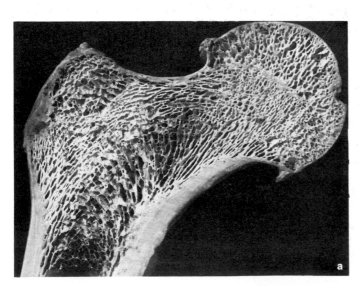

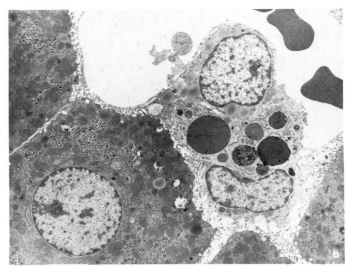

drawback. When larger film sizes are desirable, the view camera is the obvious choice.

A great deal of confusion has surrounded the terms which are used to describe photography of objects at close range. It is quite common to hear the terms "photomacrography" and "photomicrography" interchanged with "macrophotography" and "microphotography." Lenses designed for precision work at close range are often described as "macro-" or "micro-" lenses but are recommended for "close-up" work. In the interests of standardization we will follow the lead of the Kodak technical writers and define these terms as follows. *Close-up* photography covers the range from the minimum focusing distance of the basic camera to a distance about equivalent to two focal lengths from the subject, at which range the subject is being recorded at life-size (Fig. 19.1*a*). Accessory lenses, extension tubes, or bellows units may be required. *Photomacrography* overlaps this range and more specifically refers to the recording of subjects which would normally be examined visually under magnification, such as is provided by a reading glass, pocket magnifier, or a low-powered, simple microscope. Extralong extension tubes or bellows are required, special lenses are necessary for best results, and magnification may range from $1\times$ to perhaps $50\times$. *Photomicrography* refers specifically to photography through a compound microscope, a procedure which involves highly specialized manipulation and lighting techniques. Magnification may run from as low as about $20\times$ to more than $2000\times$. Electron microscopes overlap this range and extend it to an incredible $200,000\times$ or so (Figs. 19.1*b*, *c*, and *d*).

Close-up, photomacrography, and photomicrography

The term *microphotography* is used to describe the techniques of producing very small images as, for example, in making patterns for electronic integrated circuitry. This is a highly specialized field in which exotic sensitized materials and meticulous control of processing conditions are required to maintain satisfactory definition in images which are literally invisible to the naked eye. The term *macrophotography* is assigned to the making of very large images, such as photomurals.

Macrophotography, microphotography

Meter readings of close-up subjects must be taken with extreme care. Incident readings can be difficult to obtain if the camera-to-subject dis-

Meter readings must be taken with care

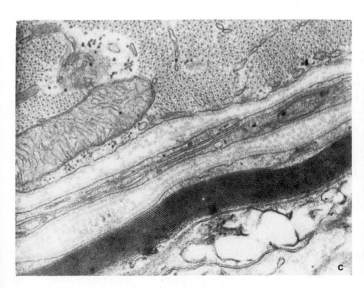
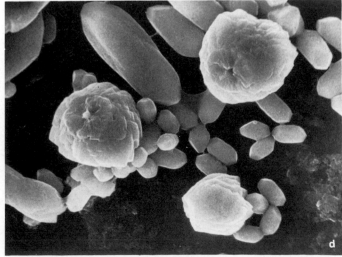

tance is very short or if the subject is likely to be disturbed. Incident readings cannot be relied on if the meter cell is not placed quite precisely in the subject plane and in a typical light condition. Conventional luminance meters are not much better for this purpose. Because of the small subject area and the proximity of the camera, accurate coverage of the subject field is difficult, and the meter will probably cast a shadow which will affect the accuracy of the reading. If the camera has a built-in through-the-lens meter, the problem is made much simpler, and very accurate readings can usually be obtained.

Usually the focal distance is similar to the focal length

When a subject is at infinity, the image is formed as close to the lens as it can be under any circumstances, and the distance approximately from lens to focal plane is called the focal length of the lens (Fig. 19.2a). In ordinary photography, the focal distance is rarely very much greater than the focal length of the lens; in fact, most popular cameras are designed to prevent much focusing adjustment.

But not in close-up work

Although there is some increase in focal distance as the subject approaches the camera from infinity, the percentage of increase, compared to the normal focal length, is insignificant until the subject reaches a point about eight focal lengths in front of the lens (Fig. 19.2b).

Figure 19.2

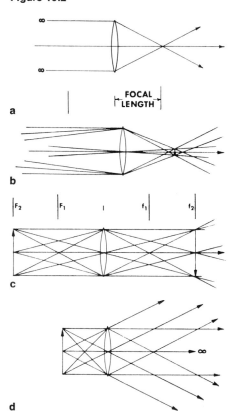

From this point on, as the subject approaches still closer, the focal distance increases very rapidly, until, when the subject has reached a point two focal lengths in front of the lens, the image is formed two focal lengths behind the lens. At this point, the subject and the image are identical in size (Fig. 19.2c), and we refer to this as the condition of *unit magnification*.

If the subject is brought still closer to the lens, the image will recede at an accelerating pace (it is now larger than the subject and growing rapidly) until, when the subject reaches a distance equal to one focal length in front of the lens, the image is formed at infinity and is infinitely large (Fig. 19.2d).

You will recall the *f* numbers marked on the aperture scale of the lens are derived from the relationship between the aperture diameter and the lens focal length.

$$f/ = \frac{\text{focal length}}{\text{diameter}}$$

Therefore, if the lens is extended in focusing to a focal distance greater than the focal length, and the aperture is unchanged, the marked relative apertures are no longer reliable.

The marked relative apertures are no longer reliable

This is what occurs in focusing on a very near object. The lens must be racked out to bring the image into sharp focus, and in so doing, the distance from lens to focal plane is increased. This in turn reduces the illumination on the film surface which, unless compensated for, will cause underexposure of the film.

An example should clarify this relationship. Imagine a lens of 6″ focal length with an aperture diameter of ½″. According to the formula above, the lens has a relative aperture of f/12. When this lens is focused on an object close enough so that the distance from lens to film measures 10″, the effective relative aperture is f/20, although the aperture pointer on the lens mount will still indicate f/12! If the same lens is focused on an object 12″ away, the image will also be 12″ behind the lens, since this is the condition of unit magnification, and the effective relative aperture will be f/24. Under this condition, if the exposure is based on the marked aperture of f/12, the film will receive only one-fourth the illumination it requires, and the negative will be seriously underexposed. Clearly something must be done to compensate for these errors.

There are several methods of computing the required exposure adjustment but the simplest and most convenient method is perhaps this one. (Use of the Macro-exposure computer scales, Figure 19.3, will save some mental arithmetic.)

How to compute the exposure adjustment

1. Focus and compose the image as desired.
2. Stop down for adequate depth of field coverage and note the aperture which you have selected.
3. Measure the focal distance (from the approximate plane of the lens diaphragm to the film plane).
4. Divide this measured distance by the lens focal length (printed on the lens mount in inches or millimeters).
5. Square the resulting number. This is the *exposure factor.*
6. Take an exposure meter reading of the subject and note the shutter speed which is indicated for use with the aperture you have selected (but don't use this shutter speed).
7. Multiply this shutter speed by the exposure factor from step 5. Use this new shutter speed to make the exposure.

For example: after focusing, composing, and stopping down you find that you have a bellows extension (total length) of 10″ and aperture scale reads f/22. The lens focal length is indicated to be 100 mm, about 4″, so:

$$10 \div 4 = 2\tfrac{1}{2}, \text{ which squared is } 6\tfrac{1}{4}.$$

This is the exposure factor. The meter indicates that an aperture of f/22 will require an exposure time of 1/125 second, but this must be multiplied by the factor just found.

$$1/125 \times 6\tfrac{1}{4} = 25/500 \text{ or } 1/20 \text{ second}$$

Use the nearest marked speed on your shutter, favoring the longer interval in preference to the shorter one. In this case, if the shutter can be set at 1/15 second, this is the speed that should be used. If the shutter calibrations provide only 1/10 and 1/25 to choose from, the 1/25 speed will probably be adequate, but the 1/10 is a little safer. If you have time and plenty of film, take one shot at each setting since an extra negative is better than none.

Here is another method using simple proportions to achieve the same ultimate result but working with the aperture numbers to affect the exposure increase.

Here is another method

Figure 19.3

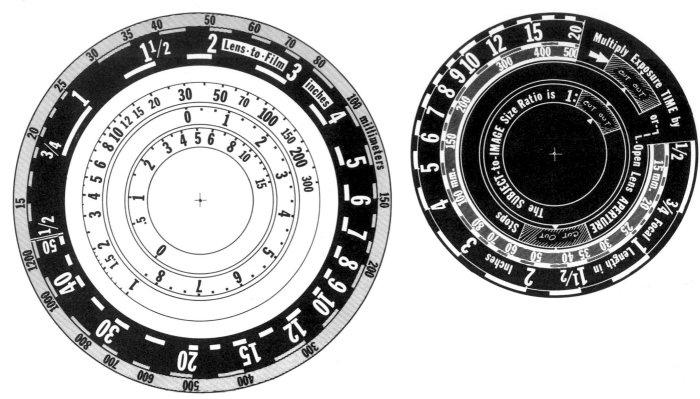

This new macro-computer will help you find the amount of exposure increase required for close-up photography if you have trouble with formulas and mathematics. Since it contains both inch and millimeter scales, it can also be used for metric conversions if desired. For example, find the measurement in inches (larger numbers) on either dial and read its equivalent in millimeters (small numbers) on the same dial. Thus, 7″ is seen to approximate 180 mm, 4″ is slightly more than 100 mm. Reading the other way, 350 mm is about 13 3/4″.

To use the computer for close-up exposure calculations, set up the camera, compose and focus on the subject, then measure the distance from lens-to-film in either inches or millimeters. Find this distance on one of the outer scales. Now move the inner scale until the lens focal length (either inches or millimeters) is aligned with the focal distance just located. Both exposure compensation and image magnification can now be read through the windows. For example, suppose you are using a 100-mm lens, extended to a total distance (lens-to-film) of 13″. Set 100 mm on the movable scale opposite 13″ on the fixed scale. The image is found to be about 2 1/3 times larger than the subject and the exposure can be compensated by either opening the lens about 3 1/2 stops or by multiplying the shutter speed by 11.

If measuring the focal distance is not convenient, and if the image size can be measured fairly accurately, you can determine the exposure compensation by setting the subject-to-image size ratio in the inner window. For example, if some subject dimension is found to be 1/2″ and the same dimension of the image measures 2 1/2″, the ratio is 1:5. Set this number (5) in the inner window and read the exposure compensation in one of the other windows. Either open the lens five-and-a-fraction stops or increase the exposure interval by 36 times. This method is convenient if you are using a view camera with inch or millimeter markings on the ground glass. It is probably the best method to follow, too, when using retro-focus or tele- lenses for close-up work.

Copy these scales on Kodalith film and print them to convenient pocket size. Mount them on thin, stiff cardboard, such as Bristol board, and cut them out neatly. You can color the white central area of the larger dial, if you want to, using a light-colored felt-tipped pen or marker; yellow is probably best for visibility. Mount the smaller disc on the larger one, so that it is free to turn, by using a single rivet, grommet, or paper fastener through the center. Although the finished scales will have a neat appearance if the prints are ferrotyped, it is likely that ferrotyping or matte drying on a heated drum dryer will deform the circles somewhat. It is recommended, therefore, that the prints be dried between blotters at room temperature. This will minimize distortion, but probably not eliminate it.

Effective aperture: Marked aperture = Focal distance: Focal length

Using the same values as in the last illustration we substitute:

$$x : f/22 = 10 : 4 \text{ then,}$$
$$4x = 220, \text{ and } x = 55 \text{ or } f/55.$$

Set the camera aperture scale for f/22 but select the shutter speed which the meter indicates for f/55 or the closest marked aperture. An obvious difficulty with this method is the fact that most meter scales do not extend past f/32 or f/45.

Most close-up photographs are of still-life material, and movement is not as much of a problem as is depth of field. Occasionally, though, it is necessary to specify some shutter speed and then determine how to set the lens to provide the proper exposure. Use of the proportion above will also make this possible. If the selected shutter speed requires an effective aperture of f/8, how must the aperture scale be set to achieve this? Using the 4″ lens working at 10″, as above, we substitute:

$$f/8 : x = 10 : 4 \text{ then,}$$
$$10x = 32, \text{ and } x \text{ (the marked aperture)} = 3.2.$$

Use your selected shutter speed, but set the aperture scale at f/3.2. The effective aperture, because of the extended bellows, is f/8.

Through-the-lens metering

You can modify these procedures, or perhaps even ignore them, if you are using a single-lens reflex with through-the-lens metering. Most cameras of this type compensate automatically for increases in focal distance because the light intensity is diminshed on the meter cells to the same degree that it is on the film surface. In some SLR metering systems the sensitive cell is included in the mirror coating or it may be inserted into the light path at some point ahead of the film. In these meters the light on the meter cell is not diminished quite as much as the actual film image light is and the meter readings may tend to underexpose the film if some compensation is not calculated. Practical experience is the best guide for coping with this condition. Cameras which meter the image light on the ground glass will usually provide almost perfect compensation for any macro-situation.

At near unit magnification, focusing can be a problem

Focusing a camera is a simple enough procedure when the object is some distance away. At distances approaching unit magnification, however, it is sometimes a very confusing task. At near unit magnification you will probably find that moving the **lens** to focus will become ineffective and it will become necessary to adjust the image sharpness by moving the whole camera, or the subject itself. If you are using a view camera it may be feasible and effective to use the **back** focusing adjustment. The problem becomes most perplexing when the subject plane and film plane are just a little more or less than four focal lengths apart. If a little more, there will be some position of the lens which will produce a sharp image but, if a little less, no adjustment of the lens will result in good focus. It will be close enough, though, to keep you working at it. The only way out of this dilemma is to increase the subject-to-film distance to four focal lengths or more. A sharp image is impossible at shorter total distances.

Reciprocity may be a factor

Because close-up photographs often require long exposure intervals, it is quite likely that the effective sensitivity of the film will be reduced by failure of the reciprocity law (see Chapter 7, "Calculating Exposure"). As a rule of thumb, it will be a good idea to double the calculated exposure if it is greater than one second, and double it again if it exceeds about ten seconds. Since films vary in their susceptibility to failure, it will be wise to bracket the exposures or make a preliminary test if the picture is important and cannot be repeated.

The rear nodal point is a hypothetical point in space

The focal length of a lens can be defined as the distance between the image plane and the *rear nodal point* of the lens when the lens is focused at infinity. In simple terms this rear nodal point is a hypothetical point in space which represents the intersection of light rays as they pass through the lens toward the film plane. It is a point, in other words, around which the lens may be pivoted slightly without displacing the focused image of an object at infinity.

It is often near or within the lens structure

In most lenses of conventional design, the nodal points, front and rear, are actually contained within the lens structure, and the diaphragm is placed between them. The position of the diaphragm, therefore, serves as a convenient and fairly accurate point from which to measure the focal distance in computing close-up exposure compensation.

This is not true with retro-focus and telephoto lenses

Although the focal lengths of telephoto and retro-focus lenses cannot be measured from the diaphragm position, because the nodal points are nowhere near it, the diaphragm position will still indicate the approximate source of light illuminating the film surface and may be used with fairly accurate results as the reference point in computing the bellows extension exposure factor. Simply consider the diaphragm-to-film distance at infinity focus to be the *focal length* of the lens. Measure again after focusing on the object and call it the focal distance. Then proceed with the normal calculation. If this, or some similar compensation is not made, retro-focus

But measure from the diaphragm position anyway

lenses will tend to overexpose, and telephotos will tend to underexpose when used for close-ups.

It is best to bracket the exposure

If the exposure increase is computed from the image magnification ratio, it will also have to be modified for use with these lenses. Exact compensation is difficult to predict, so it is advisable to "bracket" the exposure rather thoroughly, favoring underexposure with the retro-lenses and overexposure with telephotos. In practice it's unlikely that a very serious error will occur even without compensation because neither lens type is particularly easy to use for extreme close-ups. Many retro-focus lenses in particular will actually touch the subject before they will focus a life-sized image.

Neither ordinary telephoto nor retro-focus lenses can be expected to produce as good results in close-up work as do normal lenses, and it is unwise to use them in this way if image quality is of critical importance. There are some newly designed zoom lenses, however, featuring ingenious optical or mechanical refinements which permit close-up focusing and provide good macro-correction.

Cameras can be adapted with portrait lenses

Cameras which do not focus closer than eight or ten focal lengths can be adapted for close-up work by the use of *close-up* lens attachments, sometimes inappropriately called *portrait attachments*.

These lenses are generally just simple positive plano-convex lenses of low power designed to slip over the camera lens, and thereby effectively shorten its focal length. Then lens then works as if it were a shorter lens *racked out* (working at a focal distance greater than its focal length) which is the condition necessary for close-up focusing.

Since neither the lens-to-film distance nor the actual aperture diameter is changed by the addition of a close-up lens, there is no light loss of any consequence, and no close-up exposure compensation is required. The only real disadvantage of the close-up lens attachment is the generally slight loss of image quality due to the addition of the aberrations of the supplementary lens to those already existing in the normal lens system and the addition of some flare light from the two extra glass surfaces.

For most purposes the system is usually completely satisfactory, especially when stopped down somewhat. For purists who want the ultimate quality, at least one manufacturer provides achromatic, doublet close-up lenses which will maintain excellent correction of the aberrations.

Close-up lenses are often sold under the designations "plus 1" or "plus 2," etc. These numbers refer to the lens focal length in *diopters*, a term usually used by optometrists, and not often encountered in photography. A focal length of one diopter is equivalent to one meter or about thirty-nine inches. Two diopters implies a focal length of one-half meter, three diopters means one-third meter, etc. If the lens is positive, the description includes the word *plus*; negative lenses are designated *minus*.

Their focal lengths are listed in diopters

Minus supplementary lenses are not as popular as the positive ones, but they are useful as focal length extenders for long lens or telephoto effects if the camera can be physically extended enough to bring the converted image into focus. By lengthening the focal length, minus lenses convert a normal lens into a long one and reduce its speed, since the aperture is not changed. The effective relative aperture must be computed to avoid underexposure.

Minus lenses convert normal lenses to long ones

Some manufacturers provide accessory bellows units for their cameras. These units are fairly common for 35-mm cameras, and some are available for roll film cameras as well. They can only be used on cameras whose lenses can be removed and are only practical for use on single-lens reflex cameras since focusing and framing of the image are extremely critical at close range.

Bellows units usually replace the normal lens in the camera body, and the lens is attached to the front frame of the unit. The camera can no longer be focused at infinity, using its normal lens, because of the irreducible thickness of the bellows, but extreme close-ups are possible.

Bellows units replace the lens

Extension tubes provide another means of close focusing. Supplied in sets of three or four rings of different lengths, they can be interposed between camera body and lens, alone or in combination, to provide more or less continuous coverage of the range from infinity to unit magnification.

Extension tubes provide another means of close focusing

They are cheaper than the accessory bellows units and allow for moderate close-ups, which the bellows cannot accommodate, but they are awkward in use because of the number of pieces involved and the difficulty of interchanging them. They can, of course, be used in combination with a bellows unit for greater magnification of the image, and if really extreme blowups are desired, supplementary lenses can be added, too. Image quality is likely to suffer considerably, however.

Watch out for flare

Figure 19.4   The smooth, semimatte, inner surfaces of these extension tubes are a potential source of serious flare.

A potentially serious problem of flare light can be caused by extension tubes, especially the cheaper varieties, and it is a problem which is seldom mentioned in discussions of close-up photography. The flare results from light reflecting from the smooth interior surfaces of the tubes, as shown in Figure 19.4. The resulting image degradation can be disastrous (Figs. 19.5a, b). If you plan to do much serious close-up work with small cameras (this problem is rare with bellows-type cameras), check the entire camera interior for flare-producing shiny areas by pointing the camera toward a fairly strong light source and inspecting the interior surfaces through the shutter opening (Fig. 19.6). A good camera repairman can usually improvise extra baffles to eliminate the reflection or apply matte black lacquer or flocking to reduce it. You may be able to treat the surfaces of extension tubes yourself but it is best to let a professional work on the camera body if it needs extra baffling.

It may not always affect the finder image

It's worth mentioning that the flare light from these shiny surfaces is not usually apparent in the viewfinder image, especially when the surfaces causing it are part of the camera body itself. It's quite possible, therefore, to see the subject in the finder quite clearly with excellent visual contrast and still find that the film itself has been badly fogged.

Exposure compensation is necessary with both

Exposure compensation is necessary with both bellows units and with tubes since both increase the focal distance of the lens without affecting the aperture. The procedures for computing exposure are identical with those outlined for use with the view camera.

Some manufacturers provide macro-lenses

A number of manufacturers of small cameras produce special lenses for close-up photography which are intended to provide superior correction of the various aberrations in this rather critical range. They are often referred to as *macro-lenses*, and the prefix sometimes appears in the name of the lens. Such lenses for view cameras are not labelled as macro-lenses as a rule but are simply called *process* lenses and are often designated in addition as *apochromats* to indicate that correction of the color aberrations has been carried out to an unusually high degree.

Lens aberrations are not uniform at various object distances

It is one of the unpleasant facts of optics that lens aberrations are not uniform in any given lens at various object distances, and the changes become extreme and particularly troublesome in the unit magnification

Figure 19.5

a. Here is what the tubes shown in Figure 19.4 do to a hornet walking on a window pane.

b. Here is the same hornet on the same window pane, but the picture was made with well-blackened and baffled tubes.

range where the image and object relationships are subject to considerable variation. For this reason, a lens which is superbly corrected for all the aberrations at infinity may be poorly corrected at "1:1" (unit magnification) and vice versa.

Because the corrections are made for rather specific conditions of image-object relationship, it is sometimes possible to improve the performance of an ordinary lens at close range by reversing it in its mount. If it is designed to work best with a large object distance and a short image distance (infinity condition) it will probably work better at extremely close range, when the image is larger than the object, if the front of the lens faces the image. Some manufacturers suggest this practice and supply special adapters to make it possible. Reverse adapters offer no improvement in image quality unless the image is magnified, although they may permit an advantageous increase in the lens-to-subject distance. The lens will probably give better image quality in its normal position until unit magnification is reached.

One of the aberrations which is most troublesome at close range is field curvature. If the lens provides a flat field for objects at infinity it is quite likely not to at close range. It is for this reason that the use of ordinary camera lenses on an enlarger is not advisable since, of all the possible virtues of a lens, flatness of field in enlarging is most important.

This quality is so necessary in the design of high quality enlarging lenses that at least one famous manufacturer produces two separate premium quality enlarging lenses which are corrected for different magnification ratios. If used for image magnifications outside their intended range, these lenses are still very good but no longer considered superb. Within their intended magnification range, incidentally, enlarger lenses can be used as camera lenses with excellent results (Fig. 19.7).

And so you see close-up photography is not simply a matter of pushing the button. If excellent results are required, the lens must be of fine quality, well corrected for close-up work, focusing must be precise, depth of field accounted for. Both subject and camera movement must be avoided; light readings must be taken with particular care, and compensation made for the bellows extension if it is required.

Anything less than precision at every stage of the operation will show up in the print as a flaw.

Reverse adapters are no advantage unless the image is magnified

Figure 19.6

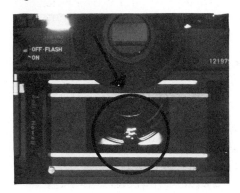

Enlarging lenses should be well corrected for field curvature

They can be used as camera lenses within their intended range

Figure 19.7 A good enlarger lens can be used for close-up work with excellent results. This penny was shot at about 3× magnification with a Schneider Componon reverse-mounted in a view camera lens board. Careful lighting has accented the contours and texture of the low-relief design.

20   Light, Color and Filters

Light is radiant energy

Light is part of a vast band of electromagnetic radiant energy which includes such familiar phenomena as radio waves, heat, ultraviolet rays, X rays, and gamma rays. All of these radiations are considered to travel through space in somewhat the same way that ripples travel across the surface of a pond, but instead of vibrating only up and down as ripples do, electromagnetic waves normally vibrate in all directions perpendicular to the direction in which the wave is travelling. The distance from the crest of one wave to the crest of the next is termed the *wavelength*, and the time interval required for the completion of a single wave *cycle*, from crest to crest or trough to trough, is called the wave's *frequency* of vibration.

The range of the electromagnetic spectrum is staggering

The range of frequencies and wavelengths in the electromagnetic spectrum is staggering. Some radio waves have wavelengths which must be measured in hundreds or thousands of feet and frequencies as low as a few thousand cycles per second. The regular AM band of radio frequencies extends from about 550 kilo-Hertz (550,000 cycles) to about 1600 kilo-Hertz (abbreviated kHz and named for the famous German physicist, Gustav Hertz).

The FM band and television frequencies are measured in millions of cycles with their corresponding wavelengths ranging from a few feet to a few inches. The VHF channels and other specialized radio waves are higher still, but still gross compared to the wavelengths which comprise the visible spectrum. Between the radio frequencies and visible radiations lies the broad band of infrared, or heat rays.

The transition from waves which we perceive as heat to those which we perceive as light occurs at a wavelength of about 7000 Angstrom units, Å. One Angstrom unit equals one one-hundred-millionth of a centimeter. Another unit of wavelength formerly used in the *millimicron*. It is equal to ten Angstrom units, which is, in other words, one millionth of a millimeter or one "nanometer" (abbreviated "nm"), which is the preferred term.

The longest wavelengths we can see we identify as red

The longest wavelength we can see, from about 650nm to about 700 nm, we identify as the color red. As the wavelengths of light decrease and frequency increases, we identify the other familiar colors, orange, yellow, green, blue, and finally deep violet, which corresponds to a wavelength of about 400 nm. Our vision is not stimulated by radiations of higher frequency, although ultraviolet "light" can cause rather serious eye damage. We are sensitive to ultraviolet in another way, too; it is the component of sunlight which causes tanning of the skin and the bleaching of hair and clothing dyes. The electromagnetic spectrum continues to still higher frequencies and shorter wavelengths through X rays, gamma rays, and beyond (Fig. 20.1).

We see narrow bands of visible frequencies as specific colors of great purity and saturation. If the frequency bands are widened, or if non-adjacent bands are mixed, we see less pure color and the colors are lighter in tone. When all the spectrum frequencies are present at high intensity, we get the sensation of white. When the intensity diminishes we see grays and when there is no light energy present, or when it is low enough to be insignificant, we perceive nothing, which we call black.

**We see narrow bands of
frequencies as colors of great
purity**

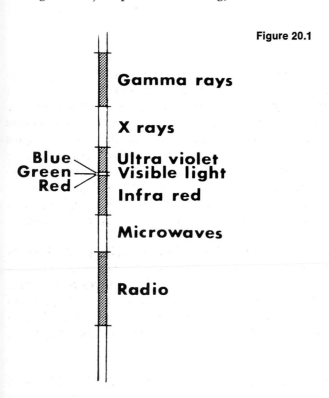

Figure 20.1

White light, then, is a scrambled conglomeration of all the visible light wavelengths, and for most photographic purposes, it is perfectly satisfactory and desirable color to work with. There are times, however, when we want to work with specific colors or mixtures of colors, and when this is so, we can resort to the use of light *filters*.

**White light
is a scrambled conglomeration**

In a sense, any object or surface which we perceive as having a color is acting as a filter because it absorbs part of the white incident light and reflects part of it. The part reflected is the part we see and identify as the object's color.

Thus a red apple is seen to be red because it absorbs the blue and green light wavelengths and reflects the remaining red frequencies to our eyes. A pink object reflects some of all the frequencies for the effect of white but is most reflective to red light which tints the white. A dark brown object absorbs a considerable amount of all the light, making it dark gray, but is particularly absorptive to blue. The remaining dark orange we see as brown.

**A red apple is red
because it absorbs blue and green**

Photographic filters absorb certain colors and transmit others

The effect is not confined to reflective surfaces. In fact the most useful photographic filters are transparent materials which absorb certain colors and *transmit* others. The materials used for this purpose are generally glass, plastic, or dyed gelatin.

If you can remember the fact that objects appear to be colored because they *reflect or transmit that color from the incident light*, you will have no trouble understanding the way in which filters work. Imagine what would happen, for example, if a green object were illuminated by a light containing no green wavelengths. None of the light which the object can reflect is present in the incident light so the object must appear dark, probably black or nearly so. On the other hand, a green object illuminated alternately with green light and white light will appear essentially the same in both, since it can reflect only the green component of the white light and simply wastes the other colors by absorbing them.

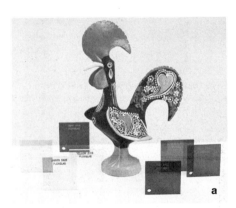

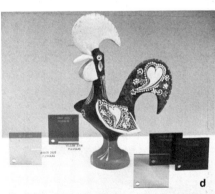
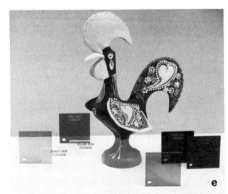

Figure 20.2 This series of photographs shows how a typical panchromatic film (in this case, Plus-X roll film) translates subject colors into values of gray. The first illustration shows the film's response without any filtration; the other photographs demonstrate the effects that several common filters produce. All photographs were made by tungsten light. For the actual colors of the subject, see the illustration on page 353.
a. No filter.
b. Yellow-green filter, similar to Wratten #11. Filter factors: Day, 4; Tung, 3.
c. Orange filter, similar to Wratten #15. Filter factors: Day, 3; Tung, 2.
d. Red filter, Wratten #25. A filter recommended for making direct-deparation negatives from the subject. Filter factors: Day, 8; Tung, 4.
e. Deep red filter, Wratten #29. A color separation filter, used in printing. Filter factors: Day, 16; Tung, 8.
f. Deep green filter, Wratten #61. This filter is commonly used to make color separation negatives for printing. Filter factors: Day, 10; Tung, 10.
g. Deep blue filter, Wratten #47B. A color separation filter, used in printing. Filter factors: Day, 8; Tung, 16.

In black-and-white photography, filters are often used over the camera lens to exclude certain colors from the film chamber. If the filtered light can't reach the film, it obviously can't affect it, and the object which reflected the light will appear dark in the final print. Parts of the subject which reflect light of the same color as the filter (which *can* be transmitted to the film) will appear in the print as comparatively light in tone and may even appear white if their light so nearly matches the filter color that none of it is absorbed (Fig. 20.2).

A similar effect can be achieved by illuminating the subject itself with colored light. Objects which are capable of reflecting the light color will appear light in the print while objects which cannot reflect the incident light, or reflect it only partially, will be recorded as black or dark in tone (Fig. 20.3).

Another method of selectively recording colors involves the use of *color-blind* film—either *ordinary* (blue-sensitive only) or *orthochromatic* (blue

**They are often used
to exclude certain colors
from the film chamber**

**Ordinary, orthochromatic, and
panchromatic films**

Figure 20.3   A practical example of selective light control with filters. This picture shows the path followed by a blind bullhead following food "smell" to its source. The fish's track, the glowing food essence in the tube and the researcher's shirt were all recorded by their fluorescent glow in ultraviolet illumination. The ultraviolet itself—to which the film is very sensitive—was restricted from the camera by an orange filter. After a thirty-second exposure which recorded the fish's meanderings a single electronic flash recorded the room and displayed the fish by visible light which passed through the orange filter only slightly attenuated. The gap in the trace near the center line was caused as the fish made a quick turn and rolled over far enough to hide the fluorescent tab briefly. (Courtesy of the University of Michigan Press)

and green sensitive). Compared to *panchromatic* emulsions which are fully color sensitive, the ordinary films are red- and green-blind and will react to colored subject matter just as pan film would if exposed through a strong blue filter. (See Fig. 11.1*a*, *b*, *c*, and *d*, p.99).

Ortho film acts like pan film with a blue-green filter and normally portrays reds in the subject as unnaturally dark in tone. Obviously, it would be unwise to try to use a red filter with ortho films since almost none of the light which the filter would allow to reach the film could affect it. By the same token, a light source deficient in blue light would be inefficient (at least) for use with *ordinary* film.

Filters absorb light intensity and necessitate a factor

Because filters work by absorbing portions of the light that strikes them, they prevent the film from receiving its full exposure unless the total exposure is increased to make up for the light loss. This necessary exposure increase is called the *filter factor* and is usually indicated by a number. Multiplying the normal shutter speed, as indicated by an exposure meter, by the filter factor number will indicate the proper exposure for use with the filter in place over the lens.

For example, if the meter indicates that an exposure of 1/100 second at f/5.6 is the right exposure to use without a filter, and if the factor of the filter to be used is 4 times (it would be written $4\times$), multiplying 1/100 by 4 gives 4/100 or 1/25 second, the proper compensated exposure at f/5.6.

The factor will vary with different films and light conditions

The factor for any given filter will probably be different for different kinds of films and for different conditions of light. Thus, a certain medium yellow filter used with pan film in daylight rates a factor of $2\times$; in tungsten light the factor is $1.5\times$. The same filter with ortho film in daylight requires a $2\frac{1}{2}\times$ increase, but only a $2\times$ increase in tungsten light. With color-blind film, the same filter in daylight has a factor of $12\times$, and $10\times$ in tungsten light.

There is no such thing as white light

In color photography, and to a lesser extent in black-and-white work involving filters, the color of the light itself is of great importance. While most people probably think of light as being "white," it usually isn't. In fact you could make a good case for the statement that there is no such thing as white light.

If you have thought that this page is white, compare it to the light coming in the window. And if you think that the window light is white hold an acetylene flame or an electric arc in front of it and watch the daylight turn gray or blue or orange. It may surprise you but your eyes are very bad judges of color—objectively; but given a reference of any sort, the human eye can establish *relative* color under terrible conditions of illumination.

Objective standards of white light have had to be established

It is for this reason that some objective standards of "white" have had to be established. The eye will adapt endlessly to changing light color and still interpret subject colors with considerable accuracy. Color film cannot do this. It has a precise notion what white is, and if it is exposed to any other color, it records it as a distinct tint or stain.

If you know precisely what color the film thinks of as white, you can adjust the existing light to that color by putting a filter of the appropriate color and intensity over the light source or the lens. This is called *balancing the light*. But we live in such a variety of light conditions that accurate filtration for the extremes is hardly feasible if only one white is acceptable. So there are several standard white light conditions and color films are balanced during manufacture to match them.

Most pictures are taken either in daylight or by the light of tungsten filament incandescent lamps. The two most common color film types are, therefore, *daylight* and *tungsten*. These sources have one important characteristic in common, their light results from the incandescence of a heated body and is a mixture of all the visible colors. In other words, both sources emit a *continuous spectrum*. The difference in color which is apparent in comparisons of the two whites is due to the different proportions of blue and red light they contain, and this results from the difference in actual temperature of the two emitting bodies.

Most pictures are taken in daylight or tungsten light

If you put a piece of black iron in a fire, it will eventually get hot and radiate heat, or infrared, rays. As the iron absorbs more energy from the fire, it will radiate at higher frequencies and eventually the radiations become visible as red light. Higher temperatures result in still shorter wavelengths and the visible color shows as yellow, then white, then bluish white (although iron would vaporize before it became noticeably blue), and the relationship between temperature and color is a predictable one.

The relationship between temperature and color is predictable

This behavior is typical of most materials heated to incandescence and is the basis for a measurement of *white* called *color temperature*. In this system a light of approximately the same color as that emitted by a non-reflective *black body* heated to 2500°K., for example, would be said to have a color temperature of 2500°K.

Color temperature is expressed in Kelvin degrees

Color temperature is expressed in Kelvin degrees, or Kelvins, since it follows the absolute centigrade scale named after the famous British physicist, Lord William Thompson Kelvin. A few common light sources and their approximate *Kelvin temperatures* are given below.

Candle flame	1900°K.
40 watt bulb	2650
75 watt bulb	2800
100 watt bulb	2900
Professional photographic flood	3200
Amateur "photoflood"	3400
Clear flashbulb	3800
Noon sunlight	5400
Photographic standard daylight (Kodak)	5500
Typical electronic flash (uncompensated)	6200
Light from north sky	15,000 to 20,000 or more.

The so-called "daylight" color films are balanced for a "white" of about 5500°K. to 6000°K., and when they are used in normal daylight, their color rendition is very satisfactory.

Daylight films are balanced for about 5500°K. to 6000°K.

Tungsten films are balanced for 3200°K., type B, and 3400°K., type A

There are two common emulsions designed for use in artificial light conditions, type *A* and type *B*. Both films are intended for use with tungsten filament bulbs and are sometimes called *tungsten* films, or *indoor* films. The type *A* sensitivity is designed for use with photoflood bulbs burning at 3400°K., while the type *B* film matches the standard professional flood and spotlight bulbs which burn at a temperature of 3200°K.

If you use any color film in a light condition which fails to match its color balance by more than a couple-of-hundred Kelvin degrees, you can count on getting obviously tinted pictures. In fact, if it is important that colors be accurately recorded, and particularly if neutral grays in the subject must be reproduced without apparent tinting, the light color and the film balance should match within 100°K. or less. If the light does not match the film, it will probably be possible to correct it by using an appropriate filter over the camera lens, but you must know what color the light is before you can hope to adjust it.

Color temperature can be measured

Color temperature can be analyzed with a *color temperature meter.* There are several models on the market, most of which obtain their readings by measuring the relative intensity of the orange and blue components of the incident light. Since the color temperature of daylight and tungsten sources follows the ideal "black body" model fairly closely, sampling the blue and orange proportions of these lights is a fairly accurate indication of their overall color.

For light sources which do not resemble the black body balance the term "color temperature" is meaningless, and their color balance must be measured by sampling at least the three light primaries, red, green, and blue. Most photographers, if they need any color meter at all, will probably be able to manage with a two-color model. Three-color meters are professional instruments and are very expensive.

If you have a color temperature meter control is simple

If you have access to a color meter, the control of color balance is quite simple. You know the color balance of the film you are using and you can read the light color temperature. Subtract the larger number from the smaller to find the difference in Kelvin degrees. The filter which can shift the light color to match the film can be found by consulting a reference such as the Kodak pamphlet, *Kodak Wratten Filters.*

For example, if you are using type *B* film, 3200°K., and find the light to be too warm at about 2950°K., you must cool the light, so you select a bluish filter—in this case an 82A. If the light had been too blue, the proper filter would have been selected from the 81 series (yellowish).

But filter selection may be confusing

Filter selection is not always as simple a matter as this illustration would imply because the *degree* of color shift that any filter can achieve will change if the light color changes. For example, the Wratten 85B filter, a rather strong orange color, is designed to convert daylight, 5500°K., for use with type *B* film, 3200°K.; in other words, it will shift the light toward orange by some 2300°K. You might expect this 2300° shift to be a constant characteristic of this filter, but this is not true. If the existing light measures 4000°K., for example, the 85B filter will correct it to about 2630°K., a change of only 1370°. On the other extreme, the 85B will change 10,000°K. light to about 4400°K., a shift, in this case, of 5600°K.

A little mathematical magic can simplify this problem significantly. If the color temperatures are converted to *mireds* (pronounced my-reds), which is an abbreviation of MIcro-REciprocal DegreeS, the new values do not vary with light color changes and every filter can be assigned a color shift factor which is a constant. The conversion is as follows:

$$\text{Mired value} = \frac{1,000,000}{\text{color temperature in degrees K.}}$$

For example, what is the mired value of photographic daylight (5500°K.)?

$$\text{Mired value} = \frac{1,000,000}{5500} = 181.8$$

Similarly, the mired value of 3200°K. is found to be 312.5. Therefore the difference between daylight and tungsten light balance is 130.7 mireds, and any filter or combination of filters which can match this number will effect the desired correction.

It is very important to remember that the mired value *of the light to be converted* must be subtracted from the mired value of the *desired light color*. Thus, if we want to convert daylight to tungsten, 5500° to 3200°, we must subtract 181.8 from 312.5, and the answer is a *positive* number, 130.7. If we wish to change tungsten to daylight, 3200° to 5500°, we must subtract 312.5 from 181.8, and the answer is a *negative* number, −130.7. In every case a *negative* number indicates a need for a *bluish* filter; a *positive* number indicates a need for a *yellowish* filter. The Kelvin Temperature Computer (Fig. 20.4) will simplify these calculations.

Following is a list of some of the available light balancing filters and their mired shift values:

COLOR	WRATTEN FILTER NUMBER	FILTER FACTOR	MIRED SHIFT VALUE
bluish	82	⅓ stop	−10
"	82A	⅓	−21
"	82B	⅔	−32
"	82C	⅔	−45
blue	80D	1 stop	−56
"	80C	1	−81
"	80B	2 stops	−112
"	80A	2⅓ stops	−131
yellowish	81	⅓ stop	9
"	81A	⅓	18
"	81B	⅓	27
"	81C	⅓	35
brownish	81D	⅔	42
"	81EF	⅔	52
orange	85C	⅓	81
"	85	⅔	112
"	85B	⅔	131

The obvious convenience of the mired system has impelled some manufacturers to produce special filter sets. The popular sets are generally

Figure 20.4

The Kelvin Temperature Scale:
This scale will help you determine the necessary filter correction whenever the existing light color is not correct for the type of color film you are using. Set the "Film Balance K.°" arrow opposite the appropriate film type on the Kelvin scale. The three normal emulsion types are labelled "Day" (5500°K.), "A" (3400°K.) and "B" (3200°K.). Next, on the Kelvin scale, find the color temperature of the existing light. The filter required for proper color rendition will be found opposite this temperature, on the Mireds scale. For example, suppose you are using clear flashbulbs with Kodachrome II, type "A" film. Set the pointer on "A." Opposite the small "f" (flash) at the 3800°K. mark read the required correction: plus 30 Mireds. The appropriate filter is the "81B" (plus 27 Mireds). Slightly warmer results will be obtained by using the "81C" (about plus 35 Mireds). The small letter "s" at 6100°K. indicates the approximate color balance of unfiltered electronic flash tubes.

Copy these scales on Kodalith film and print them to convenient pocket size. Mount them on thin, stiff cardboard such as Bristol board and cut them out neatly. Mount the smaller disc on the larger one so that it is free to turn by using a single rivet or grommet or paper fastener through the center. Although the finished scales will have a neater appearance if the prints are ferrotyped it is likely that ferrotyping or matte drying on a heated drum dryer will deform the circles somewhat. It is recommended, therefore, that the prints be dried between blotters at room temperature. This will reduce print distortion, but probably not eliminate it.

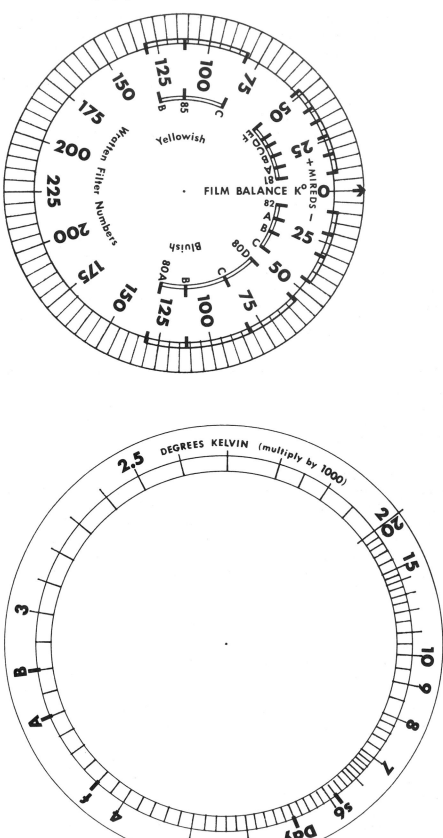

calibrated in *decamireds* (ten mireds) and they are designed to be used singly or in various combinations to provide good control of light color over quite a wide range.

A typical set of six filters consists of three red filters in strengths of 1.5, 3, and 6 decamireds; and three blue filters of 1.5, 3, and 6 decamireds. Offered separately are filters of 12 decamired strength, one red and one blue. If all eight filters are purchased and combined appropriately, the owner can reproduce any decamired value from 1.5 to 22.5 in steps of 1.5, in either red or blue.

The decamired filter sets are well thought out and are very convenient to carry and use. They do have some drawbacks, however. The most serious problem arises from the fact that many decamired values are obtained by combining two or more filters and this is always a little risky. Each filter adds two air-glass surfaces to the lens system, and if they are not very clean and accurately aligned, there is some danger of flare and loss of image sharpness. Another minor shortcoming is the relatively unsubtle color shift represented by the minimum 1.5 decamired adjustment. Another problem is cost; the sets are quite expensive.

The decamired filter sets are well thought out

For these reasons the decamired filter sets are only fairly popular. Not many amateurs are interested enough to indulge in such extensive and expensive color compensation, and most professional photographers need the much greater control and variety of compensation offered by the Wratten gelatin filter series.

In precise color work, such as photo-illustration, the Wratten light balancing filters just described are not often used, at least relatively speaking. Studio incandescent lighting is generally very close to the normal type *B* color balance, 3200°K., and studio electronic flash units usually match the daylight film balance, or are permanently filtered to match it, quite closely. The filters which are much more often encountered in this work come from the *color compensating* series. (See colorplate inside back cover.)

The color compensating filters come in six colors; red, green, blue, magenta, yellow, and cyan. Each color is available in six or seven carefully graduated strengths ranging from an almost negligible tint to a fairly saturated hue. The filters are identified by the prefix CC, a number indicating the effective density (actually density $\times 100$), and a final letter indicating the filter color. Thus for example, the term *CC30M* indicates a magenta color compensating filter whose density is .3.

Color compensating filters come in six colors

In theory, a filter density of .3 should indicate a necessary exposure increase (factor) of $2\times$, but this is not the case with the CC filters. Their density, measured for their complementary color, does not indicate exactly the amount of total light reaching the film. The actual factor, therefore, is generally less than the filter number would indicate. The discrepancy between the indicated density and the practical factor is shown by comparing the factors for the six densest filters.

Their density is measured for their own color

Filter	Peak Density	Approximate Theoretical Factor	Actual Factor
CC50Y	.5	3×	1.6×
CC50M	.5	3×	1.6×
CC50C	.5	3×	2×
CC50R	.5	3×	2×
CC50G	.5	3×	2×
CC50B	.5	3×	2.6×

The CC series filters are most useful for adjusting the color response of the film itself. Films produced for professional use include in their instructions a test sheet indicating the actual exposure index and color balance of that particular batch of emulsion. Since reciprocity failure effects are much more apparent in color films than in black-and-white emulsions, it is also customary for the manufacturer to include exposure and filtration recommendations for unusual exposure times. These color compensations will rarely require more than about a 30 filter.

Occasionally you may encounter a discontinuous spectrum

Occasionally, you may encounter a light source which emits a *discontinuous spectrum* for which no real color temperature equivalent exists. A common example is the fluorescent tube. Although the light which these fixtures produce appears white, it often shows a distinct color in photographs and color compensation is difficult. There are so many varieties of fluorescent tube colors that no general rule can be followed for filter selection, but satisfactory color can sometimes be achieved by exposing daylight film through a CC20 or 30M, or 20 or 30R, or some combination of these filters. **Trial and error is the only way to deal with these** Trial and error is the only effective way to deal with these light conditions.

It is not unusual to combine filters, particularly in color work, but as mentioned before, the number should be kept to a minimum to avoid flare and diffusion. Professionals usually use the relatively inexpensive *gelatin square* filters which are simply very thin sheets of dyed gelatin. They are optically clear and cause very little diffusion, but they are fragile and cannot be cleaned. **Professionals use gelatin squares; glass filters are common in small camera work** Many professionals simply fasten them in place over the camera lens with bits of masking tape, use them as long as possible, and throw them away when they become soiled or scratched.

Glass filters are much more often used for small camera work, especially out of the studio. They are, of course, much more expensive than gels, and relatively few colors are available, but they have the advantage of being convenient to use and are quite durable. The most accurate colors are probably produced by dyeing gelatin, and some "glass" filters are really gelatin filters cemented between clear glass plates. The modern trend, however, is toward dyed glass, and most of the commonly needed colors are available in this form.

Glass filters will cause some focus shift

Glass filters, whether solid or laminated, will cause some focus shift when placed over the camera lens because of their thickness. When they are used in front of the lens, this shift is usually negligible, but when they are placed behind the lens, they displace the image plane appreciably. If you are working with a camera which is focused through the lens, such as a single-lens reflex or a view camera, the filters can be used safely in either position as long as you focus with the filter in place. If you focus the camera without a filter and then place (a glass) one behind the lens, the image is likely to be disastrously soft. It is worth noting that a serious focus shift may occur even when the filter is in front of the lens if the subject is very close to the camera. For macro-work, therefore, it is always advisable to focus through the filter, regardless of its placement. Gelatin filters are unlikely to cause any serious focusing problems in either position.

When a beam of light is reflected from a smooth surface, the normal random vibration of the light waves is modified so that most of the vibration occurs in a single plane and the light is said to have been *polarized*. The same effect can be obtained by passing light through a polarizing filter. The filter acts somewhat like an optical venetian blind which "combs" the light into parallel vibrations.

Reflected light is polarized

Polarized light, which vibrates in a plane parallel to the polarizing axis of the filter, will pass through the filter easily; but if the filter axis is rotated so that it is perpendicular to the vibration plane of the light, the light will not pass through. Two polarizing filters, placed face-to-face, will transmit a light beam if the filter axes are parallel; but if one of the filters is rotated, the light transmission of the pair will be reduced, and when the filter axes are perpendicular to each other, the filter sandwich is essentially opaque.

It can be absorbed by a polarizing filter

Polarizing filters are valuable photographic accessories because they afford a means of controlling light selectively without affecting the light color. In fact there is no visual difference between a beam of polarized light and one which is not polarized.

The major use of polarizers in photography is in the control of reflections and surface glare. Light is strongly polarized by reflection from most smooth surfaces (polished metal is a notable exception); the effect being most noticeable when the angle of reflection is between about 35° to 50° from the horizontal. Direct right angle reflections are not polarized at all and the effect is also decreased at very small angles. Within the angular range mentioned, however, reflected light can be almost entirely absorbed by a properly oriented polarizer (Fig. 20.5).

The effect can be determined visually. Simply look through the filter at the offending glare and rotate the filter until the glare is minimized. If the filter is placed over the camera lens at the same angle, it will similarly eliminate the glare light from the picture, leaving the unpolarized portions of the subject light essentially unaltered. Because the filter is neutral gray in color, it has no effect on subject color balance and can be used with either color or black-and-white films.

The effect can be determined visually

Like any filter, the polarizing filter absorbs some of the light intensity and necessitates some exposure increase. The factor is variable, however, because its total light absorption depends upon the amount of polarized light reaching the camera from the subject. If most of the subject light is unpolarized, the filter factor may be as low as about $2\frac{1}{2}\times$, no more than you would expect from the gray density of the filter material. If a substantial portion of the subject light is polarized, and if it crosses the polarizing plane of the filter, the filter factor may be much greater.

The filter factor may vary

Figure 20.5

a. The truck as it appeared, unfiltered. From an illustration point of view there are several problems here: reflections in the paint on the side of the body, poor modelling of the hood shape, and excessive windshield glare.

b. The polarizer adjusted at the worst possible angle. Details of the side moulding are gone, the hood is still poorly defined, and the windshield glare is worse.

c. Here the polarizer is set to eliminate the windshield glare. Hood modelling is better but the side reflections are emphasized. Some art directors might prefer this "natural" look.

d. This setting is probably a good compromise: side reflections are subdued but modelling is good; the hood light pattern shows its form strongly and the windshield glare is well controlled. In color the reduced brightness of the hood would probably be an advantage.

In most situations, the polarized portions of the subject light come from localized areas of the subject and the general illumination is not polarized. Under these conditions, a factor of about $3\times$ will serve as a point of departure, but it is wise to bracket the exposure a stop or so on either side of normal to insure good results.

When used with color film, polarizers tend to increase color saturation because they eliminate some of the surface glare which is normally present throughout the subject area. Typically, too, they darken the blue of the clear sky, dramatically so in the South and especially in the North, from which direction the light is naturally strongly polarized. Maximum effect is in the sky area $90°$ from the sun position (Fig. 20.6).

When two polarizing filters are crossed, the light passing through the first is polarized in a plane which opposes the axis of the second filter and virtually no light gets through. If, however, some material which can disrupt the polarization pattern is inserted between the filters, they will again transmit (see back colorplate, p. 354).

If the disruption is local and if it is frequency-selective, the transmitted light is brilliantly colored, and the color patterns formed can be varied across the whole spectrum by rotating one of the filters through $90°$. This phenomenon is put to practical use in scientific photography such as the examination of stress patterns in plastic models of machine parts or structural members and the display of crystal structures in photomicrography.

Some of the visual effects produced are fantastically beautiful. A piece of crumpled cellophane (from a cigarette pack) placed between two polarizing filters will give you an idea of the kind of color patterns which are possible.

Polarized light can be used to illuminate a particularly reflective subject if the glare cannot be subdued by the use of a single filter on the camera lens. Oil paintings and other similar surfaces are often photographed in this way. Large polarizing screens, with their axes parallel, placed over the lights provide partial control while a polarizing filter over the camera lens removes the last vestiges of glare.

It is possible to eliminate the glare so completely from some surfaces that the texture becomes almost invisible and this may not be desirable. Rotate the camera filter slowly while observing the effect on the camera ground glass and adjust it to suit yourself.

Polarizers can be used for stereoscopic projection. The visual effect of three-dimensions depends upon the separation of left- and right-eye images. In the old parlor stereoscopes, this was accomplished by mounting the separate images side by side on a card and directing the eyes—each to its own image—by prismatic eyepieces.

This cannot be done conveniently with projected images. If, for example, the stereo images are projected through polarizing filters so that the left-eye image is vertically polarized and the right-eye image is horizontally polarized, and if the two images are superimposed on a metallic screen (which will not disrupt the polarization as a conventional surface might do), and if the viewers are provided with special polarizing glasses (left eye vertical, right eye horizontal), they will see the effect of depth clearly and convincingly.

To the naked eye, of course, the superimposed images will appear glaring and garbled. The polarizing lenses in the glasses pass only the correct image to each eye, completely eliminating the other image. The effect is particularly striking in color and motion; provided, of course, that the two screen images are accurately superimposed and synchronized.

There are a few other accessories which are sometimes referred to as filters but which do not really deserve the title because they are not selective in their action. The so-called *fog filters* are really just diffusing glass, slightly milky in appearance, intended to diffuse the image. They are available in several strengths and produce pictorial effects which suggest fog, hence the name. Somewhat similar in action are diffusing filters of clear glass into which a pattern of fine grooves is scratched or etched. In addition to contributing a kind of atmospheric softness to the image, these *star filters* produce characteristic radiating streaks around bright highlight areas.

Neutral density filters in several values are also available. Their purpose is simply to reduce the intensity of the light entering the lens by some precise amount. They are useful for reducing the exposure without affecting the aperture setting or shutter speeds, as for example, when shooting in bright light with fast film or when a wide aperture for shallow depth of field is desirable in bright light conditions.

In studio situations it is sometimes desirable to make a test exposure of some setup on Polaroid film prior to making the final shot on sheet color film. If a neutral density filter of the correct strength is placed over

Figure 20.6 In black-and-white, a polarizing filter darkens the north sky about as effectively as an orange or medium red filter would. Unlike the color filters, however, the polarizer can be used with color film without destroying the natural color of the scene. This picture was made in early afternoon with the polarizer oriented for maximum effect. Adding a red filter to the polarizer would render the sky almost black.

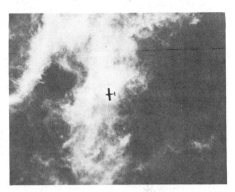

Polarizing lenses pass the correct image to each eye

Fog filters diffuse the image

Neutral density filters reduce light intensity

the lens for the Polaroid exposure, the same lens and shutter settings can be used for both the test and final exposures—an advantage if depth of field and subject motion are to be appraised in the test shot.

Filters are not a universal benefit

Filters are invaluable in certain photographic situations, but they should not be thought of as being a universal benefit. Image contrast and sharpness will suffer somewhat if a dirty filter is used, particularly if the picture is taken against the light. It is good practice never to use a filter of any kind if you do not have a specific reason for doing so, but when you do, try to keep the filter surface well shaded in use by employing a good, deep sunshade or lenshood.

Use a lens cap for protection; use your filters for light control

Use as few layers of filter material, either glass or gelatin, as possible and keep them as close to the lens surface as possible. Some photographers like to keep a clear glass "filter" over their camera lens for protection, but unless you are shooting in rain or salt spray or blowing sand conditions, this seems hardly necessary. Use a lens cap for protection and save your filters for their intended use—light control.

THE ROYAL FOREGROUND GRADED FILTER

(Patented April 14th, 1911)

The Latest and Greatest Improvement in Ray Filters

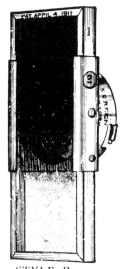

STYLE A   STYLE B

The only Ray Screen **ever** invented that will give an even, **equal exposure** to both sky and foreground, and produce a perfect cloud effect instantaneously with ordinary plates.

The Use of Light

21

Learning to be a good photographer, like learning to draw well, involves learning to see, or rather, relearning to see. As children, we knew how to accept things as they appeared without intellectualizing. As adults, we tend to lose this ability, depending upon our vision more for the identification of things, and suppressing the mere appearance of objects in favor of what our experience and knowledge tell us we ought to see. Thus we ignore much of what we look at.

Learning to photograph involves relearning to see

Merely learning to see objectively, however, is not enough to make an artist out of an art appreciator. The artist must also be able to create in his own work the visual qualities he finds appealing. This requires ability to visualize and to make comparisons between the subject as it exists and its image as it might be created.

In photography, to a greater degree than in any of the other visual arts, the technical limitations of the medium must be considered in this visualization. The photographer is tightly bound to his subject in many ways—perhaps trapped by it would be a better phrase—so that much of what he may like to think of as creativity is really only making the best of the situation. Maybe that's the same thing, at least some of the time.

The photographer is trapped by his subject

Light is one of the things over which a photographer often can have some sort of control. Even when no actual change in lighting conditions can be made, a good photographer will find a light condition which displays the subject to best advantage and will place himself and the subject to make the most of it. When the light can be controlled, photography becomes almost as free as drawing. Light can be made to explain forms, control the illusion of space, emphasize textures or subdue them, establish compositional patterns of tone, and create atmosphere and mood.

When light can be controlled, photography becomes almost free

Arranging effective lighting in the studio is made easier if there is a great deal of space around the subject, because light from a distant source is always much more even in intensity across the set than is light from a source close to the set. The reason for this is stated in the *Inverse Square Law of Illumination* which says, "Illumination (light brightness on a surface) varies inversely with the square of the distance from the light source to the illuminated surface." You may recognize this as the same law which explains the exposure increase necessary in photomacrography, because of the increase of distance from lens to film. The law does not apply to broad sources of diffused light or to pictures taken of luminous subjects,

Lighting is easier if there is a great deal of space

213

nor does the distance from camera to subject have any significant effect upon the brightness of the camera image, whether the subject is luminous or not (Fig. 21.1).

The inverse square law is valid for most situations

The law is valid for most lighting situations, however, and if only a single light is to be used, it must be placed with great care to avoid unpleasant harshness or light imbalance across the subject. As a rule, a single light should be placed no closer to the subject than about eight times the subject depth, as seen from the light position, not from the camera.

For example, if the subject occupies a space two feet by six feet, and if the light must come from the long side, it should be placed about forty-eight feet away **if it is the only source** and if the subject illumination must appear uniform from side to side. If the subject can be lighted across its two-foot dimension, the source can be placed only about sixteen feet away with good results.

In practice it is seldom necessary to go to these extremes for several reasons. Almost any light intended for photographic use will be directed by some sort of lens system (such as the Fresnel lens of a spotlight) or reflector and will be somewhat beamed. Even flood lights, which are designed to cover a relatively wide area evenly, will be found to provide brighter light in the center of their fields than at the edges.

Lights can be feathered

Such lights can be "feathered" across the subject; that is, the brighter central beam can be directed toward the farthest extreme of the subject which allows the nearest edge to be illuminated by the less-bright fringe of the beam. If this is done skillfully, and the light intensity is carefully checked with an incident meter at both extremes of the subject dimension, the light distance can often be reduced considerably with no ill effects. Occasionally, on very wide subjects, two or more lights can be feathered on the subject so that each covers only a portion of the total width. If the lights are placed so that each is at about the same distance from its own section of the subject, and if their directions are carefully matched to imply a single source, the results can be quite acceptable.

Figure 21.1 A single large studio strobe, bounced from the twelve-foot-high ceiling, provided light for this shot. The illumination is fairly even because the Inverse Square Law is not entirely valid for diffused light situations. The black paper background provides very little reflection and keeps lighting contrast high.

Reflected light is another factor which nearly always helps to even out the subject illumination. Some of the *spill* light (light that is falling outside the subject area) will usually reach the subject by reflection from walls, the floor, and ceiling and will often add significantly to the total illumination level. Because it is diffused by reflection, it is relatively directionless and uniform in intensity and will, therefore, illuminate the shadow areas of the subject quite evenly. Thus, although there may still be a noticeable decrease in highlight brightness across the subject, the shadows may seem quite uniform in tone. Of course it isn't necessary to rely on random reflection for this effect. Most photographers have plenty of reflectors available and place them with just as much care as they devote to the lights themselves.

Reflected light helps

Reflectors, in fact, *are* light sources as far as the subject is concerned. Their soft illumination, as compared to the "hard" light of a bare light bulb is due simply to the fact that they represent a large area of illumination rather than a small, or point source. It is the *area* of the light source that counts. A large source will produce a soft light, characterized by indistinct shadows and low contrast. A point source produces sharp-edged shadows and seems harsh and contrasty. Remember that distance is a factor here, too. Any light source placed close to the subject will tend to produce soft-edged shadows, and the shadows will become more distinct and harsher as the light is moved away from the subject, even though the overall lighting effect will seem unpleasantly glaring and uneven at close range and will become more uniform as the distance increases.

Reflectors are light sources

Reflectors can be made to provide either soft or hard light depending upon their size and their surface. A *flat* of white-painted canvas, evenly illuminated, will substitute for a bank of fluorescent lights or a wall of windows. On the other hand, a small reflector covered with crumpled foil can replace a flood light, and a regular hand mirror can be used to direct a more controlled spot of light than most spotlights can. The fact that the reflector is merely reflecting light, not producing it, is of no importance to the *quality* of the light. If sheer intensity of illumination is not important, reflectors can be made to do any job that a luminous source can do and often more effectively and conveniently. Of course some light source must be available to illuminate the reflector surface.

**Reflectors can do any job
that a luminous source can do**

On occasions it is inconvenient or impossible to illuminate a reflector surface adequately; perhaps because it is hidden behind a part of the subject and can't be reached with a light beam, or because there is no light outlet available on that side of the set. In these cases an almost identical effect can be obtained using a translucent screen of cloth, paper, plastic, or similar material and illuminating it from the rear. There is usually more light loss, because materials which will diffuse the light sufficiently do not transmit it well. There is also likely to be a distinct change in the color of the light—usually toward yellow or orange—due to the same effect of scattering which makes the atmosphere tint the setting sun an unusually warm tone.

Translucent screens are useful

If the effect of a direct beam of light on the subject is desirable, but some softening of the shadow edges seems necessary, a semitransparent screen can be set up between the light source and the subject. Plastic sheeting of various degrees of translucency is available and can be used for this purpose if it is not exposed to too much heat from the lamp. Another suitable material is cheesecloth. For use close to the light source, a fireproof material is preferable, and fiberglass mats and fabrics are sometimes used. Translucent screens used for this purpose or for diffusing the background details of a studio setup are sometimes called *scrims*.

Arrangement of lights should be guided by what the camera will see

Arranging a lighting setup is difficult if it is not guided by what the camera will see. The eye, no matter how skilled, does not match the lens in field of view, in point of view, or in depth of field. The photographer sees the subject as a series of related fragments which his mind integrates. The camera stares fixedly at the whole scene and will record it objectively.

Appraising the lighting at any stage of the process is easier in the camera viewfinder than with the naked eye because the composition is delimited and the effects of pattern can be seen without the confusion of irrelevant background forms. A view camera is better for this purpose than a simple viewfinder, but a reflex camera is perhaps better still. It seems easier to judge composition when the image is right-side-up and correctly oriented left-to-right. Some people think the smaller image helps, too, in the overall appraisal, since it is easier to see as a unit.

Check the lighting setup with a Polaroid picture

A great many professional photographers check their subject for composition and lighting by the obvious technique of taking a picture of it. The best and simplest method of doing this is to put a Polaroid back on your camera if it will accept it and expose a sheet of Polaroid film. It can be developed one sheet at a time and will produce a finished black-and-white print in about twenty seconds.

If your camera will not accept Polaroid film itself, it is usually possible to get a good idea of the lighting by using a separate Polaroid camera held as near to the main camera as practicable. The slight difference in viewpoint will probably not matter in the appraisal of the light condition but may not be adequate for the judgment of composition.

Or a sample exposure on regular film

If neither of these alternatives is possible and if the setup is near a darkroom, a sample exposure of the picture can be made on the regular film, unless it is to be a color shot, and quickly processed. If you cannot judge the picture from the resulting negative, it can be wiped surface-dry and printed immediately in an enlarger, without being either washed or dried. Be very careful to avoid contaminating your enlarger carrier with the hypo or other chemicals.

Beginners do not usually handle studio lighting well

Beginners do not usually handle studio lighting well. They tend to produce uneven illumination, harsh contrast, and an effect of shallow, crowded space. They are likely to distort the form of objects, confuse the separation of outlines, and tax the compositional structure of the arrangement by creating large, obvious shadows where they have no business appearing. They achieve these ugly results by making three fundamental errors in setting up their lights.

They place lights randomly; too close to the subject; and use the lights raw

First, they place light almost randomly without a guiding plan, tending to use each new light to try to correct some previous mistake; in the lighting battle they are constantly on the defensive. Second, they tend to place lights too close to the subject. Third, they almost invariably use the lights raw; that is, direct and without diffusion.

If you are having any or all of these troubles, it may help you to approach your next subject this way.

1. *Decide what visual effect you are trying to achieve.*
2. Flood the set with diffused light, bounced from walls and ceiling as evenly as possible, and of sufficient intensity to make the exposure possible. Check it with your meter to be sure.
3. Add one main light, intense enough to establish the shadow pattern and modelling effect desired. Control the sharpness or softness of the shadow edges by enlarging or decreasing the area of the source. Keep it far enough away from the subject or feather it so that there is reasonably uniform brightness across the subject.
4. Separate the subject from its background by illuminating or darkening the background to the desired degree, or by rim-lighting the subject from the rear.
5. Add reflectors as necessary to balance the overall visual effect. (Additional lights may be used if they are kept dim enough and soft enough to prevent conflict with the patterns established by the main light.) Adjust local areas by shading them with *flags* (small cards on thin wire or pole supports) or by adding necessary reflectors.

Once a setup is started it is usually possible to make adjustments and corrections to arrive at a satisfactory solution. But sometimes things just don't seem to go right. The initial setup looks fairly good, but the adjustments don't help, and finally you discover that you've ruined the whole effect. This is the time to sit down for a few minutes and think things over carefully. It often helps to turn on the lights one at a time to see what each one is doing and to see if the good effects of one light are being masked by another.

More often than not, particularly if the setup is a complicated one, the total effect will seem pointless, bland, harsh, or confusing. If this is the case, it is probable that you have arrived at the arrangement by collecting visual fragments. You should have started with a concept and built toward it. It's a little like assembling a jigsaw puzzle. Putting together a few little groups of pieces, or assembling them without regard for the picture, will result in chaos. The organized result is only obtained when the individual pieces unite to form one picture.

If you don't know where to begin, it may be helpful to consider daylight as a model for your setup. Think of some condition of daylight which you have found appealing and appropriate and analyze it. Daylight can be almost anything, but it has a couple of essential characteristics. It is almost always top light, almost never stronger from below than from above; and it almost always consists of one main light source, the sun, which casts a single set of shadows, and a substantial amount of fill light which is diffused and illuminates the shadows.

Daylight is normally a mixture of direct light from the sun and diffused light from the sky canopy. On a very clear, cloudless day the sunlight is the stronger source by far and will cast distinct dark shadows. If the atmosphere is hazy or the sky is thinly overcast, the sunlight will be reduced in intensity, and the shadows it casts will be softer in outline and less dark. As the overcast thickens, the proportion of direct light is further reduced and the skylight becomes relatively more and more effective. The shadows cast by the weakening sunlight will become indistinct in outline and light in tone. Finally, in conditions of heavy overcast, the sun is not effective as a direct light source. There are no real shadows and the completely diffused and directionless light is flat and gray.

It can be simulated indoors

Indoors the effect of bright sunlight can be simulated with a bright direct light source of a small area such as a spotlight or even a plain light bulb without a reflector. If very little light is allowed to reflect from the walls and ceiling of the room, the ratio of direct light to reflected light will be high and the illumination will be harsh and glaring. The shadows will be sharp and distinct and the effect will be similar to clear daylight.

The sharpness of the shadows will depend upon the area of the light source and its distance from the subject. Sharpness will increase if the source is narrowed or moved away from the subject. The contrast of the illumination will depend upon the relative intensity of the direct and reflected light at the subject position. A "raw" light bulb in a white room will provide a great deal of diffused bounce light from the walls and ceiling and, although the shadow patterns may be distinctly visible, the illumination contrast may be relatively low. On the other hand, a single shielded light source in a dark room will create an effect of extreme contrast at the subject position.

In any normal daylight situation, there is some reflection of light from other objects and surfaces near the subject, including the ground. In the

Figure 21.2   This "studio" shot was made out-of-doors under a heavy overcast. The background is white paper, taped down on a sidewalk and run up the side of a building. Except for problems with the wind and blowing leaves this was not a difficult picture to set up. It would have required a fairly large studio and very careful lighting if it had been made indoors. Outdoor light can make "studio" jobs simple—in addition to conserving electricity! (Courtesy of the University of Michigan Press)

Figure 21.3   Multiple banks of ceiling lights over a large area produce an almost shadow-free condition, similar to a very large skylight. (Courtesy of the University of Michigan Press)

studio these sources of diffused light can be simulated with flats, sheets of paper or cloth, or even by painting the studio walls (Fig. 21.2).

There is no reason why a studio lighting setup should duplicate daylight quality, although in many cases it may be useful to imitate it fairly closely. Daylight is believable light and it treats forms and surfaces kindly. There is danger (for the beginner at least) in departing too far from reality. Illumination which is surreal or bizarre will call attention to itself and establish a mood which may be inappropriate for the subject. It is certainly effective and desirable, however, for unusual effects.

For general purposes, it is hard to find a light condition better than the classic artist's skylight will provide. This large source of soft top light is direct enough to produce beautiful modelling of form, soft enough to avoid harshness and unpleasant contrasts, and certainly charming in its directness and simplicity (Fig. 21.3). A close second choice, at least for small objects, is the light provided by a large window. If facing away from the sun, or if curtained to diffuse the sunlight, window light is very pleasant (Fig. 21.4). The object will be most clearly modelled if it is placed close to the window and shot in cross-light. Some bounce light may be necessary to fill the shadows.

Light effects very similar to these can be produced in the studio by bouncing light from a small *fly* or *flat* fairly close to the subject, taking care to eliminate direct light or spill light from the set. The subject contrast can be controlled by adjusting the position of additional white flats around the subject position (Fig. 21.5).

Outside his studio, a photographer's control of light is considerably diminished as a rule. (It is not unusual for professional photographers to illuminate enormous areas of the outdoors with flash or flood light but this is really studio lighting, at least in intent.) Daylight, as mentioned before, is almost indefinable so no general rules can be given for coping with it, but if you are consciously sensitive to the quality of the light as it exists at the subject position, you can often see some improvement in the overall effect that can be made by simply turning the subject in the

Daylight is believable light

Skylight and window-light can be excellent

Figure 21.4   Backlighting is an excellent method of separating forms in space. Broad light source and plenty of interior reflected light prevent this group shot from becoming unpleasantly harsh and contrasty. (Courtesy of the University of Michigan Press)

light or by moving your own position. In some cases a reflector or two, strategically placed, will help reduce contrast or define a shape or an edge that might otherwise be lost.

If you can't control daylight, you can at least select it

Figure 21.5 An example of "tent" lighting. This picture of engine parts being bathed by flowing oil owes its decorative effect to controlled reflections in the oil surface. The setup was surrounded by white paper and covered by a translucent white "fly." Light, directed through the tent walls and ceiling, was adjusted by black and gray paper strips taped inside at strategic points to accent the reflection patterns. (Courtesy of the Technical Research Laboratories, General Motors Corp.)

If you cannot control daylight, you can at least select a condition of daylight which suits you (Fig. 21.6); this is a possibility that most beginners in photography ignore. Snapshooters of thirty years ago were incessantly brainwashed by the "authorities" to confine their picture-taking to the daylight hours between 10:00 A.M. and 2:00 P.M., and to keep the sun behind them while shooting. It would be hard to imagine a more ugly light condition for most purposes, and yet the habit has persisted.

Professional photographers tend to avoid high noon light like the plague and work feverishly through the fleeting minutes of dawn and dusk to make best use of the magically beautiful quality of light which exists so briefly then. No studio setup can ever duplicate the delicate, subtle quality of great natural light (Fig. 21.7), but natural light is unpredictable and constantly changing. To use it well, you must have patience to wait, and the skill and knowledge to make use of it while it lasts. It will take practice (Fig. 21.8).

Dawn and dusk are not the only workable alternatives by any means. An overcast can turn a July noon into a pleasant light condition. Rainy days are often extremely beautiful; color seems almost luminous in wet, gray weather. Heavy black storm clouds can create light conditions of spectacular quality, but the effects are often brief (Fig. 21.9). Fog, snow, mist, and all their variations and combinations will provide the sensitive photographer with enough variety of light conditions to last his lifetime. Almost every imaginable kind of light will happen somewhere, sometime, and the best conditions will transform ordinary objects into truly beautiful things (Fig. 21.10).

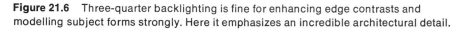

Figure 21.6 Three-quarter backlighting is fine for enhancing edge contrasts and modelling subject forms strongly. Here it emphasizes an incredible architectural detail.

Figure 21.7 Hiding the sun behind the flag has helped to avoid possible flare while allowing the water to sparkle interestingly. An approaching storm adds to this rather dramatic condition of light. You must often work fast to capture these effects; within fifteen minutes after this picture was taken the clouds obscured the sun and the scene went dead. (Courtesy of the University of Michigan Press)

Figure 21.8 Bright moonlight can be measured with a very sensitive light meter, but it is so dim that reciprocity failure is a major consideration in determining an appropriate exposure. Practically speaking, it's difficult to overexpose pictures like this one. Here the building floodlights were turned on for two seconds to register details on the underside of the reflector dish, then they were turned off and the exposure continued by moonlight alone for another four hours. The sky streaks are star trails. The glow in the sky at the horizon is from a distant small town. (Courtesy of the University of Michigan Press)

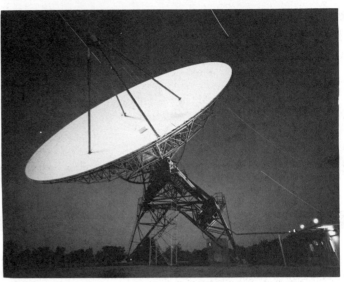

The high speed lenses and fast films available for 35-mm cameras have caused increasing interest in *available light* photography. This is usually construed to mean photography in dim light, often artificial, not specifically arranged for photographic purposes. The quality of available light is no more definable than the quality of daylight. It can be almost any sort of light—bright or dim, flat or contrasty, even or spotty, soft or harsh. It rarely seems to be "good" light to work with, but it is often dramatic and exciting light.

Available light is seldom good, but it can be exciting light

Figure 21.9 White Sands, New Mexico. During a thunderstorm a brief opening in the heavy clouds let the sun through for just long enough to make this picture.

Figure 21.10 The wide-angle lens used here emphasizes the bulk of the fish seine these men are pulling. Shooting against the light dramatizes the sparkle and texture of the flowing water and reduces background confusion. (Courtesy of the University of Michigan Press)

Contrast will probably be high; multiple shadows are common

Perhaps the most common available light condition is typified by an average house room interior at night. The general level of illumination is very low, but the light close to the various lamps is quite bright. The contrast, in other words, is likely to be very high. Home interiors are normally only moderately reflective and not much fill light will be available in most room locations. A room will usually have several lamps burning, each creating a little localized pool of light. Multiple shadows are common.

Take advantage of the breaks

Each of these conditions would be considered a problem in the studio, but this is a different kind of photography. The studio setup usually attempts to accentuate form, texture, and color and describes the object in elaborate detail. The available light picture must capitalize on mood and atmosphere. It is a case of realism versus impressionism, statement versus implication, complete control versus taking advantage of the breaks.

Technically the problems are often formidable. The low level of illumination will require a fast lens and fast film as well as a fairly slow shutter speed. The high contrast will dictate less-than-normal developing time for low *gamma*. These requirements will typically result in an image of only moderate sharpness and shallow depth of field; fairly contrasty, quite grainy, and often blurred from subject or camera motion. Also, because the small camera image is tiny, it must be enlarged greatly for use, a factor which aggravates most of the problems still more.

In such conditions keep your wits about you and do the best you can. The worst errors you can make are camera movement and overdevelopment, both of which, except in rare instances, will be disastrous. Camera movement is usually much less acceptable than subject movement, and if you must accept the risk of one or the other, put the camera on a tripod and shoot slow. The occasional exception to this rule may result in a spectacular picture.

Avoid the amateur trap of forcing development. In contrasty conditions, which most such situations are, you need low gamma, not high. The gain in film speed which the forced development provides will usually be more than offset by the loss of detail in both shadow areas and highlights and the harshness of midtone gradation. Unless subject contrast is untypically low, set your meter at **less** than normal film speed and *underdevelop.*

Because fill light is often almost nonexistent, you must depend upon other methods of balancing your composition and implying space and form. Look for larger, more dramatic areas of solid black and white to compose with, and separate forms by silhouetting them against bright areas or actual light sources. Look for rim-light conditions and glare light from shiny surfaces to delineate edges. Be particularly flexible in your choice of viewpoints, lining things up in space—light against dark, dark against light—for best separation and depth.

Make the most of the wide lens aperture. Its normal aberrations will often add a pleasing softness, and the effects of flare light can often be manipulated for decorative effects. The inevitable circles-of-confusion can be used, too. They can often be placed so as to outline a part of an essential dark foreground form. Use your head. Successful available light photography is an exercise in ingenuity and skill. "Great" shots, under these conditions, rarely just happen, but they are there for the making.

Make the most of the wide lens aperture

In working in the studio with floodlight, or in daylight, or available light condition, the exposure can be determined with a regular exposure meter in the conventional way. Exposures for flashbulbs and electronic flash units (*strobe*), on the other hand, must be measured or computed in other ways because their light is so brief that an ordinary meter will not react to it at all.

Flash exposures must be computed in other ways

If only one flash source is used, the exposure can be estimated quite satisfactorily by referring to a table of *guide numbers*, usually supplied by the manufacturer of the bulb or the strobe unit. A guide number represents the product of an f/number multiplied by some subject distance in feet.

Guide numbers will work with one source

Thus if you have set your light unit fifteen feet from the subject and find that the guide number for the light unit and the film speed that you are using is 300, the required lens opening can be found by dividing 300 by 15, which is 20, or f/20. If you decide to move the light back to 30 feet from the subject (irrespective of the camera position) you must open up the lens to f/10. If for some reason you want to use an aperture of f/32, you must place the light about 9¼ feet from the subject.

A faster film, a brighter light, or a longer effective flash duration will all increase the guide number. Placing two identical lights together so that they cover the subject from the same position will almost double the intensity and increase the guide number by up to 140 percent. If the two lights are placed at different angles to the subject, the increase will be somewhat less.

Other setups will require more sophisticated methods

More complicated lighting setups will require more sophisticated methods of exposure determination. A good one, and reasonably inexpensive, is to estimate the exposure on the basis of the guide numbers and test it by taking a Polaroid shot. This has the combined virtue of checking the accuracy of the exposure, the light balance, and composition all at the same time. It will only be accurate if the Polaroid film is fresh and the developing conditions are controlled and near-normal. Very cold temperatures (outdoors in winter) will prevent normal development and nullify the test.

Strobe meters are particularly useful for large-set work

Another good method, especially suited for use with electronic flash lighting, is to employ a special *strobe meter*. Using special light-sensitive cells with very fast response time and electronic circuitry which amplifies the cell output and stores the energy produced, these meters can measure the effective illumination within a fraction of a stop. They are essentially incident meters, but they can be used for measurement of individual light brightness if desired. They are particularly useful for large-set color work in the studio because they are adaptable to any sort of light condition and are very accurate when properly handled.

Comparing flash and flood exposures

There is one more technique for determining flash or strobe exposures which is both effective and fairly inexpensive but will require some individual calibration for good results. It involves making a practical comparison between the total effective light emitted by the flash source and some equivalent exposure in floodlight.

The light from a flashbulb is much more intense than floodlight, but it is of very short duration. Suppose you find by experimentation that good exposure is achieved using the flash at an aperture of f/11, at a flash-to-subject distance of ten feet, and using the entire light output of the bulb. If a flood bulb is set up at the same position and its intensity at the subject is measured with an incident meter, you may find the proper exposure time for that intensity and same aperture, f/11, to be two seconds. From then on, it will be possible to set up the floodlight on any subject at any distance, read the light and *select the aperture indicated for an exposure time of two seconds*. Replace the flood with the flash unit and fire away.

The camera shutter speed is unimportant provided it is long enough to use the entire duration of the flash. With ordinary flashbulbs, this will be about 1/25 second or longer. For electronic flash units, the shutter speed is immaterial, except for focal plane shutters, since the flash duration is so brief (in the order of 1/500 to 1/2000 second or faster) that it will have been completed before the shutter can close.

Using the entire flash duration is called open flash

The technique just described, using the entire effective flash duration, is called *open flash* because you rather leisurely open the shutter, set off the flash manually, then close the shutter without any attempt to rush things. If there is any appreciable amount of light at the subject position, or if the subject is moving, it is often desirable to synchronize the flash to coincide with the shutter opening at some higher speed. Then, of course, the exposure will have to be recalculated. Most modern cameras are equipped with built-in synchronizers.

Synchronization is easiest with between-the-lens shutters

Flash synchronization is easier with leaf or between-the-lens shutters than with focal plane shutters because the leaf shutters expose the entire film area at one time regardless of shutter speed. Focal plane shutters achieve their higher speeds by reducing the width of the curtain slit rather than increasing the curtain speed, and as a result, the image is "spread" across the film surface in somewhat the same way that paint is spread with a roller. The highest speed that actually exposes the entire film area at one time is usually about 1/60 to 1/125 second for small focal plane shutters. Larger cameras rarely manage this at speeds greater than about 1/30.

If focal plane synchronization is attempted at higher speeds, the flash will simply print the image of the shutter slit somewhere along the image area. Electronic flash, being much more brief than conventional flash, will stop the shutter travel and show a distinct image of the curtain slit. Flash-bulbs will usually show more of the image but most of it will be under-exposed to the point of uselessness.

Electronic flash is commonly called *strobe*—a term derived from "stroboscope" (Fig. 21.11). A genuine strobe light is one designed to flash repeatedly and at a controlled rate for the purpose of illuminating and analyzing the motion of rotating or reciprocating machine parts, as one example. Stroboscopes have also become popular with entertainers for their flickering psychedelic effect.

Stroboscopes are electronic flash, but electronic flash units are not usually stroboscopes

A stroboscope is an electronic flash unit, but electronic flash units for photography are not usually stroboscopes. Photographic flash units are intended to store a considerable amount of energy to be released in one relatively powerful flash, and they consequently require a *charging time* of several seconds between flashes. Only a few of them can be fired for very long in rapid sequence without overheating and possible damage to the flash tube.

Units designed for high power dissipation use quartz flash tubes

True stroboscopes can be adjusted to fire automatically at rates of as high as sixty flashes per second or even more. They manage this by using

Figure 21.11 Lighting contrast in this dark, cavernous room was very high. To avoid harshness and to record some details in the foreground a small electronic flash was bounced from the ceiling. Although the light on the seated figures is obviously not coming from the lamps, it is not obtrusively false and the picture is acceptable. (Courtesy of the University of Michigan Press)

high speed charging circuits, by extremely short flash duration, and by storing relatively little energy for each flash. Because of the low flash energy, the total power dissipation is kept within reasonable limits and overheating is usually avoided. Units, both stroboscopic and photographic, designed for very high power dissipation are often equipped with quartz flash tubes which can stand much greater heat than conventional glass tubes can tolerate.

Two differences between flash and strobe

There are two differences between flash and strobe. One is color. Strobe is designed to be similar to daylight in Kelvin temperature; that is, somewhere around 6000°K. Flashbulbs are naturally much warmer; the clear glass variety produce a light of about 3800°K. Most flashbulbs available now, however, especially in the amateur sizes, are dyed blue to shift their light toward daylight color. In practice, their light is warmer than strobe, as a rule, but pleasantly so. Strobe light is often a little too purplish for use raw, but that depends somewhat upon the color balance of the film in use and personal taste. For black-and-white work, the results are good with either source.

Flash is a bonfire in a bottle

The other practical difference between flash and strobe is in their firing time. Strobe, being electronic and producing its actual light by a miniature lightning flash, is instantaneous. Flash, on the other hand, is a bonfire in a bottle. After the firing current is applied to it, a flashbulb kindles itself, burns a little, then flares up into the effective flash which dies down, glows for a while, then goes out. The whole operation may take as long as 1/10 second. Regular wire-filled bulbs generally require about twenty milliseconds to reach useful brilliance after the contact is made, and their peak duration is also about 20 ms. In the larger bulb sizes the peak is somewhat longer.

Shutters usually provide separate settings for the synchronization of flash and strobe, and in some cases separate *flash posts* or flash contacts are used as well.

Shutter settings for flash

The shutter setting which indicates a 10 to 20 ms delay for normal flashbulbs is labelled "M" for "medium." At this setting the shutter release first makes electrical contact to fire the bulb, the indicated delay takes place, then the shutter is allowed to open to make the exposure.

And strobe

At the X setting of the synchronizer, the shutter opens directly and the flash firing contact is not made until the shutter is fully open. This setting is used for electronic flash, and because the flash response time is instantaneous and its duration is extremely short, it will fire to full intensity and go out before the shutter can close at even its highest speed. When strobe light is used, the shutter speed setting is not a factor in the film exposure unless there is some other light present at the subject position. With flashbulbs, the shutter determines the exposure duration at speeds above 1/30 second, and the guide numbers for these higher speeds will decrease progressively.

Mixing flash and existing light can be a vexing problem

Mixing flash or strobe light with existing light can be a vexing problem. It is perhaps easiest to start with the existing light measurement and select some combination of lens opening and shutter speed which will be adequate. Then find the guide number for the light unit in use and if it is electronic flash, divide the guide number by the previously selected aperture to find the required flash distance from the subject. This will make the flash and the existing light about equal in intensity.

The existing light effect can be reduced or increased without affecting the strobe exposure by *changing the shutter speed*. Changing the lens opening will affect both light sources equally. Changing the light-to-subject distance will affect the strobe only.

If the light is conventional flash, the situation is slightly more complicated. Changing the lens opening **or** the shutter speed will affect both light sources in the higher speed ranges. At speeds under 1/30 second, the shutter speed will only affect the existing light exposure. The simplest method of adjusting the illumination intensities relative to each other is to *move the flash unit*; farther from the subject to subdue the flash in favor of the existing light, or closer to the subject, *with a corresponding decrease in aperture*, to keep the flash exposure constant while reducing the existing light effect.

In any situation where lighting becomes this involved, it is an excellent idea to make a test exposure on Polaroid film. Lighting balance is difficult to adjust if you can't watch the effect.

It is an excellent idea to make a test on Polaroid film

Many photographers seem to feel that electronic flash light has some sort of mystical advantage over other artificial light sources which makes it produce softer light than most. It does certainly have different characteristics in some respects, but the strobe mystique is utter nonsense. Strobe lights gained their reputation for magical powers soon after they were introduced, at which time they were generally operated at very high voltage levels with relatively small capacitors for energy storage. The result was a flash of high intensity and extremely short duration.

The strobe mystique is utter nonsense

It is a well-known fact that light conditions which dictate either very short or very long exposure times will cause failure of the reciprocity law in films and will alter their normal contrast and gradation characteristics. Early strobe units did just this. The loss of film speed was unnoticed for lack of any comparison standard, but the loss of contrast was apparent. Strobe became famous for softness or low contrast, and strobe negatives were given extra development as normal procedure.

Very short exposure times cause reciprocity failure

Modern strobes, particularly the small amateur varieties, are generally low-voltage devices employing high capacity storage condensers. Their flash duration is typically in the area of 1/500 second to perhaps 1/2000 second, not high enough to cause any appreciable change in the contrast or sensitivity of most materials.

So most strobes are now "normal" lights which will produce "normal" exposures, but there are a few available which are not. There are a number of newly-designed automatic units on the market which can reach a top speed of up to 1/50,000 second under certain conditions; well into the range of reciprocity failure for all normally available films. Films exposed at speeds like this, *regardless of how the speed is obtained*, will be soft in gradation and will have to be pushed in development to reach normal contrast.

Good lighting takes skill and perception, not magic

Remember that the characteristics of any light source can be determined most accurately by noting its *area*, its *intensity*, its *color*, its *duration* (if a flash source), and its *beam spread*. If these qualities are similar or can be compensated for in two different sources, their photographic effect will be similar and they can be substituted one for the other. Good photographic lighting requires knowledge and skill and perception, but it isn't black magic.

How Color Films and Papers Work

22

There are some colors which every painter knows cannot be made from mixtures of other colors; they are called *primaries*. In pigments there are three primary colors: red, yellow, and blue; and it is theoretically possible to make any other color by mixing these colors in proper proportions. Thus orange can be made from red and yellow. Green results from mixtures of yellow and blue, and purple can be made from blue and red.

In pigments there are three primary colors

The colors which result from mixtures of two of the primaries are called *secondaries*, and they are often shown in relationship to the primaries in a classic color wheel diagram such as Figure 22.1. Colors which lie directly across from each other on the color wheel are called *complements* of each other. They are exact opposites. If two complementary pigment colors are mixed together, they are said to *neutralize* each other, and the resulting color is, in theory at least, black. The color relationships this wheel expresses are useful in paint mixing but are not very pertinent to photographic light or dye colors.

Mixtures of the primaries make secondaries

Complementary colors neutralize each other

Pigments appear colored because they absorb portions of the light spectrum and reflect the remainder. The color they reflect is the color we see, and the color we identify as being the pigment color. Because pigments produce their color effect by absorbing—or subtracting—portions of the incident light, we call the pigment color system *subtractive*.

The color pigments reflect is the color we see

In the subtractive system, the brightest most saturated color obtainable is an unmixed primary (see back colorplate, p. 353). Any mixture of pigments must become darker in tone and less brilliant than its primary components. Mixing white pigment with one of the primaries will

In the subtractive system, the brightest color is an unmixed primary

Figure 22.1

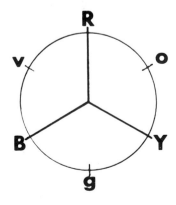

cause it to reflect more total light (making it lighter in tone) and some of all the spectrum colors, thus diluting the predominant hue into a pastel tint.

Light colors behave differently; they are additive

If you blend colored light beams on a screen, rather than colored pigments or dyes on paper, you will discover that they behave somewhat differently from pigments (see back colorplate, p. 353). In the first place, you will notice that mixtures of light result in brighter colors than the original primaries because light colors are *additive*. Turning off all the light produces black; blending the three primaries makes white.

The light primaries are red, blue, and green

But strangest of all, the primaries themselves are different. The most useful light primaries turn out to be a rather bloody red, a purplish blue, and a yellowish green. As seen in the color wheel diagram in Figure 22.2, the secondaries are magenta (red and blue), yellow (red and green), and a blue-green color called cyan (blue and green). When the light primaries are properly adjusted in their relationship to each other, their secondaries will be found to form a very useful set of pigment primaries, and they will

Light secondaries are the pigment primaries magenta, yellow, and cyan

complement each other almost perfectly. Thus, for example, an area of cyan dye on paper will appear black if illuminated by red light, etc.

There is no way, unfortunately, to record colors directly on film. The only practical light sensitive emulsions which we have available at the present time are composed of silver halides and yield black-and-white silver images after exposure and development. "But," you say, "people take color pictures all the time!" And of course that's true, but it's not done *directly* on film.

Color film is really three films in one

Color film is really three films in one. Three emulsion layers, coated one over the other on a common base, are especially sensitized and filtered so that each layer reacts to only one of the light primary colors. The bottom layer, next to the film base, is especially sensitized to red light (and, of course, blue which is basic to all silver halide emulsions) but not to green. The middle layer is sensitive to green and blue but not to red. Next comes a thin layer of colloidal silver of a strong yellow color which restricts blue light from reaching either of the lower layers, and, on top of that, a simple blue sensitive emulsion layer (Fig. 22.3).

The emulsion layers contain color couplers

Most color films contain in their emulsion layers certain exotic chemical compounds called *color couplers* which react with the oxidation products

Figure 22.2

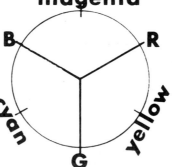

Figure 22.3

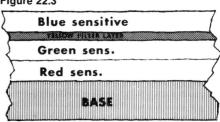

of the special *color developer* to produce dye colors. Each emulsion layer contains couplers designed to produce a particular color; cyan in the bottom layer, magenta in the middle layer, and yellow in the top layer. Notice that these dye colors are the complements of the light colors to which each emulsion layer is sensitive. Kodachrome films are different from most other color films in that they do not incorporate the usual couplers in their emulsion layers; instead they derive them from the developing baths. Each layer of Kodachrome film is developed separately by techniques and with machinery which are closely controlled and automated. These films are not intended to be processed by the user.

Some films like Kodacolor and Ektacolor are designed to produce color negatives. As the term implies, the values of the developed film image are negative like ordinary black-and-white films; but unlike black-and-white films, the image is in color, and the colors are complementary to the colors of the exposing lights. Thus a color negative of the American flag would have a light yellow field containing black stars and stripes of blue-green and black. Figure 22.4 illustrates the way a negative color film would reproduce the flag colors (see back colorplate, p. 353).

Some films produce color negatives

Color negatives are useful for making color prints, but for projection or direct viewing of the film image, we need a positive. Referring to Figure 22.4, notice that if the negative image were totally removed from the film leaving clear gelatin, and if the previously unused emulsion were allowed to develop and produce its characteristic dye colors, the resulting image would be positive.

Removing a negative image from the emulsion leaves a positive

The area of the film affected by red light would now contain a sandwich of magenta and yellow dye; the area affected by white light would now be clear; and the area resulting from the blue light exposure would now be a mixture of cyan and magenta. Seen by transmitted light, these areas would appear respectively, red, white, and blue.

Since, as you can see from Figure 22.5 (see back colorplate, p. 353), the negative image is produced solely to be discarded, and since a dye image is more difficult to eliminate than a silver image, the first step in developing a color positive film is to treat it in a conventional black-and-white type developer. This developer produces a black-and-white silver image without activating the couplers, and therefore without producing an accompanying color image (Fig. 22.5b). The unused emul-

The negative image is produced to be thrown away

Figure 22.4

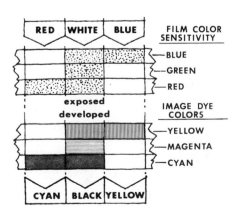

sion (neither exposed nor developed at this point) is then rendered developable by exposure to raw light or by chemical action, and the film is developed in a color-producing developer which forms simultaneously a black-and-white silver image and a dye image of the correct color in each layer (Fig. 22.5c).

After color development, the film is totally opaque; bleaching the silver leaves a dye positive

The film, at this point, is completely opaque, since it contains a complete negative silver image, a complete positive silver image, and a positive dye image. A chemical bleaching bath then removes the silver from the emulsion leaving only the positive dye image (Fig. 22.5d). There are, of course, a number of washing steps and other chemical solutions involved in the process, but they play a supporting role.

Color films are more easily damaged than black-and-white films

Since there are three separate emulsions involved, it is obvious that color film exposure and development must be more carefully controlled than is usual in black-and-white work. Color films are more easily damaged by excessive heat or humidity during storage and use, and deteriorate with age more quickly than most black-and-white films do. Variations in exposure which are insignificant in black-and-white work will become obvious, and perhaps objectionable, in color photography, and changes in processing are much more serious because they change not only density and contrast but cause shifts in color balance as well. For this reason most color developing instructions specify very precise conditions of time and temperature for the first developing bath and only slightly less rigorous control of treatment in the other solutions. A typical color process is summarized below. This is Kodak's E-3 chemistry.

First developer, 24°C. (75°F.) plus or minus 1/2° . . . . 10 mins.
Water rinse, 23–25°C. (73–77°F.) . . . . 1 min.
Hardener, 23–25°C. (73–77°F.) . . . . 3 mins.
The rest of the process can be carried out in room light.
Wash, running water, 23–25°C. (73–77°F.) . . . . 5 mins.
Reexpose both sides of film to bright light, thoroughly.
Color developer, 23–25°C. (73–77°F.) . . . . 15 mins.
Wash, running water, 23–25°C. (73–77°F.) . . . . 5 mins.
Clearing bath, 23–25°C. (73–77°F.) . . . . 5 mins.
Rinse, running water, 23–25°C. (73–77°F.) . . . . 1 min.
Bleach, 23–25°C. (73–77°F.) . . . . 8 mins.
Rinse, running water, 23–25°C. (73–77°F.) . . . . 1 min.
Fix, 23–25°C. (73–77°F.) . . . . 6 mins.
Wash, running water, 23–25°C. (73–77°F.) . . . . 8 mins.
Stabilize, 23–25°C. (73–77°F.) . . . . 1 min.
Dry, not over 43°C. (110°F.)

Kodak's E-4 process, which has now replaced this one for most films, differs in several details. E-4 is intended for 29°C. (85°F.) processing, includes different chemical steps, and effects the reversal step chemically without exposure to light.

There are other color processes available for home-processing of color film, but they are not essentially different from this one. It goes without saying that they are not usually interchangeable; that is, you cannot very successfully process GAF's Anscochrome film in Kodak's chemicals, nor

Figure 22.5

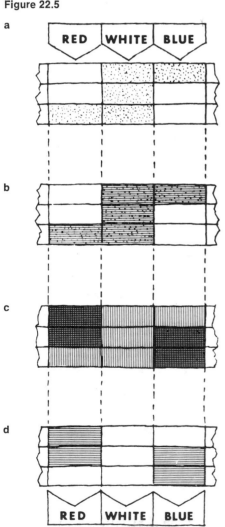

Ektachrome in Agfa chemicals since the respective developers and color couplers are not the same.

There are times when you may want to produce a color print rather than a transparency for projection. Although color prints of excellent quality can be made from positive transparencies, they are very expensive to produce and require equipment not usually found in home darkrooms. Cheaper prints are available from drugstore processors and they can also be made at home, but the quality is less than excellent, typically.

Good prints from positive transparencies are expensive

Relatively inexpensive prints of fine quality can be made from color negatives, however, and the process is easily carried out in almost any darkroom which is adequate for black-and-white printing. There are two reasons why color negatives are better for printing than positives are: they exhibit less loss of contrast in highlight and shadow areas, and there is considerably less distortion of color relationships.

Good prints from color negatives are easier and cheaper

Tone distortion occurs in every exposure-development process due to the nonlinear shape of the emulsion characteristic curve. Thus the negative image produced by one exposure-development sequence is sometimes described as being *once removed* from the original subject. If the negative is used to make a print, the printing paper emulsion contributes still further distortion to the image because of the shape of its own characteristic curve and the print image is said to be *twice removed* from reality. Each "removal," or tonal reversal, produces tonal distortion, and the more reversals that are involved in the production of the final image, the more distortion of tone will occur.

The fewer reversals the better

Color negatives produce better prints than color positives do (other things being equal) because there are fewer reversals involved, two to be exact. Printing from color positives involves four reversals;

1. The original film negative image
2. The original film positive image
3. A negative step in printing
4. The final positive printing step.

The color shift which occurs in printing is readily apparent after four reversals. Typically the magentas and pink-reds of the subject shift toward orange and the leaf-greens turn dark and bluish. Coupled with an increase in contrast in midrange tones and extreme reduction of contrast in the highlights and shadows, this slate-blue-orange color scheme is quite unpleasant.

Magentas shift toward orange, greens turn slate blue

If the image light striking the film surface were filtered with complete efficiency, one of the causes of the color shift would not exist. But the color separating filters are far from ideal in their transmission characteristics. A perfect red filter, for example, would transmit all the light wavelengths between 600 and 700 nanometers and absolutely nothing outside this range. The perfect green filter would be totally opaque to all wavelengths longer than 600 or shorter than 500 nanometers but would transmit 100 percent of the light between those limits. The ideal blue filter would begin to transmit at 500 nanometers at 100 percent efficiency and become ab-

The filters are not perfect

Figure 22.6

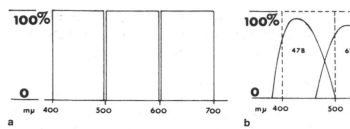

ruptly opaque at 400 nanometers. Diagramatically, filters of these ideal characteristics would behave as shown in Figure 22.6a. The best filters presently available perform about like Figure 22.6b.

Neither are the dyes

Color reproduction would still be imperfect, even with the ideal filters described, unless the image dyes were equally perfect and exactly complementary to the filters. Modern dyes are good, and year by year they are improved, but perfect they are not. Ideally the cyan dye should absorb red, and only red, light; the magenta dye should absorb only green; and the yellow only purple-blue. Practically, only the yellow dye approaches perfection. The cyan and magenta dyes both absorb appreciable quantities of blue light as well as traces of violet and green. Because of these tendencies, the image tends to be deficient in brightness in the blues, unusually bright in the yellow-orange region, and desaturation of magenta and cyan occurs.

Color negatives contain a compensating mask

These color distortions are considerably reduced in prints made from color negatives because most negative color films contain a color compensating *mask* designed to restore normal color balance in the print. The mask color in the negative is ingeniously combined with the color-forming couplers in the emulsion and is designed to have the same absorption in the cyan region that the magenta and cyan dyes have (undesirably). Since the coupler, and hence the mask color, is destroyed in the process of forming the desirable cyan image dye, the resulting cyan absorption from all sources forms an essentially uniform background for all areas of the negative.

The mask appears as a much stronger salmon-orange color in the negative than one would suspect necessary. In fact, it is virtually impossible to distinguish any colors other than cyan (from which areas the mask color has been removed). The image of a low contrast negative all but disappears in the mask stain, and only the most heavily exposed image will show the kind of visual detail that one is accustomed to in black-and-white negatives (see back colorplate, p. 353).

Printing negatives is relatively simple

Making color prints from negatives is fairly simple. The color negative is projected onto specially sensitized color printing paper in much the same way that a print is made from a regular black-and-white negative. The paper is sensitive to all colors, of course, so it requires a special safelight. Filters inserted in the light beam adjust the print color balance as desired, and herein lies the only real difficulty. Because this is a negative process, the colors are negative and correction for an off-color print must be made by adding more of the offending color to the light rather than reducing it. The orange mask must be neutralized by a strong red-orange filter before any image color correction can be attempted. The gelatin CC filters may be used under the enlarger lens for this purpose, but it is considered better practice to use large acetate filters above the enlarger condensers where they will not affect the definition of the image.

A number of enlargers are now available featuring integral filters in their light sources. Some of these employ special *dichroic* filters which are immune to fading and heat deterioration and some of the more elaborate models have provisions for coupling the filter controls to color analyzers for semiautomatic color balancing of any negative (see back colorplate, p. 353).

Dichroic filters are desirable

Color prints can also be made by exposing the paper to the three light primary colors in succession. The negative is projected, without other compensation through the red filter for a time sufficient to record all the image cyan details; then the green filter is placed under the lens and a second exposure records the magentas of the image; finally a third exposure through the blue filter builds up the image yellows to the desired intensity. Color balance is achieved by varying the relative exposure times of the three filters. Close control of print density and color balance are difficult to attain, but this sort of precision is seldom necessary for amateur work. The process is quick and easy and does indeed produce color prints.

Three-color exposure is difficult to control

A number of new color printing processes have recently been introduced and more are apparently in the offing. Color printing, which a few years ago was difficult and expensive, is becoming simple enough to compete with black-and-white. Tray processing of color prints is possible and professionals still employ drum and tank processors but the amateur can now select from a number of special canister-type tanks for fast and inexpensive print development. Chemistry has been simplified from Kodak's original five-solution, nine-step process to Beseler's recent two-solution procedure, and aerosol spray-can chemistry has been marketed. In such a rapidly changing market one can only follow the trends as best he can, relying on the dealer's recommendations in buying materials and following the manufacturer's instructions in the use of the products.

Color technology is changing rapdily

As mentioned before, prints of excellent quality can be made from color positives, but the masking corrections involved become much more formidable. Highlight contrast must usually be increased to compensate for the inevitable tonal compression and at least one color mask must be used, while two are preferred.

The best quality prints now generally available are made by the *dye-transfer process*. While this printing process can be used with either negative or positive color originals, it is usually reserved for positives. Very briefly the process works as follows:

Best print quality comes from the dye-transfer process

1. A high contrast black-and-white negative is contact printed from the transparency, exposed so that only the brightest highlights are recorded. This is called the *highlight mask*. Sometimes three highlight masks are used.
2. The transparency and the highlight mask are bound together in register and contact printed on low-contrast panchromatic film in red light. A similar exposure is made on another sheet of film in green light. These negatives are called the *principal masks*.

3. The transparency (less the highlight mask now) is bound in register with the red principal mask and contact printed on panchromatic film in red light. A similar negative is made by green light. The transparency and the green principal mask are then used to print a third negative by blue light. These are called the *separation negatives*.
4. The separation negatives are developed together (the blue negative requires more time) to achieve identical gammas.
5. The separation negatives are printed by enlarging onto special *matrix* film. After development, the matrix films are soaked one at a time in hot water which dissolves the undeveloped emulsion and produces an image in gelatin which is in relief.
6. The dried matrices are registered and punched.
7. The matrices are soaked in appropriate dye colors, complementary to the filter colors which produced them.
8. The matrices are rolled out, one after the other, on a single sheet of prepared paper. The paper leaches the dye out of the matrix gelatin and the three dye images, superimposed, comprise the final print image.

It is complicated and not for the beginner

The process is no less complicated than it sounds and is certainly not for the beginner. Success depends upon very careful control of the density and contrast of all the black-and-white films involved, and this alone is difficult. Unless you have access to a densitometer, have a large, clean darkroom, water temperature control, voltage control for your enlarger bulb, a register board and punch, a fair amount of money, lots of time and infinite patience, this is not your process.

But Cibachrome is now available

Another process capable of fine results was introduced a few years ago and called *Cibachrome*. Based on dye-destruction or controlled bleaching, it is said to produce images of superior stability and permanence. It is now available for use in the average home darkroom.

Reversal prints are of fair quality

Color prints of fair to good quality can be made from transparencies by a process somewhat similar to color negative printing. The paper used in this process is panchromatic, as is the negative paper, but the dark amber safelight which is permissible for negative printing is not safe for use with the positive reversal paper. It must be handled in total darkness. Enlargements may be made on the reversal paper directly from the transparency and color balance may be varied with filters. In this process, however, the color shift resulting from filtration is toward the filter color, not toward its complement as is the case in the negative process.

Development is similar to the processing procedure for reversal color film. There is a *first developer* which produces the necessary black-and-white negative image to be "thrown away"; a reversal exposure and development in a color developer form the positive image. The Kodak process specifies a temperature of 29°C. (85°F.), and requires about fifty minutes, not including drying time. Like Ektachrome film, the prints have a decided bluish opalescence while wet, and color balance cannot be determined accurately until they are dry.

The cheapest drugstore color prints from transparencies are sometimes made by a process like this. Somewhat better color results from the use of a color *inter-negative* copy of the transparency, followed by printing on negative paper. Because of the built-in mask in the inter-negative, both color fidelity and tonal scale are improved to some extent.

Finally, direct color prints can be made by using Polaroid's Polacolor film. Like the black-and-white emulsions, Polacolor is developed automatically in its packet and produces a finished color print in about a minute in warm weather. The film has an exposure index of about 75 and is balanced for a color temperature of 6250°K. This relatively high color temperature gives the film a characteristic warm color balance which is generally pleasing. The colors are typically very soft and muted but quite accurate.

The newest Polaroid camera uses a marvelously sophisticated film material to produce color prints which develop themselves in full daylight, right before your eyes. The prints are totally sealed in plastic and are clean and dry as they emerge from the camera. The color quality is often excellent and the dyes used are said to be very stable.

**Polacolor film gives
pleasant prints-in-a-minute**

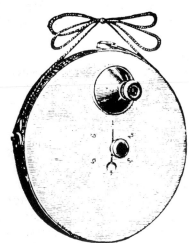

Our Cameras Photograph the World.

18,000

Sold since Oct., 1886.

Wonderful Photographic
Inventions.

C. P. Stirn's Patent
**CONCEALED VEST
CAMERAS,**

23

The Exposure-Development Relationship

Hurter and Driffield's experiments led to sensitometry

In 1876 Dr. Ferdinand Hurter, a chemist, and Mr. V. C. Driffield, an engineer, began to study the relationship between exposure and image density. Their investigations led to the science of *sensitometry*, the measurement of the sensitiveness of the photographic emulsion, and its reaction to variations in exposure and development.

Most photographers at some time in their careers experiment with films and developers to find combinations that they like. This is sensitometry in very rudimentary form, and it is both interesting and informative if done with reasonable care. But in more advanced work such as, for example, the making of dye-transfer color prints, rather exact control of negative density and contrast is necessary, and some real understanding of sensitometry is desirable.

Image formation requires both exposure and development

A film which is not exposed to any light at all, but is developed and fixed normally, will produce no appreciable image tone or density. A film which is normally exposed, but not developed, will similarly be clear or transparent after fixation. The formation of a silver image, then, requires both exposure and development. The question is, "How much?"

Figure 23.1

Suppose a sheet of film is subjected to a series of exposures which increase in intensity from some extremely low value to some equally extreme high value. Then suppose the film is developed for some reasonable time. The resulting image will show some little area of clear film where the light was not bright enough to affect the emulsion, blending into a series of increasingly dense patches indicating the areas where increasing luminance affected more and more of the emulsion. The dense patches eventually disappear into an area of complete blackness, indicating total saturation of the emulsion.

The relationship between brightness and density can be graphically demonstrated

If we think of the increasing image density as being represented by higher and higher mounds of silver particles (which, in a sense, is true), the relationship between exposure and image density can be demonstrated by a simple bar graph (Fig. 23.1a). The graph shows three steps of exposure which have produced no image (region of underexposure) and three steps (overexposure) which show no increase beyond maximum density. The steps in between illustrate the range of increasing exposures which result in corresponding increases in density.

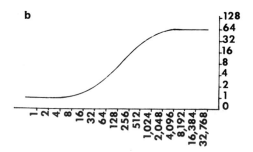

Figure 23.1b shows the same information in the form of a line graph. The horizontal axis of a graph of this kind is called the x-axis; the vertical

axis is the y-axis. The x-axis represents values of exposure, whatever they may be; 2 equals two exposure units, 4 is four units. The y-axis is similarly calibrated but it refers to the density of the silver deposit. Notice that on both axes the numbers progress geometrically; that is, each ascending number is twice as great as the preceding one, but the spaces between them remain uniform.

The x-axis represents exposure; the y-axis, density values

The exposure intervals may be labelled as *stops* if desired since exposure can be controlled by adjustment of the lens aperture, and each full stop interval represents a doubled or halved exposure relative to the preceding one. However, the standard calibration for film characteristic graphs is common logarithms. A brief review of the Log_{10} relationship to regular numbers, and to the stops interval markings should make their utility clear.

Numbers, stops, and logs

GEOMETRIC SEQUENCE	STOPS SEQUENCE	Log_{10} SEQUENCE
1		0
	1	
2		.3
	2	
4		.6
	3	
8		.9
	4	
16		1.2
	5	
32		1.5
	6	
64		1.8
	7	
128		2.1
	8	
256		2.4
	9	
512		2.7
	10	
1024		3.0

Notice that an interval of one stop is equal to a "point three" (.3) interval in the Log_{10} scale. Thus three stops equals .9; eight stops equals 2.4; five-and-one-third stops equals 1.6; and two-and-two-thirds stops equals .8. Try to become familiar with the Log_{10} numbers. They are used almost exclusively in technical literature on photography.

Figure 23.2 is a typical set of film curves taken from a technical data book. While both x- and y-axes of the graph are calibrated in Log_{10} numbers, the x-axis calibration is negative; that is, the exposures indicated are fractions of the standard exposure unit, usually meter-candle-seconds, indicating that the emulsion is sensitive to low light intensities. Similar curves for printing paper emulsions are calibrated in positive numbers indicating multiples of the standard exposure unit and lower emulsion sensitivity.

Figure 23.2

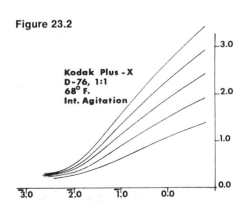

Kodak Plus - X
D-76, 1:1
68° F.
Int. Agitation

Density, opacity, and transmission

The y-axis expresses image density. Density is officially identified as the Log_{10} of the image *opacity*, and opacity is the reciprocal of *transmission*. For example, a piece of clear glass may offer no obstruction to the passage of light (let's suppose). Its light transmission is 100 percent; its opacity is 1 and its density is 0. A glass that transmits 50 percent, or ½ the light, has an opacity of 2 and a density of .3. Transmission of 10 percent means opacity of 10 and density of 1.0. The following scale shows other values of the three terms for reference.

Transmission %	Opacity	Density
100	1	0
80	1.25	.1
63	1.6	.2
50	2.0	.3
40	2.5	.4
32	3.2	.5
25	4.0	.6
20	5.0	.7
16	6.3	.8
12.5	8.0	.9
10	10	1.0
1	100	2.0
.1	1000	3.0
.01	10000	4.0

If development were invariable ... but it is not

If development were invariable, a single characteristic curve could express the entire exposure-development relationship. But it is not. Each condition of development will affect the rate or extent of image formation. It is necessary, therefore, to plot a "family of curves," sampling all the useful variations of exposure and development, for a complete analysis.

Each curve represents a certain developing time

In the usual curve family, the exposure variations are indicated as numerical values along the x-axis of the graph. The development variations are indicated by the separate curves, each curve representing a certain developing time. Image density resulting from any given amount of exposure and any given time of development can be found by reading straight up from the exposure value on the x-axis to the appropriate development curve, then horizontally across to the y-axis.

Figure 23.3

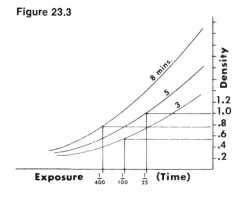

Figure 23.3 shows three examples of this procedure. Assume the light intensity to be constant for all exposure times. (1) An exposure of 1/200 second produces a latent image on the test film which is then developed for eight minutes, and the resulting negative density is .76. (2) A 1/100 second exposure developed for three minutes yields a density of .54. (3) A 1/50-second exposure developed for five minutes results in a density of 1.0. Negative densities can be read with an instrument called the *densitometer*.

Contrast is influenced strongly by development

The contrast, or density-difference between areas, is influenced strongly by the degree of development that the film receives. Extending developing time will, of course, add to the density of all the areas of the negative, but it will increase density to a greater extent in those areas which have received considerable exposure, while areas which have had relatively little exposure will gain only slightly in density. Therefore, the density difference between shadow areas and highlight areas of the negative increases as development proceeds, and proper development is achieved when the highlights and shadow areas have reached a desirable density relationship to each other.

It is usually possible, by inspection of the image characteristics, to distinguish between negatives which have been incorrectly exposed or developed. Although these clues are not infallible, the following tendencies are significant. (Refer to Fig. 23.4 to see how the negatives appear when viewed on a light-box.)

IF THE FILM HAS BEEN:	THE NEGATIVE WILL PROBABLY APPEAR:
1. Underexposed (UE) and overdeveloped (OD)	Shadows devoid of detail; highlights normal density and very harsh.
2. Normally exposed (NE) and OD	Shadow detail strong, overall high contrast, highlights may be too dense to print.
3. Overexposed (OE) and OD	Very dense and contrasty overall. Sharpness degraded. Heavy grain structure; highlight detail lost.
4. UE and normally developed (ND)	Thin, little shadow detail; midtone contrast low; highlights well formed but thin.
5. NE and ND	The perfect negative.
6. OE and ND	Dense; some loss of sharpness particularly in highlights; extreme highlight detail may be lost.
7. UE and UD	Very thin; lacking detail in shadow and midtone areas; low contrast.
8. NE and UD	Shadows thin but detailed faintly; general low contrast.
9. OE and UD	Normal density overall; sharpness somewhat degraded in highlights; low contrast.

If the negatives described above were to be analyzed graphically, they might produce the characteristic curves in Figure 23.4. In these curves, it is apparent that exposure and development have somewhat separate effects; that is, an underexposed film cannot be made into a "normal" negative by overdevelopment, nor will such a negative resemble one which has been overexposed and underdeveloped, for example.

The proof of a decent negative is in the printing. Any negative which will print easily, producing a full range of tones, and including the necessary detail in highlights and shadow areas is a "good" negative. But what is such a negative in graphic terms? The answer is deceptively simple. A good negative is one in which shadow density is about .25 or about .15 above the film *base-plus-fog* (sometimes called *gross fog*) density, whichever is greater, and in which the highlight density is about 1.35; that is, one whose *density range* (DR) is about 1.1.

The reason for this seemingly arbitrary number is that it relates suitably to the *exposure scale* (ES) of the "normal" printing paper. Most

The proof of a decent negative is in the printing

A good negative is one whose DR is about 1.1

It will print well on normal paper

Figure 23.4

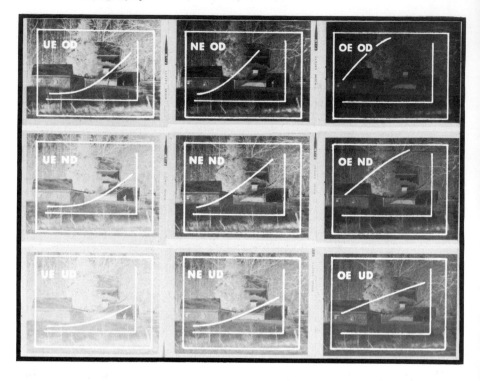

normal contrast papers will respond usefully to a maximum exposure ratio of about 1:20, which is equivalent to approximately four-and-one-third stops, or a Log_{10} range of about 1.3. The minimum useful range is typically about 3⅓ stops, or about 1.0. It is sensible, therefore, to try to develop every negative in such a way that it yields a DR of *about* 1.1. A minimum density (Dmin) of about .15 over gross fog is desirable because it guarantees a well-detailed negative of finest possible grain structure and highest possible sharpness, as well as allowing the shortest possible printing time. If you feel that you have good control over the process you can try for a Dmin of .1 over gross fog. This will still provide good shadow detailing in most cases but gives less margin for error.

Figure 23.5

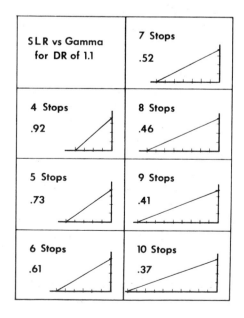

Practical subject matter will vary in luminance range from about four stops minimum to a maximum of at least ten stops. The graphs in Figure 23.5 show the idealized negative characteristic curves for each of seven subjects ranging in contrast from four to ten stops, assuming in every case a desired negative DR of 1.1. Notice that the different ratios of *subject luminance range* (SLR) to DR produce different curve slopes, indicating different developing times. This relationship is expressed by the term *gamma* which is the decimal number found by dividing the negative density range by the subject luminance range.

$$\text{Gamma} = \frac{\text{DR}}{\text{SLR}}$$

Since gamma is really an indication of the steepness of the film characteristic curve, it cannot be uniform for all densities of the negative. That is to say, in practice, the slope of any film curve changes. The slope starts out in the *toe* region (underexposure) at a small angle and gradually increases in steepness as the film exposure increases, then decreases again in the *shoulder* region of the curve (overexposure). Gamma specifically refers to the region of maximum slope, or gradient, near the center of the curve.

The terms gamma and contrast might seem to be synonymous but they are not. Contrast in a negative refers to the density-difference between areas of different tone for whatever reason; perhaps because the subject itself was or was not contrasty, or because the light condition under which the subject was photographed was unusually soft or harsh. Gamma, on the other hand, defines the relationship in contrast between the subject and the negative image and expresses the function of the film-and-developer combination in modifying subject contrast. Gamma, in other words, indicates the degree of development of the negative.

Most films are designed to work best at gammas of less than unity, which is another way of saying that they are designed to reduce the subject contrast. A gamma value greater than 1.0 indicates that the negative is more contrasty than the subject was. Such gammas are inappropriate for average work but are useful for some specialized purposes as, for example, the preparation of negatives for half-tone engraving plates. These negatives often reach gammas of 10.0 or more.

Years ago film curves were considered good if they exhibited a long *straight line* portion throughout which the steepness of the slope (and therefore gamma) was uniform. For films of this type, the gamma number is a realistic indication of actual contrast throughout most of the image range. Modern films, however, are designed to exhibit a less linear curve shape. Typically, these days a well-exposed and developed negative will display gradually increasing contrast well into the middle tones—if not throughout its entire range—and as a result, the term gamma is less useful than it used to be in describing negative characteristics. It has been replaced for practical use by the term *contrast index* which Eastman Kodak is now using to describe the average contrast of its film products (Fig. 23.6).

To find the approximate contrast index of a material for some condition of development, locate on the film curve the point corresponding to an

Practical subject matter will vary in range

Gamma refers to the maximum slope of the film curve

In other words, it indicates the degree of development

Contrast index is a more useful term

Figure 23.6

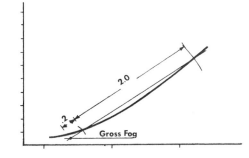

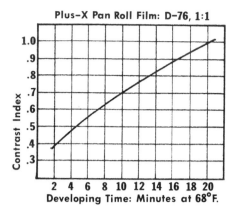

Figure 23.7

Plus–X Pan Roll Film: D–76, 1:1

Contrast Index vs. Developing Time: Minutes at 68°F.

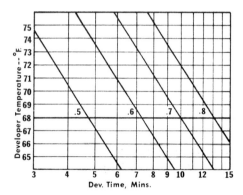

Figure 23.8

Developer Temperature — °F. vs. Dev. Time, Mins.

image density, above base-plus-fog, of .1, and, using this as a center, draw an arc whose radius is equal to an SLR of 2.0. The point of intersection of this arc with the film curve is then connected to the radius point by a straight line and the slope of the line indicates the contrast index of the material. Practically speaking, contrast index can be thought of as average gamma for an arbitrarily chosen range. Contrast index values define the density difference between the extremes of highlight and shadow density; the older gamma values expressed midtone contrast.

To help the photographer control his negative quality, most manufacturers publish characteristic curves for their various film-developer combinations and developing charts which indicate the contrast index to be expected for any reasonable developing time. This information will have to be modified somewhat, in all probability, to fit your own working conditions, but this is easily done and the information is very helpful.

A typical developing chart is shown in Figure 23.7. It illustrates the contrast index range obtainable with Plus-X Pan Professional roll film developed in D-76, 1:1. Refer to Figure 23.2 to see the characteristic curve family for this combination. Developing conditions are specified as intermittent agitation at 20°C. (68°F.). Another chart which is sometimes useful is the "time-temperature" chart shown in Figure 23.8. If it is inconvenient or impossible to adjust the developer to the ideal 20°C. (68°F.), this sort of chart can be useful to find the appropriate developing time at other reasonable temperatures.

Up to this point we have assumed that proper exposure of the film will be assured if the manufacturer's recommended ASA exposure index is used in conjunction with a good exposure meter. While the readings thus obtained will probably lead to good exposure, they may not be optimum for several reasons.

The ASA index may not lead to optimum exposure

First, the manufacturer's data are compiled from carefully regulated testing, using laboratory equipment and techniques; your equipment and control will not match theirs. They use factory fresh or carefully aged materials; yours will be aged unpredictably and under less than ideal conditions (unless you buy from the factory and refrigerate your film). They use a standard developer; you will probably use a different solution, perhaps mixed with tap water instead of distilled. They set arbitrary standards for "proper" exposure; you may not agree with them. Finally, they assign a single exposure index to the film; you will find that subjects of varying luminance range will require variations in the exposure index setting if optimum negative quality is desired.

How ASA speeds are derived

The American National Standards Institute method, from which our familiar ASA film speeds are derived, defines the film's *speed point* as the exposure in meter-candle-seconds which produces a density of .1 over gross fog, when the development is adjusted to produce a maximum density of .8 for a luminance range of 1.3—a condition equivalent to an average gradient (curve slope) of about .62. The actual ASA film speed number is then found by consulting a table or by using the formula:

$$\text{ASA speed} = \frac{0.8}{\text{Speed point in MCS}}$$

Although it is customary to assume that there is a comfortable "safety factor" built into the ASA speeds they are actually not very conservative. For subjects of fairly low contrast which require (or at least permit) extended development, the ratings are safe enough; but for contrasty subjects, requiring reduced development, the published film speeds may lead you astray.

Figure 23.9 illustrates this possibility. In the family of curves shown, the curve which approximates the ASA calibration condition is labelled "A." Its average gradient is much too steep for use with normal subject matter (a subject luminance range of 2.0, which is considered average, would yield a negative DR of about 1.4 with this development) so the development time it represents can only be used for subjects of fairly low contrast, about 1.7 or so. The film curve representing a "normal" subject is labelled "B." Its *speed point*, .1 above gross fog, falls to the right of the ASA speed point, indicating a speed loss, in this case of ½ stop. A contrasty subject curve (equivalent to a range of nine stops, or 2.7) is labelled "C." Its speed point shows a substantial shift to the right and indicates a speed loss of more than one stop. If the ASA speed of this film is 125, for example, it is effectively only 100 or so for "normal" subjects and only 64 or less for fairly contrasty ones. Bear in mind that these speeds are calculated for a film density of .1 over gross fog. The relative shift at the higher subject luminance values, which most meters measure, is substantially greater.

From these relationships you can see that subject contrast, film exposure, film development, and negative contrast are intimately interrelated and that any change in one will affect one or more of the others. It should be clear, therefore, that the popular concept of "forcing" develop-

And why they may lead you astray

Forcing development affects image quality

Figure 23.9

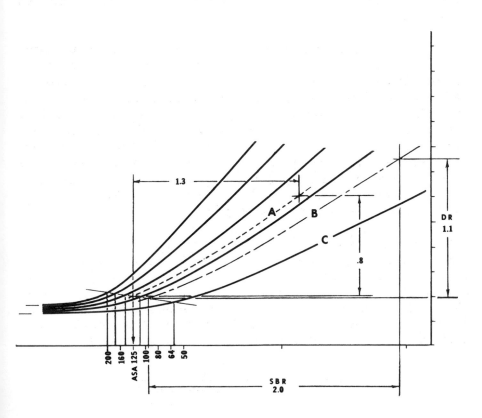

ment to increase film speed can only be accomplished at the expense of image quality, while the claims made for some of the more glamorous and expensive proprietary developers must be considered with some skepticism. "Film speed" is merely an abstract term until its implications in terms of negative density and contrast are defined.

Again, it should be emphasized that developing time should not be changed arbitrarily for the sake of adjusting film speed. If the subject contrast is not suitable, changing the developing time will simply result in unprintable negatives. A low contrast subject will permit longer development than normal, thus allowing reduced exposure and increasing film speed. A high contrast subject will require less than normal development which will necessitate increased exposure, resulting in a reduction in film speed.

There are lots of photographers, including some very successful professionals, who produce good pictures without any concern for the workings of the equipment and physical and chemical phenomena of exposure and development. Their opposites also exist. There are thousands of photographers (no successful professionals in this group) who are so charmed with the mechanics of the process that they never produce a picture worth looking at, although their negatives are perfect, their techniques exemplary, and their print gloss flawless.

Understanding the workings of the medium can improve your pictures

As in most things, either extreme is probably undesirable. You will make a mistake to become so preoccupied with the manipulation of characteristic curves, gamma, subject luminance ranges, etc., that your images suffer. On the other hand, it would seem obvious that an understanding of the workings of the medium can improve your pictures and can suggest new and increasingly more effective ways of expressing your visual ideas.

You cannot use the medium of photography creatively and effectively without knowing what to expect of it, and how to make it do what you want it to do.

Using the Zone System

24

Over the years there have been numerous procedures proposed for the control of image quality by manipulations of film exposure and development. Perhaps the simplest is the old adage "expose for the shadows and develop for the highlights," advice which can be found, slightly paraphrased, in nineteenth century writings. A much more comprehensive system, and by far the best-known, is the *Zone System* which was originated by Ansel Adams and Fred Archer many years ago. It is a remarkably ingenious approach to image control and one which has been well publicized. Adams himself has explained it thoroughly in his various writings and numerous other authors have published their own versions. Today the Zone System is taught, more or less authentically, in a large number of schools and colleges and has become a photographic tradition.

The Zone System has become a tradition

The details of the usually recommended empirical testing and calibration procedures required to suit the Zone System principles to individual use are too well known and too extensive to justify further publication. Ansel Adams' book, *The Negative*, and Minor White's little paperback, the *Zone System Manual*, are the usually recommended references.

The Zone System is based on the principle of *previsualization*, which means that the photographer, before exposing his film, will analyze the subject tonality visually to determine which areas of dark and light he wishes to preserve with adequate detail and what effect of contrast he wants to achieve in the final print. In other words, he attempts to "see" the print in the subject before the negative is made. He then measures with a light meter the tones in the subject which he judges to be significant and determines from these meter readings both the proper exposure for the film and its subsequent development conditions, based on extensive previous testing and experience with these specific materials and processes. If all goes well he produces a negative which will print easily to reproduce his previsualized image in tangible form.

It is based on the principle of previsualization

The system gets its name from the fact that certain tones of gray in the subject have been labelled as "Zones" and numbered for easy identification and convenience in calculation. Zone V (Roman numerals are always used for Zone numbers) is identified as "middle gray," for example, while a subject value one stop brighter than middle gray would be called Zone VI. Zone IV is one stop darker that Zone V; Zone III is two stops darker than Zone V.

Zones are numbered grays

Minor White's explanation of the Zone System limits the range from Zone I to Zone IX, inclusive, and defines the Zones approximately as follows.

Zone I	Maximum photographic paper black
Zone II	First printable separation of tone
Zone III	Very dark gray
Zone IV	Dark gray
Zone V	Middle gray
Zone VI	Light gray
Zone VII	Very light gray; textured white
Zone VIII	Untextured, but still toned white
Zone IX	Maximum photographic paper white

They describe print values

These definitions are descriptions of print values which will result from proper *translation* of subject Zones into print tones. The actual reflection density difference between these values on the print itself will not be uniform, nor will the nine zones represent a nine-stop range of print densities (print *reflection* densities can rarely exceed a total range of about seven stops even under the best conditions). This is a source of some confusion in many descriptions of the Zone System.

Expansion and contraction

Application of the Zone System principles must follow extensive testing to determine the minimum film exposure required to produce the first useful printing density (this is used to determine the "working film speed"), the developing time, etc., required to produce a printable representation of the nine zones, as described above, and variations in development which will effectively "expand" or "contract" the density range of the negative to compensate for unusual subject luminance ranges. *Expansion* refers to greater-than-normal development; *contraction* means less-than-normal. A final field test is recommended to verify these experimental conclusions.

A spot-meter is desirable

Careful metering is essential to the success of this system. In essence the exposure meter is used as a reflection densitometer to measure the luminance of subject areas individually. It is almost imperative, therefore, that a spot-meter be employed. No ordinary wide-field averaging meter can supply the accurate small-area readings which the system demands.

Meter scales are designed to deal with average readings. To use them with the Zone System it is convenient to modify them to display the Zones themselves as areas of graded gray. This can be done as indicated in Figure 24.1. In this homemade scale, the pointer of the calculating dial which is usually aligned with the meter light reading is replaced by the Zone V area and the other Zones are arranged appropriately on either side of it. The placement of the Zone V gray at the normal pointer position acknowledges the fact that an average gray in the subject, properly exposed and developed, will produce a medium density in the negative which can then be made to print as a middle gray.

Place the low value of the subject

The other Zones can be used similarly. For example, suppose we place some subject luminance reading opposite the Zone III mark on the meter dial. The resulting exposure recommendations will tend to produce an area of "very dark gray" (Zone III) in the print. If we place the same

Figure 24.1 Old models of the Honeywell 1/21° meter, shown, were accompanied by an instruction booklet which was complete and concise, and which included a paste-on gray-scale for the computing dial. Recent models come with an abbreviated booklet which is less informational and which omits the gray-scale. Zone System users will now have to provide their own, as has been done here.

subject light value opposite the Zone V mark (Zone System users call this "placing the value *in* Zone V") we will get a middle gray area in the print. Likewise placing some subject tone in Zone VIII will tend to reproduce it in the print as an untextured white.

If the subject contrast, or luminance range, is normal (by Zone System definition), placing some subject value in its proper Zone will automatically position all the other subject tones in their proper zones, too. Under these conditions the recommended development is "normal." For abnormal conditions of subject contrast it is customary to identify the subject value which we want to render as a very dark gray and place it in Zone III on the meter dial. Then we measure the luminance of the area we wish to render as a textured white (Zone VII in the print) and see where that value "falls" on the meter scale. If the reading falls in Zone VIII it is too high so the range must be contracted by underdevelopment. In this case, since the error is one Zone, the development recommendation would be "Normal, minus one" or "N-1." If the high value had fallen in Zone VI it would suggest that the range should be expanded by one stop and the proper development would be "N+1." Other high-value reference Zones are sometimes suggested.

See where the high value falls

One of the shortcomings of the Zone System, as it is usually explained, is its failure to compensate for expansion or contraction development by appropriate changes in the effective film speed. This is probably the reason why many Zone System users place their "detailed blacks" in Zone III or even Zone IV, on occasion. Experience has taught them that if they don't they'll get unprintably thin negatives when dealing with contrasty subject matter. This leads to the rather incongruous discovery that, although there are several numbered zones available on either side of Zone V "normal," the lower two or three are essentially useless when the subject is contrasty. That this is not a necessary condition is evident from the contours of the film characteristic curves. From even casual inspection of the curves it is apparent that the reduced development, which is what "contraction" amounts to, results in substantial loss of effective film speed. Ignoring this loss will lead to underexposure and loss of shadow details (in Zone II at least, and Zone III in extreme cases) but if the film speed is adjusted to match the development condition the lower Zones can be adequately and predictably detailed under any subject condition.

Contraction development requires exposure compensation

Figure 24.2

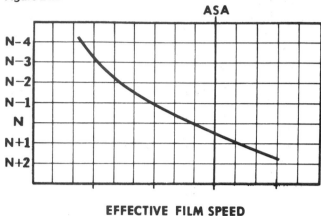

EFFECTIVE FILM SPEED

Figure 24.3

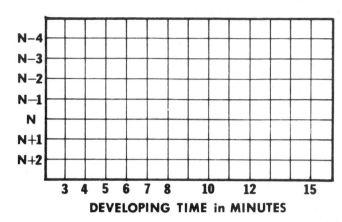

DEVELOPING TIME in MINUTES

Film speed and development charts

Ideally the necessary exposure compensation should be computed for each film-developer combination used; but, since it does not vary greatly from one film type to another and since exact calculation requires the use of a densitometer (which is not available to most students) the charts in Figures 24.2 and 24.3 are recommended for use with any film. Although they will not provide exact compensation, their use will improve the quality of negatives made of contrasty subjects and provide a more consistent minimum density than Zone System negatives often exhibit.

To calibrate the "Effective Film Speed" chart for your own use, label the "ASA" line with the actual published speed of the film you use. The spaces to the left, then, should be labelled with lower speeds; higher speeds go to the right. Each single space is equivalent to one film speed number in the standard sequence (one-third stop). Every third line is equivalent to a full stop in the sequence. For example, if you are using Plus-X film, label the "ASA" point with the number "125." The successive lines to the right will then be labelled "160, 200, 250, 320, and 400." To the left of the ASA point the numbers should read "100, 80, 64, 50, 40, 32, 25, 20, and 16.

The other chart, Figure 24.3, is provided for your own calibration of developing time versus "N-numbers." From your personal test results fill in the developing times required for the various expansions and contractions, and connect the points with a smooth curve. This will provide an accurate indication of the times required for fractional values of expansion and contraction.

How to use the charts

To use these charts, proceed as you normally would to read the subject values with a meter, and place the Zone III value. Then read Zone VII tones and see where they fall to determine the expansion or contraction required. When this has been determined consult the effective film speed chart (Fig. 24.2) to find the appropriate film speed, set it into the meter and compute the exposure settings. Make the picture using these settings (modified by such filter, bellows, and reciprocity factors as are appropriate) and mark the holder with the N-number, for identification. Back in the darkroom, develop for the time indicated in Figure 24.3. Practically speaking, this is not greatly different from normal procedure but it does require the extra step of film speed determination. This compensation will tend to assure adequately detailed shadows, however, making Zone II a useful and reliable Zone under all conditions and eliminating any necessity for intuitive "fudging" in the placement of the low values. This procedure is based on the Zone III and VII readings only. If you read other Zones for the determination of exposure and development data, you will not get entirely reliable information from the charts as they are given here.

Much of the work done with a view camera involves filtration, close-up focusing, or very long exposure times, and all of these will necessitate increasing the film exposure beyond the normal calculations. The exposure factors required by filtration and bellows extension are explained in Chapters 20 and 21. Reciprocity failure due to long exposure times or, more precisely, weak exposing light, varies with the kind of film in use. A very general guide can be given, however, and Figures 24.4 and 24.5 will supply information which will help you compensate for reciprocity failure by adjustment of both exposure and development. Lacking a more specific guide, this can be used for all normal films with good results. Notice that the exposure factors are not the same for aperture and shutter speed compensation. This is because opening the diaphragm for compensation brightens the exposing light and tends to nullify the cause of the reciprocity failure. Prolonging exposure *time*, if anything, simply aggravates the problem, although compensation will eventually occur. Reciprocity correction should be the last factor applied to the exposure calculation. Don't forget to apply it if it's needed, however. It affects both negative density and contrast.

Figure 24.5

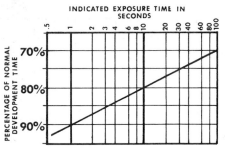

Don't forget the reciprocity factor if it applies

Figure 24.4

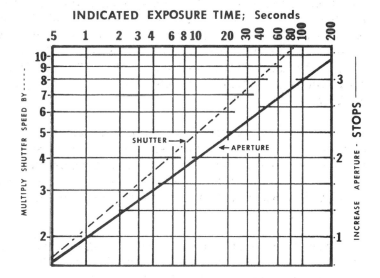

25

Darkroom Manipulation of the Image

For gammas higher than 1.0 turn to special materials

Ordinary films and developers can be made to produce gammas up to perhaps 1.0 or so, and the image contrast can be boosted still farther if these negatives are printed on hard paper grades. Sometimes, however, you will want even higher contrast than you can get conveniently this way, and that is the time to turn to the special high contrast materials.

For highest gammas try Kodalith or a similar film

For 35-mm cameras the only common one is *High Contrast Copy Film.* There is no high contrast film available now for 120 cameras. Most of the high contrast films are supplied for view camera use in the normal sheet film sizes. There are a number of useful ones, but two in particular, Contrast Process Ortho and Contrast Process Pan, will serve for most purposes in the gamma range from about 2.5 to 3.5 when processed in D-11 as recommended by Kodak.

Figure 25.1

Considerably higher gammas can be reached in D-8, but this is an extremely harsh developer containing more than an ounce of sodium hydroxide (lye) per quart and it is very hard on the hands. If you need gammas higher than about 4.0 or 5.0, the best material is Kodalith, or one of the similar films made by GAF, DuPont, or Bell and Howell.

Unlike Contrast Process Ortho or Pan, which are conventional films intended for view camera use, Kodalith is a very slow orthochromatic material coated on a thin mylar base and not notched. It is relatively inexpensive. It can be used in a view camera but since its effective ASA rating is only about 3 or 4 (Kodak says 6) it's rather too slow for general work even outdoors. It is probably most often used by photographers (other than graphic arts cameramen) as a printing material.

These films will almost eliminate gray tones

And what a printing material! Used either by contact or projection and developed in its own Kodalith developer solution, it will reach gammas of 10.0 or more and will almost eliminate the gray tones of a picture, producing an image consisting almost entirely of opaque and transparent areas with virtually no transitional tone between the extremes. The resulting image resembles a brush drawing in ink, but, of course, retains the realistic quality of a photograph (Fig. 25.1). Images of this kind are called *drop-outs,* presumably because the midtones have been "dropped out" by the high contrast treatment.

Images of this kind are called drop-outs

There are several varieties of drop-outs which are often used for esthetic as well as technical photographic purposes. All of the dropout techniques simplify the image considerably, often improving it. In fact, drop-outs are so inherently interesting as abstractions of the original that the technique has become somewhat of a crutch, used as often to save a mediocre picture as it is to create an exceptional one. In spite of its extensive use and misuse, however, the dropout technique is a basic one which will lead the creative photographer to new and exciting images.

The simplest way to make a drop-out is the most direct way—load your camera with high contrast film and fire away. Remember Kodalith is orthochromatic (although there is a panchromatic version available) and very slow. The other high contrast films can be used quite like ordinary films except that you should take exposure readings with more-than-usual care.

The simplest drop-out: load your camera with Kodalith and fire away

Kodalith, especially, is extremely sensitive to exposure variations. A one-stop error in exposure, which would be tolerable with most films, will be disastrous with Kodalith, and about four stops will be sufficient to miss most pictures entirely, yielding either a completely black or a completely blank film.

Start with an incident light meter setting (ASA) of 4 and make a series of test exposures to establish the correct index for use with your equipment. To make this test valid, you must standardize the film processing at some specific time and temperature since the effective film speed of this material depends a great deal upon the processing. For controlled results be sure to use fresh developer for each new batch of film. Used developer accumulates dissolved bromide which acts as a powerful restrainer, effectively diminishing developer activity.

Start with a meter setting of 4 and standardized processing

Use the developing time recommended for the type of Kodalith developer you obtain (there are several varieties, all suitable for this sort of work). Some other types of developer will work with this film, but the contrast is reduced, the film speed is changed and the results are generally not very good. Some general purpose developers may simply fog Kodalith completely, especially if the safelight is not quite "safe."

The Kodalith negative will display a black-and-white pattern abstraction of the subject. Variations in camera exposure will be found to produce variations in the areas of black produced in the negative; increasing the exposure will tend to increase the boldness of the image.

The Kodalith negative can be printed like any other and can be given almost any exposure greater than the minimum required to produce a black. The negative is so opaque, where it is toned at all, that no reasonable amount of exposure will penetrate it. By the same token, the paper grade hardly matters. There is only a slight difference, normally, between the prints made on either of the extreme grades of paper contrast.

The printing paper grade hardly matters

The solid black-and-white image is too harsh for some purposes, and it is occasionally desirable to separate the subject into three or more flat tones; the usual black and white plus one or more arbitrarily selected flat grays. Two or more negatives are required, and they are given exposures progressing from a minimum which barely records the highlights of the subject to one which leaves only small areas of the subject shadows unrecorded.

Figure 25.2

Exposure changes
vary the resulting image area

Posterization: making the print

Figure 25.3   The posterized negatives, printed individually, produce the images shown. When they are printed in register they combine to form this image. Color posterization is also possible and easy to do.

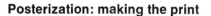

Remember that each negative will be a totally opaque-and-transparent version of the portion of the image that it records. The differences between them show up as variations in the AREA covered. This is because the film sees any gray brighter than a certain *threshold* value as totally white, and any gray darker than the threshold value as total black.

The threshold value varies with the film exposure. The underexposed film will record only the brightest subject highlights (but as totally opaque areas) and will remain unaffected by all the other subject tones. Increasing the exposure slightly will cause the film to record somewhat darker grays along with the highlights, and so on.

Finally, the overexposed film will see all the subject tones except the deepest shadows as white, and record them as opaque, leaving only tiny clear areas corresponding to the subject blacks. The various negatives will resemble a series of stencils (Fig. 25.2) and they are printed almost like stencils, too. Some people call this process *posterization* (Fig. 25.3).

Set up the enlarger for the print size desired and insert a clean sheet of white paper, not printing paper, in the easel, being careful to shove it against the paper stops so that it can be replaced exactly. Select the negative containing the most complete representation of the subject forms and project it onto the white paper. Focus, compose, and stop down. Trace the outlines of the forms on the paper with pen or soft pencil. This drawing will serve as a guide for positioning the various images on the print.

Now, with no negative in the enlarger carrier, make a test strip on the paper you plan to use to determine how much exposure time is required to produce the various grays and black. Suppose you determine that twenty seconds is required to reach full black and that you want to use two grays, corresponding to two and eight seconds exposure time respectively.

Select the most nearly clear negative, which corresponds to the highlight record of the subject, and project it onto the guide paper. Register it on the tracing if possible and trace any outlines it contains which do not appear on the first drawing. Now, without moving the easel, insert a sheet of printing paper and expose two seconds to record the lightest gray over the entire sheet except the highlights, which are opaque and protect the paper from light.

Remove the paper from the easel and immediately mark it lightly on the back with pencil to identify the top of the image. Put the printing paper sheet in a light-tight container, replace the tracing guide sheet in the easel, and check its position by projecting the negative onto it briefly. Then replace the first negative with the next most clear one and position its image on the guide sheet. Try to do this by moving the negative carrier or the negative itself in the carrier rather than moving the easel. Moving the easel very far will alter the image proportions and make exact registration impossible.

This negative has a larger opaque area than the first one and will, therefore, protect from light the original light areas plus a substantial light area around and beyond them. It will allow light to reach the paper over the rest of the image area. The highlight areas will remain white (they received no light during the first exposure and will receive none now), and the newly shielded area will remain light gray from the original two second exposure. The next gray area must receive enough light to produce the selected gray (we said eight seconds), and it has already received two seconds. This exposure will then be six seconds. Be sure the paper is inserted into the easel correctly and make the exposure.

Follow the same procedure for the last negative. It will protect most of the areas previously exposed and will add enough more exposure to the small areas to which it transmits light to produce a full black—at least twelve more seconds and a little more won't hurt.

Develop the print normally and it should appear as a four-layer image with relatively small black-and-white accents against fairly broad areas of two gray tones. The outlines will resemble the contour lines on a geological survey map or the isobaric pattern on a weather chart, and for similar reasons. They define the boundaries of areas of uniform exposure or gray tone on the original subject, just as the geological contours define equal elevations and the isobars define equal pressures. With a little imagination you can produce images in color by printing the negatives on color paper through a variety of filters. The resulting images are brilliant and striking and sometimes quite handsome (see back colorplate, p. 354).

You will probably find this sort of contour printing amusing but limited. Like most drop-out techniques this is a gimmick and tends to become tiresome unless the picture is so powerful that it can overcome the superficial appearance of the layered style. It may, however, suggest variations which are better or more interesting and will certainly increase your knowledge of the photographic process (Fig. 25.4).

One of the easiest of the darkroom drop-out techniques does not require Kodalith or any other high contrast material. It is called *bas-relief* and is perhaps even more limited than the contour method. It will provide valuable experience in tone control, however, and should be in your bag of tricks for this reason if no other.

Mark the paper to identify the top

Figure 25.4 A simple form of darkroom manipulation is shown in this photograph which was made to illustrate the principle of photo-polymerization. The test tube, the light flash, and the plastic chips were photographed separately, each against black velvet. The slight background tone in the negatives was then etched away by brief immersion in Farmer's reducer. The negatives were then superimposed in the desired positions and printed as one. (Courtesy of the Technical Research Laboratories, General Motors Corp.)

The image should appear in layers

Bas-relief printing provides experience in tone control

The negative and positive should match in density and contrast

It involves printing a positive transparency from an existing negative, and controlling the positive exposure and development to obtain a nearly exact tonal duplicate of the negative—in reverse. In other words, if the thin portions of the negative have a density of .3, the positive should also have a minimum density of .3. If the negative Dmax (maximum density) is 1.8, so should the Dmax of the positive be 1.8. If it is not possible to match the maximum and minimum tones exactly, you should at least attempt to keep the density scales alike.

If the positive is made on regular film, you will find that it will require considerably more than normal development to reach a useful degree of contrast. Specifically, since you are trying to match the original negative tone for tone, you need to reach a gamma of 1.0.

Most normal films cannot be pushed to this degree of contrast in general purpose film developers without extending development time considerably. It may be desirable, therefore, to develop the positive in a more vigorous developer such as Dektol or D-11.

They are printed slightly out-of-register

When a transparency is obtained which is a close match for the negative, the two should be sandwiched just slightly out of register and printed as one sheet. The resulting print should be essentially uniform in overall tone with the image appearing as an outline, light on one side of all the forms and dark on the opposite side. The effect of low relief in strong cross light explains the common name for the process.

The process of superimposing the negative and positive forms of an image is one of the methods of image control called *masking* and it is a valuable technique to be familiar with. In the bas-relief process, the mask (positive) is intended to cancel the negative exactly. If the two do not match in overall density, but have similar density scales, the print will be two-toned—sometimes a desirable effect. If the density scales don't match, the midtones may match but the extreme tones will show differences in density, not usually attractive.

Solarization is the colloquial title for the Sabattier Effect

Interesting images which sometimes superficially resemble the bas-relief print can be achieved by exploiting the *Sabattier Effect*, commonly, but inaccurately, known and referred to as *solarization*. Solarization, to use its colloquial title, results from the partial reversal of an image induced by flashing a partly developed film with dim white light (colored light is sometimes used in color solarizations, see back colorplate, p. 354) and continuing the development. The partly formed negative image acts as a shield for the emulsion during the second flash exposure, and the final image consists of a more or less normal negative together with a fairly fully formed positive image, the two often separated by a pronounced white outline. Properly done, the effects are often decorative and amusing (Fig. 25.5). Prints can also be solarized but the images are usually unattractively murky and fogged.

Stagnation development will thicken the outlines

The familiar outlines in the solarized image are strengthened and dramatized if the films are not agitated during development after the flash exposure. This is especially true on Kodalith which will yield very interesting patterns of heavy shaded or smeared outlines when subjected to stagnation development.

Figure 25.5

A refined and elaborate version of the bas-relief process, which produces an effect similar to a pen drawing, is Kodak's *tone-line process*, sometimes casually referred to as the *spin drop-out* or *spin-out*. This process, like the bas-relief, requires a positive mask which duplicates the negative in density and contrast. However, here the images are registered as accurately as possible but spaced apart, either by an intervening layer of acetate, or by simply placing the negative and positive films back-to-back rather than face-to-face.

The sandwich is then printed in a contact frame on Kodalith, but the frame, instead of lying stationary under the printing light, is placed on a turntable (an old phonograph turntable is ideal) and allowed to revolve during exposure. It is vitally important that the printing light be made to strike the revolving images at a rather steep angle so that the light can penetrate diagonally between the image layers. It is also important that the light be a nearly point source, and that only one source be used. No other light, direct or reflected, should be allowed to reach the frame. Normally, the emulsion side of the negative should be placed in contact with the Kodalith emulsion during printing.

The Kodalith image will probably be a very messy-looking positive or even part positive and part negative with no very heavy densities in either area. There should, however, be a distinct black line drawing of the image forms superimposed over the mottled brownish background haze. A heavy printing of the Kodalith negative, again on Kodalith, will produce a clean white line drawing on an opaque background. This is the final negative

The spin drop-out resembles a pen drawing

and, after some retouching with photo "opaque," prints are made from it in the conventional manner. (See Figs. 4.1, 8.4, 8.5 and 8.6 as examples of this technique.)

The line may be doubled, indistinct, or blurry

A number of problems can arise. If the positive and negative are not properly matched, some areas of tone will appear in the print. If the match is good, almost no tone will show. If the line is doubled, it is probably due to having the positive, instead of the negative, transparency emulsion in contact with the Kodalith during the spin printing. If the line is coarse, it may be the normal result of using a small negative. Really fine lines require an original negative of 4″ × 5″ at least, and the larger the better.

If the line is indistinct or blurry, it may indicate that the frame was rocking erratically during the spin or that the light source was too broad or that the room illumination was effective in the exposure. Similar blurring can be caused by improper contact in the frame, or perhaps most commonly, the original negative image may not have been really sharp. A blurred or out-of-focus image cannot be spun successfully.

Or it may not appear at all

If the light source is too nearly above the frame during the spin, the line will be too thin and may not appear at all in some areas. If the light is too low or if the negative and positive were not registered accurately, the line will be broad and coarse and may vary in width and sharpness. The spacing between the two films is also important. Insufficient space will result in a too-thin or nonexistent line; too much space will cause coarsening and smearing of the outline.

Kodalith is used in graphic arts to make screened images

Kodalith and other similar materials are intended for use in the graphic arts industry where they are used to form the *screened* images for *half-tone* plates. There is no such thing as a gray in most printing processes; the paper is either inked, and therefore black, or not inked, and therefore white. A plate which produces this kind of dropped-out image without gray areas is called a *line cut*.

Grays are produced by the half-tone dots

When grays are desired, they are obtained by screening the image, a process which breaks the normally solid tones into areas of tiny dots. Dark grays result from large dots close together. Lighter grays result from smaller dots with wider intervening white spaces. In most cases the dot pattern extends throughout the entire image, including both black and white, where the dots are practically undiscernible. You can see the screen pattern quite easily if you inspect a newspaper or magazine picture with a strong magnifying glass.

Crossed line screens

The screening process is an interesting one which would not be possible without the extreme high contrast characteristic of Kodalith or some similar material. For many years half-tone screens were made by ruling opaque lines on glass plates. The lines had to be virtually perfect in width and spacing, and perfectly parallel. Then two such plates were bound together with ruled sides in contact and the patterns at right angles to each other to form a single pattern composed of tiny white dots surrounded by black. These *crossed line* screens varied in coarseness from less than fifty lines per inch to 200 lines per inch and more.

Obviously, if a screen pattern were placed in contact with a sheet of film and printed on it, the film image would simply be a negative image of the pattern. If the screen and a negative were sandwiched together and printed in contact, the photograph would print with the screen, but the screen pattern would dominate and the picture would not be rendered in full gray scale.

In order to obtain an image made up of half-tone dots, varying in size to form the image tones, it is necessary to print a slightly out-of-focus image of the screen together with the photograph!

**The screen image
must be slightly out-of-focus**

In order to understand this, it may help you to visualize a single screen "dot." Consider it as a tiny window through which a beam of light is converging to a point on the film surface some little distance away. That central point will receive all the light that is available, while the area surrounding it will be partially shaded by the opaque screen. The shadow near the luminous central point is quite light, becoming progressively darker as it moves farther away from center until finally it reaches a point of almost complete darkness before lightening again under the adjacent "window."

When this pattern is printed on Kodalith and given minimum exposure, only the concentrated points of light contain enough intensity to affect the film, and the resulting image shows tiny opaque dots. As the accumulated exposure in the shaded areas becomes great enough to register the dots grow in size. Finally, when the exposure reaches maximum, all the shadow areas are recorded leaving only tiny clear areas.

In screening a picture, of course, only one exposure is given, but the variations of light intensity which are necessary for varying the dot sizes are supplied by the picture tones themselves. When the picture is focused on film through the screen, the lighter areas of the picture expose the film heavily, expanding the dot formation. The dark areas of the picture supply only a little illumination to the screen surface and therefore permit only the brightest centers to record. The other subject tones similarly control dot sizes to complete the half-tone image. Figure 25.6 shows typical dot formation in light, dark, and medium areas of a screened photograph.

**The picture tones themselves
vary the screen exposure**

Another type of half-tone screen called the *halo dot* or *contact* screen accomplishes the same result in a slightly different manner. Instead of being a pattern of opaque and transparent dots, the contact screen dots

**Contact screens
do it a little differently**

Figure 25.6

are each miniature gray scales, opaque centers surrounded by tiny halos of increasingly light gray. As the name implies, the screen is in contact with the Kodalith film during exposure since the controlled space between screen and film is unnecessary with this type screen.

It is also possible to produce a screened image directly by exposing or printing the image on a special material such as Kodak's Autoscreen film. The screen pattern is inherent in the film and when properly handled produces excellent half-tone images with a minimum of trouble. It, and a number of other interesting products, can be obtained from dealers in graphic arts materials.

An ordinary photograph can be screened for purely visual effect, and this technique is really another form of drop-out. Like the other drop-out techniques, screening abstracts the image to some extent and introduces a kind of decorative note. While the regular engravers' screens can be used for this purpose, they are not particularly exciting visually unless the patterns are enlarged tremendously or in some other way modified for dramatic visual effect.

Any pattern or texture can be made to function to a screen

If you understand the fact that screening is simply a means of introducing the effect of half-tone into a simple black-and-white drop-out, it should be apparent that any pattern or texture can be made to function as a screen. A page of type, for example, if set tight and relatively bold-face, can be made into an effective screen by simply copying it on Kodalith. Natural patterns and textures can be pressed into service too. An expanse of ivy leaves on a building side; a section of lawn; a close-up of ground pepper; crushed rock in a driveway—all these and many other things can be photographed on Kodalith and used for screen patterns.

Nonglare glass will work as a contact screen

Screens of these kinds will produce fairly obtrusive patterns which may tend to compete with the picture itself. A simpler screen pattern which is quite photographic in quality, but still decorative, can be attained by simply contact printing the negative on Kodalith while using a sheet of coarse ground glass, instead of the normal clear glass, in the printing frame. A slightly different pattern results from the similar use of nonglare glass normally sold for use in picture frames. Photographs screened in this manner retain their photographic quality while taking on some of the stylized appearance of the drop-outs. The overall effect is similar to a rather prominent but unusual grain pattern in a conventional photograph (Fig. 25.7).

The ground-glass "screens" function somewhat like the halo-dot screen and can be used in direct contact with the negative. The other patterns, made on Kodalith, must be spaced a little distance away from the printing material, like a conventional cross-line screen, so that a slightly out-of-focus image of the screen pattern will be combined with the image. If the screen and the negative are simply contact printed together, the image will be essentially a drop-out of the photograph superimposed over a uniform screen pattern. The screen dots will not vary in size and the half-tone grays will not appear.

If the screen image is too far out-of-focus, the final image will not be appreciably influenced by the screen pattern and will be a more or less

Figure 25.7

conventional drop-out. The proper degree of softness of the screen image will have to be arrived at by experimentation, although there are formulas for computing it. In all probability the best pattern technically (from an engraver's point of view) will not be the most interesting visually—and, of course, the visual effect is what this is all about. A little free-wheeling experimentation in the general area of drop-out techniques may lead you to some truly fascinating pictures.

Everyone is familiar with the use of masking techniques; for example, house painting where masking tape is used to protect window glass, metal or cardboard masks are used to protect trim mouldings, and stencil masks are used for decorative patterns. Photographic masking is somewhat similar. Masks of various shapes and sizes are used to form white borders on contact prints, and the enlarging easel often has an adjustable mask opening which frames the projected image.

There are many methods of masking

Occasionally, opaque paper masks are sandwiched with the negative in the enlarger to eliminate some area of the projected image, and sometimes a piece of cleared film is painted with photographic opaque paint and bound with the negative for the same purpose. All these are relatively obvious and unsubtle uses of masking, but there is another type which is extremely useful and much more difficult.

Masks can alter the image in many ways

One notable example of true photographic masking was mentioned in the discussion of bas-relief printing and spin drop-outs, the use of a positive mask image, derived from the negative, to modify the negative. While in the case of spin drop-out the positive is designed to cancel the negative completely, that is not always desirable. For some purposes, it is preferable to simply alter the overall contrast of the negative by registering a weak positive image over it, or to change the effective tonal distribution by using a positive which is, for example, low in density but contrasty. This, in effect, is what solarization does directly.

Masking will probably be difficult in two respects

Photographic masking will probably cause you difficulty in two respects. The control of the density and contrast of the mask is one of them, but this is only a matter of controlling exposure and development. The other is the difficulty of registering the mask image over the original. The masking film should be a polyester-based material to minimize size changes during processing. Unless the registration is precise, edge effects will be visible and will give your efforts away. To avoid them don't make the mask image sharp! If the mask is slightly unsharp, and if it is registered on the back of the original, the final image may actually appear a little sharper than normal and no edge effects will be evident.

Unsharp masks may be better than sharp ones

Unsharp masks can be made by simply separating the original and the unexposed masking film with a sheet of clear acetate to prevent close contact and exposing them in a printing frame to a diffused light source. The image softness will be increased if the acetate sheet is doubled for greater thickness, or if the light source is increased in area. Matte acetate can be used as a separator, but it will be likely to print a grainy pattern on the masking film.

Best results will be obtained with special film

Best results in the masking processes will be obtained with special films such as Kodak's Pan Masking Film. Separation Negative Film and Super XX are also good, but general purpose films such as Plus X and Tri-X may be troublesome. These films, like most modern films, have a characteristic curve featuring a long, gradually-curving toe, and the straight-line portion is almost nonexistent. This implies tonal distortion, and, in practice, makes accurate masking almost impossible. Super XX, with its long straight-line characteristic, is much more satisfactory. It is also a fine general purpose film in spite of the fact that its curve shape is not typical of the modern trend.

What Kind of Camera Should I Buy

26

There are hundreds of cameras on the market, many so similar in price and features that making a choice from among them is almost a frivolous matter. If you are a beginner in photography, the claims and counterclaims of the various manufacturers can only be bewildering. Clearly your choice should be based on something more substantial than advertising copy.

Cameras can be categorized in lots of different ways, but the most significant classification feature is possibly the viewfinder.

The first cameras were patterned after the camera obscura. The scene to be photographed was viewed, composed, and focused on a piece of ground glass (the focusing screen) in the back of the camera. The screen was then replaced with a film holder of some sort, and the film image was identical in all respects, except color, with the viewed image. Cameras which use this same method of view-finding are still made today. They are called *view cameras* (Fig. 26.1) and are very popular with professionals for work requiring the utmost precision and complete manual control of the image characteristics.

View cameras are bulky and clumsy to use and require a tripod, but in return for these disadvantages, they produce large images of highest quality.

On the other extreme are the *rangefinder* cameras which give up accuracy of image viewing for speed of handling and snapshooting efficiency (Fig. 26.2). These cameras generally provide a small optical (*brilliant*) viewfinder for framing the subject area which will appear in the picture, and focusing is accomplished by adjusting a rangefinder image, usually incorporated into the viewfinder field.

The rangefinder consists of a pair of mirrors or prisms placed two to three inches apart and arranged so that the eye, in looking through one of them, sees a double image of the subject. The other mirror can be pivoted so as to make the images converge and is connected to the focusing control of the camera so that as the lens is moved in focusing the two mirror images are always superimposed on the subject point of focus.

When the system is well made and well adjusted, it is very accurate. When viewing and rangefinding are combined in one window, composing and focusing are very convenient and fast. In addition, the eye-level bril-

Figure 26.1

**View cameras
are popular with professionals**

**Rangefinder cameras
feature speed of handling**

Figure 26.2

Focusing is fast and accurate

263

Figure 26.3

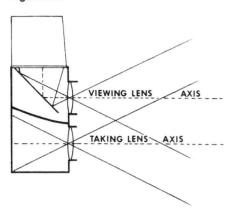

VIEWING LENS   AXIS

TAKING LENS   AXIS

Most twin-lens reflex cameras use 120 film

liant optical finder provides the brightest possible view of the subject area which facilitates work in poor light conditions. There are some disadvantages, however. The slightly different viewpoints of the subject provided by the viewfinder and the taking lens introduce an error referred to as *parallax* which simply means that the camera does not see quite what the photographer sees through his finder (Fig. 26.3).

Rangefinder cameras are made in several film sizes and styles, a few types taking 120 or 220 film to produce negatives of the so-called perfect format, about 2¼″ × 2¾″. Some larger rangefinder cameras, up to 4″ × 5″ are still available and there are a great many 35-mm cameras which use this viewing system. Not as common for a while as they were before the 1950s, the 35-mm cameras are now very popular again and many offer completely automatic exposure control.

The obvious advantages of the ground-glass image added to the convenience of small physical size and semiautomatic operation have made reflex cameras, as a group, very popular for many years. There are two types; the *twin-lens* reflex, TLR, and the single-lens reflex, SLR. They are both available in several film sizes, the most common TLRs using 120 or 220 film, while the vast majority of SLRs are designed to accept 35-mm film.

The twin-lens reflexes (Fig. 26.4) are so-called because they provide separate lenses of identical focal length for the separate functions of viewfinding and picture-taking. The lenses are placed one above the other as close together as possible to reduce the parallax error and are mounted on a common lens board so that they focus together; but they operate in separate light-tight chambers so that the viewed image and the film image are independent of each other.

The top lens (viewing lens) is usually a little faster than the taking lens for maximum image brightness, and its image is formed on a ground glass, set into the top face of the camera body. The image, having been once reflected from an inclined mirror just behind the lens, is right-side-up, unlike the view camera image, but like the view camera image, is reversed from left to right, and is the same size as the film image or nearly so.

Depth of field can be checked— at maximum aperture

Depth of field can be checked visually but only at the maximum aperture of the viewing lens. There is no way to appraise it at reduced apertures.

Most available TLRs are patterned after the famous Rolleiflex. It takes 120 or 220 film and yields either twelve or twenty-four pictures per roll, each 2¼″ square. The film transport and shutter-wind functions are combined in a single stroke of the winding crank. Parallax is partially compensated for by a moving mask on the ground glass, and the viewfinder can be used at waist-level or eye-level. A separate *open frame* finder is incorporated into the viewing hood to permit direct eye-level viewing for rapid action or dim light conditions. These cameras were enormously popular for many years but are now losing out to the single-lens reflexes.

Early SLRs were enormous and clumsy, but rugged and endearing

The single-lens reflex camera probably preceded the TLR as a design (single-lens reflex camera obscuras were used before 1800) and certainly outstripped it in popularity in the early 1900s. In those primitive days the SLR Graflex, and others like it, represented portable, hand-holdable view cameras (Fig. 26.5). They were enormous, clumsy, hard to focus, impossible to hold still for any normal snapshot speed and notable for all sorts of wheezes, groans, and clonks during actual operation. But they were also rugged, reliable, and endearing. In spite of the fact that better cameras had been available for twenty or thirty years, Graflexes were still being manufactured after World War II and can still be found occasionally; used, but often in good condition.

Modern SLRs (Fig. 26.6) represent the pinnacle of refinement in camera design and resemble the old Graflex only in fundamental respects. With few exceptions, the SLRs use focal-plane shutters and feature interchangeable lenses. The viewing and taking functions are performed by the regular camera lens by the simple expedient of making the reflecting mirror movable. During the viewing interval, the mirror is inclined behind the camera lens and reflects the image to a ground-glass screen. The film is protected from light by the focal plane shutter curtain.

Modern SLRs represent the pinnacle of refinement

When the shutter release is pressed the mirror swings upward to seal the ground-glass opening against light which momentarily blacks out the viewfinder image, and the shutter curtain travels across the film surface to make the exposure. In most modern 35-mm cameras, and some larger sizes, the mirror then returns to its position behind the lens, restoring the viewfinder image. In a few SLRs, the mirror remains up after exposure, returning to its inclined position when the film is wound and the shutter cocked for the next exposure.

The SLR principle eliminates many of the drawbacks of the TLR but has a few of its own. Certainly, the parallax-free image is preferable to the

They have eliminated many of the faults of the TLR

Figure 26.4

Figure 26.5

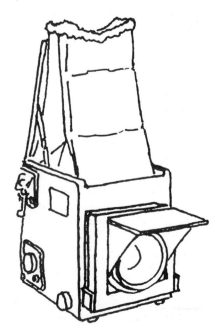

Figure 26.6

reduced parallax of the TLR, and the fact that the image is formed by the actual taking lens, rather than an "identical" substitute, is a distinct advantage. Depth of field can be inspected for general effect at any aperture; reflections and highlights can be placed advantageously with the assurance that they will appear in the picture where you thought you saw them. A very great variety of lens types and focal lengths is available, and the SLR can be used with makeshift lenses or even a pinhole if desired.

Since viewing brightness is reduced when the lens is stopped down, most SLRs provide for automatic operation of the diaphragm, allowing the lens to remain fully open during viewing (with manual provision for depth of field preview at reduced apertures) but closing it to the pre-selected aperture just before the shutter is actuated. The majority of 35-mm SLRs also include a CdS meter mechanism built into the viewfinder and coupled to the shutter and diaphragm controls. This not only facilitates aiming the meter at some significant area of the subject but also takes into account the transmission characteristics of the lens in use, and most of the systems compensate automatically, with normal lenses, at least, for the effects of extended focal distance in close-up photography.

But they are not without fault themselves

The SLR is not without fault. It is inherently larger and heavier than comparable rangefinder cameras, and mechanically more complicated. It is also noisy, mostly due to the action of the mirror linkage and the automatic diaphragm levers. Also, in spite of the fact that the viewing image is formed by the taking lens, the image in most SLRs is not as easy to focus accurately and quickly as a rangefinder image, particularly in dim light.

Most 35-mm SLRs are prism reflexes

Almost all 35-mm SLRs are now built as *prism reflexes* which means that the ground-glass image, which is normally right-side-up but backwards, is reflected laterally (reverted) by a *penta-prism* or *roof prism* and is therefore presented to the eye correct from left to right. The penta-prism, which fits over the camera ground glass, also contains a suitable magnifying eye-piece so that the image can be seen in fairly large scale and good detail. Although there is some light loss in the prism, and perhaps some loss in the CdS meter optics, the image is completely shielded from extraneous light and appears quite bright.

Penta-prisms are available accessories for larger reflex cameras

Penta-prisms are available as accessories for some of the larger SLRs and many of the TLRs. Image viewing is thereby improved and there are some advantages in focusing, but the size of the prism adds considerably to the bulk and weight of the camera. The decision to purchase an accessory prism finder has to be based upon the preference of the individual photographer. The cameras will function perfectly well without them, and will be lighter and smaller. On the other hand, the reverted image is better than the backwards one, particularly for following moving objects. In the 35-mm size, the advantages of the penta-prism clearly outweigh the relatively slight size and weight increase so that nowadays most SLR manufacturers build penta-prisms right into the camera bodies.

In summary: every camera is a compromise

Although every camera design represents some sort of compromise, each will have some specialty. If you want to be able to get some sort of picture in most situations, consider a medium priced TLR. It will give fine image quality in both black and white and color under good conditions, and is relatively light and very quiet in operation (Fig. 26.7). It

Figure 26.7   This is the sort of picture the TLR does best. Modern miniature cameras do well enough, however, and their smaller size and automated convenience are distinct advantages. Because they are not very popular anymore, used TLRs may be good bargains for the serious beginner in photography.

will not be suitable if you ever require unusual focal lengths (there are a couple of TLRs which provide interchangeable lenses) or if you must work in very poor light conditions. Nor is it suitable for close-ups because of its limited focusing range (again with a couple of exceptions) and parallax errors.

Film choice is somewhat limited, but there are certainly plenty of normal-use films to choose from, both black-and-white and color. Color transparencies in this size must be masked down to fit a standard projector (although large projectors are available). Fine color prints can be made from $2\frac{1}{4}''$ square color negatives.

The TLR is a compromise design providing some of the advantages of the view camera and some of the handling ease of the rangefinder types. It also has many of the disadvantages of both. With the aid of expensive accessories, it can be adapted to do most photographic jobs fairly well but it is really a fairly specialized camera, excelling in conservative snapshot type photography. If this kind of photography is your pleasure and if you are interested primarily in good quality images with a moderate investment, consider the TLRs.

If your tastes run toward available light situations, sports, action, candid portraits, editorial coverage of almost anything, and if you can afford to buy and equip a very expensive camera, consider a rangefinder 35-mm

The TLR excels in conservative snapshot photography

Figure 26.8 Informal portraits of this kind, which capture the subject in characteristic gestures and relaxed poses, are easy with rangefinder cameras. The bright finder image and quiet operation of the shutter permit fast, unobtrusive operation. (Courtesy of the University of Michigan Press)

camera with interchangeable lenses (Fig. 26.8). The magnificent Leica is the outstanding example of this type. Its less-expensive competitors have almost ceased to exist.

The rangefinder camera is excellent for fast hand-held shooting

The main advantages of the rangefinder cameras are handling speed and ease of focusing (particularly in dim light). They are also generally compact and quiet in operation as compared to some other types of cameras. Their disadvantages stem from the separation of viewing and taking images. Parallax is a problem, since neither the relationship of objects in depth nor the exact boundaries of the film image are accurately presented to the eye. And finally, since the brilliant finder image does not focus (everything appears equally sharp regardless of distance) there is no visual indication of depth of field nor any sign of the out-of-focus effects which, when visible, can often be used to advantage. Rangefinder focusing, however, is very fast and extremely accurate.

Figure 26.9 When precise alignment of subject forms is essential you need a viewfinder image which is totally free from parallax error—either a view camera or a SLR of some kind. This picture was made with a Hasselblad.

A 35-mm SLR is probably the best buy for the serious beginner

The rangefinder cameras are excellent for fast hand-held shooting. They are at a distinct disadvantage for close-up photography, work requiring unusual accuracy of framing, control of depth of field and optical effects, and any work in which parallax would be a problem, such as shooting through microscopes, telescopes, etc.

If speed and stealth are less important to you than accuracy of composition and framing (Fig. 26.9), and if you can accept the added size, bulk, and price of the 35-mm SLRs, look over this group carefully. There is a staggering number of them on the market, ranging in price from moderate to very expensive. Consider the number of lenses and accessories available for each in case you should want to add them later and buy the one which "feels" best to you. If you wear glasses, you may have difficulty with some SLR finders; be sure you can see the entire field of the image.

The 35-mm SLRs are better general purpose cameras than the 35-mm rangefinders but, like them, will not be entirely satisfactory if you yearn for high quality big enlargements in black and white. In summary, if you want to work reasonably fast and require an accurate viewfinder image; if you will need unusual lenses and other accessories, and will do close-ups or photomicrography; if you want the convenience and accuracy of a through-the-lens metering system, and the variety of special purpose films that are available in 35-mm cartridges, consider the 35-mm SLRs. This camera type is probably the best buy for the serious beginner in photography.

If you require the SLR viewfinder image but need better picture quality than the 35-mm film can provide, and if the bulk, weight, and noise are not a problem, consider the roll film SLRs (Fig. 26.10). There are relatively few of these now on the market, and it seems likely that several other new designs will appear. The cheaper ones may not be adequate for your needs as they are likely to be rather fragile mechanically, and the lenses may not be sharp enough to surpass the results of a good 35-mm camera.

At this writing there are only two roll film 2¼″ square SLRs which do not use focal plane shutters. Both feature interchangeable lens-shutter units which facilitate synchronization of flash and avoids the uneven exposure characteristics of large focal plane shutters. If money is no object, or if you are planning to take up photography as a profession, consider the very expensive Hasselblad or one of the other high quality roll film SLRs. The penta-prism finder hood is a worthwhile accessory. In summary, if you like the larger film size of the TLR but want some of the flexibility and versatility of the 35-mm SLRs, the roll film SLR with prism finder is indicated. It will pay you to investigate them all. There is a great variety in cost and features in this group.

The view camera will satisfy you if you work methodically and precisely and insist upon highest quality images. It is a logical choice for advertising illustration of products, in or out of the studio; formal portraits; architecture; super-sharp landscapes (Fig. 26.11) and close-ups. It is not suitable for candid portraits, available-light shooting, or any other application where you wish to travel light and work fast.

View cameras can be adapted to accept almost any lens or shutter or film type, but they are strictly tripod cameras and are slow and awkward to use, especially outdoors. These cameras are not for the casual amateur. Don't buy one unless you are serious about photography and are willing to put up with inconvenience for the sake of ultimate sharpness and quality.

If an ordinary camera won't do what you need done, you may have to look into the specialty camera market. Here you will find waterproof cameras for skin diving, motorized cameras which can run through yards of film in seconds for motion analysis or sequence photography, super wide-angle cameras which will cover 120° or more, tiny cameras which you can conceal in a shirt pocket for playing superspy, completely automated cameras for nonphotographers, etc. (Fig. 26.12).

One type worth special mention is the picture-in-a-minute Polaroid family. These cameras, available in several models and sizes, will accept

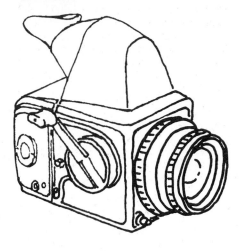

Figure 26.10

If money is no object, consider the top 2 1/4 SLRs

If you'll sacrifice everything for image perfection: the view camera

The specialty market

Polaroid cameras

only special Polaroid film. Several black-and-white emulsions and two color films are available. Most Polaroid films do not provide a conventional negative, and only one print is available from each camera exposure. The print, however, is developed and fixed automatically within seconds after removing the film packet from the camera.

Polaroid cameras will appeal to snapshooters because they are completely automated and the prints are adequate for album use. They are also widely used by professionals for documenting locations, recording and copying functions, and for testing lighting and compositional effects prior to shooting with a conventional camera. Most 4" $\times$ 5" view cameras will accept a Polaroid magazine which takes single exposure packets and this is the preferred professional model.

If you can't afford a new camera, consider a used one

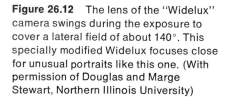

Cameras are expensive machines which depreciate in value just as automobiles do. If you cannot afford to buy a new camera of the sort you want, consider a used one. If you shop carefully, you will probably be able to

Figure 26.12 The lens of the "Widelux" camera swings during the exposure to cover a lateral field of about 140°. This specially modified Widelux focuses close for unusual portraits like this one. (With permission of Douglas and Marge Stewart, Northern Illinois University)

find a camera in like-new condition for little more than half of its new price. Although there is some possibility of buying someone else's troubles, most dealers are reliable and will let you return an unsatisfactory camera without question if it is defective. Be sure that you have this option before you buy.

Look over used equipment very carefully for signs of misuse. The lens should be free from scratches (look for very tiny abrasions on the surface, caused by careless cleaning). Check the various controls for freedom of operation. Look for burred screw heads which might indicate some amateur attempt at repairs and reject any camera or lens which shows signs of having been dropped, jammed, or abused.

Check a used camera thoroughly

Give any used camera an immediate test by shooting a roll of film under as many different conditions as possible. Check the negatives with a good magnifier for signs of scratching (both back and front of 35-mm film). Print the negatives to check for sharpness and accuracy of focus. If the equipment passes all these tests, and if the price is right, it is probably a good buy.

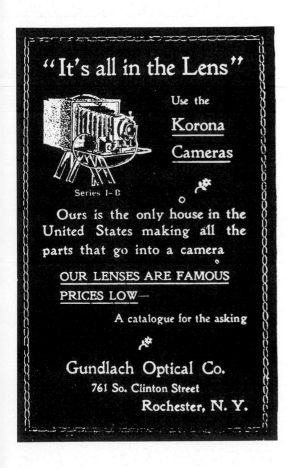

27   What Is a Good Photograph

Any photograph you like is good

Thisis a question that is sure to cause raised eyebrows or simple shock reactions in any group of photographers. They'll act as if they had never asked it (or wanted to) themselves, and if you press them for an answer prepare yourself for some of the most turgid and pretenious nonsense you've ever heard.

The answer, of course, is simply, "any photograph which you *like* is a good photograph." It just isn't any more complicated than that!

Most of us will agree in matters of taste

Now that I've revealed a great secret let me qualify it a little. Nobody can presume to tell you what you have to like, therefore nobody can tell you that a photograph you like is "bad" or that one you don't like is "good." Most of us, sharing a common culture, will agree more often than not in matters of taste, whether they be in food or music or art or anything else. Where differences in age, background, and culture exist it is quite likely that differences in taste will also exist. I'm sure you can think of lots of examples, clothing and hair styles being a currently obvious illustration of taste difference between the "hip" and the "straight" groups within our society.

It's natural to feel insecure

Within any group of generally agreeing people there will also be subgroups of specialists and laymen. The specialists, simply because they are unusually interested in their particular field and spend a lot of time thinking about it, will have generally refined and coherent attitudes about it. The laymen may enjoy some aspects of the specialists' field but their appreciation is necessarily less knowledgeable, less complete, and less subtle. It's natural for the specialist to consider the laymen's opinions rather unsophisticated or even trival. It's also natural for the layman to feel insecure in his opinions. Still, when it comes down to the simple appraisal of what's good or bad, the layman's *personal* opinion is as valid as the expert's.

We look to the experts for guidance

As laymen, we have very little confidence in our taste and habitually look to the experts for guidance. We are accustomed to accepting changes in styles of clothes and automobiles, for example, and generally take to the new models with only token resistance. Advertisers have conditioned us to view the new as "good" and the old as "bad." They tell us—and we believe—that nothing looks sillier than the styling of a two-year-old car or the length of last season's skirt. We don't form rational opinions or make considered judgments. We simply fall for the propaganda of professional tastemakers; the appointed spokesmen for industries whose profits result from a deliberate policy or forced obsolescence of consumer goods.

272

Our ability to make informed taste decisions has been diminished by the increasing complexity of our technology. The average man has no idea what goes on inside his car's engine. His television set is just a big box full of funny-looking gadgets which he comprehends only to the extent of plugging one end of it in and watching the other. He eats breakfast without ever wondering how the toast knows enough to pop out of the toaster when it's ready; reads the morning paper without any sense of amazement that it could be made up, linotyped, and printed overnight; and opens his garage door by pressing a button, explaining, if asked, that it works "by radio control."

Our ability to make judgments has diminished

We are in danger of becoming a culture of zombies, capable collectively of manufacturing incredible gadgets and elixirs and dinguses, and eagerly exchanging our precious human sensibilities, one by one, for mechancial and chemical playtoys. We have lost the individual ingenuity that our ancestors were so famous for, our respect for craft, and our pride of accomplishment. We continually aspire to gain control of our machines while we lose our self-control and self-respect.

We are in danger of becoming zombies

We can't write legibly because we all own typewriters. We don't read because it's easier to go into a mindless trance in front of the "tube." We are overweight and soft because we wouldn't dream of walking anywhere that we can reach by motorcycle or car, or that most outrageous of all mechanical nuisances, the snowmobile. We can't hear bird songs because our high-frequency hearing has been wiped out by prolonged exposure to electronically amplified guitars (not to mention the fact that the birds themselves are being wiped out by our contamination of the environment).

In short we have withdrawn ourselves from the realm of personal experience in favor of chemical and mechanical experiences and we have largely lost our ability to perceive and enjoy the simple things. We are consumers instead of producers, discarders instead of creators, spectators instead of performers. We demand constant prefabricated entertainment, since we've been robbed of all ability to amuse ourselves, and if left alone without it we bore ourselves absolutely to death.

We have lost perception and enjoyment

If you are a beginner in photography (and art), you are probably a fairly typical product of this culture. You will have well-formed calluses on most of your senses, and you will be well on your way to becoming a slave to the conventions of style, fashion, and social custom dictated by your peer group. Most disastrously you are probably blind; not in the functional sense, but rather in the ability to perceive. If you are typical, you will use your eyes to warn you of danger (so that you won't run into solid objects or be hit by cars) and to locate things you need like your gloves and coffee cups. You will also use them to inform. You'll watch television for the message or the story and you'll examine the cash register tape to see how much the groceries cost. To some extent, you will use your sight for the simple wonder of seeing, but this will be relatively rare.

You are probably blind

The ability to see is the most important single qualification that a photographer can have. The next most valuable quality is the ability to visualize. "Seeing" means perceiving the visual relationships that exist in the world. "Visualizing" means perceiving visual relationships as they might exist if manipulated, or as they will exist as translated into a pho-

Seeing and visualizing

tographic print, or other form. In the normal procedure of taking a "straight" picture, a photographer will see his subject, visualize it as he would like it to appear in his print, then select his point of view, his lens, his exposure, and the other variables of the process to make the visualized image materialize. This method of working is called *previsualization*.

Another method, called *postvisualization* is becoming increasingly popular due to the efforts of men like Jerry Uelsmann. It is based on the manipulation of images or image fragments in the darkroom to produce pictures which are evocative, diagrammatic, or surreal rather than simply descriptive of some real subject. Neither method is new; neither is better than or preferable to the other. To some extent, many photographers borrow from both styles. As a beginner, you will probably find it convenient and logical to start out with previsualization if only because straight seeing will probably seem easier at first.

The majority of pictures are snapshots

The vast majority of pictures taken are simply *snapshots*. They are taken by the millions and their production is encouraged enthusiastically by the manufacturers of photographic materials. Snapshots are sometimes attractive pictures, but they are usually of primary interest to the person who took them or the people portrayed. They are (by my definition) pictures taken without much considered selection or seriousness of purpose, hence without premeditation or previsualization. Typically, they are simple records of places or things, intended to serve as memory cues for later viewing. They are often technically poor, but a great many technically excellent photographs are snapshots, too. The name "snapshot" itself implies haste and carelessness, and often with good reason, but there is a current interest in this sort of imagery and a number of contemporary photographers are attempting to recapture and exploit its directness and naivete.

Teachers usually try to discourage snapshooting

Since snapshots are the normal and natural product of most untutored photographers, it is not surprising that teachers usually try to discourage snapshooting. This often has the immediate effect of discouraging *all* shooting, and this can be a very frustrating situation for both instructor and student. Having been stripped of his unself-conscious naivete, the student has nowhere to go. He can't snapshoot any more (it's unsophisticated) but he knows of no other approach. In desperation he is apt to simply adopt one quite randomly.

The search for the bizarre

One such gimmick is the search for the bizarre, the unusual, or the surreal. Done with taste and perception, this subject matter can yield exceptionally interesting images, but the beginner rarely manages to make it work effectively. Still working in the unsophisticated manner of the snapshooter, he now deliberately avoids the simple and obvious subjects that he used to record and looks for weird or funny situations. In the sense that these are not "his" images, they are even less desirable than his previous work.

The design photograph

Another favorite, particularly among art student photographers, is the design photograph or abstraction. To the extent that looking for design relationships does sharpen the eye, these are valuable exercises, but the vast majority of student efforts in this direction are exquisitely boring as pictures.

Then there is the art photograph which novices usually interpret to mean the nude. Male nudes seem to be artier than female nudes, currently, if their increasing frequency of appearance is any criterion. This is not to imply that the nude is a no-no. When treated seriously these images can be both powerful and beautiful, as generations of artists have demonstrated repeatedly. Done poorly, however, they are simply snapshots of people with no clothes on; neither good nor bad, just dumb. The danger here lies in the possibility that the novice photographer will begin to feel that since he is working with classic subject matter his pictures must necessarily be classics. The contrary is more likely to be true.

Male nudes seem artier than female nudes, if . . .

Beginners are almost entirely preoccupied with the content of their pictures—"who" or "where" or "what" is pictured. The student abstractionist is involved with simple demonstrations of competence in the arrangement of things (preferably unrecognizable things). A third preoccupation, usually a superficial one at this level, is pure technique. Taken together and refined, these three interests form the basis for excellent performance in straight photography. To go beyond this, the photographer must include something of himself in his work; his emotions, his comments, his philosophy.

How beginners begin

"Fine" you say, "but what should I photograph?" Anything that interests you! And I mean that without qualification. There is no preferred subject matter. Everything has been photographed and will be again and again. Your difficulty will be discovering what (if anything!) you are really, seriously interested in. You will discover, if you are honest with yourself, that it is very difficult to distinguish between what you really are interested in and what you think *should* interest you. Think about this quite a lot and don't be ashamed of what you discover. Your taste is just as valid as anyone's, and nothing is too insignificant or ordinary to be good subject matter.

What should I photograph?

How should you photograph it? Again in any way you choose. If you can't make up your mind, try simply recording the images of objects and people that attract you, and do it very simply and in a straightforward manner. Make your pictures say simple things, like "this is the house I live in," "this is my little brother, I think he's cute," "this is how the garden looks from my window." It may help you to imagine that you are entering your house or yard for the first time and are seeing it with strange eyes. What would attract a stranger in that environment? What scenes or people or buildings would you photograph to explain your home to a foreign pen pal? How could you explain snow and the fun of winter sports to a person who had never seen snow or experienced cold weather?

How should you photograph it?

I assume that you have a desire to take pictures or you wouldn't be reading this book. That desire is essential and you should pamper it. You must *want to produce images* if your work is to carry conviction; it isn't sufficient simply to want to be, or be thought of as, a photographer.

You must want to produce images

There are a few fundamental differences between human vision and camera vision that you will have to become accustomed to. In the first place, your eyes really see sharply only very small areas of any subject at any given moment. Your visual impression of things you look at is assembled mentally from a series of fragments which you see sharply in very

Human vision versus camera vision

brief, scanning glances. Added to this is a general visual orientation of the entire area of the subject obtained by your very wide-angle but unfocused peripheral vision. You use the peripheral vision to establish the relative position of objects in space, then glance at the areas that seem to need more complete analysis with your precise, central vision.

Your brain computer

This is generally a very brief, totally unconscious act. Your eyes leap from point to point without being willed to do so, and your brain pieces the visual bits together. At the same time, your brain computer is operating to make the impression intelligible. It automatically emphasizes things which it knows will interest you and suppresses things which you have programmed it, by experience, to classify as insignificant.

In addition to the purely visual impressions that you receive, your computer circuits may supply you with some information from your other senses. All of these bits add up to a general impression of the total experience. If you are paying attention, you will experience some sort of reaction, usually a mild one, of interest or boredom, pleasure or displeasure. If you experience pleasure while you are looking for photographic subject matter you will probably take a picture of the object or scene that prompted it; and if it is one casually for so trivial a reason, it will probably be a rather trivial picture.

The camera does not record what your brain records

The reason is not complicated. The camera simply does not record what your brain recorded. Your snapshot photograph really does little more than confirm the fact that you were present at the subject area when the picture was taken. It will emphasize none of the points which interested you, suppress none of the areas which bored you, illustrate a very small area of the total subject space which your peripheral vision described to you, and it will display the whole distorted mess in smaller-than-life scale, confined within artificially described boundaries, in two dimensions and, perhaps, in black and white. Obviously there can be no hint of any of the extravisual perceptions which you experienced and which contributed to your total impression.

Is it any wonder your friends fall asleep?

Is it any wonder that your friends fall asleep when you show your vacation slides? *You* can enjoy them because they help you to relive the whole enjoyment of your trip. They serve for your memory the same function that a prompter serves for an actor who has forgotten his lines. But no amount of prompting can help an actor who has not learned his part, and no amount of simple visual reminding can be of much use or much pleasure to a person who has not had the experience to remember.

Technique will affect the viewer

Here the technical refinement of your work is an important factor, too. Faulty technique will affect the viewer, if he is aware of it, as a distracting factor, breaking the spell of his interest and hampering his interpretation of your message. There is an extremely subtle relationship between the image itself and the physical craftsmanship of its presentation. When the two are compatible, the effect is a relatively strong one of "rightness" which can make the viewing experience a memorable event. When the presentation form is inappropriate to the image content, for whatever reason, the viewer's appreciation must surely be diminished, if not completely negated.

If you want to communicate your own impressions to others—and what photographer doesn't—you must supply them with complete, coherent pictures. In very simple terms of straight photography, this means that your print must display clearly, sharply, and without confusion of background details all those areas of the subject which your eye examined with pertinent interest. By the same token, your print must eliminate or subdue those areas of the subject detail which your brain classified as irrelevant or uninteresting. Your print should include enough of the subject space to indicate the feeling of the real space which you experienced. You should imply three-dimensionality (if it was important to your concept) by having selected the proper lens focal length when the picture was taken and by scaling the print size and viewing distance for best effect. Every visible feature of the print will affect the viewer in some way, and if you supply him with the wrong elements or present them to him in confusion, he will not get your message.

You must supply complete, coherent pictures

Another very important factor is the composition or visual arrangement of the image forms for the sake of the design itself. Consider it this way. The photographic print is a picture of something which conveys real information about the subject, and which, with luck and skill on your part, may suggest something of the way you related to the subject while making the picture. In addition to this symbolic aspect, the print is physically a piece of paper coated with gelatin, containing irregular areas of black, white, and gray. Even if they represented nothing at all, these areas of tone create a pattern which nearly everyone can appreciate to some small degree, at least, for its own sake. In fact, whether he is consciously aware of if or not, virtually every viewer will be at least subtly influenced by the abstract design of the image tones and textures.

The arrangement of image forms

The initial ordering of these visual elements must, of course, be accomplished when the photograph is first taken. The point of view, the lens type and focal length, the subject distance, the aperture, the exposure interval, the focus plane, light direction and contrast, etc., etc., will all have significant effect on the visual design of the final image. This is where previsualization of the picture takes place and the mental translation of the subject tones and forms to print values must occur. In straight photography the original negative contains an image which is essentially complete in all respects. Printing is simply a process of refining and enhancing the image. If you find that you must make major corrections in tone or contrast or composition while printing, it should indicate to you that you are not paying enough attention to the process of seeing with the camera. Work hard on this; it is an essential skill.

This is where previsualization takes place

As your skill and vision improve, you will probably begin to appreciate the less obvious, more subtle uses of photography. You may want to experiment with visual symbolism to convey part of your message. This may be as direct as presenting the image of a loaf of bread in such a way that it stands for "food," or it may be so personal and complex a symbol that only you will know that it exists in the picture.

The less obvious uses of photography

Whether you plan them that way or not, people may occasionally claim to recognize symbols in your pictures. This is probably good. It indicates at least that you have managed to avoid being too specific with your

Symbolism is difficult to deal with photographically

imagery. Symbolism is a difficult problem to deal with photographically because of the inherent realism of the photograph. It is very easy to take a picture which means "this is what Billy looked like on his tenth birthday." It's much more difficult to make Billy an anonymous symbol for "boyhood" without getting obvious or corny.

Alfred Stieglitz photographed clouds as equivalents

Alfred Stieglitz, at the peak of his illustrious career, turned suddenly away from conventional subject matter and began to photograph clouds. His intent was to prove that photographic subject matter, per se, is less important than the skill and vision of the photographer. Working intensively for weeks, he photographed and rephotographed clouds until he had collected a series of ten satisfactory images. According to his account (which sounds a little too good to be entirely true) the composer, Ernest Bloch, while viewing the prints, exclaimed in great excitement, "Music! Music! Man, why that is music!" Stieglitz later referred to these images and others like them as "equivalents" meaning that they could evoke an emotional response equivalent to that produced by some other experience. This concept has been nurtured and elaborated on by Minor White, and others.

The manipulated image

In the last few years, there has been a renewed interest in the "manipulated" image. These pictures take many forms; their common characteristic being that they all depart from naturalism. The most commonly seen varieties of manipulated images are the simple drop-outs, solarized images, and screened images of various sorts. Some workers retain the photographic gray scale but distort the imagery in some way. "Weegee" (Arthur Fellig) did it by printing through warped plastic sheets. Uelsmann cunningly combines parts of two or more photographs in one print by multiple printing techniques. John Wood, and others, use simple cut-and-paste techniques to produce photocollages, then work on the prints with dyes and pencil to enhance the effects. Harold Jones colors areas of his black-and-white prints with food coloring dyes. Bert Stern, Bob Fichter, Doug Stewart, and others use the bold patterns and strident colors of the silkscreen process to convey their photographic messages.

The revival of early techniques

At the same time there has been a revival of some of the very early techniques. George Tice and others are exhibiting platinum prints, an exquisite method of printing which was popular around 1900. A few photographers have experimented with daguerreotypes and calotypes. Scott Hyde is known for his composite images done in a modern version of the old "gum-bichromate" process, and Betty Hahn, and others, combine the older, more traditional methods with hand work to produce very unusual and exciting contemporary images. Todd Walker has experimented with many of the old processes and has produced some elegant solarized nudes in gum-bichromate and in the more modern offset lithographic techniques. He, and a few others, have also worked in callotype, the beautiful but difficult gelatin equivalent of stone lithography.

Their purpose is to free the photographer

The purpose of all these procedures seems to be to free the photographer from the mechanical naturalism of the straight photographic image and the cold, machine-perfect surfaces of the commercial papers. These departures from the straight tradition should not be thought of as dishonest or bad or nonphotographic even though, at first appearance, many of them are startling and even ugly if judged by conventional camera club standards. Consider them as paintings or prints if that will help you appreciate them. In many cases, it is really difficult to classify them; they are truly mixed-media expressions that can be both fresh and exciting.

It's hard to explain the fascination of image-making to a nonartist. The physical act of photography is a relatively simple procedure which anyone can learn to do passably well if he puts his mind to it. It only becomes really difficult—and engrossing—when the image itself begins to capture your imagination. Then the differences between "good" and "bad" pictures become so important to you that it's hard to think of much else. Where you go from there is up to you.

Your own interest may stop at the snapshot. That's not a bad place to be if you do it well (look up the photographs of Jacques Henri Lartigue to see how intimately delightful a family album can be). Or you may find that the straightforward documentation of your own environment is worth your attention. Look at the straight, beautifully detailed interiors of Walker Evans and the views of Paris that Atget did so naively and with such obvious affection.

Perhaps you will be attracted to social commentary. There is a great deal of material to draw on here from John Thomson, Jacob Riis, and Lewis Hine, through the incredible F. S. A. record of the depression up to the present and people like Gordon Parks, David Douglas Duncan, Bruce Davidson, and Diane Arbus. A more subdued approach to photojournalism, combined with strong visual design, is exemplified by Kertesz and, later, by Henri Cartier-Bresson.

Look at Weston and Adams for their reverence for form and light. Look at the powerful, brooding photoessays of Eugene Smith; the cool professional elegance of the work of Irving Penn; the subtle romantic Polacolor studies by Marie Cosindas. Inspect the composite images that Rejlander and Robinson produced in the 1850s and '60s and the more recent surrealistic compositions of Uelsmann. Look at the cameraless images of Man Ray, Schad, and Moholy-Nagy, and the bitterly satirical montages of Heartfield.

Investigate the work of the Photo-Secession group, a marvelously varied and skillful group of photographers. Follow the birth and growth of photojournalism from Salomon on to the present day. Look at the industrial photographs of Weston, Bourke-White, and d'Arazien and study the portrait styles of Newman, Halsman, and Karsh.

As photographers, we inevitably influence each other and this is a healthy thing. Make the most of this interchange of ideas and inspiration and use it as a springboard for your personal expression. It is far more constructive to plagiarize, to deliberately imitate someone whose work you admire, than to wait, without *doing* anything, for the spontaneous arrival of an idea which no other photographer has ever had, or a subject which no one else has ever dealt with. These things simply will not happen.

I believe sincerely that it is impossible to copy anyone else's style for very long even if you try to do it seriously. Your own personal vision will certainly intervene and you will gradually find your own expressive form

It's hard to explain the fascination of image-making

Where you go is up to you

Some of the things photographers have done

We inevitably influence each other

It is impossible to copy a style for long

in spite of yourself. The only artists who don't grow are the ones who don't work. You can't become a great photographer, or even a good one, by simply thinking about pictures. It's also true, though, that you'll have to involve your mind and your emotions as well as your trigger finger if you want to amount to very much.

Photography will return your money's worth

You'll find, in fact, if you take it seriously, that working at photography will demand as much from you and involve you as totally as anything you have ever done. In return, it will give you more than your money's worth in simple, profound, personal gratification.

A Portfolio of Photographs

This photograph of an open window and the scene beyond was done in 1896 by Frederick Evans. It is disarmingly ordinary at first glance; so ordinary, in fact, that it can easily be overlooked or ignored unless it is pointed out as worthy of attention. Studied perceptively it is still a simple image, but a charming one. It can be appreciated for its clean, economical design, its delicate rendering of light and atmosphere, and the interesting tones and textures of the handsome old buildings and courtyard seen partly through, and partly reflected in, the glass of the open casement window.

It is easy too, to identify with the photographer; to sense the shadowy atmosphere of the old house and the soft glare of the outdoor light. Is it foggy or misty? Is there a hint of stable smell and the scent of wet grass in the air? Are there bird songs? An active imagination can supply the missing ingredients of a complete scenario, and each viewer will project himself into the situation in a way which relates to his own sensitivity and experience.

For some persons the photograph may function as an "equivalent," evoking in some mysterious way an emotional response quite unrelated to the reality of the objects pictured. For others it may simply trigger recollections of past experiences, old friends, or episodes from childhood.

Any photograph can function on at least two or three levels: graphic (its two-dimensional design), representational (what it depicts, real or surreal), and evocative (what response it arouses in you); but before it can function at all, you must give it a chance by really looking at it—not casually or out of simple curiosity, but with genuine intent to perceive. The burden of communication is borne equally by the image-maker and the image-viewer!

On the following pages—and worthy of your careful attention—are examples of the work of a number of serious and dedicated photographers. Most of these men and women are well known and many of the images reproduced here are familiar. They will bear repeating, however. If you know them they will appear as old friends; if they are new to you, take this opportunity to make their acquaintance.

I have included a few photographs made in the early years of this century, mainly because they are some of my favorites and I couldn't bear to leave them out. Most of the pictures are the work of contemporary photographers, and in many cases, the choice of images was theirs. This portfolio has no theme. It includes some examples of commercial work as well as some purely expressive or creative images. It is intended to suggest some of the vast variety of work that has been done and, although it is by no means a complete summary, I hope you will find it instructive, enjoyable, and inspiring.

ALFRED STIEGLITZ, *Paula*
(Courtesy of the Art Institute of
Chicago)

EDWARD STEICHEN, *Steeplechase Day, Paris: After the Races* (Edward Steichen, GEH, courtesy of Joanna T. Steichen)

GORDON PARKS, *Favela child and father—Rio de Janerio* (Gordon Parks)

ROMAN VISHNIAC, *Boys in a One-room School in the Carpathian-Ukraine*
(Dr. Roman Vishnaic)

WALKER EVANS, *Kitchen and Dog Run, Floyd Burroughs' Cabin, Hale County, Alabama* (Library of
286
Congress)

RUSSELL LEE, *Sharecropper Mother Teaching Children, Transylvania, La.*
(Library of Congress)

ARTHUR ROTHSTEIN, *Dust Storm, Comarron County, Oklahoma*
(Library of Congress)

DOROTHEA LANGE, *Migrant Pea-pickers,*
Nipoma, California (Library of Congress)

IMOGEN CUNNINGHAM, *My Father at 90—1936* (Imogen Cunningham)

EDWARD WESTON, *China Cove*, 1940 (Cole Weston)

HENRI CARTIER-BRESSON, *Valencia, Spain*, 1933 (Magnum)

ANDRÉ KERTÉSZ, *Thomas Jefferson, Utica, N.Y.* (Magnum)

BILL BRANDT, *Policeman in Bermonday* (Bill Brandt)

MINOR WHITE, *Pacific Ocean* from "Song Without Words" (IMPGEH)

ROBERT FRANK, *Elevator girl* (Robert Frank, from *The Americans*)

CECIL BEATON, *Gertrude Stein and Alice B. Toklas* (IMPGEH)

HENRI CARTIER-BRESSON, *Roualt* (Magnum)

YOUSUF KARSH, *Pablo Casals*
(Karsh, Ottawa)

293

FRANCES B. JOHNSTON, *Stairway of Treasurer's Residence. Students at Work*, plate from an album of Hampton Institute, 1899-1900. Platinum print, 7½" x 9½". (Collection, the Museum of Modern Art, New York. Gift of Lincoln Kirstein)

BALTHAZAR KORAB, *Toronto Dominion Bank, by Mies Van der Rohe*—Two views (Balthazar Korab)

TODD WALKER, Untitled (Todd Walker)

CLYDE H. DILLEY, *Two Nudes Dancing Before Crusty Cloud Formation*, 1971
(Clyde H. Dilley)

MARIO GIACOMELLI, *Verra le morte e avra i tuio occhi*, 1968 (IMPGEH)

295

BURK UZZLE, Untitled (Burke Uzzle)

MARGERY MANN, *Park, London,*
1971 (Margery Mann)

BRUCE DAVIDSON, *East 100th St.* (Magnum)

RALPH GIBSON, *Ship to Corsica* (Ralph Gibson, from the book *Forbidden Photographs*)

GEORGE A. TICE, *White Castle, Route #1, Rattway, N.J.*, 1973 (George A. Tice)

298

LES KRIMS, Untitled (Les Krims)

ANNE NOGGLE, Untitled, 1970 (Anne Noggle)

ANSEL ADAMS, *Frozen Lakes and Cliffs*, 1937 (Collection of the author, with permission of Ansel Adams)

300

EUGENE SMITH, *Wake, from the "Spanish Village"* (Eugene Smith)

EUGENE SMITH, *Spinner* (Eugene Smith)

MAX WALDMAN, *Marat/Sade* (Max Waldman)

WILLIAM A. GARNETT,
*Sand Dunes, Death Valley
California* (by William
Garnett)

PAUL CAPONIGRO, *Stump—Rochester, N.Y.,*
1957 (Paul Caponigro)

303

BETTY HAHN, *Road and Rainbow*—A 16″ x 20″ gum bichromate printed on cotton fabric and stitching added with colored embroidery threads (Betty Hahn)

JERRY UELSMANN, Untitled (Jerry Uelsmann)

Glossary

ABERRATIONS—The several defects of a lens, inherent in its design, material and construction, which, by deforming the image points in various ways, limit the sharpness of the focused image.

ACCELERATOR—Same as ACTIVATOR, which see.

ACETIC ACID—A relatively mild acid used, in highly diluted form, as the rinse bath (shortstop) which follows the developer in the normal film and paper developing processes. The acid in vinegar.

ACHROMAT—A lens which has been corrected for two colors thus partially eliminating the effects of chromatic aberration.

ACID—A hydrogen compound having a pH value less than 7. Most acids will combine readily with certain metals to form salts. Typically an acid solution feels gritty when rubbed between the fingers, and has a sharp sour taste. Acid solutions neutralize alkaline solutions and turn blue litmus paper red. The stronger acids cause severe burns and are dangerous to handle.

ACTIVATOR—The chemical ingredient of a developer solution which stimulates the reducing agent to begin its work and accelerates it. The activator in most developers is an alkaline salt such as sodium carbonate or borax. Also called the ACCELERATOR.

ADDITIVE SYSTEM—A name for the principles of color mixing using the light primaries. Mixtures of light colors are brighter and lighter in tone than the individual colors were, and the three light primary colors, red, green, and blue, produce white light when blended.

AGITATION—The process of stirring, swirling, or otherwise causing a liquid to move freely over the surfaces of film or paper during processing.

AIR-BELLS—Tiny bubbles of air which are apt to cling to a dry surface which is immersed gently. In developing films or papers, an initial vigorous agitation is usually recommended to dislodge air-bells so as to avoid pinholes.

AIR-SPACED ELEMENTS—In a compound lens, those elements which are not cemented together.

ALBUMIN—Commercially, simply dried egg white. Used in the preparation of printing paper emulsions from about 1850, it was replaced by gelatin in the 1880s. The old spelling is albumen.

ALKALI—A compound whose pH value is greater than 7. Alkaline solutions typically feel slippery or soapy when rubbed between the fingers and are difficult to wash off, especially in soft water. They neutralize acids and turn red litmus paper blue. The stronger alkalis can cause severe burns and are dangerous to handle.

ANAMORPHIC LENS—A lens designed to compress or elongate its images usually either vertically or horizontally. They are used to make wide-screen movies on normal film stock by compressing the image width during filming, then stretching the width during projection.

ANASTIGMAT—A lens which has been well corrected for all the aberrations specifically including astigmatism and curvature of field.

ANGULAR COVERAGE—The field of view seen or covered by the lens, expressed in degrees.

ANHYDROUS—Without water; dry. Used to distinguish the dehydrated form of a compound from its crystalline form which might normally contain a substantial amount of water of crystallization while still appearing to be completely dry. When chemical measurements are made by weight, less of the anhydrous than the crystalline form will be required.

A.N.S.I.—American National Standards Institute. The present title of the organization which used to be called the American Standards Association (ASA).

APERTURE—Opening, specifically of the lens, and expressed as a fraction of the focal length. The f/ number. See RELATIVE APERTURE.

APOCHROMAT—A lens which has been corrected for three colors, thus reducing the chromatic aberrations to negligible amounts. Apochromatic lenses sometimes include the prefix "Apo-" in their names, e.g., Apo-Tessar, Apo-Lanthar, etc.

ASA—The American Standards Association, now the American National Standard Institute. A system of film speed rating now standard in the United States.

ASTIGMATISM—One of the common aberrations of photographic lenses and the human eye, characterized by the lens' inability to bring into common focus lines which are radial and those which are tangential to the image circle.

AVAILABLE LIGHT—The light condition which the photographer finds existing at the subject position. The term usually implies an indoor or nighttime light condition of low intensity requiring fast film, large lens aperture, and slow shutter speed.

B—See BULB.

BACK—That portion of a camera which contains the film; specifically, the complete assembly attached to the rear standard of a view camera (and usually removable) which includes the focusing screen, and which accepts the film holders.

BACK FOCUS—The distance from the rear surface of the lens to the focal plane when the lens is focused at infinity.

BACK LIGHT—Illumination from a source beyond the subject, as seen from the camera position, which tends to silhouette the subject. See RIM LIGHT.

BARREL DISTORTION—One of the forms of the aberration, DISTORTION, which is characterized by a bowing-out of lines near the edges of the image. See PINCUSHION DISTORTION and RECTILINEAR.

BASEBOARD—The large, flat board, usually plywood, to which the enlarger column is attached, and on which the enlarging easel is normally placed.

BASE—The transparent sheet material, usually acetate or polyester, upon which film emulsion is coated.

BASE-PLUS-FOG DENSITY—The density of an unexposed area of a developed film (negative or positive).

BAS-RELIEF—A picture printed from the slightly misregistered images of a negative and its positive mask. The print usually resembles the linear shadow pattern of the subject as it would be seen in low relief in strong slanting light.

BELLOWS—The center section of a view camera which connects the front and back standards. The bellows is usually made of leather, cloth, or plastic, is accordion-pleated for flexibility and is, of course, lighttight.

BELLOWS EXTENSION—A term often used to refer either to the total bellows length or to the additional extension of the bellows (beyond that required for infinity focus) necessary for focusing at close subject distances.

BELT—The endless canvas strip which carries prints through a motorized or manual drum dryer. Sometimes called an APRON or BLANKET.

BETWEEN-THE-LENS SHUTTER—A shutter designed to operate in a space between the elements of the lens. See LEAF SHUTTER and FOCAL PLANE SHUTTER.

BICHROMATE—Also, and preferably, DICHROMATE. Refers to the chromium salts of sodium, potassium, and ammonium which are used in various bleach baths and in the numerous variations of the Gum and Pigment printing processes. They are poisonous, and can be absorbed directly through the skin to cause painful dermatitis and ulcers.

BLACK BODY—A hypothetical, unreflecting source of pure radiant energy.

BLADE ARRESTOR—Old term for device similar to "press-focus lever," which see.

BLEACH—A chemical bath or treatment which converts the silver image into a less visible form, or which removes it entirely. See REDUCER.

BLEED—An image edge trimmed without a border; as, "the picture bleeds top and bottom."

BLIND—An emulsion not sensitive to certain colors; color blind.

BLOCKED—Also BLOCKED UP. Refers to an area of the negative image so overexposed, and therefore dense, as to obscure textures and details.

BLOTTER BOOK—A number of sheets of pure white blotting paper, interleaved with nonabsorbent tissue sheets, and bound at one edge to form a large book. Used for nonglossy drying of relatively small prints.

BLUE-SENSITIVE—The sensitivity of an ordinary silver emulsion; red and green blind.

BOUNCE LIGHT—Reflected light; specifically, light directed away from the subject toward some nearby light-toned surface so as to reach the subject diffused by reflection.

BRACKET—To make a number of exposures (some greater and some less than one considered to be "normal") in addition to the "normal" one, with the intent of getting one near-perfect exposure.

BROMIDE—Any salt of hydrobromic acid but commonly used as a shortened form of potassium bromide.

BROMIDE PAPER—A printing paper sensitized principally with silver bromide.

BSI—British Standards Institution. A system of film speed ratings used in Great Britain and essentially similar to the ASA speeds.

BULB—A marked setting (B) of most shutters which permits the shutter to be held open for an indefinite period by continued pressure on the shutter release. See TIME.

BURNED OUT—Describes an area of the print image in which highlight detail has not been recorded, usually because of severe overexposure of the negative. See BLOCKED UP.

BURNING-IN—The process of allowing some relatively small image area to receive more than the normal exposure by shielding most of the printing paper surface from the light. See DODGING and FLASHING.

CABLE—Abbreviation of CABLE RELEASE.

CABLE RELEASE—A long flexible cloth or metal braid-covered plunger which screws into a special threaded socket on the shutter or camera body. Compressing the plunger with thumb and finger pressure will release the shutter without much danger of camera movement or vibration.

CADMIUM SULFIDE CELL—A light-sensitive (photoconductive), solid-state device which is now widely used in exposure meters.

CALOTYPE—The ancestor of modern photographic processes, invented by William Henry Fox Talbot in about 1840. The camera exposure was made on sensitized paper and developed out. The prints were made by contact on salted paper, printed out, and fixed. The process came to be known as talbotype and was quite popular. It would probably have been much more widely used if Talbot's patents had not been so restrictive.

CAMERA—Literally, *room* in Latin. The instrument with which photographs are taken, consisting, at least, of a lighttight box, a lens which admits focused light, and some device or provision for holding the film in position.

CAMERA OBSCURA—Latin for *dark room*. Ancestor of the photographic camera; probably originally an actual room in which observers could watch the images of outside subjects formed by light rays entering the room through a small aperture and passing directly to the opposite wall. The camera obscura eventually evolved into a portable box, equipped with a lens and viewing screen, which was used for viewing and sketching, and finally, after the invention of suitable sensitized materials, for actual photography.

CARRIER—The negative holder in an enlarger.

CARTRIDGE—The disposable metal or plastic container in which lengths of film are sold and used. Sometimes called a CASSETTE.

CASSETTE—A metal container (usually designed to hold lengths of 35-mm film) which can be used repeatedly. Of ingenious design and construction, cassettes are made specifically for a particular camera and will not normally work in any other brand. Sometimes referred to as a CARTRIDGE.

CC FILTERS—Color Compensating filters, intended for use in color photography to modify the overall color balance of the image. They are available in six colors and several degrees of saturation.

CdS METER—An exposure meter which employs a cadmium sulfide cell as its light-sensitive element.

CEMENTED LENS—A lens composed of two or more individual glasses whose adjacent surfaces are ground to fit accurately, and bonded together with some transparent adhesive. Most photographic lenses contain some cemented components as well as some air spaces.

CHARACTERISTIC CURVE—Another name for the D logE curve.

CHLORIDE PAPER—Printing paper sensitized principally with silver chloride. A term which is seldom used any more.

CHROMATIC ABERRATION—A general name for the inability of a lens to bring all the light colors of an object point to a common point of focus in the image plane. Chromatic aberration causes simple blurring of the image in black and white, and color fringing of the image in color photography. Two forms are described, lateral and axial or longitudinal, and the effects are most severe near the edges of the image area.

CIRCLE OF CONFUSION—The tiny, but not necessarily the *most* tiny, blurred circle of light which a lens will form as an image of a point of light at the subject position. It has no significance as a measure of lens accuracy or precision, but is measured and discussed simply as a means of defining tolerable sharpness of the image, and therefore the acceptable limits of depth of field.

CLEAR—The appearance of a negative after the fixing bath has removed all visible traces of undeveloped silver halides.

CLEARING TIME—The length of time required to clear a negative. It depends on the strength, temperature, and agitation of the fixing bath and the kind of emulsion being fixed.

CLICK STOPS—Detents in the diaphragm or shutter scale of a lens which produce a tactile indication and an audible click to mark the significant scale settings.

CLOSE-UP LENS—A positive supplementary lens which, when placed over a camera lens, shortens its focal length and thereby permits closer-than-normal focusing.

CLOSE-UP PHOTOGRAPHY—The techniques and practice of using supplementary lenses, extension tubes, bellows units, etc., to take pictures at closer ranges than the normal focusing adjustment of an ordinary hand-camera will allow. Refers to image magnification ratios of up to, perhaps, $2\times$, and therefore overlaps "Photomacrography," which see.

COATING—The thin film of magnesium fluoride, or other material, deposited on the surfaces of the lens glasses which gives photographic lenses their characteristic magenta or amber color by reflected light. Its purpose is to reduce the intensity of flare light within the lens which in turn increases the brightness and contrast of the image.

COCKING THE SHUTTER—Winding or tensioning the shutter mainspring prior to making the exposure.

COLD TONES—Bluish or greenish tinge in the black-and-white image.

COLLODION—A thin, clear, slightly syrupy solution of pyroxyline in ether and alcohol. It was used in the preparation of wet-plate emulsions, a procedure described by Frederick Scott Archer in 1851.

COLOR FRINGES—The rainbowlike outlines, caused by lateral chromatic aberration of the lens, that surround dark areas of the image, and are particularly apparent in areas of high contrast near the edges of the image.

COLOR TEMPERATURE—A standard for defining the color of light based upon its similarity to the light color emitted by a black body heated to a known temperature. Color temperature is expressed in degrees Kelvin, or "Kelvins," and is only appropriate for the description of CONTINUOUS SPECTRUM light such as is emitted by the sun, tungsten filament bulbs, etc.

COMA—An aberration of the lens which causes marginal light rays from a subject point off the lens axis to fail to converge at a common image point. The effect is most severe near the edges of the lens field, and can usually be eliminated by stopping the lens down. It is a common defect of high speed lenses.

COMPENSATING DEVELOPER—A developer whose activity tends to be inversely proportional to image density. It therefore is self-limiting, working relatively vigorously in areas of underexposure, and slowing down in the overexposed areas as density increases. No practical developer is outstanding in this respect, but those containing the reducing agent, Pyrocatechol, or two-solution Metol formulas, are sometimes recommended. Almost any developer will tend to be more compensating in action if it is highly diluted, and if it is used with only occasional and gentle agitation.

COMPLEMENTARY COLORS—Any two colors in the subtractive system which, when mixed in the proper proportion, produce black or dark neutral gray. In the additive system, any two colors whose mixture results in white light.

COMPLETION—That state of development when essentially all of the exposed silver halides have been reduced to metallic silver; that is, when further prolonging the development will produce no more image density.

CONCAVE—Hollowed out. The side of a spherical surface seen from the center of the sphere.

CONDENSER ENLARGER—An enlarger employing condenser lenses to provide uniform illumination of the negative.

CONDENSER LENS—A positive lens used to concentrate light rays. Condensers are used in many enlargers to collect the light from the bulb and direct it through the negative into the enlarger lens.

CONTACT PAPER—A printing paper, usually sensitized with silver chloride, which is intended for use in contact printing.

CONTACT PRINTING—A method of printing in which the negative is placed in contact with the printing paper, emulsion to emulsion, and held in that position in a PRINTING FRAME. The exposure is made by exposing the frame to raw light so that the paper emulsion is exposed by light passing through the negative densities. Contact printers, machines which contain a controllable printing light, are also used.

CONTACT SCREEN—Type of engraving screen in which the dots are not sharply defined but, rather, are surrounded by individual haloes of decreasing density. These screens will form excellent half-tone negatives by simple contact printing methods. At least two types are used, gray screens for color work and magenta screens which permit control of image contrast in black-and-white work. Also sometimes called "halo-dot screens."

CONTINUOUS SPECTRUM—Light which contains an appreciable amount of all the visible wavelengths or colors. See DISCONTINUOUS SPECTRUM.

CONTINUOUS TONE—Describes an image containing a gradation of grays as well as black-and-white extremes. See DROP-OUT.

CONTRACTION—In the Zone System, reduced development which compensates for high subject contrast so as to produce normal contrast in the negative.

CONTRAST—Density difference, usually of adjacent areas of the image.

CONTRAST GRADE—A number or descriptive term assigned to a particular printing emulsion which identifies its contrast characteristic. In the range from 0 through 6, a normal contrast paper is usually considered to be 2, with the lower numbers indicating a tendency toward lower contrast and higher numbers indicating higher contrast. Printing filters for use with variable contrast papers are numbered similarly. In some cases low contrast is indicated by the term "soft" while high contrast papers are labelled "hard."

CONTRAST INDEX—The numerical expression of the relationship between the negative density scale and the subject luminance range when, simply, the minimum useful image density is considered to be about .1 above base-plus-fog and the useful curve length is assumed to be 2.0. It might be called the average gamma under the stated conditions.

CONVERTIBLE LENS—A lens whose two major components can be used either together or separately. They were once called "double anastigmats" because each half is separately corrected. When used together the two components yield the "normal" focal length, and a relative aperture of about f/5.6 or f/6.3. When used separately the components work as long lenses—about 1.2 to 2.5 times the normal focal length—at reduced aperture. Performance and correction of the complete lens is excellent. The individual components are fair to moderately good.

CONVEX—Bulging. The opposite of CONCAVE. The surface of a sphere seen from outside the sphere.

CORRECTION—The design and construction refinements of a lens which tend to minimize the aberrations. A practical photographic lens usually consists of several simple lenses (or glasses) since adequate correction normally requires a variety of types of glass and lens shapes, and meticulous spacing of the elements.

COVERAGE—The area of the image (formed by a lens) which is of useful quality. Also, the area of the subject which the lens can record as an image of useful quality.

CROP—To trim, or sometimes to cover, the borders of an image for any reason, but usually to improve the composition.

CROSS LIGHT—Light striking the subject from one side.

CURTAIN SHUTTER—A shutter variety in which a slit or opening in a strip of metal or cloth is made to travel past the film surface to effect the exposure. See LEAF SHUTTER.

CURVATURE OF FIELD—The tendency of a simple lens to form its image on a spherical, rather than flat, plane.

CUT FILM—Another name for SHEET FILM.

DARK SLIDE—The black plastic or fiber sheet which is inserted into a FILM HOLDER through a lighttight slot to seal the film chamber against light.

DAYLIGHT—Sunlight or skylight or any mixture of the two. For the purposes of color photography, daylight is considered to have a color temperature of from about 5500°K. to 6000°K. and this condition is likely to exist when the sun is high and slightly overcast. Under other conditions the color of daylight is likely to be quite different from the "norm" and must be filtered if "normal" color rendition is desired.

DECAMIRED—Ten MIREDS. See MIRED.

DEEP TANKS—Commercial film processing equipment in which large volumes of processing solutions are agitated by nitrogen burst, and controlled replenishment maintains the solutions at optimum strength throughout their life.

DELAY—In synchronized flash photography, the interval between the application of the firing current to the bulb and the opening of the shutter. The delay interval is controlled by the shutter. See M, F, X.

DENSE—Descriptive of a negative which is dark overall, or of an area of a negative which has a heavy silver deposit and therefore transmits only a little light.

DENSITOMETER—An instrument designed to measure the amount of light transmitted by individual small areas of a negative, thus appraising the density of the areas.

DENSITY—The common logarithm of the reciprocal of transmission. That characteristic of the image silver deposit which absorbs (or which prevents it, for any reason, from transmitting) light. Transmission density refers to the absorption of transmitted light, as by areas of a negative. Print tones are described as reflection densities, since they are seen and measured by reflected light.

DENSITY RANGE—The range of densities represented by, for example, a negative image. It is found by subtracting the lowest density value from the highest, and is expressed numerically. Also called "density scale."

DENSITY SCALE—Same as DENSITY RANGE.

DEPTH OF FIELD—The region of acceptably sharp focus around the subject position, extending toward the camera and away from it, from the plane of sharpest focus. The boundaries of the depth of field are referred to as the near limit and the far limit.

DEPTH OF FIELD SCALE—A calibrated scale, ring or chart, often a part of the camera lens mount, on which the depth of field for any distance and aperture setting is indicated.

DEPTH OF FOCUS—The little zone including the focal plane of the lens through which the film can be moved, toward, and away from the lens, and still record an acceptably sharp image.

DESSICATED—Dried. Describes a substance from which at least some water has been removed. Not necessarily "anhydrous," which see.

DEVELOPER—The solution which produces the silver image in the normal photographic process. It ordinarily contains a REDUCING AGENT, a PRESERVATIVE, an ACCELERATOR, and a RESTRAINER in water solution. A practical developer must develop only the exposed silver halide grains in the emulsion, leaving the unexposed grains unaffected. Such a developer is called clean working. A solution which develops an appreciable quantity of unexposed halide is said to produce chemical fog.

DEVELOPING-OUT—The photographic process in which relatively brief exposure produces a LATENT IMAGE which is made visible by subsequent development. See PRINTING-OUT.

DIAPHRAGM—The assembly of thin metal leaves, usually incorporated into the lens barrel or shutter assembly, which can be adjusted to control the size of the lens aperture. Same as IRIS DIAPHRAGM.

DICHROIC FILTER—A filter, usually of glass coated with a thin film of some durable material, which has the unique ability to transmit certain colors while reflecting the rest of the spectrum. Because the transmitted and reflected colors are complementary the filter appears to change color in certain lights, hence the name "dichroic." Dichroic filters are highly resistant to heat and fading and are therefore especially suitable for use in color printing applications.

DIFFRACTION—The tendency of light rays to be bent around the edge of an obstruction.

DIFFUSION—Of light, the random scattering of rays as by transmission through a turbid medium or by reflection from a matte surface.

DIFFUSION ENLARGER—An enlarger which employs diffused light to illuminate the negative.

DIN—Deutsche Industrie Normen. The German system of film speed determination.

DIOPTER—An optician's term which identifies the power of a lens. It expresses the reciprocal of the lens focal length in meters, and is usually preceded by a plus or minus sign to indicate whether the lens is positive (converging) or negative (diverging). Thus, a close-up (positive) lens having a focal length of 50 cm ($\frac{1}{2}$ meter) would be labelled a +2 lens.

DISCONTINUOUS SPECTRUM—Light radiation from which certain wavelengths (colors) are missing or present in negligible amounts.

DISPERSION—The separation of a light ray into its component colors as by a prism.

DISTORTION—Sometimes referred to as linear distortion or curvelinear distortion, it is an aberration of the lens which is characterized by variable magnification of the image. The effect increases toward the edges of the image area and will cause straight lines near the edges of the subject field to be formed near the image margins as curved lines. Two forms are identified, PINCUSHION and BARREL distortion.

D logE CURVE—The graphic presentation of the relationship between exposure and density when development is a constant. When several conditions of development are expressed the result is a "family of curves."

DMAX—Maximum Density.

DMIN—Minimum Density.

DODGING—The practice of shading a relatively small area of the image in printing so as to prevent it from becoming too fully exposed, and thus to render it, in the finished print, as lighter in tone than it would otherwise have been. See BURNING-IN.

DODGING TOOL—Any device used in dodging. Usually, a thin wire handle on which is mounted a piece of cardboard trimmed to match the shape of the image area to be DODGED.

DOUBLET—A two-element lens. If the elements are identical and there is a stop between them, the lens may be called a duplet.

DR—DENSITY RANGE, which see.

DROP-OUT—A photograph from which certain tones—usually the grays—have been eliminated.

DRUM DRYER—A machine for drying paper prints. It typically consists of a heated drum or cylinder of metal and an endless canvas belt which holds the prints in contact with the drum surface. The larger models are motorized for continuous operation.

DRY-MOUNTING—A method of mounting prints on cardboard or similar sheet materials. DRY-MOUNTING TISSUE placed between the print and mount board is softened by the heat of a DRY-MOUNTING PRESS to effect the bond.

DRY-MOUNTING PRESS—A machine for dry-mounting prints. It has a large flat metal pressure plate which can apply uniform pressure and thermostatically controlled heat on the prints to be mounted.

DRY-MOUNTING TISSUE—A thin tissue paper impregnated with shellac or some similar material, which, when heated sufficiently, softens to become an effective adhesive for paper.

DRY PLATE—Term used in the 1880s to distinguish gelatin-coated glass plates (dry plates) from the previously very popular collodion-coated plates which had to be sensitized immediately before use and inserted into the camera while still damp.

DS—DENSITY SCALE. Same as DENSITY RANGE, which see.

DYE TRANSFER—A method of making very high quality color prints, in which the final full-color image is produced by separate printings (transfers) of the three primary dye images, cyan, magenta, and yellow, from individual film matrices to a single sheet of prepared paper.

EASEL—The device, usually a frame of metal with adjustable metal masking strips, which holds printing paper flat for exposure under the enlarger, and permits adjustments of the width of the picture borders.

ELECTRONIC FLASH—A photographic light source which produces a brilliant flash of light by the discharge of electricity through a gas-filled glass or quartz flash tube. The flash duration is very short, usually less than 1/500 second and there is no firing delay. Most flash tubes produce a light which approximates daylight in color and only minor filtration is required for use with daylight color films. Electronic flash is commonly referred to as "strobe," an inaccurate nickname derived from stroboscope, a related but different device.

ELEMENT—Of a lens, one of the unit structures. A term rather loosely used to refer to a single glass unit, a cemented unit of one or more glasses, or even a complete component of several air-spaced and cemented glasses; as, "the front element (component) of a convertible lens."

ELON—Eastman Kodak's brand of p-methylaminophenol sulfate, most familiarly known as "Metol" which is itself a trade name (GAF, Agfa, Hauff, etc.). See METOL.

EMULSION—The light-sensitive coating on photographic film or printing paper.

ENLARGER—A printing machine designed to project the image of an illuminated negative onto a sheet of sensitized paper. While all enlargers can be adjusted to make prints larger than the negative image, most can also be adapted to make prints reduced in scale as well, so that the name is somewhat misleading.

ES—Exposure Scale, which see.

EVS—A system intended to simplify the determination of exposure. It assigns the EV numbers, 0 through 12, to the shutter speeds, 1 second through 1/1000 second, and the EV numbers 1 through 12, to the relative apertures, f/1.4 through f/64. Similarly, Additive Speed Values (ASV), 0 through 10 are assigned to ASA Indexes, 3 through 3200, and Light Value Scale (LVS) numbers, 0 through 10, are assigned to illumination levels of 6 footcandles through 6400 footcandles. In use, the sum of film speed (ASV) plus light intensity (LVS) yields a number which must be matched by the sum of a shutter speed EV number plus an aperture EV number. The system has not elicited much enthusiasm.

EXPANSION—In the Zone System, extended development which compensates for low subject contrast so as to produce normal negative contrast.

EXPOSURE—(1) The act of subjecting a photosensitive material to the action of light. (2) The accumulated effect of the action of light on a sensitized material.

EXPOSURE FACTOR—A number (multiplier) indicating the exposure increase required when, for example, a filter is used. The factor for a condition requiring, for example, four times the normal exposure would be written $4\times$.

EXPOSURE INDEX—A number indicating relative light sensitivity of a given film, as assigned by the American Standards Association. Usually referred to as the film speed or the ASA speed, or even simply the ASA.

EXPOSURE METER—An instrument used to measure the illumination level at the subject position or the brightness of the subject, and to equate this information with the film speed to indicate appropriate camera aperture and shutter speed settings.

EXPOSURE SCALE—The range of exposures (usually the range of light intensities with exposure time a constant) required to produce, after suitable development, the full range of densities which a given emulsion can produce. The term is relevant specifically to paper emulsions.

EXTENSION TUBES—A set of three or more (usually) rings or tubes of varying lengths, intended to be interposed between the body and lens of a small camera, so as to permit focusing the lens on subjects very close to the camera.

FACTOR—A number by which the duration or effect of some action or process must, for some reason, be multiplied.

FAILURE OF THE RECIPROCITY LAW—Refers to the fact that sensitive emulsions, when subjected to extremely intense or extremely dim exposing lights, require more total exposure than would be predicted by the Reciprocity Law. See RECIPROCITY LAW.

FARMER'S REDUCER—A water solution of potassium ferricyanide and sodium thiosulfate, proposed in 1883 by E. H. Farmer as an effective reducing solution for the silver image. It is still popular.

FAST—A term used to describe lenses of large relative aperture or films of high sensitivity. Sometimes also applied to unusually sensitive papers.

FEATHERING A LIGHT—The technique of evening the illumination across a set by directing the bright central beam of a light toward the farthest objects, thus allowing the nearest objects to be illuminated by the less intense margins of the beam.

FERROTYPE—Originally one name for the tintype process which was popular in the 1860s and '70s. It was also called the melainotype. Tintypes were made on small polished and varnished sheets of iron, hence the name *ferro*-type.

FERROTYPE TINS—After gelatin-coated printing papers became popular, prints were sometimes dried by squeegeeing them, emulsion down, on a Japanned (varnished) iron sheet or ferrotype tin. Prints so treated dried with a high gloss and the technique of glossing a print came to be known as ferrotyping. Nowadays glossy prints are dried on chromium-plated brass or plastic sheets, or chromium or stainless steel drum dryers, but the term ferrotyping persists.

FIELD CURVATURE—See CURVATURE OF FIELD.

FILL LIGHT—Light directed into the shadow areas of the subject to reduce the lighting contrast.

FILM—Generally, the familiar light-sensitive material used in cameras in the practice of photography. It normally consists of a flexible, thin, transparent sheet or strip of acetate or polyester plastic coated on one side with a light-sensitive emulsion, and on the other with a dyed layer of gelatin to reduce curl and halation.

FILM CLIP—A spring clip of metal, plastic, or wood designed to hold the film securely as it hangs in the film dryer.

FILM HOLDER—Thin container of plastic, metal, or wood, usually black, designed to hold two sheets of film in separate compartments, back to back. Film is loaded into the holder in the darkroom, and is protected from light by the DARK SLIDE. The film is positioned so accurately in the holder that, when it is inserted into the camera and the slide is withdrawn, the previously focused image falls precisely on the film surface, insuring that the photographer will actually get the picture he saw on the ground glass.

FILM PACK—A metal container of several sheets of film, so designed that when the pack is loaded properly into the camera, an exposed sheet can be removed from the focal plane into a lighttight compartment and a fresh sheet positioned for the next exposure by simply pulling a paper tab protruding from the end of the pack. After all the films are exposed, the pack can be removed from the camera, but must be unloaded in the darkroom. Film packs are not normally reusable.

FILM SPEED—The relative sensitivity of film to light.

FILTER—(1) To pass light through some material which absorbs selected wavelengths or colors or polarized portions of the light. (2) A sheet or disc of plastic, glass or other material, usually colored, which can be used to absorb selected components of transmitted light.

FINGERNAIL MARKS—Slang term for little crescent-shaped gray, black, or occasionally translucent marks which appear on negatives, resulting from pressing or crimping the film before development, as, for example, when loading roll film (inexpertly) onto a tank reel. The emulsion may be either effectively exposed or desensitized by physical violence of this kind, and the marks are authentic parts of the developed silver image. They will almost always be seen to coincide with a visible crease in the film base. They cannot be removed.

FISH-EYE LENS—A type of super wide-angle lens, or lens attachment, capable of covering a field of about 180°. Fish-eye images are circular, if the whole image appears on the film, and are notable for their barrel distortion.

FIX—To make the film insensitive to further exposure to light, usually by bathing the emulsion with a solution containing HYPO or some other effective silver halide solvent. Such a solution is called a fixing bath.

FLARE—That extraneous light, not part of the controlled image light, which passes through the lens to the film. Flare light resulting from diffusion of the normal image light by dirty lens surfaces, reflections from scratches or chips in the glass, or reflections from bright metal surfaces inside the camera usually causes a more or less general fogging of the film. Actual patterns, usually the out-of-focus images of the lens aperture, are caused by multiple reflections of strong light between the various lens surfaces.

FLASH—General name for any photographic light source which produces a very brilliant, very brief pulse of light.

FLASHBULB—A light source, similar in appearance to an ordinary electric light bulb, but containing a quantity of combustible wire and some priming material in an oxygen atmosphere. When a suitable electrical connection is made to the bulb terminals, the primer fires, igniting the wire which in turn burns very rapidly with a brilliant flash of light. Typically, the flash reaches useful intensity about fifteen milliseconds after the application of the firing current, with the peak intensity occurring at about twenty milliseconds. Total effective duration is in the order of ten to thirty milliseconds. A flashbulb can only be used once, of course.

FLASHCUBE—Small, cube-shaped assembly of four tiny flashbulbs, each with its own reflector, in a common housing. A special base design fits the flash socket of certain specialized cameras and permits the flash units to be fired in quick succession. Coupled with motorized film transport, flashcubes can be used to make four synchronized flash pictures in just a few seconds.

FLASHING—The technique of darkening an area of a print image by exposing the sensitized paper to raw white light. Flashing fogs the image unlike DODGING and BURNING-IN, both of which modify the effect of the image-forming light itself.

FLASH SYNCHRONIZATION—The adjustment of the timing of the application of firing current to a flashbulb and the actuation of the shutter release so that the peak flash intensity occurs while the shutter is open.

FLAT—(1) A large, free-standing, movable wall or panel, usually painted white, and used as a reflector or background in studio photography. (2) A term used to describe a low-contrast image, usually in reference to a print; it implies that the contrast is *too* low.

FLOOD—A photographic light source which is designed to illuminate a wide area with light of relatively uniform intensity. Almost without exception, it implies an incandescent or fluorescent source, but flood reflectors are also available for use with flash sources.

f/NUMBER—The numerical expression of the aperture diameter of a lens as a fraction of the focal length. See RELATIVE APERTURE.

FOCAL DISTANCE—The distance from the lens to the plane of the focused image. In practice, it is usually measured from the plane of the lens diaphragm.

FOCAL LENGTH—Loosely, the FOCAL DISTANCE when the lens is focused on INFINITY; more accurately, the distance from the rear nodal point of the lens to the image plane when the lens is focused on infinity. See NODAL POINT.

FOCAL PLANE SHUTTER—A CURTAIN SHUTTER operating in the camera body just ahead of the film (or focal) plane.

FOCUS—To adjust a camera, for example, so that an image is formed precisely on the film plane. Also a term applied to the adjustment of instruments such as binoculars and microscopes so as to provide a visual impression of sharpness in the image. Generally, the adjustment of any positive lens system so that light rays passing through it converge at a desired point. The convergence of light rays to a point.

FOCUSING CLOTH—Sometimes also called dark cloth. A large square or rectangular piece of black material, usually cloth, used by photographers as an aid in focusing the image on the ground-glass screen of a view camera. It is used to enclose the camera back and the photographer's head, thus excluding outside light and making the image appear bright and clear.

FOG—Any tone or density in the developed emulsion which was caused by extraneous light or chemical action, not related to the normal formation of the image.

FOOT SWITCH—A switch designed to be operated by foot pressure. Used by photographers to control the enlarger light so as to leave the hands free for dodging and burning-in.

FORCED DEVELOPMENT—Development deliberately prolonged considerably beyond the normal time. See PUSH.

FRAME—(1) To adjust the position and angle of the camera with respect to the subject for the purpose of containing or composing the image within the boundaries of the viewfinder. (2) The useful area and shape of the film image; the picture.

FRAME NUMBERS—Numbers printed on the paper backing strip and along the edges of roll film, and outside the perforations of 35-mm film strips which can be used to identify the individual pictures (or frames).

FRECKLING—Slang term describing a common flaw in ferrotyped prints. Groups or areas of tiny dull spots in an otherwise highly glossy surface.

FRILLING—The detachment (and wrinkling) of areas of the emulsion layer along the edges of the film or paper base during processing. Likely to occur with, and for the same reasons as, reticulation. See RETICULATION.

GAMMA—A numerical expression of the gradient of the straight-line portion of the film characteristic curve, it can be defined as D/logE. Loosely, an indication of the contrast of the image as influenced by development. See CONTRAST INDEX.

GELATIN—A complex protein substance made from animal hides and hooves which is used as a chemical-bearing medium and binder in the manufacture of photographic emulsions. Its many unique properties make it especially suitable for use in silver halide emulsions, but it is also an essential material in some nonsilver techniques such as the collotype and carbon processes.

GLACIAL ACETIC ACID—The concentrated, 99%, form of Acetic Acid. It is a transparent, colorless, dense liquid with a sharp, powerfully penetrating odor. It freezes at about 16°C. (60°F.); it is an effective solvent for some plastics; and its vapors are flammable. It burns the skin painfully on brief contact and should be handled with caution. See ACETIC ACID and SHORTSTOP.

GLOSSING SOLUTION—A bath in which prints are soaked briefly before being ferrotyped. It is intended to reduce freckling, prevent sticking, and generally improve the luster of the print surface.

GLOSSY—Describes a printing paper with a smooth surface suitable for ferrotyping. A print with a mirrorlike luster such as is produced by ferrotyping.

GRADATION—Variation in tone. Tonal range or scale.

GRADIENT—Slope, specifically the slope of a film characteristic curve or some section of one.

GRADUATE—A container, usually glass, enamelled steel, stainless steel or plastic, which is calibrated in fluid ounces or milliliters, or both, for use in measuring liquid volumes.

GRAIN—The visible granular texture of the silver image, caused by apparent clumping of the individual silver particles, not usually apparent until the image is enlarged or viewed under magnification.

GRAY—(1) Any of the intermediate tones of a black-and-white image. (2) Describes a print image which is without extremes of tone and is unpleasantly low in contrast. See FLAT.

GRAY CARD—A card of known reflectance, usually 18 percent, intended to be placed in the subject area and used as a meter target in the determination of exposure. Also used in color photography to establish a neutral reference for the adjustment of print color.

GRAY SCALE—(1) The gradation of an image. (2) A strip of film or paper displaying individually uniform areas of density ranging from light to dark in a series of steps. Also sometimes called step tablets, they are used in testing the sensitivity and contrast characteristics of photographic materials.

GREEN—One of the primary colors in the additive system.

GROSS FOG DENSITY—Same as "Base-plus-fog Density," which see.

GROUND GLASS—A general name for the focusing screen in a reflex or view camera.

GUM PROCESS—A method of printing in which the sensitized surface is a coating of gum arabic, a pigment, and a dichromate. The emulsion is rendered insoluble by exposure to bright light, and the image is ultimately composed of the areas of pigment which are not washed away during development in plain water.

H AND D CURVES—Film characteristic curves, specifically those plotted by F. Hurter and V. Driffield who published their procedure in 1890.

HALATION—The fringe or halo which sometimes occurs around very heavily exposed image points as the excess light, penetrating the emulsion layer, is reflected back into the emulsion from the surfaces of the film base. It is reduced in modern films by dyeing the film base material itself or by the application of a dyed gelatin layer on the film back, called the antihalation or antihalo backing.

HALF-TONE—Printer's and engraver's term for an image which has been screened so as to produce the effect of continuous tone. This is accomplished by breaking up the image into half-tone dots in a regular pattern too fine to be visually resolved under normal conditions. Tones of gray are identified by percentage numbers which indicate the total area of ink in a given area of the image. Thus a 10 percent gray would imply that the dots composing it were 1/10 as large in area as the area of the white paper separating them.

HALIDES—Metallic compounds of the halogens, namely the elements fluorine, chlorine, bromine, and iodine. The chlorides, bromides, and iodides of silver are the light-sensitive materials upon which most photographic processes are based.

HALO-DOT SCREEN—CONTACT SCREEN, which see.

HAND CAMERA—Little-used term to identify any camera that can be carried and used without a tripod. Also "hand-held" camera.

HANGERS—The frames, usually of metal or plastic, in which sheet films are placed for processing in deep tanks.

HARD—Term occasionally used to describe high contrast in images or lighting arrangements. Harsh.

HARDENER—A chemical solution for tanning or toughening the emulsion. Hardeners may be used as separate baths or they may be included in some other solution.

HARSH—Implies an unpleasant lack of subtlety of gradation or light distribution. Contrasty, glaring.

HIGHLIGHTS—The brightest light accents in the subject. Also, the areas in the image corresponding to the subject highlights. In the negative, of course, the highlights are the most dense areas.

HIGHLIGHT MASK—A deliberately underexposed, high contrast negative of a color transparency which images only the highlight areas of the transparency and which is bound in register with the transparency while the principal color correcting masks are being made. Its purpose is to increase the highlight contrast of the final color print image in the dye transfer process. Highlight masks are also useful in black-and-white photography.

HOLDER—See FILM HOLDER.

HOT-SPOT—An undesirable concentration of light on the subject in studio photography. The brilliant area of illumination produced by the concentrated central beam of a flood or spotlight. An area of unusual brightness in the projected light from an enlarger or projector.

HYDROQUINONE—Common name for p-dihydroxybenzene, a reducing agent in many popular developers. Its fine, needlelike crystals are white, lustrous, and fairly soluble in plain water and in sulfite solutions. It keeps well in dry form, but only fairly well in solution. It is a high-contrast developer, especially so when accelerated with the caustic alkalis such as sodium hydroxide. It is normally nonstaining but must be heavily restrained to prevent fog. In general use, it is almost invariably teamed with metol—a combination which not only exhibits the best features of each, but has some additional desirable characteristics of its own. See METOL.

HYPERFOCAL DISTANCE—The distance from the camera to the near plane of the DEPTH OF FIELD when the lens is focused on infinity. Also the distance from the camera to the plane of sharpest focus when the far plane of the depth of field is at infinity.

HYPO—The common nickname for the chemical sodium thiosulfate, which was originally called sodium *hyposulfite* by Sir John Frederick William Herschel who discovered it in 1819 and recommended its use to Talbot in 1839. It is still considered to be one of the best of the few practical solvents for the silver halides, and is the major ingredient in almost all of the general-purpose fixing baths. The term hypo is commonly used to refer not only to the chemical itself but also to fixing baths compounded with it, and even to those which are made with ammonium thiosulfate—the so-called rapid fixing baths.

Hypo Eliminator—A bath for films and papers, recommended for use following the fixing bath and intended to convert the chemical products of fixation into compounds more readily soluble in water, thus facilitating washing and increasing the stability of the silver image. Most such baths are more properly called hypo clearing baths since they do not really eliminate hypo but do aid in its removal.

Image—The photographic representation of the subject photographed. The visible result of exposing and developing a photographic emulsion.

Incident Light—The light reaching the subject from any and all sources.

Incident Meter—An exposure meter designed, or adapted, for the measurement of incident light intensity, or illuminance.

Infinity—For photographic purposes, that distance from the camera beyond which no further focusing adjustment is required to maintain a satisfactorily sharp image of a receding object. It varies with the focal length of the lens, the aperture, and the photographer's standard of sharpness, but for most purposes infinity can be considered to be anything beyond a quarter of a mile or so from the camera.

Infrared—Name assigned to an extensive band of invisible, long wavelength electromagnetic radiations which continue the spectrum beyond visible red light. We can perceive a portion of the infrared spectrum as heat, and some special films are capable of making pictures by infrared light.

Intensifier—A solution used to increase the density or contrast of the silver image, usually to improve the printing characteristics of underdeveloped negatives.

Interchangeable Lens—A lens which can be removed from the camera body as a complete unit and replaced by another.

Interval Timer—A device for indicating the end of a selected period of time, usually by ringing a bell or sounding a buzzer. It is used to time development and other procedures which must be carried out in darkness or where a conventional clock cannot be seen.

Inverse Square Law—A statement to the effect that "illumination intensity on a surface will vary inversely with the square of the distance from the light source to the illuminated surface."

Iris Diaphragm—See Diaphragm.

Inspection—A method of determining the extent of development by observing the image under dim Safelight illumination.

Kelvin Temperature—Temperature on the absolute Celsius (or Centigrade) scale. In photography, another name for Color Temperature.

Lantern Slide—A transparency mounted in a cardboard or metal frame or bound between glass plates for projection. Usually implies the 3¼″ × 4″ slide size used in large auditorium projectors. See Slide.

Latent Image—The invisible impression on the sensitized emulsion produced by exposure to light in the developing-out processes. Development converts the latent image to a visible one.

LEADER—A strip of film or paper attached to and preceding the useful film area of roll film which is provided for threading the film into the camera, and in some cases, for protecting the unused film itself from light during storage and handling.

LEAF SHUTTER—A type of shutter, usually operating in the space between the major lens components or immediately behind the lens, which consists of a number of thin metal leaves or blades, arranged concentrically around the lens axis, pivoted so that they can either form an opening for the passage of light or overlap to block it. An associated mechanism controls the movement of the leaves and the duration of the exposure interval.

LENS—A disc of transparent glass, plastic or other material whose opposite faces are ground into (usually) spherical, nonparallel surfaces (one face, but not both, may be plane) having a common central axis, and capable of forming either a real or a virtual image. If the center of the lens is thicker than its edges, it will form a real image and is called a positive lens. If the center is thinner than the edges, only a virtual image can be formed and the lens is termed negative. A single lens is usually referred to as a simple lens and is used for picture-taking in only the cheapest cameras. In photography, the term "lens" usually refers to the complex composite structures of two or more glasses as used in a camera. See CORRECTION.

LENS BARREL—The metal tube in which a lens is mounted. It usually also contains a DIAPHRAGM assembly. A barrel-mounted lens does not have an integral shutter.

LENS BOARD—The wooden or metal panel on which a view camera (or other) lens is mounted.

LENS HOOD—A device for shielding the front element of a lens from direct light from outside the subject area, so as to prevent or reduce FLARE.

LENS MOUNT—That portion of the camera body which holds the lens in position.

LENS SHADE—Same as LENS HOOD.

LENS SYSTEM—A group or series of lenses assembled for purpose of controlling light.

LENS TISSUE—A special soft, lintless tissue used for cleaning lens surfaces.

LIGHT METER—An instrument which measures light intensity. If supplied with a suitable computing scale, it becomes an EXPOSURE METER. The term is commonly used interchangeably with exposure meter.

LIGHT PRIMARIES—The three light colors—red, green, and blue—which, when mixed together, produce a color we recognize as white. None of these colors can be produced by mixtures of any other colors, but appropriate mixtures of the primaries can make any color desired.

LIGHTTIGHT—Describes a container, room or space which light cannot enter or leave, or a door or baffle or aperture which light cannot penetrate.

LIGHT TRAP—A device (such as, for example, a maze) which will permit the passage of air or water or objects, but will exclude light.

LITHOGRAPHY—Originally, a method of printmaking in which a drawing in greasy ink or crayon on a prepared stone could be made to produce ink impressions on paper. It is now also a very popular and efficient commercial printing process, generally referred to as photolithography because the printing plates receive their images by photographic means. The image is now prepared on a grained metal sheet but the essential process is unchanged.

Long Lens—A lens of longer-than-normal focal length. Most accurately applied to lenses of conventional construction, but also commonly used to refer to telephoto lenses as well.

Luminance—Light reflected from, or produced by, a surface.

Luminance Meter—A meter which measures luminance. Also sometimes called "reflectance meter" or "reflected light meter."

LVS—Light Value Scale. See EVS.

Macro-lens—Also occasionally Micro-lens. A term used to describe lenses especially corrected for use at short subject distances and generally applied only to those supplied for small cameras. The prefixes *Macro* or *Micro* often appear in the lens name.

Macrophotography—The process of making very large photographic images; for example, photomurals. See Microphotography.

Main Light—The light in a studio setup, usually the brightest one, which establishes the light and shadow pattern on the subject and thus describes the forms. Also sometimes called the modelling light.

Masking—The process of blocking out portions of the image area or its borders with opaque tape or paint. Also, the technique of modifying image gradation by registering negative and positive versions of the same image and printing them together to produce a new version.

Mask—A negative or positive transparency made for the purpose of masking the original image.

Mat—A wide-bordered frame, usually of cardboard, placed over a picture to define the composition, isolate the image area and improve the appearance for presentation.

Mat Knife—A short-bladed knife with a large handle and, usually, replaceable blades, intended for cutting cardboard. In use it is generally guided by a straight-edge metal ruler.

Matte—Dull, unreflective, nonglossy; referring to surface texture.

Matrix—In dye transfer printing, the final positive film image. The matrix image is in gelatin relief, and it is used to make the actual transfer of dye to the print paper surface. Three matrix images are required, one for each of the pigment primary colors. The plural is matrices, but professional printers call them simply "mats."

Maximum Aperture—The largest useful opening of the lens. Wide open.

Meniscus—In photography, describes a simple lens, one of whose faces is convex, the other concave.

Metol—Most common name for the reducing agent p-methylamino-phenol sulfate. Also known as Elon, Pictol, Rhodol, Photol, etc. It has low staining tendencies, is easily accelerated by mild alkalis and produces little fog. It is supplied as a white or slightly grayish powder which turns yellowish or brownish with age and oxidation. It keeps well in powder form, but oxidizes quite rapidly in solution. It works very rapidly, producing an image of neutral tone and very low contrast. It is considered to be toxic and will produce an irritating and painful skin rash on those unfortunate photographers who are allergic to it. It is generally used in combination with hydroquinone which complements its characteristics very satisfactorily.

M, F, X—Markings found on some shutters indicating the flash synchronization settings for use with different flash sources. *M*, medium peak, for use with regular wire-filled bulbs, provides a delay of about twenty milliseconds. *F*, now rarely seen and intended for fast peak bulbs which are obsolete, provides a delay of about five milliseconds. *X*, zero delay, is recommended for use with electronic flash units and makes the flash contact when the shutter blades are fully open.

MICROPHOTOGRAPHY—The photographic production of extremely small images, as in the preparation of masks for electronic microcircuits.

MICRO-PRISM—Descriptive of the structure of a type of focusing aid incorporated into the ground-glass viewing screen of some miniature cameras. Consisting of a multitude of minute 3- or 4-sided transparent refracting pyramids arranged in a regular pattern, and placed in the center of the viewing screen, it functions as an area of rather coarse-textured ground glass for viewing, but provides a more sensitive indication of image sharpness than ordinary ground glass does.

MILLIMICRON—One millionth of a millimeter, one nanometer; formerly, and still occasionally, used to describe wavelengths of light. Equivalent to ten Angstrom Units. See WAVELENGTH.

MIRED—Pronounced "my-red," it is a contraction of *micro-reciprocal degrees*. It is a value found by multiplying the reciprocal of a COLOR TEMPERATURE by 1,000,000. The expression of color temperatures in mireds rather than the usual Kelvin degrees simplifies considerably the problem of filter selection for color photography in unusual conditions of light color.

MIRROR LENS—Optical system which employs a (usually) spherical mirror surface, rather than a positive glass lens, to form a real image. Most such lenses for photographic use incorporate one or more glass lenses in addition to the main mirror element to improve the system performance. These composite systems are called catadioptric systems.

MONO-BATH—Processing solution, usually for use with film emulsions, combining the functions of developer and fixing bath.

MONOHYDRATE—The stable form of sodium carbonate, and the one commonly specified in formulas calling for this chemical. If either the anhydrous or crystalline form is used in place of the monohydrated form, the amount, by weight, must be adjusted. See ANHYDROUS.

MQ—Nickname for developers compounded with the reducing agents *M*etol and (Hydro-) *Q*uinone. Also sometimes called MH, for *M*etol-*H*ydroquinone.

NEGATIVE—Any photographic image in which the subject tones have been reversed. Specifically, the reversed-tone image resulting from the simple development of the film exposed in the camera in the conventional process of taking a picture.

NEGATIVE CARRIER—The frame of glass or metal which holds the negative in printing position in the ENLARGER.

NEGATIVE LENS—A diverging lens, thinner at the center than at the edges, which can produce only a virtual image.

NEUTRAL DENSITY FILTER—A thin sheet or disc of glass, plastic or gelatin having plane and parallel faces, toned to some uniform and specific shade of gray, and intended to be used over the camera lens during exposure for the purpose of reducing the intensity of the exposing light without changing its color. Sometimes called ND filters, they are available in accurately calibrated densities from 0.1 to 4.0.

NODAL POINT—A point on the axis of a lens around which the lens can be rotated slightly without displacing the focused image of an object at infinity. Specifically, the point from which an accurate measurement of the lens focal length can be made.

NORMAL LENS—Any lens whose focal length is approximately equal to the diagonal measurement of the film frame. See FRAME, 2. The angular coverage of a normal lens is usually about 55° across the film frame diagonal. See ANGULAR COVERAGE.

NOTCHES—Specifically, the notches which film manufacturers cut into one of the short edges of a sheet of film which identify the type of film by their number, shape, and position, and the emulsion side of the film sheet by their placement.

OBJECT—The thing photographed. Often used interchangeably with subject, but usually applied to inanimate things. See SUBJECT.

OBJECTIVE—In optics generally, the lens or lens assembly which faces the object. The objective normally forms an aerial image which (in a microscope, for example) is then viewed through the eyepiece or ocular lens. In photography, the term objective is sometimes used to refer to a camera lens.

ONE-SHOT DEVELOPER—A developing solution, usually compounded and stored in very concentrated form, intended to be highly diluted for one-time use, then discarded.

OPAL BULB—Electric light bulb having an unusually dense, translucent envelope of white opal glass, intended for use where uniform diffusion of light is important, as for example, in an enlarger.

OPAQUE—(1.) Incapable of transmitting light. (2.) A special fine-ground tempera paint, usually brick-red or black, for use in blocking out (opaqueing) unwanted areas of the negative image prior to printing.

OPEN FLASH—Method of taking pictures with flash in which the shutter is opened on *time* or *bulb* and the flash is fired manually.

OPENING—Refers to lens opening and is used, loosely, to mean either aperture or relative aperture.

ORDINARY—Refers to emulsions whose color sensitivity has not been extended beyond visible blue light. Ordinary films are not really ordinary any more. The vast majority of available film types are now Panchromatic. See ORTHOCHROMATIC.

ORTHOCHROMATIC—Type of emulsion which is sensitive to visible blue and green, but not to red. See PANCHROMATIC.

OVEREXPOSED—Refers to a photographic image which has received too much light.

OYSTER SHELLING—A defect in glossy prints dried on flat ferrotype tins, which shows itself as a series of concentric rings or ridges of torn or strained emulsion, caused by uneven drying. Not common in prints dried on glossy drum dryers.

PAN—(1.) Abbreviation of PANCHROMATIC. (2.) To swing a camera during the exposure to follow a moving object, and thus to render the object sharp against a blurred background.

PANCHROMATIC—Describes an emulsion sensitive to blue and green and some, or all, of the red region of the spectrum. See TYPE A, 2; TYPE B, 2; and TYPE C.

PAPER—The sensitized paper used in making photographic prints.

PAPER NEGATIVE—A negative image on a paper base, prepared either by exposing the paper directly in a camera or by printing from a positive transparency. The term implies that the image is not in its final form, and that another printing step will follow. If the image is finished for presentation as a negative, it would more likely be referred to as a negative print.

PARALLAX—In photography, the differences, in both the framing of the subject forms and their spatial relationships, between the image seen by the camera viewfinder and that recorded on the film. Sometimes referred to as the parallax error.

PHOTOFLOOD—A type of incandescent light bulb of high efficiency but limited life, designed to burn at 3400°K. Formerly popular with amateur photographers because of their small size, modest cost, and low current requirements. They are now being superseded by quartz-iodine lights.

PHOTOGRAM—A shadow image made by simply placing objects on the sensitized surface of a sheet of photographic paper and exposing it to light. If the light is sufficiently intense and the exposure long enough, the exposed portions of the paper will turn dark, and the image is a light-toned record of the shadow pattern on a dark background. This is called printing-out the image. Relatively brief exposure to light will form a latent image which can be developed-out like a conventional print image. Developed-out images are more neutral in tone and more contrasty. Both types must be fixed to be preserved for any great length of time.

PHOTOMACROGRAPHY—The photography of objects under some magnification, usually employing accessory bellows units, extension tubes, supplementary lenses or simple microscopes. Image magnification may range from about life-size (1:1) to perhaps 50×.

PHOTOMICROGRAPHY—Photography through a compound microscope.

PIGMENT PRIMARIES—The primary colors in the subtractive color system, normally considered to be red, yellow, and blue, but in photography specifically magenta, yellow, and cyan.

PINCUSHION DISTORTION—One of the two forms of curvelinear distortion in which image magnification is disproportionately greater near the edges of the field than near the center. Thus, for example, the image of a large square, placed concentric with the image center, would assume the shape of a pincushion. BARREL DISTORTION is the other, and opposite, form.

PINHOLE—(1) A very small aperture in the front panel or lens board of a modified or contrived camera for the purpose of forming an unfocused but useful image on the film. (2) A small transparent spot, usually circular, in a negative image, marking the position of an air-bell which, by shielding the emulsion from the developer, prevented the formation of silver in that area.

PLANE OF FOCUS—The position of the focused image in space; the image plane, as distinguished from the film plane which will usually, but not necessarily always, coincide with it. Actually, the term is misleading, since the image of any three-dimensional subject closer to the camera than infinity is not plane but three-dimensional—and even the image of a flat subject is plane only under unusual conditions, usually being warped into one or more spherical curves.

PLATE—A sheet of glass or occasionally metal, coated with light-sensitive emulsion and usually intended for exposure in a camera.

POLARIZED LIGHT—Light waves which have been caused to vibrate uniformly in, or parallel to, a particular plane.

POLARIZER—A transparent material such as certain natural crystals and some plastics, capable of polarizing transmitted light.

PORTRAIT ATTACHMENT—Another term (and a rather inappropriate one) for a close-up lens. See CLOSE-UP LENS.

PORTRAIT LENS—A lens designed to produce soft-focus images, and popular with portrait photographers. See SPHERICAL ABERRATION.

POSITIVE—An image in which the tones or colors are similar to those of the subject.

POSITIVE LENS—A converging lens; one which has relatively thick center and thin edges and which can focus light to form a real image.

POSTERIZATION—Popular name for a printing process in which the image gradation is arbitrarily limited to two or three tones of unmodulated gray (or color) resulting in a simplified posterlike pattern.

PRESERVATIVE—The ingredient in a developing or fixing solution which tends to prevent or retard spoiling, usually sodium sulfite.

PRESS-FOCUS LEVER—A device incorporated in many leaf shutters which permits opening, or holding open, the shutter blades regardless of the speed setting. On some old shutters this was called a "blade arrestor."

PRIMARY COLORS—Those fundamental colors, in light or pigment, which cannot be created by mixing any others. See LIGHT PRIMARIES and PIGMENT PRIMARIES.

PRINT—In photography, the term is generally used to identify an image on paper, produced by photographic means. It is usually understood to mean a positive image, and implies a final image rather than an intermediate one in some longer process.

PRINT FINISHING—The process of producing a permanent, presentable photographic print, sometimes including treatment in the fixing bath and the final wash, but certainly referring to drying, spotting, cropping, mounting, and matting and related operations.

PRINTING FRAME—A shallow, rectangular frame of wood or metal equipped with a removabe front glass and a separate folding back which can be fastened to the frame with leaf springs so as to hold a negative and a sheet of printing paper against the glass smoothly and tightly. In use, light is allowed to shine through the front glass and through the intervening negative to reach the printing emulsion. Also called a contact printing frame. See CONTACT PRINTING.

PRINTING-OUT—A method of photographic printing in which a visible image is formed by the action of light directly, and without subsequent development.

PRINTING PAPER—Photographic printing paper. Any paper coated with a light-sensitive substance, to be used for making photographic images, but generally in reference to commercially manufactured papers coated with gelatin emulsion containing silver halides as the sensitive materials.

PRINT QUALITY—This term refers to the craftsmanship of the print and whatever evidences there are of the photographer's technical understanding and competence (or lack of them). But there are often intangibles involved which influence the viewer in ways difficult to explain, and these factors, whatever they are, must be included in the term. Print quality is unrelated to pictorial content.

PRISM-REFLEX—A type of camera, usually small, in which the viewfinder image is focused, right-side-up and correct from left to right, on a ground-glass screen, and viewed through a magnifying eyepiece. The optical system which accomplishes this includes both a mirror and a penta-prism, hence the name.

PROCESS—(1.) To subject photographic films or papers to chemical treatment, such as, for example, development. (2.) The sequence of chemical steps required to produce the desired image or result.

PROCESS LENS—A photographic lens especially designed and painstakingly constructed for the purpose of producing images of the highest quality at object distances of only a few focal lengths. Usually nearly symmetrical in construction and corrected apochromatically, these lenses are exceptionally free from distortion, of relatively long focal length, slow, and very expensive. They are used almost exclusively by professionals in industry and the graphic arts. The nearest equivalent for the small-camera user is the *macro*-lens.

PROJECTION PRINT—Any print made by projection, rather than by contact. Usually interpreted to mean an enlargement.

PROJECTOR—In photography, usually a machine used to project enlarged images onto a viewing screen, such as a slide projector or movie projector.

PUSH—To prolong the time of development of film in an effort to compensate for underexposure. Also, to underexpose a film deliberately with the intention of attempting compensation in development. To force, but moderately. See FORCED DEVELOPMENT.

PYRO—Common contraction of pyrogallic acid or 1, 2, 3-trihydroxybenzene. One of the first organic reducing agents to be used as a photographic developer, it is usually in the form of white prismatic crystals of irregular size and shape. It is a very active developer. It keeps well in dry form or in suitable stock solution, but oxidizes very rapidly in most working dilutions. It is usual to prepare the stock as three separate highly concentrated solutions: Sol. *A* containing the pyro, the restrainer and a substantial quantity of an acid sulfite as a special preservative; Sol. *B* containing the normal preservative; and Sol. *C* containing the accelerator. Pyro developers of this kind typically produce a heavy yellowish stain image and also tan or harden the image gelatin as they work so that the final image combines silver, stain, and gelatin relief. Pyro stains the hands and utensils badly but is relatively nontoxic.

QUARTZ LIGHT—Also quartz-iodine light or quartz-halogen light. An incandescent electric light of small size and high efficiency employing a tungsten filament burning in an atmosphere of iodine or bromine vapor and enclosed in a quartz envelope. Characterized by exceptional resistance to blackening or dimming with age, long life, and uniform color temperature.

RC PAPERS—RESIN COATED PAPERS, which see.

RACKED OUT—Referring to the bellows of a view camera, the term means extended.

RANGEFINDER—Primarily refers to an optical device consisting of a system of lenses and beam-splitting prisms, which, viewing the subject through two slightly separated objective lenses, presents the images together in the viewfinder. When the two images are made to coincide by turning a dial, the subject distance can be read from a calibrated scale. Now also used to refer to a simple arrangement of two small prisms incorporated into the viewing screen of some single-lens reflex cameras as a focusing aid.

RANGEFINDER CAMERA—A camera featuring a built-in, coupled, optical rangefinder, usually incorporated into the viewfinder and linked mechanically with the focusing mount of the lens so that bringing the rangefinder images into coincidence also focuses the lens.

RAW LIGHT—Unfocused light.

REAL IMAGE—An image which can be projected onto a surface and seen with the unaided eye. See VIRTUAL IMAGE.

RECIPROCITY LAW—A law which states that exposure varies uniformly with changes in either time or intensity.

RECTILINEAR—Free from linear distortion.

REDUCER—A solution of chemicals capable of dissolving the developed silver image, thereby reducing its density.

REDUCING AGENT—In chemistry, a substance capable of reducing the positive charge of an ion by supplying electrons. Many reducing agents are capable of reducing silver halides to metallic silver, but only a few are appropriate for use as photographic developing agents. See DEVELOPER.

REEL—The metal or plastic spool featuring parallel spiral flanges (sometimes adjustable) on which roll films are wound for small tank processing.

REFLECTANCE—Describes the ability of a surface to reflect light.

REFLECTANCE METER—Luminance meter, which see.

REFLECTION—The rebounding of light from a surface, especially a plane polished surface. Also the image seen by reflection, such as the image "in" a mirror.

REFLECTOR—A surface used to reflect light. Photographic reflectors are usually sheets of cardboard, plywood, masonite, or stretched fabric, painted white or covered with metal foil.

REFLEX CAMERA—A type of camera in which the viewfinder image is formed by a lens and reflected by an inclined mirror onto a ground-glass screen mounted in the top of the camera body. See SINGLE-LENS REFLEX and TWIN-LENS REFLEX.

REFRACTION—The bending of light rays as they pass obliquely through the interfaces of transparent mediums of varying or different densities.

REGISTER—To superimpose one image on another of identical outline so that the forms and edges coincide.

RELATIVE APERTURE—The relationship between the diameter of the lens opening and the focal length of the lens. It is found by dividing the focal length by the diameter and is, strictly speaking, the number so found—as distinguished from the APERTURE which includes the prefix f. This is a niggling distinction—photographers use the terms interchangeably.

REPLENISHER—A solution of chemicals, similar in composition to a developer but usually more concentrated, intended to be added in measured quantities to a developer after each use for the purpose of restoring the strength of the developer and extending its useful life.

RESIN COATED PAPERS—Printing papers employing a special base material, treated during manufacture with a "Resin Coating" which, by limiting water absorption, allows for very rapid processing and reduces drying time.

RESTRAINER—An ingredient in a developer solution intended to inhibit the development of unexposed halides. In most solutions which contain one, the restrainer is potassium bromide.

RETICULATION—The pattern of tiny wrinkles or tears in the emulsion of a negative which sometimes results when the film is subjected to temperature extremes or harsh chemical treatment during processing. In extreme cases, the emulsion may be detached from the film base in large patches. See FRILLING. Mild cases of reticulation are often over-looked or confused with the image grain. See GRAIN.

RETRO-FOCUS LENS—A type of wide-angle lens supplied for reflex cameras which has a BACK FOCUS greater than its FOCAL LENGTH. This is made possible by special reversed telephoto design, and provides clearance for the reflex mirror.

REVERSAL—(1.) The transformation of the original tonal scale from negative to positive or vice versa, which occurs whenever a conventional photographic emulsion is exposed and developed. (2.) A special process by which exposed film is made to produce a positive image of the original subject. Actually a double reversal of the subject tones, the film is first developed to form a conventional negative image which is then bleached out of the emulsion. The remaining unexposed silver halides are then fogged by exposure to raw light or chemical treatment and developed to form the final positive image.

RIM LIGHT—Back light which illuminates the edges of the subject, producing a bright outline.

RISING FRONT—One of the shifts of a view camera, this refers to that adjustment of the camera lens board which permits vertical displacement of the lens while allowing the lens board to remain parallel with the film plane.

ROLL FILM—Film supplied in rolls rather than sheets, but especially those films protected from light by paper leaders rather than those supplied in protective cartridges of metal or plastic.

SABATTIER EFFECT—The partial reversal of image tones caused by exposure of the emulsion to light during development, usually after the image has been partially formed. Named after Armand Sabattier who first described the effect in 1862. Commonly referred to as solarization which is a misnomer. See SOLARIZATION.

SAFELIGHT—Illumination, used in various darkroom processes, which is of a color and intensity which will not appreciably affect the emulsions being handled. Blue-sensitive emulsions can be handled in a yellow safelight and orthochromatic emulsions are generally unaffected by orange or red safelight. Image density resulting from excessive exposure to safelight, or to an inappropriate safelight color, is known as safelight fog.

SALTED PAPER—Photographic printing paper such as was described and used by Talbot in his calotype process. It can be prepared by soaking a sheet of good-quality paper in a weak solution of salt, then coating it with one or more layers of a silver nitrate solution. The halide formed is silver chloride. The paper is used for printing-out and the image is an elegant purplish tone which, unfortunately, changes to brown during fixation.

SBR—See SUBJECT BRIGHTNESS RANGE, for which this is a contraction. "Subject Luminance Range" is preferred.

SCATTERING—Loss of intensity of light in passing through a turbid medium. The shorter wavelengths are typically absorbed most readily, causing the transmitted light to appear yellowish or reddish. This is the atmospheric effect which is responsible for the warmth of color in late afternoon sunlight and in sunsets.

SCREEN—(1.) The surface upon which images are projected for viewing. Usually made of special fabric painted white, or covered with tiny glass or plastic beads, or metallized for maximum reflectance. (2.) The sheet of glass or film containing a fine pattern of lines or dots, through which films are exposed in the production of half-tone printing plates. See HALF-TONE and SCREENED IMAGE. (3.) Occasionally used to refer to the ground glass of a camera, as the viewing or focusing screen.

SCREENED IMAGE—A photographic image composed of minute dots which vary individually in size in proportion to the intensity of the light which formed them. Photographs or other continuous-tone images must be screened for reproduction by letter-press or offset techniques in order to preserve the gradation of the original subject. See HALF-TONE.

SENSITIVITY—In photography, the susceptibility of an emulsion to alteration by light energy.

SENSITOMETRY—The science of the measurement of the sensitivity, and related characteristics, of photographic materials.

SEPARATION—(1.) The visual quality of any image area which makes it visible against its background. (2.) The process of recording, on individual black-and-white films, the extent and intensity of each of the primary color components of a photographic subject or image.

SHADOW AREA—Any region of a photographic image which corresponds to an area of shade or shadow in the original subject. Loosely, any dark area of a positive or light area of a negative image.

SHARPNESS—The subjective impression of clarity of definition and crispness of outline in the rendering of the detail and texture of the photographic image.

SHEET FILM—Film supplied in individual pieces; also called cut film.

SHEET FILM HOLDER—See FILM HOLDER.

SHIFTS AND SWINGS—The various adjustments of the front and rear standards of a view camera, provided for the purpose of facilitating framing, control of perspective, and the efficient use of the available depth of field. See RISING FRONT.

SHORT LENS—A lens of less-than-normal focal length; a wide-angle lens. See WIDE-ANGLE LENS.

SHOULDER—The upper, diminishing-gradient portion of a film characteristic curve, which represents the region of overexposure.

SHUTTER—The mechanism, sometimes electronically controlled, which opens and closes to admit light to the film chamber of a camera and control the length of the exposure interval. See LEAF SHUTTER, FOCAL PLANE SHUTTER, and BETWEEN-THE-SHUTTER.

SHUTTER RELEASE—The lever or plunger which, when pressed, allows the shutter mainspring to operate the shutter mechanism and make the exposure.

SHUTTER SPEED—(1.) The duration of the interval of exposure. (2.) The marked settings on a shutter dial. The numbers represent the denominators of fractions of which 1 is the numerator.

SILK SCREEN—(1.) A method of producing pigment prints on almost any material by squeegeeing a thick ink through a taut screen of silk or synthetic fabric. The image areas of the screen are left untreated to allow the ink to pass through, while the background areas of the screen image are covered with some impermeable material which prevents the passage of the ink and leaves the print paper surface clean. Silk screen printing is becoming popular with some exhibiting photographers for making large, stylized images notable for their posterlike simplicity and bold color. (2.) The fabric-covered frame used in silk screen printing.

SINGLE-LENS REFLEX—A reflex camera in which the viewfinder image is formed by the camera lens and reflected to a top-mounted viewing screen by a hinged mirror normally inclined behind the camera lens. During exposure of the film, the mirror flips up to seal the ground-glass opening, allowing the image light to pass through to the film chamber. In most designs, a focal plane shutter is employed.

SLIDE—(1.) A transparency mounted in cardboard, metal, plastic, or glass, for projection onto a screen for viewing. (2.) A shortened name for the dark slide of a film holder. See DARK SLIDE.

SLOW—A term used to describe the longer exposure intervals provided by the shutter, as "one-half second is a slow speed." Also applied to relatively insensitive emulsions, as a slow film.

SLR—Abbreviation for SINGLE-LENS REFLEX, which see.

SODIUM THIOSULFATE—One of the few chemicals which, in solution, can dissolve the silver halides, and one of a still smaller group which is suitable for photographic use. It is the principal ingredient of ordinary fixing baths and is somewhat less active, but also less prone to attack the developed silver image, than is ammonium thiosulfate which is used in the so-called rapid fixing baths. Available in both anhydrous and crystalline form; the crystals are generally used and are sometimes sold as hypo-rice. See HYPO.

SOFT—(1.) Describes an image which is not sharp; that is, one which is blurred, diffused, or not accurately focused. (2.) Photographic emulsions, specifically printing papers, which tend to produce images of lower-than-normal contrast; for example, the paper grades 0 and 1, and some others of similar characteristics, are called soft papers.

SOLARIZATION—Originally, the reversal of image tones occurring in the early printing-out processes resulting from extreme overexposure; now almost universally used to describe the Sabattier effect. See SABATTIER EFFECT.

SPECTRUM—A complete and ordered series of electromagnetic wavelengths, usually construed to mean the band of visible wavelengths which we perceive as colors. The visible spectrum consists of wavelengths of from about 400 to 700 nanometers, a band which represents a gradual color transition from deep violet, through blue, green, yellow, orange, and red. The spectrum colors can be displayed by dispersing white light with a prism. A natural example, resulting from the dispersion of sunlight by raindrops, is the rainbow.

SPHERICAL ABERRATION—The tendency, inherent in any simple positive lens whose surfaces are spherical, to focus light rays passing through the peripheral areas of the lens at points closer to the lens than the focal point of the central rays. This results in a zone, rather than a plane of focus, and produces a film image which is generally well defined, but overlayed and blended with a kind of ethereal diffusion. It is a common and troublesome defect in fast lenses, but can be greatly reduced by stopping down. It is deliberately left uncorrected in lenses intended for portraiture so as to produce a pleasing softness of image.

SPIN DROP-OUT—Slang term for Kodak's Tone-Line Process, which see.

SPLIT-IMAGE RANGEFINDER—A variety of rangefinder in which the opposite halves of the image are displaced along a dividing line when the instrument is not properly focused. Correct distance is indicated when the image halves are adjusted to match. See RANGEFINDER and SUPERIMPOSED RANGEFINDER.

SPOTMETER—An exposure meter which measures reflected light or luminance, over a field of only a degree or two. The portion of the subject being read is outlined on a viewing screen to facilitate accurate appraisal of the individual luminances of small areas of the subject.

SPOTONE—Trade name of a popular spotting dye available in several shades of warm, neutral, and cool colors to match almost any black-and-white print image tone.

SPOTTING—The process of bleaching or painting out blemishes in the print image for the purpose of improving its appearance.

SPOTTING COLORS—The dyes and especially the pigments used in spotting.

SPRING BACK—The entire assembly, attached to and usually removable from the rear standard of a view or press camera, which includes the ground-glass viewing screen and the frame and springs which secure the filmholder in position.

STABILIZATION—The process of rendering the unexposed halides in the developed image resistant to further visible change by the action of light. Stabilized prints are not permanent and they are heavily contaminated with chemicals, but the process is a valuable one for many purposes because it is fast and convenient. It does, however, require a special machine called a stabilization processor and uses special papers and chemicals.

STAIN—Colored or toned area, generally of a print, caused by chemical oxidation or contamination and not usually stable, permanent, premeditated, or desirable. The exceptions are the stain images, formed by such developing agents as pyrogallic acid, which have certain virtues.

STAR FILTER—A glass disc etched or scratched in a regular pattern, intended for use over the camera lens for the purpose of producing radiating streaks around the highlights of the image. A square of shiny window-screening or a stretched piece of nylon stocking will produce a similar result.

STEP TABLET—A gray scale composed of regular areas of density increasing in incremental progression. Film step tablets are intended for use with transmitted light; paper step tablets are used with reflected light. See STEP WEDGE and GRAY SCALE.

STEP WEDGE—A stepped gray scale for attenuating transmitted light, specifically one formed by increasing thicknesses of a uniformly dense material, but also applied to scales consisting of areas of uniform thickness but increased density.

STOCK—(1.) The base or support material such as paper on which sensitized photographic emulsions are coated. (2.) The concentrated form of a photographic chemical solution which is commonly diluted into the working solution for use.

STOP—(1.) Originally a metal plate, centrally perforated, and intended for insertion into a slot in the barrel of a lens for the purpose of limiting the amount of light passing through the lens. Sometimes referred to as Waterhouse stops (after James Waterhouse, who devised the system in 1858) these stop plates were supplied in sets with apertures of different sizes. (2.) The aperture or f/number of a lens. (3.) A change in exposure, from any cause, which doubles or halves the preceding one. For example, changing the shutter speed from 1/25 second to 1/100 second, other things being equal, is said to reduce the exposure by two stops. (4.) Contraction of shortstop, the acid rinse bath which commonly follows the developer.

STOP DOWN—To reduce the size of the aperture of a lens.

STRAIGHT LINE PORTION—The central length of the D logE curve, between the toe and the shoulder, which represents a progression of image densities which are uniformly proportional to their corresponding increments of exposure. The portion of the curve exhibiting uniform gradient.

STRETCH LENS—An anamorphic system of movable prisms for use over the camera lens, and used by photographic illustrators to elongate or compress the image, as for example, when photographing automobiles.

STROBE—Contraction of the word stroboscope. A special form of electronic flash unit capable of firing repeatedly and automatically at rates which can be varied from a few flashes per second to hundreds. This term is applied inaccurately, but almost universally, to ordinary photographic electronic flash units which usually require several seconds to recharge after each flash, and do not flash repetitively. See ELECTRONIC FLASH.

STUDIO—Generally refers to the large room in which a photographer arranges and photographs his subjects, but is also used to refer to the complete physical plant, including darkrooms, offices, etc., and occasionally to the entire enterprise, as for example, "What studio do you work for?"

SUBJECT—The thing or view photographed. There is some implication that the term subject refers to animate things, and that object refers to inanimate things, but the terms are generally used interchangeably.

SUBJECT BRIGHTNESS RANGE—See SUBJECT LUMINANCE RANGE, a preferable term.

SUBJECT LUMINANCE RANGE—The numerical difference between the light intensities of the shadows and highlights of a subject as expressed in arithmetic or logarithmic terms, or in terms of the number of stops represented. Sometimes called "Subject Brightness Range."

SUBTRACTIVE SYSTEM—The system of color mixing involving pigments or dyes in which the primaries represent the most intense and brightest colors available and any mixture of them must necessarily be darker and less intense. Pigments, and dyes, are seen to be colored because they reflect that color of the incident white light, absorbing the remaining wavelengths. The absence of all pigment color is assumed to be white, as represented by the untouched ground or surface which reflects light without selective absorption. Since each of the three pigment primaries absorbs one of the three light primaries, a mixture of the three pigments will absorb virtually all of the incident light, providing, theoretically, the visual effect of black. See ADDITIVE SYSTEM and PIGMENT PRIMARIES.

SUPERIMPOSED RANGEFINDER—A type of rangefinder in which the two images appear to overlap. One is usually slightly tinted for easy identification, and the instrument will indicate the correct subject distance when the images are adjusted to coincide by superimposition. See SPLIT-IMAGE RANGEFINDER.

SUPPLEMENTARY LENS—A simple lens or lens system to be used over a camera lens for the purpose of altering effective focal length.

SURFACE—A term relating to printing paper, referring specifically to the texture of the emulsion coating.

SWINGS AND TILTS—Another name for the adjustments of a view camera. See SHIFTS AND SWINGS.

SYNCHRONIZER—The device, usually included in the shutter mechanism, which fires a flash unit at the precise moment required to provide peak light intensity during the instant that the shutter is open.

TACKING IRON—A small, electrically heated, thermostatically controlled tool used to tack or attach dry-mounting tissue to the back of a print or to the mount board, so as to hold it in place while the print is being trimmed and heated in the dry-mount press.

TAKING LENS—The lens which forms the film image in a twin-lens reflex camera, as distinguished from the viewing lens which forms the view-finder image.

TANK—A small, lighttight container, usually of plastic or metal, in which film is placed for processing. Also the larger rectangular containers of hard rubber, plastic, or stainless steel used in sheet-film processing and sometimes called deep tanks.

TANNING DEVELOPER—A developer solution which hardens the gelatin of the emulsion in the same areas and at the same time that it develops the silver image.

TELEPHOTO—A type of lens constructed in such a way that its physical length is unusually short in relation to its focal length. Telephoto lenses are usually more compact, and sometimes lighter in weight, than conventional lenses of similar aperture and focal length. They are invariably used as long lenses, since their angular coverage is inherently restricted, and they are more likely than are conventional lenses to suffer from distortion and chromatic aberrations.

TESSAR—A modified and improved version of the Cooke triplet lens, in which the rear element of the triplet was replaced by a cemented pair. Designed by Paul Rudolph for Zeiss in 1902, it was enormously successful and is still considered to be an excellent design for lenses of normal coverage and moderately wide aperture. It has been widely copied, and virtually every lens manufacturer in the world now has a few Tessar-type lenses among his offerings.

TEST STRIP—A piece of paper or film which is subjected to a sequence of regular and cumulative exposures and controlled development, so as to sample the estimated range of useful exposures in an effort to determine the optimum one.

THIN—Describes the appearance of a transparency image (usually the negative) of low overall density.

THIN-EMULSION FILM—One of a group of modern roll and 35-mm films coated with an unusually thin layer of silver-rich emulsion, and capable of producing images of high resolution, relatively fine grain, and brilliant gradation. They are typically of medium or low speed and tend to produce high contrast unless specially processed.

TIME—One of the marked speeds on most shutters. A shutter set on *Time* will open when the shutter release is pressed and will remain open until the release is pressed again. It is a convenient setting for exposure intervals of more than a few seconds. See BULB.

TIME-AND-TEMPERATURE—The method of controlling film development, when the film is processed in small tanks or in total darkness in large tanks or trays, by maintaining the process solutions at a known temperature and limiting the duration of development to a selected interval. See INSPECTION.

TIME EXPOSURE—Specifically, a camera exposure made by setting the shutter dial on *T*, but generally used to refer to any exposure, timed manually, of longer than a second or so.

TIMER—A mechanical or electronic device used to terminate an exposure interval or ring a bell or otherwise indicate the end of some selected interval of time.

TLR—See TWIN-LENS REFLEX.

TOE—The lower segment of the D logE curve, characterized by its progressively increasing slope or gradient. Its lowest extreme represents the region of underexposure of the emulsion.

TONAL SCALE—The range of grays or densities of a photographic image. Gradation.

TONE-LINE PROCESS—A method of producing a photographic image which resembles a pen-and-ink drawing. It includes a step in which a high-contrast film material in contact with a fully-masked negative is exposed to slanting light while being rotated on a phonograph turntable, and is, therefore, sometimes called the spin drop-out process.

TONER—Any solution of chemicals used to alter the color of the silver image, either during development or, usually, as a postdevelopment treatment.

TRAILER—The length of opaque film or attached paper which follows the useful image area of the film strip and, when wrapped in several layers around the exposed film roll, serves to protect the image exposures from raw light.

TRANSLUCENT—Describes a diffusing material which will transmit light, but not focused light.

TRANSPARENCY—An image which is viewed by transmitted light. Specifically a film image, usually positive and often in color, intended for projection.

TRAY—The shallow, rectangular, open containers in which prints, and sometimes films, are processed. In England they are called dishes.

TRIPLET—A lens of three elements, specifically the three-glass lens designed in 1893 by H. D. Taylor and known as the Cooke Triplet. It was considered a breakthrough in lens design and is the ancestral prototype of a great many modern lenses.

TRIPOD—A three-legged stand, usually adjustable in height and provided with a tilting and swivelling head, on which a camera can be fastened for support and stability during use.

TTL—Through-the-lens; describes a type of exposure meter, incorporated in the structure of a camera, which reads the intensity of the image light transmitted by a lens.

TUNGSTEN LIGHT—Generally, the light emitted by a heated tungsten filament such as is contained in conventional electric light bulbs. Sometimes used to refer specifically to the light of special photographic tungsten-filament bulbs which are designed to burn at either 3200°K. or 3400°K. Also often used loosely to apply to artificial light in general, as distinguished from daylight.

TWIN-LENS REFLEX—A type of reflex camera which uses separate but similar lenses in separate compartments of the camera body for the individual functions of viewing and recording the image. See SINGLE-LENS REFLEX.

TYPE A—(1.) Refers to those color films which have been balanced or specially sensitized for use in tungsten light of 3400°K. (2.) Very occasionally refers to panchromatic emulsions whose sensitivity to red light is minimal.

TYPE B—(1.) The group of color films intended for use in tungsten light of 3200°K. (2.) Commonly, the designation of panchromatic films whose red-sensitivity approximates that of the human eye.

TYPE C—Panchromatic films whose red-sensitivity exceeds that of the human eye.

ULTRAVIOLET—The common name for the band of short wavelength, high frequency electromagnetic radiations which border the visible spectrum beyond visible violet light.

UNIT MAGNIFICATION—The formation by a lens system of an image identical in size or scale with the subject.

US—Uniform System. The name of an obsolete system of lens aperture scale marking which expressed, inversely, the arithmetic relationship of the light transmission of the various apertures. In the system, the number 1 was assigned to the aperture f/4.0, 2 was equivalent to f/5.6, 4 equalled f/8.0, 8 equalled f/11.0, etc.

VARIABLE CONTRAST PAPER—A type of printing paper coated with a mixture of two emulsions which are separately sensitized to (usually) yellow and purple light. Since one emulsion has a high-contrast characteristic and the other low, the overall contrast rendition of the paper can be controlled by varying the proportions of yellow and purple in the exposing light. With most such papers, a yellowish light will produce an image of low contrast, while high contrast will result from exposure to purplish light. Light color—and therefore image contrast—is controlled by filters, each numbered to indicate the paper grade it corresponds to.

VIEW CAMERA—A type of camera in which the image is viewed and composed on a ground-glass screen placed precisely at the film plane. The viewed image is therefore identical to the one presented to the film during exposure. After the image has been focused and composed, the ground glass is replaced by the film in a suitable holder and the picture is made. Most view cameras provide for considerable adjustment of the relative positions of the lens board and film plane. They are typically designed to accept sheet film in the larger sizes and must be used on a tripod, or other firm support. See SHIFTS AND SWINGS.

VIEWING LENS—In a twin-lens reflex camera, the lens which forms the viewfinder image. See TAKING LENS.

VIRTUAL IMAGE—An image, such as is typically formed by a negative lens, which can be seen in the lens or as an aerial image, but cannot be formed on a screen.

WARM TONES—In photography, shades of red or orange (browns) in the black-and-white silver image. Generally, similar shades in the color or tone of any material.

WASHED OUT—A term to describe a pale, lifeless, gray print image, usually implying loss of highlight detail, such as might typically result from underexposure of the print.

WAVELENGTH—The distance from crest to crest, or trough to trough, of adjacent, cyclic waveforms. The completion of a single waveform, including crest and trough, is called a cycle, and the number of cycles which are completed in a second of time is called the frequency (of vibration) of the waveform. The traditional units of wavelength measurement in light are the Angstrom Unit, abbreviated "Å" and equal to 1/10,000,000 of a millimeter, and the millimicron, equivalent to 1/1,000,000 of a millimeter. The preferred unit is now the "nanometer" which is equivalent to the millimicron. The unit of frequency is the Hertz, cycles per second.

WEAK—Describes an image which is not fully formed or which is unpleasantly low in contrast or density. Pale, gray, lifeless.

WEDGING—The deviation of a light ray in passing, for example, from air through a glass plate with plane, but not parallel, faces. Also sometimes used loosely to describe the lateral displacement of an image being projected through a thick glass or plastic filter which is slightly tilted in the light beam.

WEIGHT—The thickness of printing paper stock.

WET-MOUNTING—Methods of attaching prints to their mounts by means of liquid, especially water-based, glues or adhesives.

WET-PLATE—Another name for the collodion process, in which glass plates coated with a thin film of salted collodion were sensitized in a solution of silver nitrate and immediately loaded into the camera for exposure while still damp. The process was popular from about 1850 until about 1880 when it was largely superseded by gelatin-coated dry plates.

WHITE LIGHT—Generally used (as distinct from safelight) to refer to any light which is capable of exposing an emulsion. Also, in color photography, it describes light of a Kelvin temperature suitable for use with a particular emulsion type. Thus, white light for daylight film is considered to be of about 5600°K., while for "Type A" film white light is 3400°K., etc.

WIDE-ANGLE—Describes a lens whose angular coverage is substantially greater than that of a "normal" lens. Also sometimes called "wide field."

WORKING SOLUTION—Any solution used in photographic processing, as distinguished from stock or storage solutions which are usually more concentrated for better keeping qualities. Stock solutions are almost invariably diluted for use, to make the working solution.

ZONE—In the Zone System a specific subject tone as it will be rendered in the print. Seven to nine Zones are usually described as covering the useful range of print tones and each is assigned a number; thus, Zone III is considered to represent very dark gray or textured black in the print, Zone V is middle gray, Zone IX is maximum paper white, etc. In the subject the Zones are defined as being luminances and the interval between adjacent Zones of a "normal" subject is one stop.

ZONE SYSTEM—A method of exposure and development determination advanced by Ansel Adams, and later propounded by Minor White, which involves analysis of the luminances of the significant areas and the tonal extremes of the subject and the previsualization of their translation into print densities. It is a logical theory, but one which tends to become pseudoscientific, if not actually intuitive, in practice.

ZOOM LENS—A type of lens of very complex structure which can be adjusted in use to provide a continuous range of focal lengths within its design limits. They are very popular with cinematographers and are also widely used in still photography with small cameras.

Bibliography

The following bibliography lists only a few of the books available which treat the subject of photography in words or pictures. It is not intended to be a definitive list but does represent a selection of titles which would form a fine reference library. I am sure there are many valuable books which are not included and, no doubt, some of these selections could be contested but within this listing there should be something of interest for almost any photographer, regardless of his background or specialty. The bibliography emphasizes picture books and books of historical interest because, it seems to me, these are major sources of inspiration for students. The relatively few instructional books listed are basic; extremely technical or specialized scientific works have not been included.

Two fairly recently published groups of books are worth special mention. The *LIFE Library of Photography* series, published in 1971, consists of seventeen volumes which, taken together, cover most aspects of photography quite satisfactorily. Their particular strength is in their illustrations, both photographic and graphic. Not all of this set has been listed here because of the limited appeal of some of the titles. The other major publishing effort was completed in 1973 by the Arno Press, a New York Times company. Their *Literature of Photography* series, consisting of sixty-two volumes, makes available facsimile editions of a great many rare and significant works, some dating from the very earliest years of photography. Anyone interested in the history of this medium should certainly become familiar with this collection as well as the few other facsimile editions published by other organizations.

Because students often ask for references and recommendations about books to buy, I have indicated with asterisks my personal choices for a ten-volume personal library. It is a difficult choice to make, but the starred titles are the ones I'd take with me to the proverbial desert island if I could only have ten. I expect that a great many photographers will disagree with some of these choices but I feel sure that almost everyone will agree with my first choice, the *Daybooks of Edward Weston*, Volumes I and II. I recommend them most sincerely.

PICTURE BOOKS

ABBOTT, BERENICE, and McCAUSLAND, ELIZABETH. *New York in the Thirties.* Unabridged republication of 1939 edition (formerly titled *Changing New York*). New York: Dover Publications, Inc., 1973.

*ABBOTT, BERENICE. *The World of Atget.* New York: Horizon Press, Inc., 1964.

ALDRIDGE, JAMES. *Living Egypt.* Photographs by Paul Strand. New York: Horizon Press, Inc., 1969.

André Kertesz, Photographer. Intro. by John Szarkowski. New York: The Museum of Modern Art, 1964.

The Appalachian Photographs of Doris Ulmann. Intro. by John Jacob Niles. Pennland, N.C.: The Jargon Society, 1970.

Barbara Morgan Monograph. Foreword by Peter Bunnell. Hastings-on-Hudson, New York: Morgan & Morgan, 1972.

Berenice Abbott, Photographs. Foreword by John Szarkowski. New York: Horizon Press, Inc., 1970.

The Best of LIFE. New York: Time-Life Books, 1973.

Brassai. Intro. by Lawrence Durrell. New York: Museum of Modern Art, 1968.

BROWN, JOSEPH EPES, ed. *Edward Curtis.* Photographs of the American Indian. Millerton, N.Y.: Aperture, 1972.

BRY, DORIS. *Alfred Stieglitz: Photographer.* Boston: Museum of Fine Arts, 1965.

BULLOCK, BARBARA. *Wynn Bullock . . . Photographs.* San Francisco: Scrimshaw Press, 1971.

CALLAHAN, SEAN, ed. *Photographs of Margaret Bourke-White.* Intro. by Theodore M. Brown, afterword by Carl Mydans. Greenwich, Conn.: New York Graphic Society, 1972.

CAPA, CORNELL. *The Concerned Photographer.* New York: Grossman Publishers, Inc., 1968.

————. *The Concerned Photographer II.* New York: Grossman Publishers, Inc., 1972.

CAPA, ROBERT. *Images of War.* New York: Grossman Publishers, Inc., 1964.

CARPENTER, EDWARD. *They Became What They Beheld.* Photographs by Ken Heyman. New York: Outerbridge & Dienstfrey, 1970.

*CARTIER-BRESSON, HENRI. *The Decisive Moment.* New York: Simon & Schuster, Inc., 1952. (Out of print)

————. *World of Henri Cartier-Bresson.* New York: Viking Press, Inc., 1968.

CLARK, LARRY. *Tulsa.* New York: Lustrum Press, 1971.

CURTIS, EDWARD S. *Portraits From North American Indian Life.* Intro. by A.D. Coleman and T.C. McLuhan. New York: Outerbridge and Lazard, 1972.

DAVIDSON, BRUCE. *East 100th Street.* Cambridge, Mass.: Harvard University Press, 1970.

DeCOCK, LILIANE, ed. *Ansel Adams Monograph.* Foreword by Minor White. Hastings-on-Hudson, New York: Morgan & Morgan, 1972.

DeCOCK, LILIANE, and McGHEE, REGINALD. *James Van Der Zee.* Intro. by Regina A. Perry. Dobbs Ferry, N.Y.: Morgan & Morgan, 1973.

Diane Arbus. An Aperture Monograph. Millerton, New York: Aperture, 1972.

Dorothea Lange. Intro. by George P. Elliott. New York: The Museum of Modern Art, 1966.

EISENSTAEDT, ALFRED. *The Eye of Eisenstaedt.* New York: Viking Press, Inc., 1969.

ERWITT, ELLIOTT. *Photographs and Anti-Photographs.* Greenwich, Conn.: New York Graphic Society, 1972.

EVANS, WALKER. *Message From the Interior.* New York: The Eakins Press, 1966.

The Family of Man. Intro. by Edward Steichen. New York: The Museum of Modern Art, 1955.

FEININGER, ANDREAS. *Forms of Nature and Life.* New York: Viking Press, 1966.

FRANK, ROBERT. *The Americans.* Photographs by Robert Frank, intro. by Jack Kerouac. New York: Grossmann Publishers, Inc., 1969.

FRIEDLANDER, LEE. *Self Portrait.* New York: Haywire Press, 1970.

GERNSHEIM, HELMUT, ed. *Alvin Langdon Coburn, Photographer.* New York: Frederick A. Praeger, 1966.

HAAS, ERNST. *The Creation.* New York: Viking Press, Inc., 1971.

The Hampton Album. Intro. by Lincoln Kirstein. New York: The Museum of Modern Art, 1966.

Harry Callahan. Intro. by Sherman Paul. New York: The Museum of Modern Art, 1967.

HENDRICKS, GORDON. *The Photographs of Thomas Eakins*. New York: Grossman Publishers, Inc., 1972.

HUGHES, LANGSTON. *The Sweet Flypaper of Life*. Photographs by Roy DeCarava. Philadelphia: Hill and Wang, 1967.

HUNT, ROBERT. *A Popular Treatise on the Art of Photography*. A facsimile edition with intro. and notes by James Yingpeh Tong. Athens, Ohio: Ohio University Press, 1973.

HURLEY, F. JACK. *Portrait of a Decade*. Baton Rouge, La.: Louisiana State University Press, 1972.

Imogen Cunningham: Photographs. Intro. by Margery Mann. Seattle, Wash.: University of Washington Press, 1970.

Jerry N. Uelsmann. An Aperture Monograph. Intro. by Peter Bunnell. Millerton, N.Y.: Small, 1971.

KERTESZ, ANDRÉ. *Sixty Years of Photography: 1912–1972*. New York: Viking Press, Inc., 1972.

KIRSTEIN, LINCOLN. *Eugene Smith, Photographs*. Millerton, N.Y.: Aperture, 1969.

Larry Burrows: Compassionate Photographer. New York: Time-Life Books, 1972.

LARTIGUE, JACQUES HENRI. *Boyhood Photos of J. H. Lartigue*. Lausanne, Switz.: Ami Guichard, 1966. (Out of print)

———. *Diary Of a Century*. Ed. by Richard Avedon. New York: Viking Press, Inc., 1970.

LEVITAS, MITCHEL. *America In Crisis*. Photographs by Magnum photographers. New York: Holt, Rinehart & Winston, 1969.

LYON, DANNY. *The Bikeriders*. New York: Macmillan Company, 1968.

———. *Conversations With The Dead*. Photographs by Danny Lyon, drawings and writings by Billy McCune. New York: Holt, Rinehart & Winston, 1971.

LYONS, NATHAN, ed. *Aaron Siskind, Photographer*. Intro. by Nathan Lyons. Rochester, N.Y.: George Eastman House, 1965.

———. *Photography In The Twentieth Century*. New York: Horizon Press, Inc., 1967.

LYONS, NATHAN; LABROT, SYL; and CHAPPELL, WALTER. *Under the Sun: The Abstract Art of Camera Vision*. New York: George Braziller, 1960. (Limited edition)

MANOS, CONSTANTINE. *A Greek Portfolio*. New York: Viking Press, Inc., 1972.

McCARTHY, MARY. *Portugal*. Photographs by Neal Slavin. New York: Lustrum Press, 1971.

MICHALS, DUANE. *The Journey Of The Spirit After Death*. New York: Winter House, 1971.

NATALI, ENRICO. *New American People*. Hastings-on-Hudson, N.Y.: Morgan & Morgan, 1972.

*Newhall, BEAUMONT. *Frederick H. Evans*. An Aperture Monograph. Millerton, N.Y.: Aperture, 1973.

NEWHALL, NANCY. *The Eloquent Light*. A biography of Ansel Adams. San Francisco: Sierra Club, 1963.

———. *Yosemite Valley*. Photographs by Ansel Adams. Redwood City, Calif.: Five Associates, 1959.

*NORMAN, DOROTHY. *Alfred Stieglitz: An American Seer*. Millerton, N.Y.: Aperture, 1973.

Looking At Pictures: One Hundred Photographs From the Collection of the Museum of Modern Art. Notes by John Szarkowski. Greenwich, Conn.: New York Graphic Society, 1972.

PARKER, FRED. *Manuel Alvarez Bravo*. Pasadena, Calif. Pasadena Art Museum, 1971.

Paul Caponigro. An Aperture Monograph. New York: Aperture, 1967. Revised and enlarged, 1972.

Paul Strand: Photographs 1915–1968. Text by Alfred Stieglitz, Nancy Newhall, Paul Strand, and others. Millerton, N.Y.: Aperture, 1972.

PORTER, ELIOT. *In Wildness Is The Preservation Of The World*. New York: Sierra Club-Ballantine, 1967.

———. *The Place No One Knew . . . Glen Canyon*. San Francisco: Sierra Club, 1966.

*Sander, August. *Menschen Ohne Maske*. Luzern and Frankfurt: C. J. Bucher, 1971.

Steichen, Edward, ed. *The Bitter Years 1935–1941*. New York: The Museum of Modern Art, 1966.

Szarkowski, John. *The Photographer's Eye*. New York: The Museum of Modern Art, 1966.

————, ed. *The Photographer and the American Landscape*. Greenwich, Conn.: New York Graphic Society, 1972.

Tucker, Anne, ed. *The Woman's Eye*. Intro. by Anne Tucker. New York: Alfred A. Knopf, Inc., 1973.

Walker Evans. Intro. by John Szarkowski. New York: The Museum of Modern Art, 1971.

Weiss, Margaret R., ed. *Ben Shahn, Photographer*. Intro. by Margaret R. Weiss. New York: DaCapo Press, 1972.

Weston, Cole. *Edward Weston: Fifty Years*. Millerton, N.Y.: Aperture, 1973.

White, Minor. *Mirrors, Messages, Manifestations*. Millerton, N.Y.: Aperture, 1969.

Winningham, Geoffery. *Friday Night At The Coliseum*. Houston, Texas: Allison Press, 1971.

Winogrand, Garry. *The Animals*. New York: The Museum of Modern Art, 1969.

INSTRUCTIONAL AND REFERENCE BOOKS

Adams, Ansel. *Camera and Lens*. Hastings-on-Hudson, N.Y.: Morgan & Morgan, 1970.

————. *Natural Light Photography*. Hastings-on-Hudson, N.Y.: Morgan & Morgan, 1965.

————. *The Negative*. Hastings-on-Hudson, N.Y.: Morgan & Morgan, 1968.

————. *The Print*. Hastings-on-Hudson, N.Y.: Morgan & Morgan, 1968.

Eaton, George T. *Photographic Chemistry*. Hastings-on-Hudson, N.Y.: Morgan & Morgan, 1965.

The Focal Encyclopedia of Photography. New York: McGraw-Hill Book Company, 1969.

Life Library of Photography. New York: Time-Life Books, 1970.
   The Art of Photography
   The Camera
   Color
   Frontiers of Photography
   Great Photographers
   Light and Film
   Photojournalism
   The Print
   The Studio

Neblette, C. B. *Fundamentals of Photography*. New York: Van Nostrand Reinhold, 1970.

————. *Photographic Lenses*. Hastings-on-Hudson, N.Y.: Morgan & Morgan, 1972.

————. *Photography: Its Materials and Processes*. New York: Van Nostrand Reinhold, 1972.

Pittaro, Ernest M., ed. *Photo-Lab-Index*. Hastings-on-Hudson, N.Y.: Morgan & Morgan, 1972.

Procedures For Processing And Storing Black and White Photographs for Maximum Possible Permanence. Grinnell, Iowa: East Street Gallery, 1970.

Stroebel, Leslie. *View Camera Technique*. New York: Hastings House Publishers, Inc., 1967.

Todd, Hollis N., and Zakia, Richard D. *Photographic Sensitometry*. Hastings-on-Hudson, New York: Morgan & Morgan, 1969.

White, Minor. *Zone System Manual*. Hastings-on-Hudson, N.Y.: Morgan & Morgan, 1968.

Zakia, Richard D., and Todd, Hollis N. *101 Experiments in Photography*. Hastings-on-Hudson, N.Y.: Morgan & Morgan, 1969.

Zone Systemizer. Hastings-on-Hudson, N.Y.: Morgan & Morgan, 1972.

AESTHETICS AND CRITICISM

COFFIN, CHARLES. *Photography As A Fine Art.* Intro. by Thomas Barrow. Hastings-on-Hudson, N.Y.: Morgan & Morgan, 1971.

COKE, VAN DEREN. *The Painter and The Photograph.* Albuquerque, N.M.: University of New Mexico Press, 1971.

GERNSHEIM, HELMUT. *Creative Photography, Aesthetic Trends 1839–1960.* Boston: Boston Book and Art Shop, 1962.

LYONS, NATHAN, ed. *Photographers On Photography.* Englewood Cliffs, N.J.: Prentice-Hall, Inc., 1966.

SCHARF, AARON. *Art and Photography.* Baltimore, Md.: The Penguin Press, 1969.

————. *Creative Photography.* New York: Van Nostrand Reinhold, 1969.

BOOKS OF HISTORICAL INTEREST

The following are titles from a recently issued collection of facsimile editions published by the Arno Press, New York, all dated 1973.

ANDERSON, A. J. *The Artistic Side of Photography in Theory and Practice.* London, 1910.

ANDERSON, PAUL L. *The Fine Art of Photography.* Philadelphia and London, 1919.

BECK, OTTO WALTER. *Art Principles in Portrait Photography.* New York, 1907.

BINGHAM, ROBERT J. *Photogenic Manipulation.* Parts I and II. London: 1852.

BUNNELL, PETER C., ed. *Nonsilver Printing Processes: Four Selections, 1886–1927.* New York: 1973.

BURBANK, W. H. *Photographic Printing Methods.* 3rd ed., New York: 1891.

BURGESS, N. G. *The Photograph Manual.* 8th ed., New York: 1863.

CROUCHER, J. H., and LEGRAY, GUSTAVE. *Plain Directions for Obtaining Photographic Pictures.* Parts I, II, & III. Philadelphia: 1853.

DRAPER, JOHN WILLIAM. *Scientific Memoirs.* London: 1878.

EMERSON, PETER HENRY. *Naturalistic Photography for Students of the Art,* 3rd edition, including *The Death of Naturalistic Photography,* London: 1891. New York: 1899.

FOUQUE, VICTOR. *The Truth Concerning the Invention of Photography: Nicephore Niepce—His Life, Letters and Works.* Translated by Edward Epstean from the original French edition. Paris, 1867; New York, 1935.

GILLIES, JOHN WALLACE. *Principles of Pictorial Photography.* New York: 1923.

HARRISON, W. JEROME. *A History of Photography Written As a Practical Guide and an Introduction to Its Latest Developments.* New York: 1887.

HARTMANN, SADAKICHI (SIDNEY ALLAN). *Composition in Portraiture.* New York, 1909.

————. *Landscape and Figure Composition.* New York: 1910.

HICKS, WILSON. *Words and Pictures.* New York: 1952.

JONES, BERNARD E. ed. *Cassell's Cyclopaedia of Photography.* London: 1911.

LEREBOURS, N. P. *A Treatise on Photography.* London: 1843.

MORTENSEN, WILLIAM. *Monsters and Madonnas.* San Francisco, 1936.

PRITCHARD, H. BADEN. *About Photography and Photographers.* New York: 1883.

ROBINSON, H. P. and ABNEY, CAPT. W. DEW. *The Art and Practice of Silver Printing,* American Edition. New York: 1881.

ROBINSON, H. P. *Picture Making by Photography.* 5th ed. London: 1897.

SOBIESZEK, ROBERT A., ed. *The Collodion Process and the Ferrotype: Three Accounts, 1854–1872.* New York: 1973.

————. *The Daguerreotype Process: Three Treatises, 1840–1849.* New York: 1973.

SPARLING, W. *Theory and Practice of the Photographic Art.* London, 1856.

TISSANDIER, GASTON. *A History and Handbook of Photography.* 2nd ed. Ed. by J. Thomson. London: 1878.

VOGEL, HERMANN. *The Chemistry of Light and Photography.* New York: 1875.

WILSON, EDWARD L. *The American Carbon Manual.* New York: 1868.
————. *Wilson's Photographics.* New York: 1881.

ANDREWS, RALPH W. *Picture Gallery Pioneers.* New York: Bonanza Books, 1964.
BRAIVE, MICHEL. *The Photograph, A Social History.* New York: McGraw-Hill Book Company, 1966.
Camera Work: An Anthology. Millerton, N.Y.: Aperture, 1973.
Daguerre. Intro. by Beaumont Newhall. New York: Winter House, Ltd., 1971.
DOTY, ROBERT. *Photo Secession, Photography As A Fine Art.* Rochester, N.Y.: The George Eastman House, 1960.
French Primitive Photography. Intro. by Minor White. Millerton, N.Y.: Aperture, 1970.
GARDNER, ALEXANDER. *Gardner's Photographic Sketchbook of the Civil War.* New York: Dover Publications, Inc., 1959.
GERNSHEIM, HELMUT. *Lewis Carroll, Photographer.* New York: Dover Publications, Inc., 1970.
GERNSHEIM, HELMUT and ALISON. *A Concise History of Photography.* New York: Grosset and Dunlap, 1965.
————. *The History of Photography 1685–1914.* New York: McGraw-Hill Book Company, 1969.
GUTMAN, JUDITH M. *Lewis W. Hine and The American Social Conscience.* New York: Walker & Co., 1967.
HENNEY, KEITH, and DUDLEY, BEVERLY, eds. *Handbook of Photography.* New York: Whittlesey House (McGraw), 1939.
HORAN, JAMES D. *Timothy O'Sullivan. America's Forgotten Photographer.* New York: Bonanza, 1966.
LOTHROP, EATON S., Jr. *A Century of Cameras.* Dobbs Ferry, N.Y.: Morgan & Morgan, 1973.
MEES, C. E. KENNETH. *From Dry Plates To Ektachrome Film.* Ziff-Davis, 1961.
MUYBRIDGE, EADWEARD. *The Human Figure In Motion.* New York: Dover Publications, Inc., 1955.
NEWHALL, BEAUMONT. *The Daguerreotype In America.* Greenwich, Conn.: New York Graphic Society, 1961. Revised in 1968.
*————. *The History of Photography.* New York: The Museum of Modern Art, 1964.
————. *The Latent Image.* Garden City, N.Y.: Doubleday & Co., Inc., 1967.
*NEWHALL, NANCY, ed. *The Daybooks of Edward Weston, Vol. I, Mexico.* Millerton, N.Y.: Aperture, 1973.
*————, ed. *The Daybooks of Edward Weston, Vol. II, California.* Millerton, N.Y.: Aperture, 1973.
POLLACK, PETER. *The Picture History of Photography.* New York: Harry N. Abrams, 1969.
RIIS, JACOB A. *How The Other Half Lives.* New York: Dover, 1971.
RINHART, FLOYD and MARION. *American Daguerreian Art.* New York: Clarkson N. Potter, 1967.
ROBINSON, H. P. *Pictorial Effect In Photography.* Pawlet, N.H.: Helios, 1971. (A facsimile edition first published in 1869.)
RUDISILL, RICHARD. *Mirror Image: The Influence of The Daguerreotype On American Society.* Albuquerque, N.M.: University of New Mexico Press, 1971.
SNELLING, HENRY H. *Art of Photography.* Hastings-on-Hudson, N.Y.: Morgan & Morgan, 1970. (Facsmilie edition.)
STEICHEN, EDWARD. *A Life In Photography.* New York: Doubleday & Co., Inc., 1963.
TAFT, ROBERT. *Photography And The American Scene.* New York: Dover Publications, Inc., 1964.
TALBOT, WILLIAM HENRY FOX. *The Pencil of Nature.* A facsimile of the 1844–46 edition, with intro. by Beaumont Newhall. New York: DaCapo Press, 1969.
THOMSON, JOHN and SMITH, ADOLPHE. *Street Life In London.* New York and London: Benjamin Blom, 1969. (Reissued.)
TOWLER, J. *The Silver Sunbeam.* A facsimile of the 1864 edition, with intro. by Beaumont Newhall. Hastings-on-Hudson, N.Y.: Morgan & Morgan, 1969.

Index

DEVELOPMENT CHARTS

The charts which follow provide developing information for a number of popular films and several developers. These data have been compiled from published information and are believed to be reasonably accurate at the time of publication; but, since photographic materials are being modified and improved constantly, information of this kind soon goes out of date. The best guide to follow is the information printed on the data sheet which is included in the film package. This will at least be pertinent for the film it accompanies. If you do not have a film data sheet, consider these charts a reasonable alternative; they will not get you into any serious trouble.

Because there are so many factors which affect the rate and extent of development of film, it is impractical to try to predict results with real precision without testing the film and developer for yourself. For that reason these charts do not specify values of gamma or contrast index but, rather, indicate general degrees of contrast which can be expected if the instructions are followed carefully. If you find that your negatives are consistently over or under developed when these data are used, pick times on the charts which will give more or less contrast as desired, whether these times fall within the so-called normal range or not.

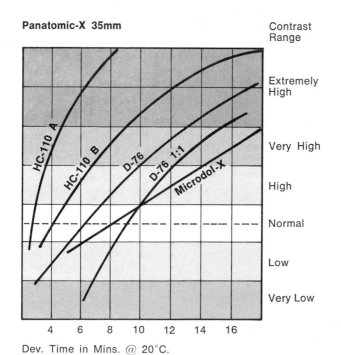

Panatomic-X 35mm

Dev. Time in Mins. @ 20°C.
Intermittent Agitation in Small Tank

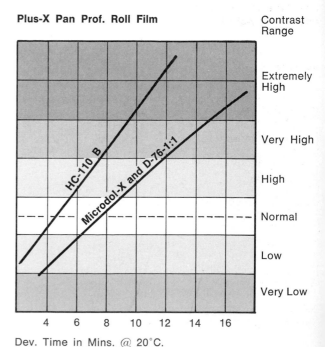

Plus-X Pan Prof. Roll Film

Dev. Time in Mins. @ 20°C.
Intermittent Agitation in Small Tank

350

Tri-X Pan Film Roll and 35mm

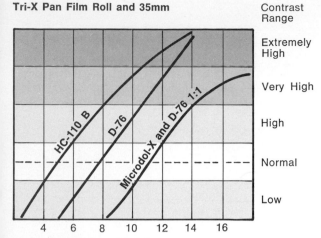

Contrast Range

Extremely High

Very High

High

Normal

Low

Dev. Time in Mins. @ 20°C.
Intermittent Agitation (Tank)

Plus-X Pan. Prof. 4147 Sheet Film

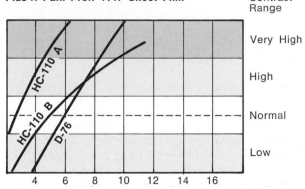

Contrast Range

Very High

High

Normal

Low

Dev. Time in Mins. @ 20°C.
Constant Agitation. For **Intermittent**
Agitation **Increase** Times by 30%

Tri-X Pan Prof. Rolls and Packs

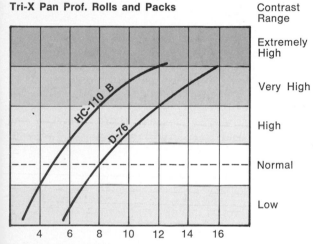

Contrast Range

Extremely High

Very High

High

Normal

Low

Dev. Time in Mins. @ 20°C.
Intermittent Agitation (Tank)

Tri-X Pan Prof. 4164 Sheet Film

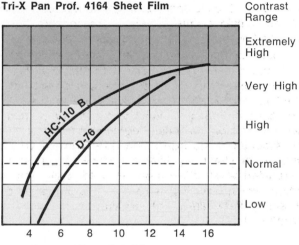

Contrast Range

Extremely High

Very High

High

Normal

Low

Dev. Time in Mins. @ 20°C.
Constant Agitation (Tray)

Verichrome Pan Roll Film

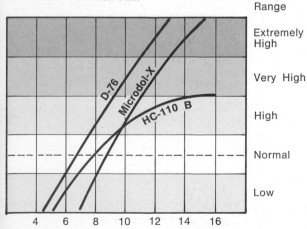

Contrast Range

Extremely High

Very High

High

Normal

Low

Dev. Time in Mins. @ 20°C.
Constant Agitation (Tray)

Super-XX 4142 Sheet Film

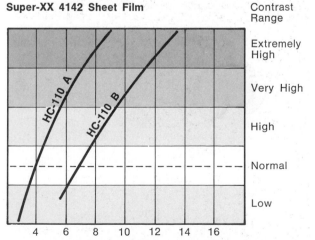

Contrast Range

Extremely High

Very High

High

Normal

Low

Dev. Time in Mins. @ 20°C.
Constant Agitation (Tray). For **Intermittent**
Agitation **Increase** Times by 25%.

Ektapan 4162 Sheet Film

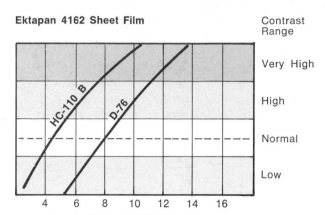

Dev. Time in Mins. @ 20°C.
Constant Agitation (Tray). For **Intermittent**
Agitation **Increase** Times by 25%.

Ilford HP-4 35mm Film
Developed in ID-11 or D-76

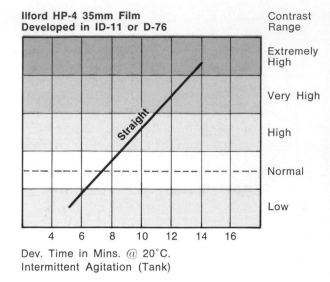

Dev. Time in Mins. @ 20°C.
Intermittent Agitation (Tank)

Ilford Pan F 35mm
Developed in ID-11 or D-76

Dev. Time in Mins. @ 20°C.
Intermittent Agitation (Tank)

Ilford HP-4 Roll Film
Developed in ID-11 or D-76

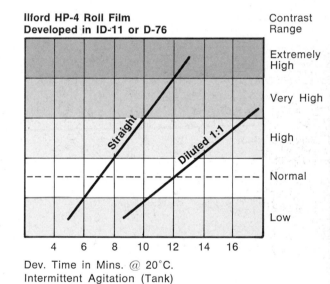

Dev. Time in Mins. @ 20°C.
Intermittent Agitation (Tank)

Ilford FP-4 Rolls and 35mm
Developed in ID-11 or D-76

Dev. Time in Mins. @ 20°C.
Intermittent Agitation (Tank)

Ilford HP-4 Sheet Film
Developed in ID-11 or D-76

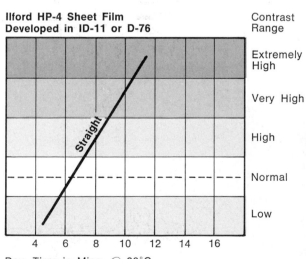

Dev. Time in Mins. @ 20°C.
Constant Agitation (Tray)

a and b. Negative color image formed by direct development.

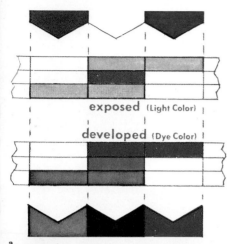

exposed (Light Color)

developed (Dye Color)

a

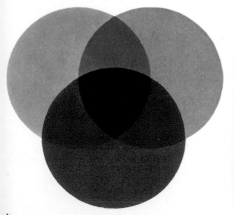

b

EXPOSURE (Light Colors)

1st DEVELOPMENT (Silver)

COL. DEV. (Silver plus Dye)

BLEACH (Removes Silver)

FINAL DYE IMAGE

c

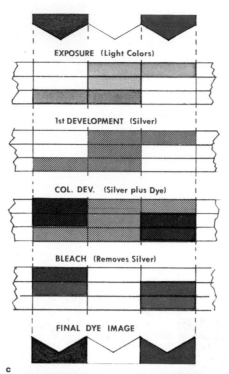

c. Diagram of reversal color film producing a positive transparency image.
d. This is how a typical color negative material records the colors of the American flag, and how the colors are reproduced in a print made from it.

d

e

f

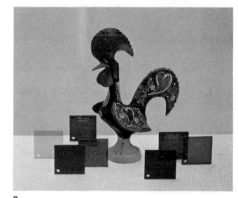

g

Color transparencies. Compare the color balance of the unfiltered transparency (e) with the slight tints produced by the CCO5R (f) and the CCO5C (g).

h. Dye primaries, subtractive system.
i. Light primaries, additive system.

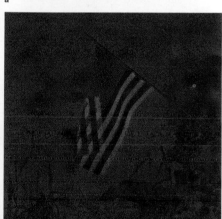

h

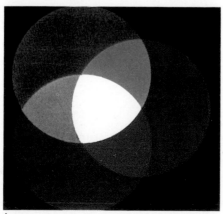

i

a

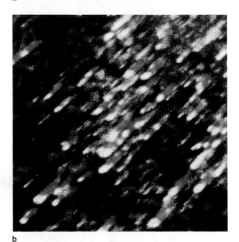

b

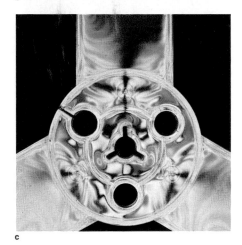

c

d

e

a. An ordinary color filter will transmit a portion of the spectrum and absorb the rest of the light energy which it dissipates as heat. Dichroic filters, on the other hand, reflect most of the light which is not transmitted, and it can be seen as a color which is complementary to the transmitted color. Because of their high efficiency, durability, and resistance to fading, dichroic filters are especially useful in enlarger color heads. Here three dichroic filters convert a beam of white light into a vari-colored pattern, demonstrating their unique ability to split the spectrum.

b. Here is a thirty-diameter enlargement of a corner of a color transparency which was taken with a long telephoto lens. Although this is a rather extreme example, the chromatic aberration shown is a common problem with telephoto lenses.

c. The rainbow patterns in this photograph of a tape reel demonstrate the ability of polarized light to reveal internal stresses in certain transparent or translucent materials. Here the two pola-screens were crossed, almost totally blocking the background illumination.

d. Color posterization by Dick Stevens, Notre Dame.

e. Color solarization by Michael Lonier, University of Florida. (Courtesy of Dick Stevens)